Island of Guanyin

Budaluojia guanyin xianshen shengjing 補怛洛迦觀音現神聖境 (c. 1350).

Island of Guanyin

Mount Putuo and Its Gazetteers

MARCUS BINGENHEIMER

OXFORD
UNIVERSITY PRESS

Oxford University Press is a department of the University of Oxford. It furthers
the University's objective of excellence in research, scholarship, and education
by publishing worldwide. Oxford is a registered trade mark of Oxford University
Press in the UK and certain other countries.

Published in the United States of America by Oxford University Press
198 Madison Avenue, New York, NY 10016, United States of America.

Library of Congress Cataloging-in-Publication Data
Names: Bingenheimer, Marcus, author.
Title: Island of Guanyin : Mount Putuo and its gazetteers / Marcus Bingenheimer.
Description: New York : Oxford University Press, 2016. |
Includes bibliographical references and index.
Identifiers: LCCN 2015034121 | ISBN 978–0–19–045619–1 (hardback : alk. paper)
Subjects: LCSH: Buddhist temples—China—Putuo Shan Island. | Putuo Shan Island (China)—
Description and travel. | Putuo Shan Island (China)—History.
Classification: LCC BQ6345.P82 B56 2016 | DDC 294.3095124/2—dc23 LC record available at
http://lccn.loc.gov/2015034121

9 8 7 6 5 4 3 2
Printed by Sheridan, USA

CONTENTS

FIGURES

ACKNOWLEDGMENTS

This book started out as a project to digitize a collection of mountain and temple gazetteers. From 2007 to 2011, the Digital Archive of Buddhist Temple Gazetteers (http://buddhistinformatics.ddbc.edu.tw/fosizhi/) was funded by the Chung-hwa Institute of Buddhist Studies and created with the help of many friends, among others: Ray Chou, Jenjou Hung, April Ke, Axian Lee, Miao Lin, Xiuli Lin, and Chuanqin Peng. To date it contains text and images of more than 230 gazetteers. So much new information was added to the digital texts of some gazetteers that in a follow-up project we decided to produce improved print editions of them with detailed indices, annotation, and new punctuation. In 2013, twelve gazetteers were published as *The Zhonghua Collection of Buddhist Temple Gazetteers* 中華佛寺志叢書 (Taipei: Shin Wen Feng). The two gazetteers on Mount Putuo in that collection were especially valuable to me and will be often cited here. Having been interested in Buddhist historiography for some time, I was naturally curious as to how the gazetteers depicted a sacred Buddhist site over time. What comes into focus and what is obscured by looking at a sacred site through the lens of its gazetteers?

The book itself was written between 2012 and 2015, when I enjoyed working with my colleagues and the graduate students in the Department of Religion at Temple University. I am grateful for their company.

The study was helped in many ways by Chün-fang Yü's groundbreaking work on Guanyin, and I am very fortunate to have received Professor Yü's support in my own efforts to understand the manifestations of the Bodhisattva. Her help and advice in the publication process is gratefully acknowledged. It was wonderful to work with Cynthia Read and Gina Chung at Oxford University Press, who skillfully managed the review and production process. Reviews by two anonymous readers provided new perspectives and led to significant additions to the manuscript.

Drafts of chapters were presented at several conferences and lectures over the last few years. Thanks to all who came to listen and cared to comment.

Some friends and colleagues have read parts or even all of the manuscript, and their insightful comments and suggestions saved me from many embarrassing mistakes. Special thanks therefore go to Wendi Adamek, Jinhua Chen, Douglas Gildow, Sujung Kim, Karen Kingsbury, Tingyu Liu, Pierce Salguero, Ting Shen, and Simon Wiles.

Many other friends and colleagues have in various ways contributed by answering questions, sending info, making one of those small remarks that change everything, or just by lending a patient ear: Susan Andrews, Timothy Brook, Sara Chiesura, Wen-shing Chou, Douglas Duckworth, Hilde De Weerdt, Shih-shan Susan Huang, Weining Huang, Venerable Huimin, Seinosuke Ide, John Kieschnick, Chaoheng Liao, Wendy Lochner, Karen Lucic, William Magee, Justin McDaniel, Max Moerman, Christine Moll-Murata, Joseph O'Leary, James Robson, Stephen F. Teiser, Christian Wittern, Li Wei, and Dorothy Wong.

Island of Guanyin is dedicated to all those who try to be compassionate like Guanyin.

Island of Guanyin

Introduction

THIS BOOK IS ABOUT Mount Putuo, a Buddhist sacred site in China, and how it is presented in a certain genre of Chinese historiography—the Buddhist temple gazetteer.[1] To a degree the book replicates the structure of a gazetteer and—with the exception of this introduction—it is organized by genre in the way gazetteers are. After a chapter on prefaces there follow chapters on maps, miracle tales, landscape, biographies, inscriptions, poems, and travelogues. Each of the eight chapters is a variation on a certain type of record that appears in gazetteers as part of the feedback loop between text and site. In this loop, text is made manifest in landscapes, architecture, or practices, and these in turn are shaped by various interests, by loss and increase, until they are again recorded as text. Gazetteers are important for understanding the ways in which sacred sites are constructed—textualized—in a multiplicity of genres. As they document the textualization of sacred space through prefaces, maps, miracle stories, poems, biographies and other forms, the information about a single person, event, or place is often found scattered across different chapters. Thus, in their own disjunctive and encyclopedic manner, gazetteers deny any single genre the power to provide a unified viewpoint from which to observe events and explain their causes. At the same time, the gazetteers often preserve rare sources that allow us to examine the history of Chinese Buddhism, especially of the last five hundred years, in great detail.

Using the gazetteers of Mount Putuo as a case study is, I believe, a reasonable choice. For Mount Putuo we have nine extant gazetteers, the first dated 1361—sufficient material to observe how the depiction of the site has evolved over time. Furthermore, Mount Putuo is a truly significant site. Throughout the last millennium it was widely known in China as a center of Buddhist pilgrimage dedicated to the Bodhisattva Guanyin (Skr. Avalokiteśvara)—one of the most popular deities in East Asia who is widely worshipped in China, Tibet, Mongolia, Korea, Japan, Taiwan, and Vietnam.

My aim is to show how gazetteers operate and how different generations of gazetteers reflect changes in the site and the circumstances of their production. To this end each chapter focuses on one genre, presenting and discussing examples taken (mostly) from the gazetteers of Mount Putuo. Individual texts are framed as "exhibits," and readers are invited to walk through the chapters of the book as they would through rooms in a museum. The genres are arranged in the order in which they would typically be found in gazetteers, but, as in a real museum, the rooms and exhibits in this "gazetteer" can be explored out of numerical order. Readers interested in how poems, for instance, are used in gazetteers might proceed directly to Chapter 7.

The Site and Its Gazetteers

Where Is Mount Putuo?

Sacred sites are founded on text. Some form of shared text is required to communicate about a place and agree on its sacredness. Sacred sites are not only remembered in text; they are born of it, and therefore the "same" site can exist in different geographic locations. Especially where the foundational text is not a unique local legend, but part of a tradition's canonical corpus, a place can be instantiated in different locations.[2] Such is the case with Mount Potalaka (Skr. *potalaka parvata*), which is described in the *Gaṇḍavyūha* section of the *Avataṃsaka Sūtra* as the abode of the Bodhisattva Avalokiteśvara, known as Guanyin in China.[3]

There are a number of sites in the Buddhist world that are held to be Mount Potalaka. Internationally, the most famous is perhaps the mountain-shaped Potala Palace in Lhasa. From the seventeenth century until 1959, the Potala Palace served as residence of the Dalai Lamas, who, not incidentally, are worshipped as manifestations of Avalokiteśvara. In East Asia, Mount Potalaka sites were established far earlier: the Naksan Temple 洛山寺 in South Korea, for instance, was founded by Uisang in the seventh century.[4] In Japan the Fudarakusan Temple 補陀洛山寺 on the Kii peninsula was established in Heian times and became one of the starting points of ritual, suicidal sea voyages in search of Avalokiteśvara's paradise.[5] In China the Potalaka was emplaced on a small island in the

Zhoushan archipelago off the coast near Ningbo.[6] This island, today called Mount Putuo 普陀山, is the focus of this book.[7]

In keeping with the description of Mount Potalaka in the *Avataṃsaka Sūtra* and the ocean imagery in many texts related to Guanyin, the East Asian sites are all close to the ocean shore. However, there seems to have been little, if any, awareness of the existence of different Potalaka sites in East Asia until the twentieth century. The sites themselves were obviously advertised as unique, and there is no record comparing the sites in Korea, Japan, and China. In the Qing dynasty the name "Putuo" or "Southern Putuo" was assumed by several temples in China, most importantly by the *Nan Putuo*, the "Southern Putuo" Temple 南普陀寺 in Xiamen.[8] "Putuo" became quite a popular temple name, and Taiwan alone is home to more than twenty-four Putuo Temples, the earliest founded in Tainan in 1889.[9]

In spite of these and other competitors, however, it was the island of Mount Putuo near Ningbo that came to represent the abode of Guanyin in the Chinese world.[10] Though located in what was a border area where the influence of the central government ebbed and flowed, Mount Putuo was closer to the urban centers of late imperial China than was either Mount Wutai or Mount Emei.[11] The literati of the Lower Yangzi delta, who produced the Mount Putuo gazetteers, appreciated the proximity of Mount Putuo and remarked on its strategic location. In one of the earliest descriptions Wu Lai 吳萊 (1297–1340), who visited Mount Putuo in 1324, writes: "To the east it rules the three Han [Korea] and Japan. To the north it connects to Denglai and Huaisi [in Shandong and northern Jiangsu], to the south to Chingyuan [in Fujian]."[12]

Ningbo, the nearest city to Mount Putuo, was an international trading hub. A major port for trade with the Islamic world, Ningbo even had a sizable community of Arab merchants. The city also played an important role in domestic trade and was, as Yoshinobu Shiba has remarked, "in effect the southern terminus of the Grand Canal."[13] Rice and tea from south China was moved north and west through Ningbo heading to Hangzhou, Nanjing, and Beijing; iron and silk went south. For centuries the city played a crucial role in international communication networks. During the Song all official visitors from Japan or Korea had to enter China through Ningbo. Key figures in the transmission of Buddhism to Japan such as Saichō, Kūkai, Eisai, and Dōgen passed through its busy port and spent time in the city waiting to enter or leave China. Even during the Edo period (1603–1868), when all Chinese trade to Japan was routed through Nagasaki, a large number of ships went from Ningbo to Japan carrying raw silk, sugar, and books (including many gazetteers).[14]

Mount Putuo was therefore far from isolated and was situated on one of the busiest shipping lanes in the "East Asian Mediterranean."[15] From the Song dynasty onward it was also considered a major Buddhist pilgrimage mountain, and since the Qing, Mount Putuo was counted among the "Four Great and Famous Mountains" (*si damingshan* 四大名山) of Chinese Buddhism alongside Mounts Wutai, Emei, and Jiuhua.[16] Today Mount Putuo is still one of China's most popular Buddhist sites and draws hundreds of thousands of visitors every year.[17]

History of Study

The academic study of Chinese Buddhist sites began in the late nineteenth and early twentieth centuries when Jan J. M. de Groot, Édouard Chavannes, Ernst Boerschmann, Johannes Prip-Møller, Daijō Tokiwa, Tadashi Sekino, Katsutoshi Ono, Willem Grootaers, and others went to China to explore Chinese religion "on the ground." This ground, always overshadowed by colonialism and military intrusions, shifted when early Communist rule and the Cultural Revolution made the study of Chinese religion in situ infeasible. Since the 1990s the study of religious sites has reemerged in a less contentious setting. In English alone we have the pioneering collection of essays on sacred sites and pilgrimages edited by Susan Naquin and Chün-fang Yü (1992), as well as monographs by Timothy Brook (1993a) on local literati patronage, Susan Naquin (2000) on the temples of Beijing, Brian Dott (2004) on Mount Taishan, James Hargett (2006) on Mount Emei, Amy McNair (2007) on the Longmen Grottoes, James Robson (2009) on Nanyue, Michael Walsh (2010) on the Tiantong Monastery, María Ríos Peñafiel (2015) on Nanwutai, and a fair number of works on Mount Wutai (Tuttle and Elverskog 2011; Cartelli 2013; Andrews 2013; Lin 2014), to name only a few.[18] Sacred Buddhist sites in Japan too have increasingly attracted attention (Grapard 1989, 1992; Moerman 2005; Ambros 2008). These efforts have shown repeatedly how the study of sacred sites yields the kind of "thick descriptions" that deepen our understanding of religious practice beyond the doctrinal discourse, which is often oblivious to its own geographic and historic context. The increase in scholarship on sacred sites in East Asia has also revealed how much work remains to be done. For Chinese Buddhist sites alone we have temple and mountain gazetteers for more than 240 sites, a rich trove of primary sources filled with information from the religious to the economic.[19] Only a handful of these sites have so far been researched.

To write about emplaced religion in the genre of the academic monograph is, necessarily, an etic endeavor, based on historical, epigraphic, literary, or visual sources. As with the discourse on doctrine, however, there are self-descriptive, emic accounts in which the tradition, or at least some of its voices, speaks of itself. Buddhist traditions often have a strong sense of their own history, and Buddhist historiography exists in a large number of cultures, languages, and genres. We need to understand the formal characteristics of local historiography regarding sacred sites, just as we need to understand the textual mechanisms of sutra and commentarial literature. Therefore the emphasis here is on the workings of the most important emic genre that was used to describe sacred sites in late imperial China: the temple gazetteer. Chün-fang Yü first pointed out the importance of the Mount Putuo gazetteers as primary sources: "Together [the gazetteers] might form one of the most persuasive means of transforming the island into Mt. Potalaka and serve as one of the most influential media proclaiming and broadcasting this fact. Even though the gazetteers range across some six hundred years, they form a self-contained cumulative tradition."[20] Much of this book is an extended comment on this remark. In his magisterial study on the Daoist sacred site of Mount Wudang (2010)—subtitled "A History of Foundational Narratives"—Pierre-Henry De Bruyn has formulated a similar approach. He notes: "The methodological separation of the different gazetteers of Mount Wudang, which are the privileged witnesses to its struggles and specific historical mutations, has made it possible to better discern [. . .] discontinuities."[21] As we will see, for Mount Putuo too the different editions of its gazetteers reveal significant changes and continuities in the development of the site.

What Are Temple Gazetteers?

The term "gazetteer" or "local gazetteer" has come to translate the Chinese term *zhi* 志.[22] The *zhi* is a peculiar format of Chinese chorography that combines cultural and topographic description with local historiography. The problem with the term "gazetteer" is that its sinological usage as a translation for *zhi* differs considerably from other meanings of "gazetteer," in particular its usage in geography. The *Oxford English Dictionary* defines "gazetteer" as "geographical index or dictionary," which is not really what a *zhi* 志 is about.[23] German and French sinology seem to prefer a more literal solution and render *zhi* as "monograph" ("Bergmonographie"/"monographie locale"[24]). This takes its cue from the beginning of the *zhi* genre in the *Shiji* 史記 (c. 109 BCE). As part of the

Shiji, the *zhi* treatises can well be considered "monographs," but of course a *zhi* in the context of the later *difangzhi* 地方志 literature is just the opposite. It is not a treatise of one author on a single topic but rather a container format that includes texts from many different authors in different genres. Everything considered, and while sympathizing with those who prefer other renderings (e.g., "regional description / Regionalbeschreibung"[25]), the translation "gazetteer" for *zhi* is so widely used in Asian studies that I will adopt it here.

The local gazetteers of later imperial China have their origin in the guidebooks that were compiled by government officials for their colleagues in order to assist in the administration of a region. "Official" gazetteers for administrative units had to be updated and reworked from time to time. Population figures, land use, irrigation canals, and building sites changed, at times considerably, over just a few generations, and so did the roster of the local worthies whose biographies and poems had to be included. During the Song and Yuan only a small number of gazetteers were produced.[26] In the Ming and Qing, however, the writing of gazetteers became popular among local historians, who produced them not only for administrative reasons but also out of antiquarian interest. Members of the local gentry commissioned or compiled new gazetteers and underwrote the printing costs.[27] The compilers gathered texts relevant to a place or region ranging from topographic descriptions, edicts, biographies, essays, poems, and *epigraphia* to maps and images. For this they often drew on previous gazetteers, updating information and adding more recent material, while omitting some of the older sources.[28]

The description of religious sites had a precarious status in official gazetteers. Entries on Buddhist and Daoist temples tended to be short and did not have a well-established, fixed position in the contents in gazetteers of administrative units.[29] Conservative Confucian compilers sometimes omitted even these brief sections on ideological grounds, and the information on temples in official gazetteers decreased during the Qing.[30]

The temple or mountain gazetteer about Buddhist and Daoist sacred sites is, like its secular model, a container format that collects texts about a religious site (or a group of sites) and arranges them according to genre. With temple gazetteers, however, geographic description cannot be purely descriptive, nor history merely historical. Buddhist and Daoist temple gazetteers must tie their sites into their respective religious *imaginaires* by documenting their religious meanings. A gazetteer series of a sacred site in China thus provides a detailed, diachronic record of the textualization of that site, documenting the recursive process whereby religious meanings associated with a place are encoded and negotiated in text and how the texts in turn influence the site itself and how it is perceived.

Buddhist temple gazetteers of the Ming and Qing usually have between five and twenty-five fascicles (*juan* 卷). Organization and chapter order varies, but a typical temple gazetteer might look like this: before the text proper there are a number of prefaces (*xu* 序), usually by the compiler, his friends, the sponsors of the gazetteer or representatives of the Sangha. After that follow a table of contents (*muci* 目次), then perhaps some maps and groundplans together with explanations (*tukao* 圖考). Readers can then expect topographic descriptions of famous sites and temples (*xing-sheng* 形勝, *fancha* 梵刹), which are among the few chapters actually authored by the compiler. Often there are chapters on history that provide a rudimentary, annalistic chronicle of the development of the site (*jianzhi* 建直). The middle part of a temple gazetteer often consists of miracle tales (*lingyi* 靈異) and various biographical accounts of monks (*chande* 禪德), lay patrons (*jinglan* 精藍), and famous visitors (*liuyu* 流寓). Sometimes a compiler adds a chapter on local products (*fangwu* 方物) or landholdings. Literary texts and poetry (*yiwen* 藝文, *shiwen* 詩文) connected with the site are generally included toward the end.[31]

Smaller sites might have only a single gazetteer, while over the centuries the larger and more popular sites accrue more than ten. A recent edition of gazetteers, for instance, counts eleven extant gazetteers for Mount Wutai and thirteen extant gazetteers for Mount Emei.[32] The edition history of individual gazetteers is often complex, and what should be counted as gazetteer is to some degree arbitrary.[33] For the purpose of this book nine works will be considered "gazetteers" of Mount Putuo and cited frequently.

1. Sheng Gazetteer 1361: *Butuoluojia shan zhuan* 補陀洛迦山傳. By Sheng Ximing 盛熙明 (fl.1361). 1 fascicle (*juan* 卷) in 4 parts (*pin* 品).[34]

Although brief, this first description of Mount Putuo already follows the comprehensive approach and structure of the mature gazetteer format. After an introduction Sheng includes sutra passages, which are considered scriptural evidence for the connection between Avalokiteśvara and the Potalaka. This is followed by an annotated list of places on the mountain and a chronicle of miracle tales and imperial patronage. Toward the end Sheng includes a eulogy to Guanyin and other poems. About Sheng Ximing himself not much is known. Born in Kucha, on the Silk Road, he lived during the Yuan dynasty—one of the more open and international periods of Chinese history. Of Central Asian background, he was familiar with Tibetan Buddhism and included (in *siddhaṃ* script) the mantra *Oṃ māṇi padme hum*, which according to him was hardly known in South China in those days.[35]

2. Hou-Tu Gazetteer 1590 [1598]: *Butuoluojia shan zhi* 補陀洛伽山志. By Hou Jigao 侯繼高 (1533–1602); Tu Long 屠隆 (1543–1605). 1 + 6 fascicles.[36]

The Hou-Tu Gazetteer was the first gazetteer produced after the revival of Mount Putuo in the late Ming. The gazetteer is relatively informal in that it reproduces most of the Sheng Gazetteer and adds mainly personal observations and poems. A large number of prefaces and postscripts are presented in the original calligraphy of their authors. The whole project has a collaborative, congenial air to it, and most of the poems were written by members of the lively circle of Ningbo literati to which Hou and especially Tu belonged. In spite of its private tone, the gazetteer was produced by the local military and literati to support the newly recovered site. Both Hou (see esp. Chapter 8, Exhibit 2) and Tu (see esp. Chapter 7, Exhibit 2) are key figures for the history of the site. Tu Long's collected works fill twelve volumes in modern print, and we know far more about him than about any other compiler in this gazetteer series.

3. Zhou Gazetteer 1607 [1641]: *Chongxiu Putuoshan zhi* 重修普陀山志. By Zhou Yingbin 周應賓 (1554–1626). 1 + 6 fascicles.[37]

The Zhou Gazetteer is in many ways a reaction to the success of its predecessor, the Hou-Tu Gazetteer, and partly a product of the debate about Mount Putuo's revival to which the earlier compilation had contributed. Zhou Yingbin was a scion of the Ningbo Zhou clan and a high-ranking official. As Vice-Minister of Rites Zhou was, at least nominally, responsible for the Daoist and Buddhist institutions throughout the whole of China. He was the "man in Beijing" of the local Mount Putuo supporters of Ningbo and possibly only minimally involved with the compilation of the gazetteer that bears his name. Zhou did write a preface, and several of his poems are included as well, but he was probably not mainly responsible for the contents of this gazetteer. As the title page attests, it was the eunuch Zhang Sui who oversaw the printing, and it was probably Zhang who coordinated the edition with a team of local literati, whose names are found at the beginning of each fascicle. The aim of the Zhou Gazetteer was to show that Mount Putuo had gained full imperial patronage. As such it was successful, and for the remainder of the Ming the status of Mount Putuo as a pilgrimage site was not called into question again.

4. Qiu-Zhu Gazetteer 1698–1705 [1735]: [*Nanhai*] *Putuoshan zhi* [南海]普陀山志. By Qiu Lian 裘璉 (1644–1729, *jinshi* 1715); Zhu Jin 朱謹 (fl. 1702); Chen Xuan 陳璿 [also 璇] (fl. 1702). 15 fascicles.[38]

Like the Hou-Tu Gazetteer, the Qiu-Zhu Gazetteer is the result of a period of revival. The edition history of this gazetteer is especially complicated, and we know little about the compilers. From its own prefaces and a discussion in the Qin Gazetteer of 1832 (*Fanli* 凡例: 3a), the following outline emerges: In 1698 the abbots of the Puji and the Fayu Temples together commissioned a gazetteer from Qiu Lian 裘璉 and others. For unknown reasons, it was published in 15 fascicles under the auspices of the Fayu Temple alone. In 1702 the Puji Temple asked Zhu Jin 朱謹 and Chen Xuan 陳璿 [also written 璇] to edit Qiu's work, and a revised version was published in 1705.[39] Both the Qiu and the Zhu-Chen gazetteer had 15 fascicles. The differences between the two editions are not clear, but according to the Qin Gazetteer they were not significant (凡例: 1b–2a). Due to the lack of extant witnesses of the Qiu version, the exact relationship between the work of Qiu and that of Zhu and Chen is difficult to determine. In the woodblock edition used here, starting with Fascicle 2, and for most of the following fascicles, all three authors—Zhu Jin, Chen Xuan, and Qiu Lian—are credited, often alongside other contributors, such as the military governor Lan Li 藍理 (Chapter 5, Exhibit 2). Some fascicles, however, credit only Qiu and Chen, or, rarely, only Zhu (Fasc. 7). This is in accord with the description of this edition in the Qin Gazetteer. Everything considered, it is possible that the two editions never circulated independently. Thus, although the Qiu and the Zhu-Chen gazetteers are sometimes listed separately (cf. Yü 2001: 562, Hong 1984: 513–514), I will reference them here as one single edition as our copy suggests.

5. Xu Gazetteer 1740: *Chongxiu Nanhai Putuoshan zhi* 重修南海普陀山志. By Xu Yan 許琰 (*jinshi* 1727). 20 fascicles.[40]

While the Qiu-Zhu gazetteer was tightly connected to the patronage of the Kangxi emperor, who sponsored Mount Putuo to an unprecedented degree (see Chapter 6, Exhibit 3), the Xu Gazetteer was produced under

Qianlong. The Qianlong emperor emulated his grandfather in many ways, but he was not interested in Mount Putuo, and imperial support for the site dried up during his reign. Nevertheless, in the early years of Qianlong, Mount Putuo was still a vibrant pilgrimage center, and a new gazetteer was compiled. There seems to have been a certain rivalry between the Puji and the Fayu Temple, and this dynamic is probably responsible for the short interval between the Qiu-Zhu Gazetteer, which was printed under the auspices of the Puji Temple, and the Xu Gazetteer, which was commissioned by the Fayu Temple. As its name says, it is a revision of the previous *Nanhai putuoshan zhi*, i.e., the Qiu-Zhu Gazetteer. According to Qin Yaozeng (Qin Gazetteer 凡例: 1b), who relied heavily on both works for his own gazetteer, the Xu Gazetteer is more skillfully executed than the Qiu-Zhu Gazetteer.

6. Qin Gazetteer 1832: *Chongxiu Nanhai Putuoshan zhi* 重修南海普陀山志. By Qin Yaozeng 秦耀曾 (fl. 1809–1839). 20 fascicles.[41]

The Qin Gazetteer makes copious use of both the Qiu-Zhu Gazetteer (referenced as "Old Gazetteer" 舊志) and the Xu Gazetteer.[42] It was commissioned in 1825 by Nenglun 能侖, the abbot of the Puji Temple. Wang Hengyan considered it biased toward Puji Temple, which it depicted as the main temple, giving only minimal exposure to the Fayu Temple.[43] The Qin Gazetteer was the last gazetteer to be produced before Mount Putuo entered a period of decline. During the Opium Wars and the Taiping civil war, pilgrimage decreased and with it maintenance of the site. The Qin Gazetteer was reprinted several times until it was replaced by the Wang Hengyan Gazetteer.

7. Wang Hengyan Gazetteer 1924–1934: *Putuoluojia xin zhi* 普陀洛迦新志. By Wang Hengyan 王亨彦 (1865–?). 12 fascicles.[44]

The Wang Hengyan Gazetteer is the first Mount Putuo gazetteer that was set in movable type. It makes a first, helpful attempt at punctuation, even distinguishing between two types of punctuation marks, roughly corresponding to the comma and the period in English. After the Taiping civil war Mount Putuo again experienced a revival period, and by 1875 steamboats from Shanghai were bringing pilgrims and tourists to the island on a regular schedule. The eminent Pure Land master Yinguang 印光 (1862–1940) took up residence on the island in 1893 and stayed for more than thirty years, corresponding with his lay followers and disciples. Yinguang was involved in new editions of gazetteers for all four "great and famous mountains."[45] One of his correspondents was the district magistrate Tao Yong 陶鏞, who commissioned a new gazetteer from Wang Hengyan in 1923. The gazetteer is often dated to 1924, but the ZFSH copy that is used here was actually printed in 1934.[46]

8. Fang Gazetteer 1995: *Putuoshan zhi* 普陀山志. By Fang Changsheng 方长生. Shanghai: Shanghai shudian 上海書店. 377 pp. ISBN: 7–80622–011–9.

The Fang Gazetteer is the first modern gazetteer, in that it aims to describe the island and its history in a way that is "based on evidence, scientific and readable" (Fang Gazetteer 凡例: 1). For the first time photos and architectural ground plans become part of a Mount Putuo gazetteer. Like most gazetteers, the Fang Gazetteer was produced by an editorial team.

9. Wang Liansheng Gazetteer 1999: *Putuoluojiashan zhi* 普陀洛迦山誌. By Wang Liansheng 王连胜. Shanghai: Shanghai shudian 上海書店. 1125 pp. ISBN: 7–5325–2647–x.

The Fang Gazetteer was quickly superseded by the much larger Wang Liansheng Gazetteer. The relationship between the two is difficult to assess, but there seems to have been a situation similar to that in the early eighteenth century, when different factions could not agree on one edition of the gazetteer. Wang Liansheng was involved in the production of the Fang Gazetteer, and his name is listed first among the editors, who usually do the bulk of the work. The Fang Gazetteer was commissioned by a government institution, the Management Office for Mount Putuo (Putuo shan guanliju 普陀山管理局), and none of the prefaces were written by a monk. In contrast, the Wang Liansheng Gazetteer was explicitly approved (*jianding* 鑑定) by Miaoshan 妙善 (1909–2000), who was for many years the leader of the Buddhist community on Mount Putuo. Miaoshan and his successor Jieren 戒忍 both wrote prefaces for the Wang Liansheng Gazetteer, and the editor, Wang Liansheng himself, is shown in photos with Miaoshan, a common demonstration of patronage and approval in Chinese publications. The existence of the Fang Gazetteer, although obviously an earlier version of the Wang Liansheng Gazetteer, is not acknowledged anywhere in its prefaces or in Wang's postscript. In the world of Chinese publishing this usually indicates a somewhat acrimonious relationship. In the late twentieth century, just as in the late Ming and again in the eighteenth century, different views of Mount Putuo and its role in Chinese society affect the compilation of its gazetteers.

Besides these full-fledged gazetteers, there are three shorter, single-fascicle works:

> The "Gazetteer of Mount Putuo, the Famous Site of the Southern Sea" *Nanhai shengjing putuoshan zhi* 南海勝境普陀山誌, author unknown, eighteenth/nineteenth century.[47]
>
> Zhu Defeng's 祝德風 "The Famous Sights of Putuo" *Putuo quansheng* 普陀全勝 (1830).[48]
>
> Shi Chenkong's 釋塵空 "Small Gazetteer of Mount Putuo" *Putuo shan xiao zhi* 普陀山小志 (1948).[49]

These should be considered guidebooks rather than full-fledged gazetteers, but the distinction is somewhat arbitrary. All three are much shorter than gazetteers of that era and have a different structure.[50] Another primary source for the study of Mount Putuo is the "Record of the lineage of Putuo Patriarchs" *Putuo lie zu lu* 普陀列祖錄 (X.1609, dated Oct. 1696) by Tongxu 通旭 (1649–1698), which contains biographical information about the abbots of Puji Temple. (Tongxu's attempt to integrate the history of Mount Putuo into the Chan lineage narrative is discussed in Chapter 5, Exhibit 1.)

Textualization

A sacred site consists of more than a location and the socio-economic arrangements of its inhabitants. A location becomes a place by the meanings attached to it.[51] These meanings must be encoded in some form of text in order to be remembered and communicated. This text then is preserved in a wide range of media: orally or in writing, in architecture, in ritual objects, and the performance of ritual itself.[52] Without its meanings encoded in text, a place is but a point in space, unsighted by humans, uncited and uncitable. The process is dynamic—places keep changing, text is always on the move. What is here called the textualization of a site is the process by which meanings associated with a place are encoded in text; meanings, place, and text change in time, and memories of change again leave their traces in text and landscape. Topographic facts and historical events inspire the production of texts; the texts in turn influence how people perceive a site and what is proper to do there. The feedback loop of textualization begins with the naming of a site and ends only with its complete oblivion: the state in which we have forgotten that a site ever existed. This process of textualization is characterized by being *cumulative* and *self-reflexive* and by being *lossy and distortive.*[53]

Textualization is generally cumulative because the media that store cultural memory have evolved to preserve ever-larger amounts of text. With regard to gazetteers, one measure of this accumulation is the rising number of texts on the site, while another is the increasing differentiation of the texts into various genres. This increase in complexity continues independently of the varying fortunes of a site and can be found in virtually all Buddhist temple gazetteer series.[54] Here we compare eight of the Mount Putuo gazetteers.[55]

TABLE I.I   Growing Number of Texts Collected in Gazetteers

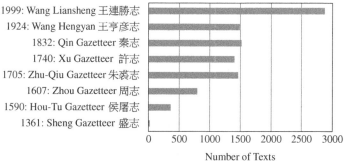

Table I.1 shows the difference between the proto-gazetteer of 1361 and the later woodblock and movable type editions. The plateau during the Qing and early Republic, when gazetteers had a volume of about 1,400 text units, reflects the influence of market forces, such as production costs and selling price. Larger works would have found no investors or buyers. Wang Hengyan (1924/1934) was the first Putuo gazetteer printed with movable type, but it still operated under the constraints of the *juan* fascicle format and comparatively high printing costs. Fang (1995) (not included in Table I.1), and Wang Liansheng (1999) show the cumulative effects of collecting and publishing texts from previous gazetteers.[56]

The growth of text about the site continues in the twenty-first century, though it is now moving out of print and into the amorphous realm of the Internet. As Franco Moretti has observed: "For every genre comes a moment when its inner form can no longer represent the most significant aspects of contemporary reality."[57] The gazetteer genre reached its limit in the twentieth century. Although gazetteers are still compiled in print, I expect they will soon follow other container formats, such as encyclopedias or bibliographies, and dissolve into linked digital text. The process of textualization itself, for which gazetteers proved useful for about five hundred years, is of course not dependent on any particular format and is bound to continue.

Another characteristic of textualization is that it is self-reflexive or self-referential. New textual formations are aware of and react to older strata just as the buildings on Mount Putuo are constructed, rebuilt, and expanded in relation to existing habitats. Analogizing from the distinction between first- and second-order observation in system theory, it is possible to distinguish different orders of how the textualization of Mount Putuo proceeds.[58] First-order textualization such as foundation legends and miracle stories connect the location with figures from the religious *imaginaire*. A passage of the *Avataṃsaka Sūtra* or a local legend is remembered and linked with a site in memory. Locations on the site are named in reference to these texts and to new, emerging local legends, asserting both identity (this island is that place) and distinction (this island is special, unlike that other, ordinary island next to it). Second-order texts such as inscriptions or travelogues reflect on the site *qua* sacred site. They are created in reference to previous first-order operations and their consequences on the ground. An imperial edict affirms patronage of Mount Putuo, citing support by the emperor's predecessors. A traveler records his visits to the island (where the edict is now inscribed on a stele), and his travelogue inspires fellow literati to make the journey themselves. Second-order texts observe first-order texts.

Each gazetteer is a particular constellation of first- and second-order texts. They themselves function as archives, as containers, but not merely so. The prefaces and postscripts add another layer, which reflects on the collection. The compilers are aware not only of the site as sacred site but also of the textual tradition that has accumulated around it. Textualization of this kind does not just passively observe the observation by other second-order texts. Its function is to select those expressions that seem admissible or desirable at a certain time. Still seen from the perspective of system theory, the task of gazetteers is to reduce complexity by filtering, ordering, and categorizing sources. Functioning as a container genre they, furthermore, aid the dissemination of the gathered texts.

Like every communication this process introduces its own distortions. Textual transmission is prone to loss; it suffers what in information theory is called transmission or generation loss.[59] In a less technical idiom, "buried under the footprints of memory and history then opens the empire of forgetting."[60] Information loss or distortion manifests both at the level of whole texts and at the level of passages or even single characters. Gazetteer compilers select texts from previous editions. They keep some, drop others, and add a few new ones. Although in principle more and more texts are available for inclusion, the selection process keeps the amount of text manageable for printing. As texts drop out of sight, the discourse about the site also changes, which in turn might affect the site itself. When, for instance, the set of illustrations of the "Twelve Views of Putuo" in the Qiu-Zhu gazetteer (see Chapter 2, Exhibit 3) replaced Tu Long's set of poems on the same theme (see Chapter 7, Exhibit 1), visitors started to write poems about these new locations. As a result of these poems other visitors seek out these newer places. Even repeated inclusion in gazetteers, however, results in information loss. On the passage level the loose editorial standards that operate in gazetteers have often resulted in altered, usually shortened, versions of texts. When Zhou Yingbin included Hou Jigao's postscript in his gazetteers, he cut about a third of the text, not unlike a newspaper editor, taking out passages and words here and there (see Chapter 1, Exhibit 3). Intentional editorial interventions that made silent changes to the text could happen for political and ideological reasons—for example, to gloss over the destruction wrought on the site by government soldiers or a scandal involving an abbot. Compilers, however, also took liberties for stylistic reasons and might sometimes have shortened pieces simply for lack of space.

Lossiness can thus be the result of intentional editorial intervention or the unintended consequence of a scribal error or a lost page. There is a question as to the degree to which lossiness matters, and to whom. Forgetting is, after all, indispensable for memory, both personal and cultural.[61] The texts collected in gazetteers are treated with much less care than Confucian classics or the canonical works of Buddhism. They are outside the purview of textual criticism and critical editions, just as no one would attempt critical editions of different Baedeker or Lonely Planet travel guides. Interesting as it might be, the market constraints of print publication make such an effort unlikely, though here, as elsewhere, digital text offers new possibilities.

The connection between the culturally constructed, semi-stable formations of the environment that we call landscape and the culturally constructed, semi-stable formations of meaning that we call text has been noted by geographers for some time. In a chapter titled "Religion and Landscape," Chris Park declares: "The landscape is a manuscript on which is written the cultural history of the area, although some traces of the past are more enduring than others. . . . Landscape is a palimpsest, or a manuscript on which two or more successive texts have been written, each one being erased to make room for the next. Quite how much is erased varies from place to place. . . ."[62] As we will see in Chapter 4, the changes in the landscape of Mount Putuo have been just as cumulative, self-referential, and marked by loss and erasure as the changes in the texts about it.

The monuments, both textual and material, to the production of emplaced meaning are manifold. Temple gazetteers are merely one expression, one medium of the textualization of sacred place. Historically, they belong to the period between the sixteenth and the twentieth century. There were some earlier "proto-gazetteers,"[63] and doubtless a few more printed gazetteers will be produced in the twenty-first century. Today, however, the textualization of Mount Putuo—the common weave of site and text—continues mainly in the relatively less constrained realm of cyberspace. There digital images and videos amplify new genres (wikis, blogs, travel sites, digital editions of gazetteers) to create a new textual record far beyond the confines of the gazetteer. I will not attempt to describe these formations here. To analyze the movement of text in cyberspace requires different methods and procedures. The texts that will concern us in this book are thus mainly those collected in the printed editions of the Mount Putuo gazetteers.

Historical Overview

Beginnings until the Yuan

Besides some short entries in the local gazetteers of the Ningbo region, much of our information on the history of Mount Putuo before the Ming comes from the proto-gazetteer by Sheng Ximing 盛熙明 (d.u.). Sheng's *Butuoluojia shan zhuan* 補陀洛迦山傳 (1361) has chapters on buildings and sights, miracle stories, a chronicle of major events, and a section of eulogies to Avalokiteśvara. It already exhibits the encyclopedic interest in topology and history that was the driving force in the formation of the genre, but it does not yet have the size and the self-awareness of later gazetteers.

Mount Putuo became established as Buddhist pilgrimage center during the Song and the Yuan, when it received intermittent support from central and local government. The Sheng Gazetteer records financial support from the court in 1081, 1151, 1210, and 1248 CE under the Song, and in 1298,

1313, 1327, 1328, and 1331 CE under the Yuan.[64] Legend ties the beginning of Buddhist activity to a nameless Indian monk, who is mentioned in the earliest accounts, and to the Japanese monk Egaku, whose story will be examined in Chapter 3 (Exhibit 1). Other early stories connect the site to Korean merchants and Chinese envoys to Korea. Wang Shunfeng 王舜封 (d.u.) saw an apparition of Guanyin at Mount Putuo in 1080, while on their return to China in 1103 the envoys Liu Da 劉達 and Wu Shi 吳栻 were guided by a ray of light. The connection to India, Japan, and Korea in the early accounts reminds us that Putuo was located on busy shipping lanes and was established in an era of close and relatively harmonious contacts between China, Korea, and Japan.

Information on Mount Putuo in the Song is complemented by short records preserved in three early gazetteers of the Ningbo area. From the description in the *Qiandao Siming tujing* 乾道四明圖經 (1169)[65] we know that at least until the twelfth century Mount Putuo was officially called "Mei's Peak" (*Meicen* 梅岑), though its association with the Mount Potalaka in the *Avataṃsaka Sūtra* was already established. The name Mei's Peak alludes to the Han dynasty official Mei Fu 梅福 (fl. 7 BCE), who allegedly withdrew to the island and became a Daoist immortal.[66] His name is remembered in the gazetteers in poems and biographic sketches, as well as in some place names on the island. "Mount Putuo" was used informally for the island as early as the eleventh century. The name is first attested in two poems by the eminent Song dynasty statesman Wang Anshi, who traveled to Mount Putuo in 1047 or 1048.[67] The *Qiandao Siming tujing* also contains a first inventory of sites on the island, which already lists the Sudhana and Tidal Sound Caves. The *Baoqing Siming zhi* 寶慶四明志 (1229) is the first gazetteer that names the island Mount Putuo (*Butuoluojia shan* 補陀洛迦山).[68] In the Yuan the *Dade Changguozhou tuzhi* 大德昌國州圖志 (1298) first groups Mount Putuo with Mount Wutai and Mount Emei as one of the "Three Great and Famous Mountains."[69] The dynastic change does not seem to have affected its popularity.

From the sources above the following picture emerges: the island Mei's Peak was first called Mount Putuo in the eleventh century and was established as a pilgrimage center by the twelfth. By the thirteenth century the number of pilgrims had increased to a point where new infrastructure beyond Mount Putuo was required. In 1277 the monk Ruzhi 如智, later abbot of the Puji Temple, organized the construction of a guest house in Shenjiamen on Zhoushan Island, the last ferry stop on the way to Putuo.[70]

What drew the visitors to the island? One note in Zhang Bangji's 張邦基 (fl. 1123–1148) *Mozhuang manlu* 墨莊漫錄 describes a visit to Mount

Putuo during the time of the Xuanhe reign (1119–1126). This account is one of the earliest descriptions of Mount Putuo.[71]

When I [Bangji] was in Siming, . . . my colleague Wang Zao, whom we called Cuizhao, was dispatched by the Prefect to pray for rain at the Guanyin cave of Mount Putuo in the Changguo district. On his return he gave me the following account of his journey:

"Mount Putuo is two days off Changguo. The mountains on the island are not very high and more than a hundred families live there. They make their living on salted fish and some agriculture. There is one temple with fifty to sixty monks. On top of the main hall live two Kalaviṅka Birds, who have built their nest in the roof beams. They are about the size of doves. The hue of their feathers is purple mixed with green and the clarity of their voice surpasses that of a jade chime. Every year they breed and fly away with their offspring—we do not know whither.

On the island there is a cave too deep to measure and impossible to enter. The water [rushing] in the cave sounds as if a hundred drums are being struck; one cannot hear what others say. One top there is an opening where the sun light falls in at least some dozen meters. It is in here that the image of the Bodhisattva appears.

Being under orders of the Prefect I prayed silently and hoped for a vision. After a short while I saw a railing of several feet, all made of jade and decorated with engravings, just like at the way leading to a worldly palace. There also appeared a pattern of red coral only several feet away from us, brightly radiant. After some time we saw an image of Guanyin in the very deepest part of the cave. However, we only saw the lower part of the body [clearly] from the waist down, the upper body was unclear. She was clad in white and adorned with necklaces and bracelets, so clear one could have counted them, but her head was not visible at all. A monk from the temple said that long ago someone had seen her face and it was bright red. This is why the image [in the temple] on the island now was done in this color.

The kingdoms of Korea are far beyond the sea. Whenever their boats arrive at Putuo they pray [at the temple]. The temple has many bronze items such as bells and sounding boards which were donated by merchants from Korea, and which often bear dates in their calendar. There are also many inscriptions by foreigners, which are written very tastefully. The monks [also] said that those who pray at the cave see different things. Some see a shining vase or a necklace, some see Sudhana or a bridge. There are also those who see nothing. In front of the cave, under a big boulder there is something sparkling and translucent like white jade, called the Bodhisattva Stone."

Cuizhao is not the gullible type, and his words can be believed.[72]

The account of Wang Zao's visit offers a rare glimpse into the life on the island in the twelfth century. It confirms that the early development of the site was connected with traders and envoys from and to Korea. Outgoing vessels would make a last stop at Mount Putuo before crossing the East Chinese Sea to Korea or Japan. Incoming ships would stop there before venturing on to Ningbo. These stopovers were perhaps not always religiously motivated; a stop outside the scrutiny of government officials could be used to take on or unload contraband. Zhang also provides a first head count of monks: he reports fifty to sixty monks at the Puji Temple. It was a mid-sized monastery, therefore, well able to take care of visitors and cater to envoys but not nearly the busy scene with several monasteries and the several thousand monks that lived on Mount Putuo in the Ming and Qing.

The Song-Yuan transition, which was traumatic in many ways for China, has left little trace in the records on Mount Putuo. There is reason to believe that Buddhist institutions in general received more support under the Yuan than under the Southern Song. In North China the Mongol conquest in fact strengthened the participation of Buddhism and Daoism in local and regional administration.[73] The Yuan court continued and even increased imperial support for Mount Putuo, which kept expanding and now attracted visitors not only from East Asia but also from Inner Asia. Sheng Ximing himself, the author of the first gazetteer, was from Kucha on the Northern Silk Road.[74] Unlike the Song emperors, the Mongol rulers considered themselves Buddhists. Their patronage of Buddhist art and institutions, and the translation of Buddhist texts into Mongolian are well attested.[75]

Caesura and Revival—Mount Putuo During the Ming

After Sheng Ximing, it was almost two hundred years before the next gazetteer was produced. The long hiatus between the Sheng and the Hou-Tu Gazetteer coincides with what has been called the decline of Buddhism during the early and middle periods of the Ming dynasty.[76] During that period the prevailing form of Confucian orthodoxy was hostile to Buddhism and literati interest in Buddhism was generally low. Institutionally, Buddhism was severely constrained by the restrictive legislation of the Ming Code that was instituted by the founding Hongwu emperor and upheld by most of his successors.[77] The new dynasty had started relatively well for Buddhism. The Hongwu emperor in his early years had been a monk for some time before joining the uprisings that ended the Yuan dynasty, and after ascending to the throne he wrote a number of works on Buddhism and Buddhist sutras.[78] While Hongwu's early policies toward Buddhism were lenient, this changed as his rule descended into the cruel despotism that ushered in a long period of ideological and intellectual stagnation. Although—or perhaps because—he was in many ways deeply involved with Buddhism, his absolutist instincts led him to enforce an unprecedented degree of state control over monastic hierarchies, the ordination of monks, temple construction, and the dissemination of Buddhist texts.[79] His Amalgamation Order of 1391, as Timothy Brook has put it, "altered institutional Buddhism in China more thoroughly than any previous suppression, and there would be nothing like it again until the 1950s."[80]

After Hongwu, most Ming emperors of the early and middle period were interested in Tibetan Buddhism, which regained a strong presence at court and in the capital until 1536 when the Daoist Jiajing emperor closed all Buddhist establishments in the Forbidden City. Previously, the court had even commissioned new translations of tantric texts, though no attempt was made to promulgate these teachings beyond a relatively small circle of insiders.[81] Eunuchs and palace women were generally seen as sympathetic to Buddhism but were not able to influence religious policy. Thus, during the early and mid-Ming the institutional—and arguably the intellectual—development of Buddhism was stymied by legal repression carried out by a strong central government. Ideologically this was legitimized by a hegemonic Neo-Confucian discourse, which ruled supreme in politics and education.[82]

Mount Putuo bore the full brunt of the Hongwu emperor's strict policies. In 1387 the Buddhist establishments on the island were destroyed on the orders of Tang He (1326–1395), Duke of Xin, as part of a campaign against coastal piracy.[83] The destruction and suppression of Mount Putuo was not in the main religiously motivated, but it was typical of the centralized form of autocracy that developed under the early Ming, where *raison d'état* trumped all other ideological, social, and economic concerns. The monks and the other inhabitants of Putuo were moved to the mainland. This resulted in a hiatus of almost two hundred years during which little or no religious activity is recorded for Mount Putuo. The hiatus in the early and mid-Ming was brought about by the government and continued due to a lack of support for Chinese Buddhism from the literati, as well as due to the restrictive legislation of the Ming Code, which prohibited the construction of temples without government approval. Another reason, of a more regional nature, was the government's failure to maintain a robust coastal defense. As a pilgrimage site, Mount Putuo relied on safe passage for its visitors. Travel in the archipelago, however, became more and more precarious in the fifteenth and early sixteenth centuries as China increasingly turned its back on international trade, which was first restricted and finally prohibited. Partly as a consequence of this shift, the maritime frontier saw a new surge in "Japanese pirate" incursions.[84] As former trading partners in China and Japan continued their now illegal trade, the Ming government tried to suppress it. The situation grew increasingly violent, and in the mid-sixteenth century sizable bands of Japanese and Chinese pirates raided the coasts of Fujian, Zhejiang, and Jiangsu. The pirates were able to engage the Ming navy in protracted sea battles with hundreds of boats, and at times their raids penetrated deeply into the coastal hinterland. Only with great difficulty was the central government able to defeat Wang Zhi 王 (*v.l.* 汪) 直 (d. 1559), a powerful pirate-insurgent, who was executed after having surrendered in exchange for a promised amnesty. The strategic importance, or rather vulnerability, of the Zhoushan archipelago, which was a major center of pirate trade, became a national issue during the 1540s and 1550s. In 1553 the Ming General Yu Dayou 俞大猷 (1503–1579) fought a battle against pirates on Mount Putuo, in which more than 1,500 men were killed.[85] After the death of the Jiajing emperor in 1567, the pirate problem was resolved by maintaining a strong naval presence while allowing normal trade to resume, and the archipelago was resettled.

The expansion of maritime trade coincided with a number of other developments. China's education system had for some time produced more far more literati than could be incorporated into the bureaucracy. This resulted in a sizable reading public, trained in the Confucian classics, but without the kind of government work which the classics idealize. A large number of these men, recognizing that the chances of official appointment were slim, turned toward local family networks for power and a wide array of cultural pursuits for pleasure.[86] The pendulum of power swung back from an absolutist central government to the regional elites. The rise of local historiography, of which the Putuo gazetteers are an example, is one of the consequences of this development; another was increased support for Buddhist institutions in general.[87] Thus the overall situation for large Buddhist sites like Mount Putuo improved in the late Ming when Chinese society regained some of the commercial and demographic dynamism it had had in the Song and Yuan.[88]

Although the economic and cultural conditions had shifted in favor of the regional gentry, the religious policy of the central government still mattered. Only with the death of the Jiajing emperor in 1567 did his anti-Buddhist policies give way to the moderately tolerant attitude of the Longqing and Wanli emperors, thereby allowing a resurgence of Mount Putuo as a pilgrimage site. The Jiajing emperor (r. 1521–1567), on the advice of his Daoist advisers and against the preference of the eunuch faction, had pursued a stridently anti-Buddhist policy that stopped just short of outright persecution.[89] His successor, the Longqing emperor (r. 1567–1572), quickly retired the influential Daoists at his father's court. His wife, the mother of the Wanli emperor, was a committed Buddhist who came to play an important role in the late Ming revival of Buddhism. The Wanli emperor (r. 1572–1620), who for most of his later reign was at odds with the Confucian bureaucracy, offered qualified support to institutional Buddhism. In this he was at least partly influenced by his mother, the empress dowager.[90] Both patronized monastic communities, mainly around Beijing and in the Jiangnan region. Their support was aligned with the interests of the eunuch faction and some literati, but it did offend the more conservative segments of the Confucian elite.[91]

As will be discussed in Chapter 1 (Exhibit 3), an alliance between some officials, the eunuchs, and the empress dowager managed to reopen Mount Putuo as a pilgrimage site. A watershed was reached in 1580 when the monk Dazhi 大智 (1524–1592) founded what would later become the Fayu Temple on the northeastern shore of Mount Putuo. Dazhi was well connected among the local literati; his friends included authors like Wang Shizhen and Tu Long, and both the Hou-Tu and the Zhou Gazetteer contain a large number of poems dedicated to him.

Around 1589, after the island had been resettled, Navy Commander Hou Jigao commissioned the poet and playwright Tu Long to update Sheng Ximing's gazetteer. Tu Long compiled the gazetteer as requested, complete with new maps. He included most of Sheng Ximing's text and added a large number of poems by local literati.

For some time there was considerable resistance to Mount Putuo among conservative officials, who preferred to see the site closed. After the Puji temple burned down in 1598, unsuccessful attempts were made to prevent its reconstruction (see Chapter 1, Exhibit 3). It was only after the appearance of the Zhou Gazetteer, produced by the vice minister of rites Zhou Yingbin (a Ningbo native) and the eunuch official Zhang Sui, that these efforts ended, and Mount Putuo became firmly reestablished in the religious landscape of Chinese Buddhism.

More Revivals: Mount Putuo During the Qing and the Early Republic

The Ming–Qing transition was a messy, violent affair in general and for the Jiangnan region in particular. The Ming dynasty did not go quietly. Although the north was quickly brought under Manchu control after the fall of Beijing in 1644, it was another forty years before the Manchus had quelled all remnants of Ming loyalist forces. One of the loyalist groups, grouped around Zhu Yihai (1618–1662), fought their retreat through Zhejiang and along the Zhoushan archipelago before fleeing further south to Fujian. Mount Putuo was touched by the fighting only peripherally. In 1649, however, the loyalist commander Ruan Jun, who had taken refuge on Zhoushan island decided to sell the precious copy of the Buddhist canon, given to the Fayu Temple by the Wanli empress dowager, to Japan. In a desperate attempt to raise money for loyalist troops, two boats were dispatched to Nagasaki. The mission, however, was not successful. The *bakufu* commissioner at Nagasaki was not willing to assist the struggling Ming loyalists, and the Tripitaka was returned to Mount Putuo.[92]

Even after the loyalist forces had been defeated, the Qing, like the Ming a hundred years before, found the silver-driven commerce along the southeastern coast difficult to control. Japan had by then retreated into isolation with the promulgation of the *sakoku* 鎖国 edicts of 1633, but Spanish, Dutch, and English traders now competed with Chinese coastal pirate-traders for the shipping lanes of East Asia. In the summer of 1665, three years after the final defeat of the Ming pretender in Fujian, the Dutch repeatedly raided the temples of Mount Putuo and made off with bronze images and other goods worth more than 200,000 *tael* of silver.[93] The Qing response to these and other incursions was the tried-and-trusted evacuation of the archipelago, a drastic measure to prevent pirates and privateers gaining a foothold on the islands. In 1671 the monks residing on Mount Putuo were once more moved to temples in the Ningbo region. In 1675, the Puji Temple, which had been rebuilt only seventy years earlier, burned down again as "local bandits" tried to melt off the metal decoration on the large statues in the abandoned temple.[94] Again the contingencies of dynastic change had caused Mount Putuo to be abandoned. This time, however, the hiatus did not last long. As had been the case a century earlier, a military leader, Navy Commander Lan Li 藍理 (1649–1720), was at the center of a clique of local gentlemen who wanted the site reopened. Once the

Kangxi emperor had consolidated his reign in the west and southwest, the "ocean embargo" (*haijin* 海禁) was revoked in 1684. The Fayu Temple was immediately reopened under the abbot Xingtong 性統 (1661–1717), and a large ordination ceremony was held there only three years later, reestablishing a Sangha with ordination ties to Mount Putuo. Kangxi continued to patronize Mount Putuo during the second half of his reign by granting inscriptions, funds, and, crucially, in 1718, a tax exemption for some of the land holdings. In Chapter 5 we will discuss this "early Qing revival" of Mount Putuo in greater detail, focusing on the military and monastic actors operating under imperial patronage.

The main witnesses for the "early Qing revival" are the Qiu-Zhu (1705, reprinted c. 1735) and Xu (1740) gazetteers. The Qiu-Zhu Gazetteer is considerably longer than its three predecessors but was quickly followed and surpassed by the Xu Gazetteer in 1740. As with the "late Ming revival" the first gazetteer after the recovery is quickly succeeded by another, more polished edition. The Xu Gazetteer superseded the Qiu-Zhu Gazetteer in the same way as the Zhou Gazetteer (1607) had superseded the Hou-Tu Gazetteer (1590). In the late twentieth century this pattern was repeated, when the Fang Gazetteer (1995) was quickly superseded by the more comprehensive Wang Liansheng Gazetteer (1999). On all three occasions this was not because the earlier gazetteer had become unavailable. It was rather that during and right after the "revivals" there were varying opinions as to what and who had brought the revival about. Conflicting emphasis led in all cases to revision and re-edition of gazetteers by another compiler, who put a different spin on recent events. Pierre-Henry De Bruyn noted a similar pattern when studying the gazetteers of Mount Wudang: "Every gazetteer is witness to a specific struggle."[95]

The Qianlong reign was a prosperous and peaceful time for Mount Putuo, but government support dried up after Yongzheng. Nevertheless, the site expanded in 1793 when a third major temple was built on top of Huading Mountain above the Fayu Temple. The Huiji Temple 慧濟寺 continued the move northward up the island by Buddhist institutions (see Chapter 4, Exhibit 2). Even today, pious pilgrims prostrate their way from the Fayu Temple upward along the scenic pilgrimage trail, which takes about half an hour to ascend. For two centuries, from the late eighteenth century until very recently, the Puji, the Fayu, and the Huiji were considered the three main temples on Mount Putuo.[96]

In 1832, the Qin Gazetteer was compiled at the request of Hongkun Nenglun 鴻崑能崙 (1770–d. after 1832), abbot of the Puji Temple.[97] This gazetteer is considered biased toward including texts on Puji Temple at the expense of other establishments.[98] The re-emergence of competition between the Puji and the Fayu Temple might have been the result of the general decline of the site in the early nineteenth century. The Qin Gazetteer shows a precipitous drop in government support after the Yongzheng reign. In the sections describing donations, temple construction, and other events there are only few entries for the Qianlong reign. This is confirmed by the next gazetteer (Wang Hengyan 1924). In the digital edition of the Wang Hengyan Gazetteer, the Kangxi emperor and his sixty-year reign are referenced 208 times, the thirteen years of Yongzheng are referenced 60 times, while the sixty years of Qianlong are only referenced 44 times. It is unlikely that both the Qin Gazetteer and the Wang Hengyan Gazetteer have been negligent and that we are dealing with a lacuna in historiography rather than history. It seems rather that after Yongzheng, the court had indeed lost interest in Mount Putuo.

This probably did not translate into an immediate decline of the site. As we have seen, a major temple was added in 1793, and in the fascicle on buildings (fansha 梵刹) the Qin Gazetteer still lists a number of structures as "renovated" besides the many glossed as "now abandoned."[99] A decline in religious activity might, however, be inferred from the lack of new of miracle stories for this time in the gazetteers (see Chapter 3).[100]

There is a strange lacuna in our information relating to Mount Putuo for the time between the compilation of the Qin Gazetteer 1832 and what could be called the "late Qing revival" of Mount Putuo after 1870. During that period Mount Putuo as a pilgrimage center was in decline as both the Opium Wars (1840–1842, 1856–1860) and the Taiping Rebellion (1851–1864) disrupted travel to the island. British forces twice invaded Zhoushan during the First Opium War and for six years (1840–1846) occupied Dinghai, its main harbor.[101] During that time a number of Europeans visited Mount Putuo and, not surprisingly, found it in disrepair.[102] It is difficult to determine whether stagnation had already set in before the Opium War, but it stands to reason that the destruction of Dinghai in 1841 and the British occupation of Zhoushan would have affected pilgrimage travel and therefore the economics of Mount Putuo, dependent as it was on the delivery of rice from the mainland. The botanist Robert Fortune, who traveled to Mount Putuo in July 1844, reports that "almost all these places are crumbling fast into ruins. There are a few exceptions, in cases where they happen to get a good name amongst the people from the supposed kindness of the gods; but the great mass are in a state of decay."[103] Besides the three major temples Fortune estimates there were sixty to seventy smaller temples on the island all of which together housed about two thousand monks.[104] Fortune and other naturalists like Theodore Cantor, Évariste Huc, and Ferdinand von Richthofen visited existing or potential overseas domains to collect intelligence about the local climate, geography, and fauna and flora. We owe to Fortune an observation about a pastime of Putuo monks: "I was also informed that the resident priests were fond of collecting plants, particularly Orchidaceae, and that their collections were much increased by the itinerant habits of the begging priests, who visit the most distant provinces of the empire, as well as by the donations of the lay devotees, who come to Poo-to at stated seasons of the year, to worship and leave their offerings in the temples."[105] Not all visitors came to bring orchids, however. Around 1845 Captain William Edie pilfered five large and valuable bronze statues of Bodhisattvas from the Puji Temple.[106] They were displayed at the monumental Manchester Arts Treasure Exhibition in 1857 and are now in the National Liverpool Museum.

The dearth of information about Mount Putuo for the period between 1800 and c. 1870 in its gazetteers is indicative of difficult times. Chinese Buddhism of this period is little understood,[107] but it seems that institutional Buddhism was stagnating, although Qianlong had lifted ordination restrictions in 1754.[108] The nadir for the lower Yangzi region was the widespread destruction of Buddhist (and Daoist) temples during the Taiping rebellion (1850–1864). This vast civil war, in which more people were killed than in World War I, affected especially the Jiangnan region, where its consequences were felt for many decades.[109] The Taiping never attacked Zhoushan or Putuo, and their occupation of Ningbo in winter 1861/62 was a relatively bloodless affair. Thus Mount Putuo was not directly affected by the war, but pilgrimage travel and grain supply were greatly diminished.

According to the sources preserved in the gazetteers, a "late Qing revival" of Mount Putuo took place after 1870, again mirroring what seems to have been a nation-wide trend.[110] In *The Buddhist Revival in China*, Holmes Welch famously discusses the problematic dimensions of the term "revival" for what occurred in the late Qing and the early Republican periods.[111] Still, *The Buddhist Revival in China* by and large does assume a revival period between 1850 and 1950, and Welch begins his narrative of the Chinese Buddhist "revival" around 1870, when Yang Wenhui restarted the printing presses in Nanjing. This is also when the coverage in the Mount Putuo gazetteers picks up again. For the years 1820 to 1875 we do not even know the exact sequence of the abbots of Puji Temple. In 1875, the first steam ships went from Shanghai via Ningbo to Mount Putuo, and the island became famous among the expat community for its beaches, a popularity it would enjoy into the 1920s.[112] Already in

1879, Butler remarked on "an era of rebuilding, on a large and permanent scale. . . . Now that merchant steamers are daily passing back and forth in sight of its shores . . . the fears of the priests [of pirates] have been quieted."[113] In the early twentieth century visitors like Boerschmann (1911) and Johnston (1913) found an active and wealthy pilgrimage site, with "well over a thousand" monks in residence.[114] Johnston reports that one to three hundred monks from all over China were ordained on the island every year. The beginning of the difficult twentieth century thus saw Mount Putuo in good form, and the prefaces of the Wang Hengyan Gazetteer are accordingly confident and optimistic.

Mount Putuo in the People's Republic

The Fang (1995) and the Wang Liansheng (1999) gazetteers collect an unprecedented amount of texts about the site (see Table I.1). Impervious to political change while recording it, the gazetteer tradition stays on track. Religious activity on Mount Putuo was severely affected by the fall of the Yuan and the Ming, the Opium Wars and the Taiping rebellion, the Sino-Japanese and the ensuing civil war, as well as by the Cultural Revolution, but the production of texts about the site has continued unabated.

Our discussion of Mount Putuo and its gazetteers will mention recent developments only rarely. The most recent exhibit (Chapter 5, Exhibit 3) is Sun Yat-sen's account of the vision he had on Mount Putuo in 1916. This is not for lack of information in the gazetteers. The Fang and the Wang Liansheng gazetteers, in many ways typical (and perhaps the final) exponents of the Putuo gazetteer tradition, offer a number of records for the more recent past. However, to illustrate the textualization of the site in the twentieth century, a narrow focus on gazetteers does not seem appropriate. Plenty of other sources are available for this period, especially newspapers and magazines, as well as infinitely more images. Also, for the last fifty years, the memory of eyewitnesses arguably takes precedence over the texts gathered in gazetteers. Fieldwork could give us access to the religious aspirations and customs of pilgrims that are hardly ever documented in the gazetteers.[115] To show how Mount Putuo has been constructed as a sacred site in the twentieth century merits another book altogether, one that would be based on a much more diverse range of sources. Were it written, however, I suspect that the underlying mechanism of how the site was suppressed and recovered would prove to be not all that different from the cycles of previous centuries that left their textual traces in the gazetteers.

Whereas the effect of early Communist rule has been documented to a degree,[116] the impact of the Cultural Revolution on Chinese and Tibetan Buddhism is understood only in its depressing outlines. For Mount Putuo the Cultural Revolution was a short and disastrous caesura. In the current political climate it is not possible to give a full account of the damage wrought. Most of the sources are declared "sensitive," and eyewitnesses cannot easily be named. To its credit, the Wang Liansheng Gazetteer records occasionally which sites and artifacts have been lost or destroyed when the Red Guards invaded Mount Putuo from September to November 1966. According to Wang, more than seventeen thousand images were taken from the temples and destroyed. The Red Guards raided the libraries of the three main temples and burned more than 34,000 fascicles, presumably including the editions of the canon gifted by the Ming and Qing emperors. The monks and a few nuns, who had found shelter on the island after the war, were defrocked and dispersed. Only some ten elderly monastics were allowed to retire in the Mei Fu Hermitage.[117] After the "lost decade" of the Cultural Revolution, Mount Putuo experienced its most recent revival. Local devotees started to reconstruct the site, uprighting toppled steles and restoring effaced images and inscriptions. This (dare we call it the "early PRC revival"?) resulted in the vibrant pilgrimage site that is visited by several hundred thousand people every year.

The pattern is by now familiar. As during the Ming and Qing, Mount Putuo suffered as a result of the instability following a regime change. While the Ming suppression led to a long hiatus, the early Qing evacuation, the nineteenth-century decline, and the Cultural Revolution were relatively short interludes. All interruptions were caused by the failure of governance in the Zhoushan archipelago.[118] All resulted in revival periods that included the compilation of new gazetteers. Like their predecessors, today's gazetteers prefer to dwell not on the barbaric destruction but on the optimism of the renaissance, and I too will follow that custom.

CHAPTER 1 | "We Confucians"—Prefaces and Postscripts

> I believe Buddhism differs from our Confucianism in what it holds
> to be real and what to discard as unreal. But Buddhists too want to
> benefit society, practice the Way and transmit it to posterity, and in
> this they are similar to us Confucians.

—YANG YONGJIAN[1]

IN 1698 YANG YONGJIAN 楊雍建 (1627–1704), high-ranking official, scholar, and writer, received a visitor in his home near Hangzhou. The abbot of Mount Putuo's Fayu Temple, Bie'an Xingtong 別庵性統 (1661–1717), had come to ask Yang for an inscription.[2] Xingtong planned to build a stūpa for the robe and alms bowl of his late master Sanshan Denglai 三山燈來 (1614–1685). Yang, who had known Denglai from a previous posting in Sichuan, remembered him well and thus "did not dare to refuse." The result was a short, thoughtful piece on Confucian and Buddhist attitudes toward death, which will be discussed as Exhibit 4 of this chapter.

Renowned literati were often commissioned to write commemorative inscriptions, and the scene above is typical for how the texts collected in gazetteers, and indeed many of the gazetteers themselves, were produced. Most of them were created not by Buddhist monks but by Confucian literati, people who had received an education in the Confucian classics and, as members of a "writing elite," were able to write certain genres appropriate to the occasion.[3] Already the first proto-gazetteer, the sixth-century *Record of Buddhist Monasteries in Luoyang* (*Luoyang qielan ji* 洛陽伽藍記), was, in John Kieschnick's description, "an urbane official's nostalgic look back at a sophisticated, flourishing city rather than the pious record of a Buddhist devotee."[4] As with other forms of Buddhist historiography in

China, temple gazetteers are an adaption of a genre that was first devised by Confucians to record *their* history for their own purposes.[5] Therefore, although it might seem strange to begin this book on a Buddhist site with a chapter on Confucian sentiments, those sentiments inform the characteristic perspective of gazetteers and deserve a closer look. As we will see, the development of Mount Putuo as a pilgrimage site was influenced by how much support the site received from government officials and local literati, all of whom generally considered themselves Confucian.

How did the Confucian author-compilers of temple gazetteers go about their Buddhist task? After the anomaly of the early and mid-Ming, when literati engagement with Buddhism was largely absent, in the late Ming Buddhism again became one of the issues about which Confucian gentlemen could be of different opinion. In the spectrum between highly sympathetic versus hostile attitudes toward Buddhism, those who subscribed to the latter obviously were unlikely to become involved in the compilation of temple gazetteers. It is worth remembering, however, that this hostility existed and that at times the Buddhist history of a site was written with literati assistance against literati resistance. Kubota (1931 [1986]) has shown how the relationship between Buddhism and Confucianism since the Tang consisted of a creative tension, which time and again brought forth both syncretistic attempts to resolve it as well as stern opposition to any such moves.

The conservative branch of Neo-Confucianism, the *daoxue* 道學 associated with Zhu Xi and the Cheng brothers (Cheng Yi and Cheng Hao), was generally unfriendly, if not outright hostile, toward Buddhism. During the Yuan it had become the hegemonic discourse within Chinese literati culture through its dominant role in the examination system.[6] According to Benjamin Elman, "in effect, by the early Ming, the values of the state educational system for elite men were automatically linked with the Dao Learning sympathies of local elites."[7] That fact that literati were able to express their Buddhist sympathies again more freely in the late Ming was in part due to the influence of Wang Yangming's 王陽明 (1472–1529) comparatively liberal interpretation of Neo-Confucianism, which was widely perceived as being close to or inspired by Buddhism.[8] Yangming's teachings drew explicitly on the thought of Zhu Xi's antagonist Lu Xiangshan 陸象山 (1139–1192) and created an alternative within Confucianism to the anti-Buddhist attitude of the *daoxue*. His philosophy emphasized individual, inner experience and exhorted Confucians to develop and bring forth "innate knowledge"—concerns akin to those of Chan Buddhism. Thus, within Confucianism a more nuanced spectrum on which intellectuals could position themselves with regard to Buddhism was reopened. The syncretistic attitudes, collectively labeled "Three Teachings Harmonize as One" (*sanjiao heyi* 三教合一), which in earlier periods had allowed literati to combine aspects of Confucianism, Buddhism, and Daoism, was reestablished. The Buddhist revival of the late Ming was in many ways a return to modes of literati–Buddhist interaction that had been generally available in previous dynasties. As a result, Buddhism and Confucianism were again described as compatible both by Buddhists such as Hanshan Deqing 憨山德清 and Yunqi Zhuhong 雲棲株宏, as well as by sympathetic Confucians such as Li Zhi 李贄, the Yuan brothers,[9] and Tu Long 屠隆, the main compiler of the Hou-Tu Gazetteer.[10]

In spite of these options for rapprochement, Confucian literati in the Ming remained, in Timothy Brook's words "Neo-Confucianism's captive audience."[11] The success of Wang Yangming and his students was strongly resisted by adherents of Zhu-Cheng orthodoxy, who accused them of being too Buddhist.[12] It was difficult for literati in late imperial China to admit Buddhist sympathies if they held government office and the authors whose works appeared in temple gazetteers were rarely purely religiously motivated.[13] Nevertheless the gazetteers reflect a nuanced range of Confucian attitudes toward Buddhism.

These attitudes surface in the various prefaces (*xu* 序, *xu* 敘), the sections on editorial principles (*fanli* 凡例), and the postscripts (*houxu* 後序, *ba* 跋) attached to the gazetteers.[14] Besides writing his own preface, a compiler would invite friends and local officials to contribute. Gazetteer prefaces and postscripts are therefore not only individual statements but an ensemble that provides information about how local cliques worked together and supported a site. Prefaces are not always placed before the main body of the text; sometimes they are prefixed to individual chapters. Both prefaces and postscripts are generally attached to the main text with their own page numbering and do not appear in the table of contents. This makes it possible to add prefaces of sponsors in later print runs. Woodblock editions often preserve prefaces in the original calligraphy of the author, resulting, in effect, in a collection of autographs. Autographs are relatively "firm" texts compared to those collected in the main body of the gazetteer, which went through various rounds of editing and copying and which, as we will see, were often changed considerably by the compilers.

The forces of textualization—accumulation, self-awareness, and distortion—are in full swing not only on the level of the gazetteer as a whole but also on the level of each individual genre. First, in the case of prefaces and postscripts, although their number varies among gazetteers, it tends to increase with each new edition. In a series of gazetteers, later editions often preserve several prefaces from previous gazetteers in a special section.[15] On the other hand, the only gazetteer for a site or the first gazetteer of a series might have only one or two prefaces.[16]

Second, prefaces and postscripts are among the most self-referential genres because they relate to the production of the work they are part of. Prefaces are also our main source for the edition history and editorial policy of a series. The sections on editorial principles (*fanli* 凡例), which generally follow the preface of the main compiler, are especially helpful for understanding the criteria by which texts were collected. The Pure Land master Yinguang, for instance, had strong views about what a gazetteer ought to be and wanted to expand the religious content of gazetteers. In the editorial principles of his Mount Emei Gazetteer, he complains about how previous versions had given too little space to the deeds of Bodhisattva Samantabhadra.[17] Elsewhere Yinguang pays a rare compliment to his fellow monastic Zhencheng 鎮澄 (1547–1617), the compiler of the late Ming edition of the Mount Wutai Gazetteer, recommending Zhencheng's edition over the later Kangxi era edition.[18]

Third, as to distortion, even the preface of the main compiler cannot always be relied on. The compiler of the Aśoka Temple Gazetteer, for instance, says that the structure of his edition is modeled after the Hou-Tu Gazetteer, which is not the case.[19] Incongruities between an edition and its prefaces occurred in part because the compilation process was a collaborative enterprise and the main editor was not always fully involved at all stages.

In what follows, exhibits 1 and 2 illustrate some of the Confucian and Buddhist attitudes at play in the production of temple gazetteers for various sites during the Ming and Qing. The material in Exhibit 3 is solely concerned with the debates surrounding the late Ming revival of Mount Putuo and the editorial differences between the Hou-Tu and the Zhou gazetteers. Exhibit 4 brings us back to Yang Yongjian and the essay he attached to the stūpa inscription for Xingtong's teacher. Yang's reflections on the relationship between Confucianism and Buddhism are typical for the Kangxi era in which the relationship between the two belief systems was fairly amicable, and the chapter ends on a relatively harmonious note.

Exhibit 1: We Confucians

The term *wuru* 吾儒, "we Confucians" or "our Confucianism," appears frequently in the prefaces and postscripts of Ming and Qing dynasty gazetteers.[20] It asserts the identity of the writer and signals that in spite of the Buddhist subject matter, the author is writing with the detached attitude of a literatus addressing his fellow Confucians. Sometimes Buddhism is conflated with Daoism, both being systems that a gentleman might make use of, without putting them at the center of his identity.

Miao Sui 繆燧 (1650–1716) became involved in the early Qing revival of Mount Putuo after he was appointed district magistrate of Dinghai in 1695. In a typical statement he explains:

> Since the Han and the Jin dynasties, Daoism and Buddhism have both been actively propagated in the world, Buddhism has been somewhat more popular than Daoism. Those who follow them blindly are silly, while those who deny them are narrow-minded. Only accomplished men can put both of them to good use. The emperor [Kangxi] has . . . pronounced that the "loving-kindness" (ci 慈) of the Buddhists is just like the "benevolence" (ren 仁) of us Confucians (wuru 吾儒). The [Buddhist idea of] "ferrying people across out of compassion and pity" is not different from [the Confucian motto] "generously provide and assist others."[21]

In spite of the wide availability of the syncretistic move during the late Ming and Qing, officials often felt they had to justify why they supported Buddhist institutions. The gazetteer of the Huangbo Temple in Fujian preserves, attached as "prefaces," two fund-raising appeals.[22] The first was written by Ye Xianggao 葉向高 (1559–1627) some time between 1614 and 1620.[23] Ye, whose family was from Fujian, rose through the ranks to become one of the most influential grand secretaries of the late Ming. He begins his preface with a line describing the mountain scenery from a poem (*Journey to Mount Huangbo* 游黃檗山) by the Liang dynasty poet Jiang Yan 江淹 (444–505): "The dazzling Luan birds glide by sunlit peaks, in shaded brooks gush dragon springs; on the crimson cliffs the cries of birds; monkeys shout in clear and empty spaces."

The reference to Jiang Yan, who traveled to the Huangbo mountains before Buddhist activity is recorded there, sets the tone for a secular recommendation of a religious institution. Ye keeps his text largely devoid of Buddhist imagery. He recounts how the Wanli emperor donated a set of the Tripitaka to the monastery and uses this and earlier land donations by the dynasty's founder, the Hongwu 洪武 emperor, as precedents to justify his own support for the fund-raiser.[24] He also alludes to the fact that official support may not be taken for granted:

> Some say the Buddhist teachings are sheer nonsense, are to be avoided by Confucians, and do not merit respect. [These people] do not realize that

in the universe this Way does exist after all, and cannot just be abolished. [Nevertheless, in spite of the example] of his majesty Emperor Gao [the founder of the Ming] himself, there are [still people] saying this. When I stayed in the capital, I saw how in its vicinity everywhere are landholdings that temples had received from Emperor Gao. Huangbo [Monastery] is more than a thousand years old, and again our Emperor has ordered [to support it]. How could one not admire this?[25]

Ye supports the rebuilding of the temple, which had been destroyed by a fire in the Jiaqing period (1522–1569), and urges the "believers of the four directions" to help with the task. A second endorsement was written about two hundred years later, when Mount Huangbo was again in dire straits. The monks approached Zhang Jinyun 張縉雲, an official posted in the area. In a *Preface for the Donation Ledger* 黃檗寺緣簿序 (c. 1823–1826) Zhang writes:

> When I came to this area in 1823, I visited first Lingshi [monastery] then Huangbo. Both temples had fields that have been appropriated by the populace. I sent someone to make inquiries, and the people returned the fields to the temples, without charging for it. . . . [A while ago] the monks from the [neighboring] Lingshi monastery asked me to write an endorsement [for a fundraiser]. I consented and less than one year later, the monks from Huangbo too asked me to write an endorsement to raise funds. Huangbo's buildings are even more numerous than those of Lingshi, the repair costs are huge and the monks have no choice but to ask for help. The teachings of the two masters [Buddhism and Daoism] are not greatly admired by [us] Confucians, but I felt that as the local official I would be at fault if I would not see to the repair of the famous sites of the area that have existed for centuries.[26]

Both Ye and Zhang are hedging against possible criticism from conservative Confucians with good reason. The conservative reaction against the assimilation of Buddhism had teeth. In 1602 Li Zhi 李贄 (1527–1602), a radical champion for a synthesis of Confucian and Buddhist ideals, committed suicide in prison after being impeached for heterodoxy. A memorial endorsing the suppression of his writings criticized Li Zhi's championing of Buddhist ideals over "Our Way" (*wudao* 吾道).[27] Ye, who probably knew Li, a fellow Fujianese, personally, certainly remembered the case well. And even two hundred years later, Zhang Jinyun would have known about the incident, as the indictment against Li Zhi was widely circulated in later times.[28]

Although both Ye and Zhang were supportive of Buddhism on other occasions as well, it is difficult to gauge the depth of their interest in Buddhism. Belonging as they did to "Neo-Confucianism's captive audience," they had to frame their support as part of their administrative duties and put rhetorical distance between themselves and their Buddhist subjects.

Exhibit 2: Buddhist Rhetoric Toward Confucianism

The literati rhetoric, which tends to downplay both a religious motivation on part of the authors and the religious meanings of the site, was not limited to literati authors. In the Ming and Qing, Buddhist monks too when compiling gazetteers often used a rather muted, secular register. Only now and then did apologetic comments find their way into gazetteers. The 1624 gazetteer of Hangzhou's Jingshan Temple 徑山寺 contains a short rebuttal of Neo-Confucian views, which ends: "Therefore doubting that the Buddhist tradition is 'without father' and 'without ruler' shows only that the teaching was not fully understood. This obscures the Way of Confucius as well as causing great harm to Buddhism. What a pity!"[29] The author singles out the Zhu-Cheng school of Confucianism for criticism and does not reject Confucianism as such. Unqualified criticism of Confucianism was not advisable, and monastic authors knew to treat the hegemonial discourse with respect. Consider, for instance, Yuanxian's 元賢 (1578–1657) preface to the gazetteer of the Quanzhou Kaiyuan temple 開元寺 written in 1643:

> The first records [about the Kaiyuan temple of Quanzhou] were composed in the Song, when Xu Lie 許列 wrote the "Biographies of Eminent Monks of the Kaiyuan Temple." The Yuan dynasty master Mengguan 夢觀[30] accused Xu's work of being unreliable and based on hearsay, its explanations being unfounded and labored, coarse and unrefined, and not worthy of being read. Master Mengguan then wrote the "Biographies of Bodhisattvas," and his work was erudite and knowledgeable. . . . Since then more than 300 years have passed and today's Chan cannot compare to that of yesteryear. In these days of decline there hardly seems anything worth reporting. Nevertheless, the ups and downs, the continuities and changes should be recorded somehow. In 1596 Master "Zhizhi" Chen first produced a gazetteer, but his research was superficial and people felt he did not do a very good job of it. Then in the winter of 1635–1636 some gentlemen of Wenling asked me to teach at the Kaiyuan temple. [Yuanxian is asked several times to write

a history of the Kaiyuan temple.] Though I do not have the ability to write a gazetteer—me being just a rustic from Nanzhou who, not successful in studying Confucianism, gave up and studied Buddhism instead [!]—I have followed the wishes of these gentlemen. . . . I have just tried to fill a gap. Someday a better writer will come and this gazetteer may be replaced.[31]

Two things should be noted here: First, the overview of previous gazetteers of the site illustrates the change in genre: while in the Song and Yuan dynasties the history of a temple was written in the then well-established form of collected *biographies* (*zhuan* 傳), in the late Ming Yuanxian is asked to write a *gazetteer*. The gazetteer genre replaces earlier formats for writing about the history of a temple. Second, Yuanxian, in spite of his humble rhetoric, deftly disparages previous attempts by lay writers to write about the Kaiyuan temple. And yet, that the monk Yuanxian, during the last days of the Ming, only one year before the fall of the capital, wrote passages like "not successful in studying Confucianism, gave up and studied Buddhism instead" 學儒不成棄而學佛 testifies to the strength of the Confucian discourse.

It was only in the twentieth century that Confucian hegemony was broken. In 1905 the examination system that had welded Confucian ideology to political power was abolished. After the end of Confucian hegemony, Buddhist monks and laymen were free to create gazetteers from a more Buddhist perspective. As part of the Buddhist revival of the late Qing and Republican era, Buddhists could to a degree redefine their sacred sites. The eminent monk Yinguang 印光 (1861–1940)—along with Taixu, Hongyi, and Xuyun one of the most influential monks of the Republican era—was especially active in promoting new gazetteer editions. Between 1924 and 1938 he was involved in the creation of new gazetteers for all four "Great and Famous Buddhist Mountains," collaborating with local officials and editors.[32] He felt that previous editions had neglected the religious content of the sites and that the impact of imperial patronage had been unduly emphasized.[33] In the preface to the 1938 edition of the Mount Jiuhua Gazetteer, Yinguang writes:

The earlier editions of this gazetteer were written by literati who would not even dream of the Buddhist teachings. To them, to believe or to doubt the miraculous stories about [the Bodhisattva] Dizang was all the same, and they included Dizang's biography among those of [ordinary] humans, which were placed *after* the chapters with literary texts and biographies of Daoist immortals. In our new edition of the gazetteer the first chapter is dedicated to the saintly traces [of Dizang's deeds]. . . . The earlier editions gave pride of place to those temples that were established by imperial decree or had received the inscription above their gate from the court. Those temples that were built by private donations, or for which the funds were collected [by the clergy] were called "hermitages," "chapels," "groves," or "halls," and placed after the former. . . . From the Tang to our days more than a thousand years have passed. There have been many upheavals, and [dynasties] rose and fell. [Today] only a few monks might live in what was once designated a "temple," and what was called a "hermitage" or a "chapel" might now house many. Society too has changed and no longer follows the will of a king. In this gazetteer we therefore put the large public (conglin 叢林) monasteries, where monks from all directions gather, first. After that we include the smaller family temples [where the monks from one tonsure lineage reside].[34]

Yinguang seems to have enjoyed the freedom gained after the fall of the empire. During the Republican era it was possible for Buddhists to claim superiority for their religious sites in an unprecedented way. Being liberated from the need for rhetorical tributes to the greatness of imperial power, Yinguang wryly comments on the lack of devotion the five sacred mountains of the imperial cult now inspired:

When talking about Mount Jiuhua people often used to regret that it was not included in the five marchmounts (wuyue 五嶽) where the imperial court makes offerings. Did they not know that at the marchmounts' temples no one but the local government officials in charge make offerings, two per year, one in spring and one in autumn? At Jiuhua mountain, however, devotees from all over the country offer their sincere respects, and the burning of incense and the prayers do not cease from dawn to dusk. How could the five marchmounts ever hope to compare?[35]

Yinguang lived on Mount Putuo between 1893 and 1928 and commissioned the Wang Hengyan Gazetteer in 1922. Nevertheless, he had to compromise with his collaborators about the form and content of the gazetteer. In his negotiations with the district magistrate Tao Yong 陶鏞 about a new Putuo Gazetteer, it became clear that his vision was not necessarily shared by the local literati. As a consequence his involvement with the actual production was reduced to a preface and approval of the end product. Tao Yong and the compiler Wang Hengyan agreed to keep the traditional gazetteer format in the main body of the text while accommodating Yinguang by including a series of hymns to Guanyin before the main text.[36] This is revealed only by their correspondence and is never mentioned in the gazetteer.

Exhibit 3: The Late Ming Revival of Mount Putuo as Hidden in Prefaces and Postscripts

As so often in Chinese history, there was a precedent for those early twentieth-century discussions about what a gazetteer for Mount Putuo should look like. In the late Ming, the Hou-Tu and the Zhou gazetteers competed for the best way to textualize the site. These differences are only rarely made explicit in the gazetteers themselves. Much remained unsaid and becomes understandable only within the context of contemporary politics.

The Hou-Tu Gazetteer contains eight prefaces and postscripts, two of which were added for a reprint in 1598.[37] Hou and his friends were on the Buddhist side of the Confucian–Buddhist syncretist spectrum and broadly sympathetic toward Buddhism. Most of them did not openly take on a Buddhist lay devotee identity by adopting a Dharma name, but they might have taken refuge as part of the Buddhist rituals in which some of them participated.

Tu Long's preface begins with the arrival of Buddhism in China: "The teaching of Nirvana is a teaching from the West. In the past the awe-inspiring Ancient Buddha broke through the darkness and dispelled the gloom."[38] Tu then continues to explain how Guanyin is able to manifest in many bodies and teachings. Commander Hou, whose preface is translated below, also dwells on the Buddhist nature of the site: "Mount Putuo is now the place where the Bodhisattva [Guanyin] appears. It is one of the three[39] great places of the [Buddhist] Way in the realm: from ancient times until now, veneration for it has grown, and [its fame] has spread through the generations." Tu Long organized the gazetteer in a way that privileges literary texts and half of the Hou-Tu Gazetteer (fascicles 4 to 6) consists of poems.

Only eighteen years after the Hou-Tu Gazetteer first appeared, and less than ten years after its reprint a new "revised" gazetteer appeared in 1607 under the name of the Hanlin scholar Zhou Yingbin 周應賓 (1554–1626). The Zhou Gazetteer privileged communications from the court and topographic descriptions,[40] while Buddhist elements such as miracle stories and monk biographies were arranged toward the end. The three prefaces in the Zhou Gazetteer were clearly not written from a Buddhist perspective, and their *jinshi* authors, mainly praise emperor and landscape and emphasize the role government officials played in reconstructing the site.[41] Clerics and the patron Bodhisattva Guanyin are barely mentioned. The prefaces and postscripts of the Hou-Tu Gazetteer were preserved but, as was customary in such cases, moved into a separate section.[42]

Why was a new gazetteer compiled after only 18 years? The Hou-Tu Gazetteer was recent, had even been reprinted, and was certainly available. Zhou's short preface addresses this question:

Introduction to the new edition of the Putuo Gazetteer

Putuo already has a gazetteer, why compile another one? [Because Putuo] has been reestablished by imperial favor. A gazetteer is to guide the future by exhibiting the past. Now the numinous power of the landscape has been renewed by the imperial orders. There should be a trace of its decline and revival, [therefore, and] although there is a record [already], it can be improved.

What could represent the Eastern Sea if not Putuo? In a far away corner, it can not compare to the winding presence of Yellow River of the Central Plains, but still is one of the four great [sacred sites of Buddhism]. The pole of heaven in the northwest is where [the emperor] the master of sages reigns; while at land's end in the southeast, the "old Buddha" [Guanyin] appears.[43] The teachings of the deities were not abolished by the sage [emperor], [but rather] are protected and maintained by imperial edicts. How could we allow them to perish?

The temples of Putuo were raised and destroyed, destroyed and raised many times. This time the funds [for the Puji Temple's reconstruction] were provided by the court, and an overseer [the eunuch Zhang Sui] was sent from the palace. The temples were rebuilt and its fame and administrative structures reestablished. This time its revival is a great occasion and therefore it was said "although there is a record [already], it can be improved."

This gazetteer has five fascicles [covering] seventeen topics.[44] It gathers works by the hands of many erudite men, that I, in spite of my incompetence, have selected. The previous gazetteer emphasized the scenery and the Buddhist spirit of the site. This gazetteer emphasizes the temples and highlights the contributions of the emperor. These are the main principles of this edition.

Respectfully offered, May 11th 1607, Hanlin Academician Zhou Yingbin[45]

Zhou's concern was the role the central government played in the reconstruction of the site, and this is borne out by the structure and content of the gazetteer. One might infer that he was not happy with the Buddhist sympathies of the Hou-Tu Gazetteer and that he wanted to produce a gazetteer that brought the narrative under control. This is only part of the story, however. Zhou is a complex figure, of whom we will hear more in later chapters. He included three of his own poems in his gazetteer that were dedicated to monks on Putuo.[46] The poems are respectful and friendly, sometimes even striking a personal note. The Zhou Gazetteer also contains a remark prefixed to the chapter on temple construction:

> In all ages temples are destroyed and rebuilt, but why is it that during our Ming they met with so much destruction? Considering the radical exercise of control during the Hongwu and Jiajing reigns, who would have thought that today again there could be two temples with three halls as before? How extraordinary! As long as the "Ocean Office" [ruled by the Dragon King] is unharmed, the Iron Lotus will always open, thousands of years in wondrous firmness.[47]

The last sentence is an allusion to a number of miracle stories about Guanyin and Mount Putuo. It is also a veiled critique of state encroachment on the religious institutions on the island: in legend the iron lotuses open on the ocean whenever someone wants to carry off something from the island and prevent the ships from leaving.[48] The dragon king appears in these stories as protector of the Dharma and in particular of Guanyin. The idea is that his "office" protects the interest of Mount Putuo, a hint that Zhou's fellow administrators would have understood. Was Zhou Yingbin, Hanlin academician and high-ranking vice minister in the Ministry of Rites, perhaps not as uninterested in Buddhism as the rhetoric of his preface seems to imply? Or was the passage above written not by Zhou but rather by Zhang Sui, the eunuch official who arranged for the printing of the gazetteer and who played such an important role in the rebuilding of the Puji Temple?

Zhou's preface must be read in the context of the dispute about the rebuilding of the Puji Temple.[49] In November 1598 a fire had destroyed not only the main buildings but also the first Tripiṭaka donated in 1586 by the Empress Dowager Cisheng 慈聖 (1546–1614)—a gift much celebrated in the Hou-Tu Gazetteer. The Puji Temple was at that time the major religious center on the island, as the Fayu Temple had only just been established and was not yet equipped to serve as pilgrimage center. The rebuilding of Puji, however, met with strong opposition. Already before the fire, local officials had argued against allowing Buddhist activities on the island.[50] They were complaining about "deviant monks" (*jian seng* 奸僧), who alleg-edly turned the island into a pilgrimage site and thus provided a cover for pirates, making it more difficult to patrol the archipelago. A document of 1596 regarding Putuo says: "The Puji and the Fayu Temples invite pil-grims from afar, and provide them with food. Vagrant monks of all direc-tions hear of this custom and gather. Certainly some among them keep the precepts, but many of them are deviants and vagabonds."[51]

The strategic argument must have been considerably undermined by the endorsement of Mount Putuo by military figures such as Hou Jigao, who were actively involved in re-creating the site as well as in the fight against pirates. Nevertheless, more so than previous dynasties, the Ming was sus-picious of religious travel and sought in general to tightly control domestic and international travel. It was in the interest of the local authorities to be able to ascertain the identity of all inhabitants of the archipelago. This was undercut by the Buddhist building activities on Putuo, because in a net-work of smaller temples or hermitages, monks and laypeople could move about without leaving a record. For the opponents of the pilgrimage site, the fire was literally a godsend: "In the tenth month of last year (1598–10–30 to 1598–11–27), the spirits were disgusted with the blasphemy, and the temple buildings burned down without [apparent] cause. Orders were given to move the Buddha images to the mainland."[52]

In 1599 the monk Rude 如德, since 1596 abbot of the Fayu Temple,[53] was collecting building material for the reconstruction when he was appre-hended on orders of Li Fang 李方 (d.u.), the prefect of Ningbo. The lum-ber donated thus far was confiscated.[54] Li's explicit aim was to prevent the reconstruction of Puji Temple. Other opponents of Mount Putuo harshly criticized the pilgrimage activities there. They were especially exasperated by the pilgrimage of women to the island, which had been explicitly for-bidden on several occasions: "deviant monks band together, openly trans-gressing the prohibitions concerning [groups such as] the White Lotus and others. . . . In Ningbo, all along the rivers, incense shops were opened and . . . hostels with bedrooms and bathrooms, where all the men and women first stop over on their pilgrimage to Putuo."[55]

Confucian literati culture viewed female pilgrimage with deep sus-picion. The organization of women outside the family was threatening to patriarchal conservatism and had no place in the Confucian social order. Late Ming vernacular novels often reflect these anxieties. In the seventeenth century novel *Xingshi yinyuan zhuan* 醒世姻緣傳, the fam-ily patriarch Mr. Di instructs his son: "I wouldn't mind if we were in an ordinary way of life. But now you are a member of the academy, we count as a cultured family. How can we send our young womenfolk to join a society on a pilgrimage?"[56] Pilgrimage by women was a fact, but there was a strong conservative sentiment among the educated to discourage it.

The anti-pilgrimage sentiment also reflects Neo-Confucian concerns with sexual control, which in those days was challenged by the fledgling bourgeois society forming among the literati, especially in the Jiangnan region. While late Ming literature often depicts sexual mores as negotiable, the *de jure* rules against "fornication" (*fanjian* 犯姦) in the Ming Code were draconian.[57] Vernacular stories reveal again and again how the male imagination of the time was obsessed with illicit sexual activities allegedly taking place in monasteries.[58] Their fantasies ranged from rape by deviant monks in a "Monastery of Debauchery"[59] to the relatively innocent concerns voiced by a relative of Mr. Di: "How can a tender young lady mount the summit? Haven't you seen people riding in those mountain chairs? It's all right the way up, but on the way down they sit in the chair facing backward, the women face to face with the carrier; if the women falls backwards her feet are more or less right on the carriers' shoulders!"[60]

The Confucian ideal of patriarchal control of the family was mirrored on the level of autocratic government, which resented all public spheres not entirely controlled by the state. The Ming and, based on it, the Qing codes prohibited women from visiting Buddhist temples and sacred sites.[61] As Vincent Goossaert has remarked, such rules were "on first glance comical," because obviously the temples were frequented and supported by women throughout these eras.[62] According to Goossaert, the prohibition "was aimed not so much at elderly ladies spending time with their friends in their neighborhood temple, but at young women on pilgrimage or during festivities staying at temples overnight (*sushan* 宿山)."[63] Women had to organize their own pilgrimages in groups out of necessity. For them, pilgrimage alone or even in small groups for longer than a day was not acceptable and, strictly speaking, illegal.[64]

As it turned out, perhaps not incidentally, the camp that supported reopening Mount Putuo was led by a woman, too. In the same year that Abbot Rude was arrested for trying to rebuild Puji Temple, the Empress Dowager Cisheng convinced her son, the Wanli emperor, to send another set of the Tripitaka to Putuo in order to renew and affirm imperial patronage. In this she was supported by the court eunuchs and, crucially, by a group of literati officials. One imagines that the pro-Putuo faction also had firm support among the local populace. Almost everybody in Ningbo and on Zhoushan, from ship and hostel owners to incense sellers and beggars, had an interest in maintaining and expanding the pilgrimage economy. The strategic concern of military officials, that further temple construction on the island would abet pirates, was probably not widely shared as the last major pirate incursions lay forty years in the past.

Buddhist monks, of course, also used whatever influence they had to reopen the pilgrimage site. In 1601, Zhenzai 真宰, the designated abbot of Puji Temple, went to Beijing to directly petition the government to allow the reconstruction. His illness and death there in the same year actually might have helped his task. It was framed as a sacrifice brought about by his heroic effort to fulfill his duty as abbot.

Nevertheless, the discussion about whether to reopen Puji Temple continued for some years. In June 1602 the eunuchs Zhang Sui 張隨 and Wang Chen 王臣 were sent to Putuo with 1,000 *tael* of silver to assess the fire damage and the prospects for reconstruction. Later in 1602, as a reaction to their recommendation to rebuild Puji on a larger scale, the Grand Coordinator Liu Yuanlin 劉元霖 compiled a memorial opposing the reconstruction: "Mount Putuo rises steeply from the sea close to the realm of the [Japanese] island-barbarians. At the beginning of the dynasty a strict prohibition [of settlement] was decreed, the temples were destroyed and the monks dispersed, after wise and thorough deliberation."[65] In addition to Liu's memorial, there are various endorsements supporting the ban on reconstruction from both civil and military officials.[66]

This time around the reasons against rebuilding the Puji Temple were strategic, not ideological, and local, not general. The authors do not seem to oppose Buddhism as such. Most start their statement by remarking on the proximity of Putuo to Japan, "only four or five days away," and express their worries about espionage and infiltration if untrammeled pilgrimage to Putuo was allowed again. All authors were acutely aware of the history of pirate incursions, their suppression, and settlement prohibitions in the archipelago. Several mention the "pacification" of the islands in 1387 when Tang He 湯和 (1326–1395), one of the Hongwu emperor's most seasoned generals, had the island evacuated and the temples destroyed.[67] Several authors reminded the court of the battles against the pirate leader Wang Zhi and his son, who in the 1550s repeatedly managed to defeat government forces.[68]

In the following year (1603), to resolve the dispute between the anti- and the pro-Putuo faction, the court dispatched Yin Yingyuan 尹應元 (*jinshi* 1574). Yin was, in spite of his rhetoric below, probably not on a fact-finding mission, but was sent to convey the will of the emperor and make sure everybody was "on message." To make his point, Yin had a short account of his journey inscribed on a stele and erected near the Puji Temple.[69]

When in the fifth month of the thirty-first year of Wanli in the Great Ming (1603–06–09 to 1603–07–08) [I], the Grand Coordinator[70] of Zhejiang [p. 378], Censor-in-Chief Yin Yingyuan inspected the navy, the Regional Commander and Assistant Commissioner-in-Chief of Chuzhou, Li Chengxun expected me with several thousand elite marines.

I had heard that Putuo rises high out of the sea, and that climbing the mountain, one can point out and know all strategic points from there. In recent years the Empress Dowager and his Majesty the Emperor have sent the Palace Eunuch Zhang Sui and the Palace Eunuch Wang Chen with funds to rebuild the temple buildings and the library. The previous Grand Coordinator [Liu] has submitted a memorial asking to discontinue this practice [p. 379]. Since I believe that seeing something once is better than hearing about it hundred times, I decided to pay a visit.

The Regional Commander prepared the boats and troops, and, checking the winds and tides, set a date for our departure. The Coastal Vice Commissioner Wang Daoxian of Tong'an, the Assistant Regional Commander of Suzhou Yuan Shizhong, the Prefect of Ningbo Zou Xixian of Jian'an, his Associate Administrator Huang Ju of Jinxi, the Judge He Shijin of Yixing, the District Magistrate of Dinghai Zhu Yi'e of Zhangpu— they all accompanied me.

It is noteworthy that the party included at least three of the authors of the 1602 memorial discussed above—Li Chengxun, Yuan Shizhong, and Huang Ju. All were military men who had argued against the reconstruction of Puji Temple. For another member of the party, Zhu Yi'e, we can assume Buddhist sympathies, expressed in his poem "Traveling to Putuo," which was perhaps written on this very occasion and included in the Zhou Gazetteer.[71] The list therefore includes both military and civil officials, and both supporters and opponents of the reconstruction. Yin's account continues:

On the thirteenth (1603–06–21) we heaved anchor and on the fifteenth we arrived on Putuo. After offering incense and paying our respects to the Bodhisattva Guanyin, we visited Fayu Temple, and ascended the steep slopes, looking over the ocean, almost glimpsing Japan. Looking around the whole island, I had the best sight-seeing in all my lives [p. 380].[72]

The Puji and the Fayu Temples are both of the same mountain. The buildings of Fayu seem peaceful as before. The [destroyed] Puji Temple, however, is much more famous. The reasons for its restoration after the fire are not ordinary. It has in short time been favored by the emperor's orders on several occasions. This will certainly be noted with awe by people far and near. Attacks by the Japanese pirates are hard to predict, thus our defenses must be strong and alert. The Regional Commander and all officials are entrusted with leading the army and maintaining the defenses. That way they are able to assist as soon as they hear a warning, and peace and safety can forever be maintained. Never allow our fatherly emperor to be troubled. The Regional Commander and all officials by different methods, but united in intent, are to ensure a time of growth [p. 381]. This is to be carved in stone to commemorate the occasion and proclaim it to later generations.[73]

Yin Yingyuan was a seasoned diplomat. Couched in compliments about the importance of the military for the region, he affirms the decision of the emperor to rebuild Puji Temple. He seems to have been understood: after his trip in 1603 Mount Putuo became again a vibrant pilgrimage site and no further dispute is recorded. To underline his support, the Wanli emperor in 1607 added 2,000 *tael* to a 3,000 *tael* donation by his mother. Again Zhang Sui was dispatched to deliver the funds, this time with orders to supervise the reconstruction of the temple. The imperial envoy made sure that the money was put to the intended use and that the project was not obstructed by the local anti-Putuo faction. Zhang Sui was one of the more influential voices at court for the reconstruction of Mount Putuo and he is mentioned in Zhou's preface. The eunuchs at the imperial "inner court" were often, but not always, as this example shows, in competition with the Confucian officials of the "outer court." We will hear more of Zhang Sui and other eunuch officials in Chapter 6 (Exhibit 2).

What was the role of the Wanli emperor in all this? The Zhou Gazetteer includes three edicts: two imperial "prefaces" and one inscription by the Wanli emperor. Wanli addressed his missives "To the Abbot and the Monks of Mount Putuo."[74] He justifies his support as fulfilling his filial duty to follow the wishes of his mother, Empress Dowager Cisheng, who is mentioned in all texts. The record leaves little doubt that Cisheng influenced her son on the matter of Putuo. The emperor, however, deeply frustrated with the bureaucratic apparatus, had his own reasons to support the pro-Putuo faction. He was clearly aware of the Confucian–Buddhist tension and had no intention of siding with the Confucians: "I reckon that from ancient times kings and emperors have ruled the world according to the Confucian way; but apart from the craft of the Confucians there are also the teachings of Buddhism. As they are complementary, I use them both."[75]

Mount Putuo's final breakthrough came in 1607. The rebuilding of Puji Temple was completed, and a stele bearing the "Imperial Inscription on the Reconstruction of Puji Temple"[76] was erected next to it. When Abbot Rujiong received the purple robe and was promoted to "Buddhist Patriarch of the Left" (*zuo shanshi* 左善世), the highest Buddhist office in the state hierarchy, Zhou Yingbin pointedly offered a poem in congratulation (see Chapter 7, Exhibit 3). In 1601, Rujiong had become the successor of the unlucky Zhenzai, who had passed away in Beijing trying to petition the court to assist Mount Putuo. As Buddhist Patriarch of the Left, Rujiong had to reside in Beijing. He had become one of the most influential Buddhist monks charged with overseeing ordinations, confirming abbot appointments, and involved in many issues concerning the oversight of Buddhist activities.[77] Making the abbot of Mount Putuo's main temple part of the official court hierarchy signaled a strong endorsement of Mount Putuo as pilgrimage site, and for the rest of the dynasty the status of Mount Putuo as a pilgrimage site was never again questioned.

This then is the background story to Zhou Yingbin's re-edition of the Putuo Gazetteer: his gazetteer was part of the efforts of the pro-Buddhist faction at court to smooth the waves and placate the opposition that had sought to prevent the rebuilding of Puji Temple. By shifting the emphasis of the gazetteer from a record of a Buddhist site to a record of imperial patronage, Zhou manages to silence those critics who had argued for a more tightly controlled management. He does so subtly, without mentioning them by name, and the whole affair is only alluded to in half sentences, as in the account by Yin Yingyuan above. In other words, the ostensibly "secular" gazetteer served as medium for propagating texts that place Mount Putuo under imperial patronage. To this end Zhou had to overwrite Hou Jigao's "Buddhist" gazetteer.

We will now turn to Hou Jigao's postscript, which he wrote in 1589; his gazetteer was printed the following year and is a fascinating record of the opinions of a late Ming military official. Educated in the literati tradition and having spent years in government service, Confucianism was an important part of Hou's life-world. His status as military official, which was hereditary in the Ming, gave him a certain independence, however. He did not have to spend years preparing for the official examinations that were the main gateway for the civil service. His Buddhist sympathies even allowed him to look critically at certain aspects of the prevailing military ideology. Hou's reflections about the relationship between Confucianism, Buddhism, and his own role as navy commander reveal a sophisticated man coming to terms with the ideological issues of his time. Below is a translation of the full, authorial version of Hou's postscript as contained in the 1590 edition of his gazetteer. Underlined are those passages that were omitted in the Zhou Gazetteer. Zhou, or whoever the actual compiler was, takes great liberty with Hou Jigao's postscript, deleting almost a fourth of the text. The deletions appear to have been made in order to dilute the Buddhist sentiments expressed by Hou Jigao. Noticeably, the compiler of the Zhou Gazetteer has often elided passages that profess Buddhist sympathies or allude to tensions between Confucianism and Buddhism.[78]

[p. 1a] Postscript to the Gazetteer of Mount Potalaka

Cities and villages, mountains and rivers have their gazetteers, like families have their family registers and countries their official histories, to record their fortunes and reflect on their development, in order to illuminate the past and pass it on to those who come after. How could we do without them?

Mount Potalaka [p. 1b] is now the place where the Bodhisattva [Guanyin] appears. It is one of the three great Buddhist sites[79] in the realm. From ancient times until now, veneration toward it has grown and through the generations [its fame] has spread. Many worthies have again and again described it in songs and poems,[80] but there is no gazetteer tradition yet by which these texts [p. 2a] can be preserved forever.

During the times of the vanquished empire [i.e., the Yuan dynasty] Sheng Ximing, a descendant of a family from the Western Regions, was well versed in the secret scriptures [of esoteric Buddhism]. He first wrote "A Chronicle of the Potalaka Mountain" in four chapters. In these the merit-power of the Bodhisattva, the numinous sites among the mountains and streams, and, throughout the ages, the auspicious power of prayers [p. 2b] and miracles brought about by sympathetic resonance were vividly presented.[81] However, it is only a thin book, short and concise, never well distributed. Though it was known and liked in all the provinces and cities of the realm, in the end no one could obtain a copy for some armchair traveling anymore.

How could that not be [p. 3a] to the regret of those eminent officials and good men wishing to venerate the Buddha, or the hermits seeking out good places for practice? Now the monasteries [on Putuo] were destroyed in the uprising of the Japanese pirates some years ago, and were just rebuilt again. Although they have not yet attained their former greatness, these developments [p. 3b] should not go unrecorded.

As for myself, of little competence, it was only when I was posted here, to fill this position in Zhejiang, that I first crossed the sea to visit the Bodhisattva at Putuo. Apart from looking around on the island, I talked to the monks in the temples and asked them: "Does the Mountain have a gazetteer?" That was when they brought out Sheng Ximing's chronicle. The moth-eaten paper was brittle and the ink had faded. From Ximing's time until our days more than 230 years [p. 4a] have passed. What is recorded in his four chapters is only a general outline. When it comes to our Ming, with the incense fires [at Putuo] increasing, the [literary] writings about the place also grew in number. Until now, no one like Sheng Ximing came and turned them into a chronicle.

I said with a sigh: "How could it be that there are no historical records of such a famous mountain and its auspicious places [p. 4b] to make them known to the world?" All the more these days, under a benevolent ruler and with able ministers at court, the realm is inwardly and outwardly pacified, the northern and southern [regions] are at peace, the Buddha sun is shining, benevolent numinous powers manifest themselves everywhere; we are living through a splendid era [p. 5a]. *Fortunately*, the Saintly Mother of our Emperor had the canon [of Buddhist scriptures] printed and the Emperor, in his pure piety, seeking to fulfill her wish ordered a palace eunuch[82] to bestow the sutras and some incense upon Puji Temple [p. 5b]. On occasion of the imperial order, lofty as Mount Meicen and profound like the ocean, I had [inscriptions] carved in precious stone, so that they may stand erect together with the mountains.

Regarding the creation of a gazetteer, this should be continued in our days so I ventured to ask [p. 6a] the Coastal Censor[83] Master Liu [Zhishang] 劉志尚 of Qianshan to write the gazetteer. He passed the request on to one of the commandry's literati, Master Long [Defu] 龍德孚 (1531–1602) of Wuling, [who in turn passed it on] saying: "This can only be done by Tu Zhangqing 屠長卿, [formerly at] the Ministry of Rites. Perhaps he will accept this task." So we went to Sir Zhangqing and asked him for help, and he agreed.[84] Soon the edition was completed [p. 6b] and given to me, the Student Hou Jigao, who arranged for its printing. Myself, of little competence, added some content to the end [i.e., this postscript].

The rise of Buddhism started in the Eastern Han and the honors bestowed on it [by the court] in those days are too far away to be recorded now. Starting with the essay of Han Changli from the Tang onwards the Confucians avoid discussing Buddhism. [p. 7a] Since the Daoxue elders [i.e., Neo-Confucians] of the Song dynasty it has become almost forbidden to talk about it.

Those in the military [on the other hand], the warriors, who command soldiers and fend off intruders, they always talk of "sternness overcoming love,"[85] which seems indeed very different from the ideal of compassion.

To a foolish person [like me], <u>it seems [Confucians and military officials] all just hold on to their respective truths and have not really started to address the main principle of Buddhism</u> [p. 7b]. I hold the main principle in Buddhism is to take compassion as the central meaning (*ti*) and guiding and educating others as the application (*yong*). This principle causes people to be disposed to the good and turn away from evil.

<u>When it comes to those teaching Daoxue, none are like Confucius and Mencius.</u> When Mencius said: "If with a lenient mind one governs in a lenient way . . . [then governance will be easily successful]," is this not the same as [the Buddhist idea of] "compassion"? When Confucius said [p. 8a]: "If one wishes to prosper one helps others to prosper, if one wants to succeed one lets others succeed," is this not the same as "guiding and educating"? <u>If the people in this world honestly took the Buddhist [principle of] compassion to heart, they would do no evil, and [perceive] everybody within China as part of themselves. Reminding themselves of the Buddhist [principle of] guiding and educating others, they are able to empathize with others, and [even] those living beyond the reaches of the empire [p. 8b] will be like family [to them]. With this kind of leadership applied to rule the world, how could people turn away from ethical conduct and go against tradition, steal and take life? This was the spirit out of which the Empress Dowager bestowed the sutras and venerated the Buddha. [p. 9a] As was well said by Master Liu [Shangzhi in his preface]: "Why should it not be possible for a person of great learning to let our Confucian ways govern his actions and decisions, while making use of Buddhism to improve his essence and return to the truth?"[86] Believing these words there is no need to avoid discussing Buddhism out of veneration for Daoxue.</u>

I am a warrior [p. 9b], uncouth and without learning, and I <u>don't dare to say I have understood either Confucianism or Buddhism,</u> but still in my days I have snapped up something of what my elders said and I have tasted the purport of "compassion" as well as of "guiding and educating." All the more pleased am I to see this gazetteer completed, in these splendid and well-ordered days of our dynasty.

[p. 10a] This year (1589) in the second month of spring, on an inspection tour of the outposts [of our naval defenses], our ships stopped at Mount Putou. I respectfully visited the Bodhisattva and prayed: "Our powerful, radiant Buddha! Grant my soldiers success through discipline, so that I will be able to repay [the kindness] of the emperor in a small way." Soon after this the Japanese slaves secretly rose and spied at our borders [p. 10b]. This angered the Emperor greatly and I defeated them at Hua'nao and Langgang.

How could I have done so without the silent assistance of the Bodhisattva? This happened just after the gazetteer was completed, so I record it here in order to show that for a long time now the power of our Buddha has never stopped to manifest itself for the benefit of the country [p. 11a] and the protection of the people. This is no small matter.

[Therefore] this preface. Written by the Grand Defender appointed by the Emperor, the Regional Commander of Zhejiang and environs [p. 11b], Rear Guard Assistant Commissioner in Chief, Hou Jigao of Yunjian on the 16th[87] of the fifth month in the seventeenth year with the cyclical sign Jichou of the era Wanli of the Great Ming (1589-6-28).

Many deletions marked in the text above are not in themselves extraordinary—edition policies for gazetteer compilation were generally lax, especially when compared to editions of Buddhist sutras or Confucian classics. Omissions, the use of variant characters, and even insertions were well within the purview of the compilers, who changed documents for stylistic reasons or cut them simply to save space. In the transition from the Hou-Tu to the Zhou Gazetteer, however, we can see that at times editorial changes were also made for ideological reasons, in this case in order to tone down the Buddhist sentiment. Overall, text in gazetteer literature was very much in flux, from the level of individual texts, which could be dropped or newly included, down to the level of the single character.

Exhibit 4: Yang Yongjian on Confucianism, Buddhism, and Death (c. 1698)

We started this chapter on Confucian attitudes toward Buddhism with Yang Yongjian, who had been approached to write an inscription for a stūpa enclosing Sanshan Denglai's robe and begging bowl. As a preface to the inscription Yang added a short and original meditation on Buddhist and Confucian attitudes regarding death:

Chan Master Sanshan Denglai from Eastern Shu died in the Gaofeng Temple [near Chongqing] in the autumn of 1685. His Dharma heir Qianfu Xingyi and others put his ashes to rest in the ancestor's stūpa at Qingzhong Temple [in Chongqing]. That was 13 years ago. Now, Master Bie'an [Xing]tong, his last and most renowned disciple, has built a stūpa for his master's robe and bowl next to Zhengling Brook [on Mount Putuo], and came to ask me for an inscription. Since, back when I was posted in Jiaxing, I was acquainted with Denglai, I would not dare to refuse this.

I believe Buddhism differs from our Confucianism (*wuru*) in what it holds to be real and what to discard as unreal. But Buddhists too want to benefit society, practice the Way and transmit it to posterity, and in this they are similar to us Confucians. Concerning the border between life and death, everybody says that we Confucians take it as real and the Buddhists as an illusion, but actually that is not the case.

We Confucians have a saying: "Life is but a temporary dwelling, in death it is that we return home." This means that the gentleman should always keep the eminent teachings in mind and be ready to "sacrifice his life in times of danger."[88] In the end this is the meaning of "[some] deaths are heavy as Taishan" [while others are "light like a goose feather"[89]]. Whoever regards death as a rule to return to, has already freed his breast [from anguish]. Those, however, who, mired in the ten-thousand things, cling to life and are afraid of death, are but foolish children.

As for the Buddhists, they say: "Life and death are matters of great importance." However, there are a few mediocre followers, who, wiggling their way into the Chan tradition,[90] and pretending they have reached attainment and broad vision, believe everything material is "empty" and [only] Nirvana brings happiness. Saying this is facile, to practice it is difficult. Thus those among Buddhists, who by true practice and actual insight have attained understanding, all carefully diminish their wants and relinquish their desires. They deeply dislike every mention of rebirth and return.

Put thus, the Confucians make little of death, because true Confucians are ready to sacrifice their life for their principles. And Buddhists take death seriously, because true Buddhists understand where they are heading. True Buddhists and true Confucians both will stop only when they have attained their goal, though mostly for Confucians what is to attain lies before death, for Buddhists after death. . . .[91]

After describing admiringly how Bie'an Xingtong has continued his teacher's lineage and built a stūpa for his relics, Yang continues:

With regard to our parents we Confucians (*wuru*) bury them, hold the funeral rites, and that is it. One who lives far from his ancestral home, simply hands over the responsibility for the graves to his brothers in the family line. Though we have the idea of filial piety, we do feel not compelled to do more. But among the teachings of the Buddhists there is an honest concern and a readiness to move [even the master's secondary relics]. Therefore I say when it comes to the border of life and death, actually it is the Confucians who take it lightly, while the Buddhists take it seriously.[92]

In his balanced comments Yang avoids the ethnocentric and parochial overtones that often mar Confucian comments about other traditions, but instead conveys the generous tolerance that too is part of Confucianism. Compared with Yang's measured comparison, Commander Hou's postscript of a hundred years earlier reads as defensive. Personal style aside, this was also because Hou lived at a time when the relationship between Confucianism and Buddhism was more contested. Hou had to work harder to make the "syncretistic move" and to explain how the two traditions can complement each other.

Conclusion

Ostensibly the role of the preface/postscript genre is to remark on the occasion of a gazetteer's compilation and its edition principles. As we have seen in the case of Zhou Yingbin, however, the texts often seem more straightforward than they are, and the wider political context will reveal additional layers of meaning. De Bruyn has commented on the importance of understanding what is "unsaid" in gazetteers, and our analysis of the transition between two Mount Putuo gazetteers corroborates what De Bruyn has found in his work with the gazetteers of Mount Wudang, namely that "only the historical and political context 'says' the true reasons."[93]

The late Ming prefaces and postscripts of the Putuo gazetteers reveal a concern with the relationship between Buddhism and Confucianism. The literati authors move along the spectrum from devout Buddhists to moderately sympathetic Confucians. In late Ming, as well as in later revivals of Mount Putuo, these literati supporters of Buddhist sites served as a crucial link between the central government and the religious professionals and nonelite adherents of Buddhism. Different researchers have highlighted the relative importance of different groups for the development of Buddhism. Zhang Dewei (2010) makes the case for the importance of the central government (high-ranking officials in the capital and the inner court, the court itself, with the emperor, palace women, and eunuchs) for the late Ming revival. Timothy Brook (1993a) and Jennifer Eichman (2005) draw attention to how Buddhism was supported by regional gentry or literati networks. The works of Daniel Overmyer (1976) and Barend Ter Haar

(1992) emphasize the vitality of nonelite "folk-Buddhist" activity that should be seen as the driving force and basis of religious institutions but which is not well documented in the sources that concentrate on famous benefactors or monastics. The gazetteers rarely give voice to the concerns of the nonelite adherent or pilgrim. Although they remain "unsaid" in the sense that De Bruyn has diagnosed for the gazetteer discourse, it must be remembered that sites like Mount Putuo exist because of the support of nonelite Buddhists.

A study of sacred sites can show how these three levels—imperial center, local gentry, and "grass-roots" religious believers—are linked in the growth of religious institutions: certain sections of society have a fundamental interest (religious or not) in a pilgrimage site. This is understood by members of the local literati. Sympathetic members of the literati class take up the cause out of their own interests (religious or not). They support religious institutions directly themselves and/or communicate their support to the court. The court decides whether it is in its own interest (religious or not) to support the site and bestow imperial recognition.

For Mount Putuo, representatives of all three levels appear together in an inscription, which was never included in the gazetteers. In 1632 two steles were erected commemorating the donors for a sturdy, stone-paved pilgrimage road that was built between 1627 and 1630 on Mount Putuo.[94] The first stele with the names of lay adherents (*xinshi* 信士) lists members of the imperial court and local worthies as well as less powerful local lay believers, whose names do not appear elsewhere. A second stele records donations by individual monastics. Their contributions were more modest but would have ultimately come from lay supporters as well.

The collaboration between these three groups will become visible again in Chapter 5, which introduces some of the actors involved in the "early Qing revival" during the Kangxi era. First, however, true to the chapter order in the gazetteers themselves, we will turn to the representation of Mount Putuo on maps and in images.

CHAPTER 2 | Landscape and Map—Visual Representations of Mount Putuo

In ancient times the borders of the nine provinces were cast on ritual
bronzes. Today Mount Putuo on Sea surely is a sacred site. Without
maps and images, how could its perfect shape be shown throughout
the myriad worlds? If you say: "The ocean of suffering is boundless,
but turn your head and there is the shore" or "All material things will
be destroyed, only emptiness does not decay," then why should it
matter whether there is a Mount Putuo or not? Mountain and Map—
erased with one flick.

—ZHOU YINGBIN[1]

TEMPLE GAZETTEERS OFTEN CONTAIN maps or images of some kind. From
the rich, meticulously labeled maps of the Mount Jizu Gazetteer (1692),
to the small, single-panel sketch of Mount Wutai (1833), to the surprising absence of any maps in the *Tiantaishan waifang zhi* (1601 [1894]),
visual depictions of sacred Buddhist sites exist along a broad spectrum.[2]
Although the gazetteers are mainly a medium for text, wherever maps are
included they bring their own dynamic to the cultural construction of the
site. As Denis Cosgrove remarks, maps are "not merely traces or sources"
but rather "active, constitutive elements in shaping social and spatial practices."[3] Maps in official local gazetteers played a role in how a region was
administered. The maps in Buddhist and Daoist temple gazetteers, on
the other hand, offered mainly scenic views to enhance the experience
of "armchair traveling" (*woyou* 臥遊).[4] The notion of armchair traveling
is invoked by several editors, including Yinguang in his editorial principles for the Mount Emei Gazetteer.[5] There also existed shorter, illustrated

guidebooks that were structured around a series of views of a pilgrimage way, which a pilgrim could follow, book in hand in his armchair or on site, to learn about the history of a particular spot.[6] As full-fledged gazetteers were too bulky and expensive for people to bring along on an actual visit, there was a market for pilgrim maps and short guidebooks that helped visitors find their way around the famous sights.[7]

Maps and images in gazetteers were usually gathered in their own section (*tukao* 圖考 or *tushuo* 圖說) at the beginning of the gazetteer, either before or as part of the first fascicle, but always after the prefaces. Although there are different types of maps, they are not distinguished terminologically. Some show an overview of the site as a whole, but many are split in different panels following a path through the landscape. Within the confines of the woodblock print, this technique, modeled on the landscape scroll painting, was an efficient way to convey both breadth and detail. The image section sometimes also included ground plans of monasteries and portraits of famous persons associated with the site.

Accuracy was rarely important for the maps in premodern gazetteers and none of them are scaled. What mattered was to find places of interest on a mountain for those who took the guidebook along and to depict them nicely for those who stayed at home. The relationship of the maps to the main text of a gazetteer varied. Sometimes they are not mentioned at all in the text because they were added later. Sometimes they were updated without changes in the text.[8]

In line with the accumulative tendency of textualization, the maps and illustrations within a gazetteer series tend to become more detailed over time. This, of course, is also tied to progress in printing, marketing, and audience expectations. In contemporary gazetteers, photos have taken on the role of illustrations, but the maps and ground plans are still alive and well.[9] The latest Putuo gazetteer of 1999 includes four colored foldout maps: an elevation map, a two-dimensional map, a three-dimensional remote sensor map, and a map connecting points of interest to photos. Besides the maps there more than one hundred images of people, inscriptions, ground plans, scenery, and artifacts connected to Mount Putuo.

The illustrated sections of modern gazetteers also contain instances of self-reflexivity. Thus the Fang Gazetteer reprints previous illustrations of the twelve views from the Qiu-Zhu Gazetteer (see Exhibit 3), and the Wang Liansheng Gazetteer includes photos of previous gazetteers. The photos are too small to make out characters, and they are included merely to showcase the tradition of gazetteers themselves: a late representative of the tradition pointing to its own beginning.

The maps and images of Mount Putuo embedded in its gazetteers show how visitors perceived the site but also instructed visitors in what and how to see. They moreover reveal facts about the changing geography of the island, which are otherwise undocumented. The first exhibit will be about a precious fourteenth-century map-painting of Mount Putuo, which has survived in Japan. Exhibit 2 explores how Mount Putuo was depicted in the maps commissioned by Hou Jigao on the eve of its late Ming revival. Exhibit 3 shows why and how Mount Putuo came to be perceived as a series of scenic views in the eighteenth and nineteenth centuries.

Exhibit 1: The Earliest Map of Mount Putuo (c. 1350)

The first time a "Mount Potalaka" is mentioned as an actual geographic site is in Xuanzang's *Datang xiyu ji* 大唐西域記 (T.2087). Xuanzang says:

> To the east of the Malaya mountains is Mount Potalaka. The passes of this mountain are very dangerous; its sides are precipitous and its valleys rugged. On the top of the mountain is a lake; its waters are clear as a mirror. From a hollow proceeds a great river which encircles the mountain as it flows down twenty times and then enters the southern sea. By the side of the lake is a rock-palace of the Devas. Here Avalokiteśvara, in coming and going, takes his abode. Those who strongly desire to see this Bodhisattva do not regard their lives, but, crossing the water (fording the streams), climb the mountain forgetful of its difficulties and dangers; of those who make the attempt there are very few who reach the summit. But even of those who dwell below the mountain, if they earnestly pray and beg to behold the god, sometimes he appears as *Īśvāra-deva*, sometimes under the form of a yogi (a *Pāṁśupata*); he addresses them with benevolent words and then they obtain their wishes according to their desires.[10]

In medieval China, the *Datang xiyu ji* was the single most important source of knowledge about the geography of Central Asia and India. In conjunction with Xuanzang's biography, the *Daciensi Sanzang fashi zhuan* 大慈恩寺三藏法師傳 (T.2053), it inspired a cartographic tradition in China and Japan that depicts India as Jambudvīpa with places labeled according to Xuanzang's travelogue. The earliest known instance of this tradition is a map of India in Zhipan's 志盤 comprehensive history of Chinese Buddhism, the *Fozu tongji* 佛祖統紀, which was published between 1265 and 1270.[11] Zhipan's "Map of the West and the Five Regions of India" (*Xitu wuyin zhi tu* 西土五印之圖) follows Xuanzang's account closely and places Mount Potalaka—labeled *Danluojia shan* 怛洛迦山—in the sea south of India.[12] In Japan there is a series of maps that depict Mount Potalaka to the south of India in greater detail.[13] These depictions seem to fuse Xuanzang's account with the topography of the Chinese Mount Putuo and the Japanese practice of the *Fudaraku tōkai*.[14] While in the thirteenth and fourteenth centuries some Chinese and Japanese cartographers, based on Xuanzang's travelogue, imagined Mount Potalaka as an island south of India, the Chinese site too attracted the interest of at least one painter-cartographer. Mount Putuo near Ningbo first appears on two maps in the *Baoqing Siming zhi* 寶慶四明志 (produced 1227–1272), it is labeled Meicen shan 梅岑山 on one and Butuo shan 補陀山 on the other.[15] The more detailed of the two adds labels for the Putuo Temple and the Tidal Sound Cave; on both maps, however, Mount Putuo is shown as but one of many islands in the Zhoushan archipelago.

The earliest dedicated map of Mount Putuo is a painting (see frontispiece) titled *Budaluojia guanyin xianshen shengjing* 補怛洛迦觀音現神聖境 (below *Budaluo shengjing*), which is preserved at the Jōshō Temple 定勝寺 in Nagano.[16] The *Budaluo shengjing* is an impressive work and quite distinct from the other known paintings depicting the Potalaka as Guanyin's Pure Land.[17] It offers a comprehensive visual record of Mount Putuo, roughly contemporary with the earliest gazetteer by Sheng Ximing. Like Sheng Ximing's gazetteer, the *Budaluo shengjing* is primarily a religious work that depicts the island as a sacred site and not as a destination for the pilgrim-tourist, as do the later maps in the Qing gazetteers. Just as the Sheng Gazetteer included hymns to Guanyin, the *Budaluo shengjing* centers the map in an iconographic ensemble with an image of Guanyin. Guanyin and attendants hover prominently above a birds-eye view of Mount Putuo. The hanging scroll (113 × 57 cm) is oriented north toward the top. Its composition is not topographically accurate.[18] On the island itself more than eighty sites are meticulously labeled. Based on the place names, it has been dated to the period between 1278 and 1369.[19] Below I will argue for a more narrow window between 1334 and 1369.

The entire upper third of the *Budaluo shengjing* is given to the image of a willow-branch Guanyin sitting in a round halo. On her proper right Guanyin is flanked by the Elder Somachattra (*Yuegai zhangzhe* 月蓋長者) in the attire of a Chinese scholar, to the left by the barefooted Sudhana.[20] Below, in the southwest, the *Budaluo shengjing* shows the landing pier where visitors arrive at the island. It is not yet called "Pier of the Sister-in-Law," as in later gazetteers, but labeled "Korean Pier" (*Gaoli daotou*

高麗道頭); another indication for the importance of the presence of Korean merchants during the Song and Yuan. In the lower left corner of the *Budaluo shengjing*, the painter has drawn the temple hostel (*jiedai si* 接待寺) in Port Shenjia, where monks and pilgrims found shelter until they could be ferried over. The hostel was first built in 1277, at a time when Mount Putuo was already considered one of three sacred mountains of Chinese Buddhism, alongside Mount Wutai and Emei.[21]

Toward the southeast the Tidal Sound Cave is featured prominently. In its grotto a white-robed Guanyin floats on a lotus petal, her face identical to that of the main icon depicted in the halo above.[22] The opening on the roof of the grotto, where pilgrims would try to catch a glimpse of the Bodhisattva, is labeled "Sky Window." To the right pilgrims make prostrations, as they do further to the west at the Sudhana Cave, in which Sudhana stands with folded palms facing toward Guanyin in the Tidal Sound Cave. This is one of the earliest pictorial representations of an appearance of Guanyin at Mount Putuo.

Moving north from the caves, there is the Puji Temple. At its northern end is a label for the "Pavilion of the Dragon Writ" (*Longzhang ge* 龍章閣). The pavilion was built in 1214 to accommodate two imperial plaques gifted to Mount Putuo. It was already gone by the time of the Zhou Gazetteer 1607, and the Qiu-Zhu Gazetteer of 1705 repeats that "no remains of it can be found."[23] Puji was the single, dominant temple on the island at the time, as the Fayu Temple, with which it later had to compete, was only established in the sixteenth century (see Chapter 4, Exhibit 2). Strangely, however, on the *Budaluo shengjing* there is a place labeled "Foundations of the Old Temple" (*gusi ji* 古寺基) at the spot where the Fayu Temple came to be built. This suggests that the Fayu Temple might have been built where a shrine or temple had been before, but the texts do not provide further information.

In front of the Puji Temple, half hidden behind a hill, is the famous stūpa that today is called Prabhūtaratna Buddha Stūpa (Duobao(fo) ta 多寶(佛)塔). It is labeled "Fenfeng ta 分奉塔." The words *fenfeng* ("to offer [one] part") appear in a Lotus Sutra passage, where Guanyin divides her adornments. She offers one half to the stūpa of Shakyamuni and the other to that of Prabhūtaratna Buddha.[24] Both names, Fenfeng Stūpa ("Stūpa of the Offering of One Part") and Duobaofo Stūpa ("Prabhūtaratna Buddha Stūpa"), therefore reveal the stūpa to be an architectonic reference to this passage in the Lotus Sutra. The stūpa is an intrinsic part of the temple ensemble; Guanyin after all is the central image in the main hall of Puji Temple. According to the Sheng Gazetteer, a "stone stūpa" was sponsored in 1334 by the Prince of Xuanrang 宣讓.[25] On account of the imperial sponsor the stūpa was called "Stūpa of the Prince" in the late Ming.[26] Probably, it was first called Fenfeng Stūpa and the original name was forgotten during the early Ming hiatus of the site.[27] If this is correct and the Fenfeng Stūpa on the *Budaluo shengjing* is indeed the later "Stūpa of the Prince" (a.k.a. today's "Prabhūtaratna Buddha Stūpa"), it has implications for the dating of the *Budaluo shengjing*. In view of the characteristic top ornaments that are visible in the *Budaluo shengjing*, there is indeed little room to doubt that the Fenfeng Stūpa is today's "Prabhūtaratna Buddha Stūpa." This means the *Budaluo shengjing* must have been painted after 1334, when the stūpa was constructed, and before 1369.[28]

Judging from the *Budaluo shengjing* and the maps in the Hou-Tu Gazetteer (see Exhibit 2), the stūpa used to be directly in front of the main temple. It appears in its current spot to the west of the lotus pond only in the Zhou Gazetteer of 1607. Probably it was moved around 1605 when the pond in front of the main gate was created. Restorations and movement notwithstanding, the square, five-storied stūpa is one of the oldest structures on the island. According to Hou Jigao it was quite dilapidated by 1588, and inscriptions show that it was restored four years later in 1592.[29] By the late nineteenth century the first photos by Shufeldt and Boerschmann show it again badly decayed.[30] Yinguang, the famous Pure Land patriarch and longtime resident on the island, had the stūpa restored once more in 1919.[31] Finally, like many other sites on Mount Putuo, it was defaced during the Cultural Revolution but is now again restored.[32]

The topography of at least one major site on the *Budaluo shengjing* is problematic. The famous Pantuo Rock, which is mentioned in all accounts, appears in the northeast of the island and not to the west as one would expect. Moreover, it is labeled "The great Pantuo Rock / a place to watch the sun rise" (*pantuo dashi guan ri chu chu* 盤陀大石/觀日出處), and we see white-clad pilgrims prostrating toward the east. The Sheng Gazetteer, too, seems to imply that the site was oriented toward the east.[33] However, as Hou's map of 1589 shows, at least since the late Ming the Pantuo Rock has been located on the west of the island, and at least since Tu Long's set of poems it has been regarded as a place to watch the sun set, not rise.

The sites found on the *Budaluo shengjing* are generally in accord with the descriptions in the early local gazetteers and the Sheng Gazetteer of 1361. There are, however, also a large number of places that fell out of use and were not re-established in the late Ming revival. We do not know, for example, what happened to the "Stone Guanyin" (*shi guanyin* 石觀音) that is shown in the northwest of the island. Based on the *Budaluo shengjing*, it probably was a stone formation resembling a Guanyin statue, but it is never mentioned in the gazetteers. Also the "Wisdom Sun Cliff" (*huiri an* 惠日岸) in the northeast, the "Plateau where Mei Zhen practiced internal alchemy" (*meizhen lian dan tai* 梅真練丹臺), and the two structures labeled "Utmost Purity" (*ji qingjing* 極清淨) and "Realm of the Clear Spring" (*qingyuan jingqie* 清源境界) are nowhere to be found today. This loss of places that made up Mount Putuo in the fourteenth century highlights the caesura that the site underwent between the end of the Yuan and its revival in the early Wanli era. Besides being evidence for continuity, the *Budaluo shengjing* is also a witness to the disruption that the repressive early Ming policies caused at Mount Putuo.

Exhibit 2: The Maps in the Hou-Tu Gazetteer (1590)

The set of maps contained in the first chapter of the Hou-Tu Gazetteer shows the site around 1600 CE. The set consists of one overview map of the island (Figure 2.1) and detail maps of the area around the Puji Temple and the Tidal Sound Cave (Figure 2.2), as well as a ground plan of the Fayu Temple (Figure 2.3). The Fayu Temple is treated more prominently, presumably because its leadership was better connected to the circle around Hou Jigao, Tu Long, and Long Defu, the editors of the gazetteer. On its detail map the Puji Temple appears smaller, embedded in its surroundings, though it was actually the larger compound. The overview map shows the two temples horizontally aligned, indicating their equal status. It is clear from the map that Putuo has now two centers. For the next two hundred years these would compete for preeminence until the addition of the Huiji Temple in the late eighteenth century added a third large temple to the constellation. Left of the Puji Temple small characters report laconically "Burnt down in 1598–10–25." This might mean that the maps were not part of the first edition but were added only to the reprint in late 1598 or 1599.[34] Another possibility is that only this remark was added by making changes to the woodblock on the occasion of the reprint. Considering that the position of the date on the print does not overlap with any other elements in the composition, the text might have been inserted into the empty area next to the temple.

In the southwest there is, as in all maps of Mount Putuo, the landing pier where visitors enter the island. Only the Hou-Tu map, however, shows a *Sanguan tang* 三官堂, a shrine to the Daoist "Three Officials of Heaven, Earth and Water," near the pier.[35] When the map was drawn the Three

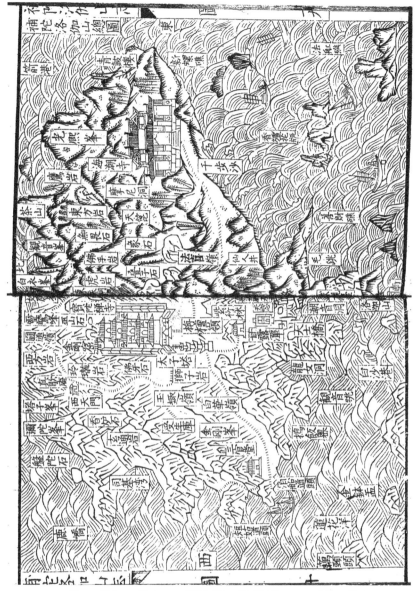

FIGURE 2.1 Map of Mount Putuo, c. 1589 (Hou-Tu PT-Gazetteer 19b – 20a)

Officials' Shrine was still relatively new; it was built only in 1577 to "give the [pilgrims] arriving on the ships a place to rest."[36] At least one of the three officials, the Official of Water, has an iconographic connection with ocean crossings by Buddhist figures.[37] Like Guanyin, he is depicted riding a dragon across the waters, and, like the Bodhisattva, he and the Official of Earth have salvific aspects.

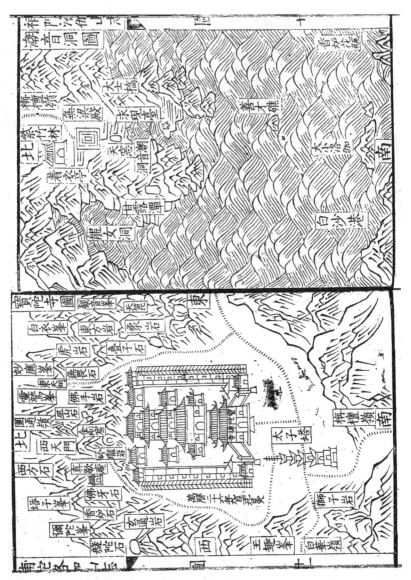

FIGURE 2.2 Detail Maps of the Tidal Sound Cave (right) and the Puji Temple, c. 1589 (Hou-Tu PT-Gazetteer 20b – 21a)

Daoist or folk-religious shrines often existed at or near Buddhist sites, and Buddhist establishments were sometimes found near Daoist centers. Especially in late imperial China the two traditions had come to an arrangement, at least at a grassroots level. A shrine to the Three Officials on Mount Putuo would have instilled a sense of orderliness and recognition in the pilgrims as they disembarked after the at-times dangerous

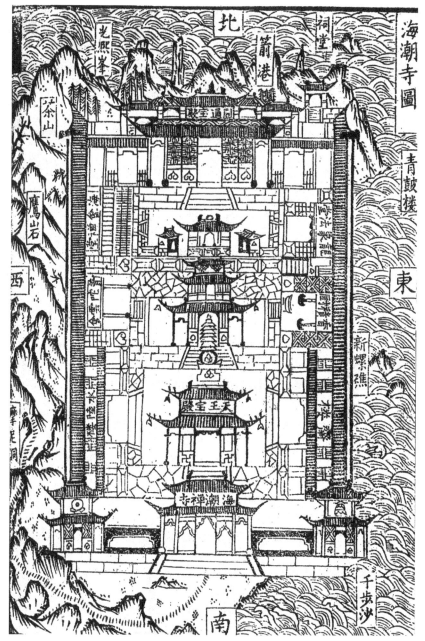

FIGURE 2.3 Detail Map of the Fayu (Haichao) Temple, c. 1589 (Hou-Tu PT-Gazetteer 21b)

passage. Perhaps it assured them that the numinous Buddhist site they were going to visit was, though liminal, still within the boundaries of Chinese civilization.

Buddhist mountain sites were often founded in already existing sacred places, and there is evidence for Buddhists appropriating Daoist sites during the Sui and Tang.[38] Therefore, at many sacred mountain sites, such as Nanyue, Buddhists and Daoists were co-present and interacted in "both amicable and inimical" ways.[39] In the case of Mount Putuo, however, there is little evidence of a Daoist presence either before or after the place was used by Buddhists. This did not preclude, as we will see in Chapter 7, that Mount Putuo was often described in terms of a Daoist literary *imaginaire* of sacred islands such as Mount Penglai 蓬萊山 (or 島) or Mount Fangzhang 方丈山. Also, the place names associated with Daoist masters (Mei's Peak, Ge Hong Well), who allegedly lived on the island in the distant past, is not unusual. Although there is no hint of Daoist activity on the island since the beginning of the Song, either in the gazetteers or in official sources, references of "traces" to a legendary past are quite usual in Buddhist descriptions of sacred sites. As James Robson has pointed out "layering—of whatever kind—increased the perceived sanctity of a site" and accordingly the presence of traces was faithfully recorded in the chronicles.[40] Nevertheless, in the case of Mount Putuo, the claims to a Daoist past wear thin, and elsewhere I have argued that Mount Putuo is in fact the most exclusively Buddhist of the four "great and famous" Buddhist mountains.[41]

Indeed, the Shrine to the Three Officials is the only Daoist establishment on record, and according to the gazetteers even this ostensibly Daoist site was founded by a Buddhist monk. The shrine vanished in the seventeenth century, perhaps destroyed in the chaos that engulfed Putuo Island between 1665 and 1684. It is not mentioned in the Qiu-Zhu or any later gazetteer, but Boerschmann on his visit in 1908 found a miniature version of a Shrine to the Three Officials, a small altar niche, located near the Fayu Temple. Clearly, the three officials had not been forgotten.[42]

The pier area that is named "Korean Pier" in the *Budaluo shengjing* is labeled twice in the Hou-Tu set (see Figure 2.1), both prosaically "Pier for Mooring" (*bochuan daotou* 泊船道頭) and, alluding to legend, "Pier of the Sister-in-Law."[43] As maritime trade was increasingly restricted by ocean embargoes (*haijin* 海禁) during the Ming, culminating in its complete suppression between 1522 and 1567, the trade among China, Korea, and Japan was pushed underground and lost the ritual, diplomatic dimension on which Mount Putuo had drawn in the Song and Yuan.[44] Even after the Chinese relaxed the restrictions in the Wanli period, coastal bans were again promulgated by the Qing dynasty[45] in the seventeenth century. International communication was further limited as the Japanese instituted their own strict seclusion policy (*sakoku* 鎖国) after 1633. As much as Mount Putuo profited from the international trade and contacts in the Song and Yuan, its location turned into a liability when maritime trade was discouraged or recast as piracy under the Ming and the Qing. Thus the name change of its modest pier is—as so often—indicative of larger and more far-reaching changes in the fortunes of the island.

The Hou-Tu maps are oriented north-up like the *Budaluo shengjing*, but are topographically closer to the current layout of the site. The Pantuo Rock and the Immortal's Well are firmly in place, as are many other sites, which are located roughly where they can be found today. For the first time a "Tea Mountain" is labeled to the north of the island, although tea trees on Mount Putuo are already mentioned in the Sheng Gazetteer.[46] The names of the various hills and mountain peaks on the island vary greatly from map to map, perhaps reflecting not so much actual name changes but a lack of interest in and cartographic effort to represent the mountainous terrain.

The cave west of the Tidal Sound Cave is named "Cave of the Dragon Girl" (*longnü dong* 龍女洞) instead of Sudhana Cave. The name change must have occurred in the Ming, perhaps around the time Mei Kui 梅魁 (fl. 1568) wrote the poem titled "Sudhana Dragon Girl Cave."[47] The combination of Sudhana and the Dragon Girl is of course not surprising as both are often depicted together as attendants of Guanyin.[48] Moreover, their iconography overlaps at times, they are both depicted as children, and they also have entered Daoist literature and iconography.[49] The Dragon Girl appears first in the Lotus Sutra, while Sudhana features in the *Gandhavyūha* part of the *Avataṃsaka Sūtra*. The rise of the Dragon Girl at the expense of Sudhana near the Tidal Sound Cave might also be connected to the relative importance of the Lotus Sutra, which was extremely popular in late imperial China. The name change from Sudhana Cave to Dragon Girl Cave is part of the "move" of the Sudhana Cave away from the Tidal Sound Cave, which will be discussed in Chapter 4.

The differences between the maps in the Hou-Tu Gazetteer and the maps in the Zhou Gazetteer (1607) reflect the movement away from the depiction of Mount Putuo in the relatively exact style of the maps toward more impressionistic "views" for the armchair traveler.[50] From the layout and the style of the illustrations in the Zhou Gazetteer, it is clear that something new was intended.[51] The Zhou Gazetteer maps are a large set of fourteen tableaux, each arranged to fit on two pages.[52] They are drawn in a distinctive guidebook style that allows readers to armchair travel from the northern tip of the island to its southern shore. Similar, though much shorter, tableaux series can be found for instance in the gazetteers of Mount Jizu or Mount Huayin.[53] The tableaux transition into each other seamlessly. Like in a scroll painting, the gaze is guided by the pathways to create the impression of a walk along the deserted mountain ways passing by temples and famous sites. The panels thus merge into a single panoramic view of the island. In spite of this, the illustrations are clearly intended to work as maps as well, with labels attached to important places and an emphasis on the paths that connect them. Unlike the Hou-Tu maps, the Zhou Gazetteer illustrations give much space to the sea surrounding Mount Putuo, which is drawn in great detail. Both the first and the final tableau, clearly more landscape painting than map, merely show a barren shoreline next to an empty expanse of water.

Exhibit 3: The "Twelve Views of Putuo" in the Qiu-Zhu Gazetteer (c. 1705)

The images created for the Qiu-Zhu Gazetteer depict the island in the time around 1700. Besides an overview map (Figure 2.4) and ground plans of the Puji and the Fayu Temple, there is a set of "Twelve Views of Putuo" (*putuo shier jing* 普陀十二景). The set was successful and it was re-used in the two subsequent Qing editions, the Xu and the Qin gazetteers. The "Twelve Views" continue the movement away from the relatively exact but prosaic map style of the Hou-Tu Gazetteer that the panoramic set in the Zhou Gazetteer had begun. Their arrangement, however, is now informed not by topography but literature. The images do not form a single panoramic view but work in the way of snap shots. The touristic impression is enhanced by the fact that the views show pilgrim-tourists interacting with these sites. The overview map shows for the first time the lotus pond and the bridge in front of the Puji Temple, which were constructed around 1606. Also for the first time, the Brahma Voice Cave east of the Fayu Temple, with its characteristic bridge, appears on a map.

The "Twelve Famous Views" are inspired by poem cycles on "Twelve Famous Views of Mount Putuo," the first of which seems to have been written by Tu Long (see Chapter 7, Exhibit 2).[54] The "Twelve Views" of the Qiu-Zhu Gazetteer, however, depict a different set of sites than the poems. The editors of the Qiu-Zhu Gazetteer thought "the old names [by Tu

FIGURE 2.4 Overview of Mount Putuo (Qiu-Zhu PT-Gazetteer, c. 1705)

Long] were all far-fetched, vulgar, unrefined, and unrealistic" and wanted to include only the most famous sites on Mount Putuo.[55] The criticism of Tu Long's poetry seems overly harsh. It is true, however, that in his poem cycle he included poems on some outlying islands that were of little interest for pilgrims to Mount Putuo. We will discuss Tu Long's poems in Chapter 7 and focus here on the set of images that became the standard depiction of Mount Putuo during the Qing.

1. The "Buddha" Chooses the Mountain[56]

The first image (Figure 2.5), alluding to the central foundation legend, shows Guanyin arriving at Mount Putuo by boat. It is, however, not a mere illustration of the legend, but instead of the monk Egaku and the Bodhisattva image Guanyin herself arrives at Mount Putuo as a pilgrim would do. Thus the panel evokes a sense of chronological progression both in terms of the history of the site as well as in the course of pilgrimage. Readers start their virtual "armchair" pilgrimage with the legendary beginnings of Mount Putuo—the arrival of Guanyin.

2. Guanyin Appears to the Rebuked Sister-in-Law

This dual progression in time and topography is continued in the next panel (Figure 2.6). It shows the pier where pilgrims arrive on the island and illustrates the legend from which it takes its name: "Pier of the Sister-in-Law."[57] Beginning with the Zhou Gazetteer the legend is repeated in all gazetteers, if in slightly different versions. It must have formed between the Yuan and 1590, when the name "Pier of the Sister-in-Law" was first used on the map of the Hou-Tu Gazetteer.[58] It is one of the few tales about women on pilgrimage and offers a glimpse into their concerns.

The standard version is as follows: Two sisters-in-law went to Mount Putuo on pilgrimage. On arrival, the younger discovered she was having her period. Since it was considered taboo to visit a temple or sacred site while menstruating, the elder woman went ashore alone, but not before having berated her younger sister-in-law. The younger sister-in-law, rebuked and ashamed, stayed behind on the boat. With the rising tide the stone mooring was submerged and she could not leave the boat. She was also getting hungry. At that point an old woman appeared on the shore and, throwing stepping-stones into the water, went up to the boat and brought her some food. When the older sister-in-law returned and heard about this, she looked for the old woman but was unable to find her. Convinced that the old woman was an appearance of Guanyin, she went back to the temple to pray. As she looked up to the Guanyin statue in the main hall, she noticed that the skirts of the image were wet.

The image shows the younger sister-in-law sitting unhappily under a tent in the small boat. She has not yet noticed Guanyin, who is going to step over the narrow stretch of water between boat and shore carrying her basket. The size of the boat is probably typical for pilgrim ferries of the time. Even

FIGURE 2.5 Guanyin arrives on Mount
Putuo (Qiu-Zhu PT-Gazetteer, c. 1705)

FIGURE 2.6 Legend of the Sister-in-
Law (Qiu-Zhu PT-Gazetteer, c. 1705)

FIGURE 2.7 The Tidal Sound and the
Brahma Voice Caves (Qiu-Zhu
PT-Gazetteer, c. 1705)

FIGURE 2.8 The Pantuo Stone
(Qiu-Zhu PT-Gazetteer, c. 1705)

much later, in 1922, regulations limited the passenger load for ferry boats from Zhoushan to Putuo to ten persons. The very same regulations single out "women and children," admonishing them to dress modestly and avoid wearing gaudy jewelry.[59]

That women from the same family traveled together without their husbands is considered unremarkable in the legend. We have seen in Chapter 1 (Exhibit 3) that orthodox Confucians might have found this objectionable. The story also shows that the site was safe enough for women to remain unattended at what was probably not the deserted shore we see in the picture but a rather busy pier.

3. The Tidal Sound and the Brahma Voice Caves

The image in Figure 2.7 shows the Tidal Sound Cave and the Brahma Voice Cave separated by a stretch of sea. Although the perspective is topologically impossible, it has its own logic as the use of both sites relies on the spectacle of the incoming breakers crashing into the grottoes. In the panel people are shown at both sites, prostrating themselves on the famous bridge at the Brahma Voice Cave and standing at the Tidal Sound Cave. These postures capture the different geography of the sites well. At the Brahma Voice Cave the bridge allows a panoramic view of the grotto, before which one can prostrate. At the Tidal Sound Cave one has a better view from above if one remains standing.[60]

The Brahma Voice Cave became established only in the seventeenth century and had not appeared on maps contained in previous gazetteers. In Chapter 4 (Exhibit 2) we will argue that the Brahma Voice Cave is a functional copy of the Tidal Sound Cave. That by 1705 it was depicted equal in prominence to the Tidal Sound Cave shows how quickly developments at the site were reflected in its textualization.

4. Sunset at the Pantuo Rock

Figure 2.8 shows three figures sitting on the large boulder as they watch the sun set behind the mountains of Zhoushan Island west of Mount Putuo. A fourth figure is ascending the steep steps to join them. The presence of visitors in the panels encourages the viewers to imagine themselves at the island. We have noted above that in the Yuan, the Pantuo Rock was considered a place to watch the sun rise, but at least since the late Ming the name Pantuo Rock has been firmly associated with the characteristic natural stone platform on the western end of the island. The woodcut shows the stone precariously balanced, tilting somewhat to the left. Probably the artist had actually seen the stone—it is indeed perched on the supporting rock tilting to the west. The Wang Hengyan Gazetteer reports: "The women coming on pilgrimage who climb up to this stone, all carry some copper coins. They rub these against the stone until they shine. Then take them back and give them to their little sons to make them brave."[61]

Today the stone bears the brightly red inscription "Pantuo Rock" 磐陀石, allegedly in the calligraphy by Hou Jigao. The inscription seems to have been added in the eighteenth or the nineteenth century as it is not listed among the stone inscriptions in the Qiu-Zhu Gazetteer.[62]

5. The Numinous Fahua Cave

The panel of the Fahua Cave shown in Figure 2.9 is remarkable because for the first time we see a child on Mount Putuo. That children accompanied their families on pilgrimages is not in itself surprising, but given that the texts concerning Putuo were written by men and women and children are rarely mentioned, this view is a precious reminder that in all likelihood most visitors of the island were women and that a pilgrimage to Mount Putuo might well have been a family outing. In his travelogue of a visit in 1617, Zhu Guozhen states that it was in the main donations by women that supported Mount Putuo, a fact that is probably true for all periods.[63] The pilgrims are seen walking through a stone formation, which appears to have been quite different from the area surrounding the Fahua Cave today.

6. The Immortal's Well at Mei's Peak

Figure 2.10 evokes the image of the legendary Daoist recluse Mei Fu. It shows a small house next to a hexagonal roofed well. Through an open wall, a common device in Chinese painting, we look into a study where one man sits next to a table. It seems a simple enough depiction of the site where Mei Fu practiced inner alchemy, but, as is often the case, the relationship between the place and its view is more complex.

Like several other sites, the well has undergone a "copying" (see Chapter 4, Exhibit 2) and there are now two wells on Mount Putuo associated with Mei Fu. The *Budaluo shengjing* shows a "Well of the Immortal Mei [Fu]" (*Meixian jing* 梅仙井) to the west, northwest of Puji Temple. This became part of the Mei Fu Hermitage (*Mei Fu An* 梅福庵), which was built in the Wanli era and is today called "Mei Fu's Cinnabar Well" (*Mei Fu dan jing* 梅福丹井). This well (actually a spring) is clearly one of Mount

FIGURE 2.9 The Fahua Cave (Qiu-Zhu PT-Gazetteer, c. 1705)

FIGURE 2.10 The Immortal's Well (Qiu-Zhu PT-Gazetteer, c. 1705)

FIGURE 2.11 Watching the sun rise from the morning tide (Qiu-Zhu PT-Gazetteer, c. 1705)

FIGURE 2.12 Walking on Thousand-Step Beach (Qiu-Zhu PT-Gazetteer, c. 1705)

Putuo's oldest sites, and its name points to the time before the arrival of Buddhism. It is fully possible that recluses on the island built their huts here on this scenic but sheltered spot on the western ridge of Mei's Peak. By the late Ming, however, this site too, like the Puji Temple and the Tidal Sound Cave, was doubled and a second Immortal's Well had been established to the east of Puji, where it is recorded in the overview map of the Hou-Tu Gazetteer. This, the more recent Immortal's Well, is the one we see in the "Twelve Views." It was never fully integrated into the Buddhist *imaginaire* of Mount Putuo by legends or architecture, however, and today it stands as a pointer to a Daoist past, which for all we know was completely legendary.

7. The Morning Sun Rises from the Ocean

After a series of numinous sites associated with ancient legends, which were sought out by pilgrims for vision and prayer, with the panel shown in Figure 2.11 the "Twelve Views" change track and present more generic depictions of aesthetic landscapes. Here, the sun is drawn as if rising from out of the ocean itself. This is in line with the literal Chinese title of the scene: we see the morning sun indeed "bubbling up" (*yong* 湧). "The Morning Sun Rises from the Ocean" is another view that gained currency only in the seventeenth century. As the Pantuo Rock had become the site for watching the sun set, there was an opening for a sunrise site. This spot was found at the southern end of the Thousand Step Beach, where a rock formation juts out into the ocean. It is easily accessible from the area around Puji Temple, where the guest houses that accommodated pilgrims overnight were located. The scene shows the Morning Sun Cave Retreat (*Zhaoyang dong an* 朝陽洞庵), which was built during the Kangxi era. It must have been fairly new when the woodcut was made. Originally constructed on an outcrop in front of the small cave, it was torn down during the Cultural Revolution,[64] but the foundations of its outer walls are still visible today. The small cave is still in use today and contains a shrine with statues of various Buddhist and Daoist deities. As the panel shows, however, the best place to observe the sun rise "out of the sea" is on top of the rock. It is one of the most scenic spots on the island, and in 1992 the tasteful "Watching the Sun Pavilion" (*Guan ri ge* 觀日閣) was built there.

8. The Golden Thousand-Step Beach

The longest beach on the island (Figure 2.12) had been a landmark for visitors since Mount Putuo became a pilgrimage site. It is first mentioned in a fourteenth-century poem appended to the Sheng Gazetteer.[65] Since the late sixteenth century most pilgrims would have passed along the beach on their way to the Fayu Temple. The panel shows a pagoda near the beach, which does not seem to be attested in the text or in the panoramic view of the beach in the Zhou Gazetteer maps. The calm and leisurely postures of the visitors on the beach are in contrast to the stylized, fierce breakers that seem to loom above them.

9. Waves of Clouds at Peak Hua and 10. On Guangxi Peak after Snowfall

The panels in Figures 2.13 and 2.14 show a mountainscape with small figures of visitors hiking on steep trails. The views do not reference any religious sites, and neither peak has been mentioned as particularly scenic in previous accounts. The panels intend to show the pleasing landscape of Mount Putuo for the sake of the armchair traveler. The main difference is that of season: panel 10 shows Guangxi Peak in winter, and sea and sky are darkened against the landscape. A cape worn by the figure in the foreground suggests the cold, as do the leafless trees. Snow falls rarely on Mount Putuo, and perhaps the snowscape was especially appreciated.

11. Listening to the Bell near Baotuo Stūpa and 12. Watching the Moon in the Lotus Pond

The last two scenes (Figures 2.15 and 2.16) can also be considered together. After the grand vistas of the previous panels, the armchair traveler returns to the more intimate environment of the Puji Temple. The temple closes its gates in the late evening, and visitors in the surrounding guesthouses would have spent time in the area around the Lotus Pond and on the bridge in front of it. Although the area around the temple gates was probably one of the most lively and busiest spots on the island, the scenes evoke a silent and introspective mood. The lone visitor that listens to the temple bells near the Baotuo Stūpa seems to have stopped on his way for a quiet moment, and the two figures on the bridge contemplate the "moon in the pond," a well-known trope in Chan Buddhism.

Read together with the poem cycles, we can understand how the "Twelve Views" served as a template to create or recreate for the viewer the experience of visiting Mount Putuo, much as picture books of tourist destinations do in our time. Even if some of the views are generic, with little effort toward realism, they do relate both to the actual landscape of Mount Putuo and to its religious *imaginaire*. The "Twelve Views" might

FIGURE 2.13 Waves of clouds at Peak
Hua (Qiu-Zhu PT-Gazetteer, c. 1705)

FIGURE 2.14 On Guangxi Peak after
snowfall (Qiu-Zhu PT-Gazetteer, c. 1705)

FIGURE 2.15 Listening to the bell near
Baotuo Pagoda (Qiu-Zhu PT-Gazetteer,
c. 1705)

FIGURE 2.16 Watching the moon in
the lotus pond (Qiu-Zhu PT-Gazetteer,
c. 1705)

be less religiously charged than the *Budaluo shengjing*, but they too use the web of religious meanings around the island to create an inviting series of tableaux. Interestingly, none of the views show monastics or Buddhist rites or images. Guanyin herself, who is shown in the first panel standing on the small junk on her first "arrival" on Mount Putuo, is used much less conspicuously than in our first exhibit, the *Budaluo shengjing*. The Qing dynasty gazetteers were aimed less at committed pilgrims or monastics than at a literati audience interested in religious sites and travel.

Conclusion

The visual record discussed above is witness to the textualization of Mount Putuo in the wider sense of text as encoded in images. It helps us to understand how previous generations experienced—literally "saw"—the site. Its analysis also adds to our factual knowledge about the site and its sources, such as the original name of the Duobaofo Stūpa or an improved dating of the *Budaluo shengjing*. Seen in conjunction, the Yuan dynasty painting, the Ming woodblock maps, and the "Twelve Views" of the Qing dynasty depict Mount Putuo in their own, idiosyncratic ways. Nevertheless, all are representative for their times. The *Budaluo shengjing*, itself not part of a gazetteer, presents the island in religious terms, dominated and protected by Guanyin. The set of maps commissioned by Hou Jigao is topographically the most exact, reflecting the strategic concerns of Commander Hou. The illustrations in the Zhou and the Qiu-Zhu gazetteers were created for the literati armchair traveler and emphasize neither the religious nor the strategic but the aesthetic dimension of Mount Putuo.

After the sections on prefaces and images, most temple gazetteers begin the compilation proper with a description and enumeration of the numinous places and buildings that make up the sacred site. Some, however, launch their show of genres in a more religious key and start out with foundation legends and miracle tales, to which we will turn in the next chapter.

CHAPTER 3 | Foundation Legends and Miracle Tales

Of those who ask the Bodhisattva to appear, some see her and some don't. Why is that?

—ZHU JIN[1]

TALES OF SUPERNATURAL EVENTS— miracle tales[2]—are a vital part of the religious *imaginaire* surrounding pilgrimage sites and are often at the very center of their textualization. The general theme of the miracle tales at Buddhist sites is closely related to the local focus of worship. While most miracle tales in the Mount Putuo gazetteers are about visions of Guanyin, the Mount Wutai Gazetteer of 1933 recounts twenty-two carefully crafted stories of encounters with Mañjuśrī.[3] In the Aśoka Temple Gazetteer most of the tales are about miracles surrounding the relics and the reliquary for which the temple is famous.[4] For Mount Tiantai, where both Buddhist and Daoist sites are present, the ecumenical *Tiantaishan waishan zhi* distinguishes between Daoist and Buddhist miracles and groups them in different sections.[5] As a result, the extraordinary events around the monks Fenggan and Shide are listed in the Buddhist section and that of their poet friend Hanshan in the Daoist section. Such a distinction might not be useful in a literary or art historical context, but categories, in gazetteers as elsewhere, develop their own dynamics and force their inventors to discriminate in unforeseen ways.

Miracle tales are arranged chronologically in their own sections. While some compilations tend to leave the miracles in the past and do not give credit to tales of their own time, other compilers include miracle tales of their own generation.[6] Some gazetteers have no separate section for miracle tales at all. The compilers of the gazetteers of Suzhou's Hanshan Temple or the Huiyin Temple in Hangzhou, for instance, took a secular approach to compilation and kept the supernatural at a minimum, but such cases too reflect local religious practice.[7] As city temples, neither the Hanshan nor the Huiyin is a religious pilgrimage site. Their fame rests on their doctrinal or literary heritage rather than on numinous events, and their gazetteers accordingly give emphasis to those aspects and provide their readers with strong sections on inscriptions and poetry.

Skepticism about the value of miracle tales in gazetteers is not limited to secular authors. The Mount Huangbo Gazetteer, compiled by monks, includes only a few miracle tales appended to the poetry section, which are prefixed by an apologetic remark. But then Mount Huangbo is famous as a lineage temple and for its role in the transmission of Chan to Japan, not for its miracles.

A large pilgrimage site such as Mount Putuo, on the other hand, needs miracle tales. It acquires a reputation for being numinous because people tell stories about it, which—in their way—attest the extraordinary powers of the place. The tales are seen as evidence that the borders between the mundane and the transcendent at that particular place are thin and that the site might be worth a journey. While some places might be remembered for but a single miraculous event, large pilgrimage sites like Mount Putuo or Lourdes generate new tales with every generation. The appeal of a pilgrimage is in part the possibility to witness a miracle. Religions have different doctrinal explanations for supernatural events. Whereas the miracles associated with Christian saints are based on the notion of intercession, the tales surrounding Bodhisattvas in China are explained in terms of *ganying* 感應[8]—the idea that beings or things can be affected (*gan*) by others and respond (*ying*) to this in unexpected ways.

The concept of *ganying* originated and was widely used in traditional Chinese cosmology. It entered Buddhism only in China; there is no direct parallel in Indian Buddhist literature.[9] *Ganying* is a conveniently flexible concept that allows for the extraordinary within Confucian naturalism; but it can also explain the intervention of supernatural beings in Daoism and Buddhism. In the traditional sense *ganying* occurs "naturally," i.e., without a pronounced sense of agency, especially on the side of the respondent. When Bo Juyi (772–846) was asked in his *jinshi* exam whether to believe the story of Zou Yan, who changed the temperature of a valley by playing his zither, or that of Lu Yang, who changed the direction of the sun by swinging his halberd,[10] he answered using the concept of *ganying*: "Nature has no constant mind, it takes the mind of men as its mind.

Thus, by a deeply inspired mind one can affect (*gan*) responsive (*ying*) nature. By utmost honesty one can affect [even the course of] sun and moon which have no self [of their own]."[11]

Buddhists have used *ganying* to describe the miraculous response of Buddhas and Bodhisattvas to the prayers of the supplicant. Shifting the emphasis from a purely natural "resonance" to that of supernatural intervention, the Buddhist use of *ganying* has served as the conceptual basis for the "miracles" (*lingyi* 靈異) and "apparitions" (*shixian* 示現)[12] that were reported at Mount Putuo. Because of its ambivalence regarding agency, *ganying* could appeal to Buddhists and Confucians alike. The former understood that the miraculous event was brought about by the agency of a Buddha or Bodhisattva. The latter could appreciate the miracle tales without being overly invested in the Buddhist pantheon.

The term *ganying* appears already in the *Yijing,* the Classic of Changes (fifth to third century BCE), a fact of which the gazetteer compilers were well aware. Zhu Jin, the co-editor of the Qiu-Zhu Gazetteer, was much interested in the metaphysical dimension of *ganying*. He explains: "Everywhere all things mutually affect (*gan*) and penetrate (*tong*) each other. The *Yijing* says: '[The principle of Change] is still and without movement; but when affected it penetrates all things under heaven. If it were not the most spiritual in the world, how could it do that?'"[13] We will return to Zhu Jin and his ideas of why Guanyin appears at Mount Putuo in Exhibit 4. Exhibit 1 discusses the partly legendary, partly historical origin stories of Mount Putuo. Exhibits 2 and 3 show how the established genre of Guanyin miracle stories was put to local use for describing the apparitions of the Bodhisattva at the Tidal Sound Cave.

Exhibit 1: Origins

Religions often attach great importance to miracle stories surrounding the birth of a religious figure. In the same way, the foundation legends of a sacred site are an important part of the textual landscape draped around the place. As myths of origin, foundation legends of sacred sites must fulfill two functions equally well: they must tie the location into the wider *imaginaire* of the religion and establish a plausible local connection that explains why the sacred came to manifest itself in this very place. Tradition abhors chance. In religious discourse events are always meaningful, they never "just happen." This two-fold task of foundation legends is compounded in Chinese Buddhism by the challenge to provide both an Indian and a

Chinese connection for a given site, institution, or practice.[14] There are two important foundational texts concerning Mount Putuo, which are not parallel but complementary in the sense outlined above. Both are needed to turn a small island in the East China Sea into the abode of Avalokiteśvara. The first is a passage in the *Gaṇḍavyūha* part of the *Avataṃsaka Sūtra*.[15] The *Gaṇḍavyūha* tells the tale of young Sudhana, who in his quest for enlightenment visits fifty-three teachers or "benevolent friends" (*kalyāṇamitra*) to receive instruction. The setting of his meeting with Avalokiteśvara is described as follows:

> Then, the merchant's son Sudhana . . . arrived in due order at Mount Potalaka, and climbing Mount Potalaka he looked around and searched everywhere for the Bodhisattva Avalokiteśvara. Finally, he saw the Bodhisattva Avalokiteśvara on a plateau on the western side of a deeply forested mountain in a clearing, abundant with young grass, adorned with springs and waterfalls, and surrounded by various trees. He was sitting leisurely on a diamond rock surrounded by a multitude of Bodhisattvas firmly seated on rocks of various jewels. He was expounding the teaching called 'the splendor of the door of great friendliness and great compassion' belonging to the sphere of caring for all sentient beings.[16]

The existence of different Potalaka sites in Tibet and East Asia exemplifies how a single passage from an Indian Buddhist text was able to influence Buddhist religious life in distant cultures. The description itself, however, is fairly commonplace (grass, clearing, waterfalls, etc.). Any forested mountain slope could be called Mount Potalaka based on this account.[17] Only Avalokiteśvara's throne, the diamond rock, which on Mount Putuo was mapped as the Pantuo Rock (Chapter 2, Exhibit 1), is slightly out of the ordinary. Although Sudhana's visit in the *Gaṇḍavyūha* is the most famous and probably earliest example, there are other sutra passages that associate Avalokiteśvara with Mount Potalaka.[18] Such canonical passages were generally not considered miracle tales by the gazetteer compilers and were at times gathered and placed before the section on miracle tales proper.[19] For believers the existence of Mount Potalaka was thus proved by scriptural evidence, the word of the Buddha. The problem was now one of localization, as the *Gaṇḍavyūha* and other texts were all set in India.

The second foundation legend brought the Potalaka to China and started to turn a small island called Meicen into the pilgrimage site of Mount Putuo. According to this tale, the ninth-century Japanese monk Egaku 惠萼[20] was on his way back from a pilgrimage to Mount Wutai, where he had acquired a statue of Guanyin. Soon after leaving Ningbo his ship was caught in a storm near the island that is today Mount Putuo. It ran aground, and only after Egaku agreed to leave the statue behind was his boat freed again and he and the crew allowed to return to Japan. The statue was duly enshrined on the island and called the "Guanyin Who Did Not Want to Leave" (*buken qu guanyin* 不肯去觀音).

Here is the tale as told in the Zhou Gazetteer of 1607:

At the time of the [Later] Liang (907–923) the Japanese monk Egaku obtained a Bodhisattva image from Mount Wutai. When he was about to return [to Japan], his boat ran aground on a reef and could not be moved. He made a silent prostration toward the Tidal Sound Cave [on the island] and was able to reach the shore. There he put the image at the entrance of the cave. [Later] a man named Zhang built a small temple to enshrine it. People often observed miracles and strange occurrences there. When the prefect heard of this, he "welcomed" the image to the city where people could pro- pitiate it.[21] Soon after, a monk came to Mount Putuo and asked for some good wood. Behind closed doors he carved an image [of the Bodhisattva]. After a month had passed the image was finished. The monk, however, was nowhere to be found.[22]

Once the connection between this particular island and Guanyin had been formed, the religious life on the island took place in a new context. The process of textualization that turned the geography of Meicen Island into Mount Potalaka had begun. It was never a straightforward process. As information is added, lost, or distorted, even the presumably "original" foundation legends change. In our case, there are reasons to believe that the legend of the "Guanyin Who Did Not Want to Leave" became associ- ated with Egaku only later. Its earliest version is found in a short passage titled "Meicen" (Mei's Peak), which is part of Xu Jing's 徐兢 (1091– 1153) account of his mission to Korea.[23] Xu stopped over at Mount Putuo/ Meicen in the summer of 1123. His note shows that in the early twelfth century the island's Buddhist identity was not yet clearly established. Like the early local gazetteers of the region, Xu still calls the island Meicen. His account will be discussed in greater detail in Chapter 8, but here is what he says concerning the numinous image:

In the deep forest at the foot of a mountain there is the Puji Temple that was built in the Southern Liang dynasty. The shrine hall had a Guanyin image of numinous power that was once brought by a Silla merchant coming from Mount Wutai, who had the image carved because he wanted to take it back to his country. When he set out to sea the boat got stuck on a reef and would not advance until he left the image on the shore. A monk from the temple enshrined it in the main hall and from that time on, whenever the crew of a ship on an oversea voyage came here to pray for good luck [for the crossing] their prayers were invariably answered. Under the house Qian of Wu and Yue (907–978) it was brought to the Kaiyuan temple in the city [on the mainland]. The image venerated today on Mei's Peak was carved later.[24]

Xu, or his informant, got the founding dynasty wrong. It was an easy mistake to make, but the Liang dynasty that seems likely for the founding is the Later Liang (907–923), not the Southern Liang (502–557). Another detail that deserves attention is that the name of the main temple (above translated as Puji Temple) is actually *Baotuo Yuan* 寶陀院 in the text. This is slightly unusual, as the court had fully recognized Baotuo as a *si* 寺 temple already in 1080. Perhaps the site was still small and the older name still in use when Xu Jing visited in 1123.[25]

What is most interesting here, however, is that the founding is not tied to the Japanese monk Egaku but to an anonymous Korean trader. Egaku was one of the more peripatetic Japanese student monks.[26] The records are incomplete, and unfortunately he did not leave a travelogue, but we do know that he went to China at least three times—in 840 or 841, in 844, and again in 862—and that he visited Mount Wutai twice.[27] On at least some of his journeys he entered and left China at Ningbo and, by extension, must have passed by Mount Putuo. However, none of the scarce twelfth-century sources about the site—the report by Zhang Bangji of a visit between 1119 and 1126, Xu Jing's account of his stay in 1123, and Nanhu Daoyin's description of Mount Putuo of c. 1165[28]—mention Egaku. They do, however, all tell of merchants and diplomats from Korea. This is not necessarily a contradiction. Egaku was known to have traveled with Korean traders as many Japanese monks of the Sui and Tang did before him.[29] Moreover, Xu Jing's account is short, and his informant might not have mentioned Egaku's name. Still, one assumes Xu would have noted the presence of a foreign monk in the foundation legend.

Thirteenth-century versions of the story "Guanyin Who Does Not Want to Leave," on the other hand, all have the monk Egaku as the lead character, and it is this version that is most often told.[30] In the *Baoqing siming zhi* (1226)[31] and later local gazetteers, as well as in the *Fozu tongji* (1269)[32] and other works of Buddhist historiography, it was Egaku who brought the image from Mount Wutai. At least by the early fourteenth century the story was also known in Japan, and it appears in Egaku's biography in the *Genkō shakusho* 元亨釈書 (1322).[33] Is it possible that the connection with Egaku is a thirteenth-century invention? This is important not so much for the function of the legend itself but for the dating of the earliest religious establishment. If a connection with Egaku can be proven, then we are able to point to 863 as the year in which Egaku returned to Japan for the final time. If Egaku was added to the foundation legend later, a founding date somewhere during the Later Liang (907–923) is more likely.

Wang Liansheng draws attention to the fact that some thirteenth-century sources cite the Tang poet and official Wei Xuan 韋絢 (801–866) as a source for the association of Mount Putuo with Egaku.[34] According to the *Baoqing siming zhi* (1226), Wei Xuan had left a record concerning the events of Egaku's return voyage, which must be considered contemporary.[35] Unfortunately, Wei Xuan's text is now lost, but I agree with Wang Liansheng that this reference in the *Baoqing siming zhi* makes it likely that Egaku was indeed involved in the founding of Mount Putuo. In all likelihood his visit took place in 859 or 863 CE.[36] Therefore, if one insists on putting a particular date to the beginning of the site, Egaku's visit is the earliest occasion by which the island is connected to Buddhism in historical sources.

Exhibit 2: Apparitions of Guanyin at the Tidal Sound Cave

In gazetteers miracle tales are usually arranged chronologically. The miracle tale sections are presented as annals of supernatural events, a structure that in China is associated with the authoritative air of an ancient classic, the *Spring and Autumn Annals*, as well as with the "chronicles" (*biao* 表), which are a prominent part of the official dynastic histories (*zheng shi* 正史). Miracle tales add a veneer of factuality by providing dates and often the name and rank of the main protagonist. Like other genres, they follow the general pattern of textualization in gazetteers in that their number increases over time:

1. 1361: Sheng Gazetteer (Ch. *Ganying xiangrui* 應感祥瑞): 13 tales
2. 1590–1598: Hou-Tu Gazetteer (Ch. *Ganying xiangrui* 應感祥瑞): 15 tales. This includes verbatim the text of the *Ganying xiangrui* chapter of the Sheng Gazetteer; two tales were added by Hou Jigao.
3. 1607: Zhou Gazetteer (Ch. *Lingyi* 靈異): 14 tales.

4. 1698–1705: Qiu-Zhu Gazetteer (Ch. *Linggan shixian* 靈感示現): 31 tales. This includes verbatim the text of the *Ganying xiangrui* chapter of the Sheng Gazetteer.
5. 1739: Xu Gazetteer (Ch. *Lingyi* 靈異): 41 tales.
6. 1832: Qin Gazetteer (Ch. *Lingyi* 靈異): 36 tales.
7. 1924: Wang Hengyan Gazetteer (Ch. *Lingyi* 靈異): 63 tales.
8. 1999: Wang Liansheng Gazetteer (Ch. *Lingyi* 靈異): 68 tales.

Considering the cumulative character of textualization, the decrease in the number of recorded tales from the Xu to the Qin gazetteer is an anomaly. Other sections in the Qin Gazetteer were brought up to date. It seems that the editors of the Qin Gazetteer were not so interested in miracle tales and indeed the tales in its miracle story section are simply copied verbatim (with some omissions) from the Xu Gazetteer.[37]

Guanyin miracle tales do not follow a single plot, but one can distinguish a number of recurring motifs. These were not necessarily exclusive to Guanyin worship but appear frequently in tales of the Bodhisattva. Guanyin can appear to her followers both in waking and in dream. Visions of her are invariably beneficial. And, like other Bodhisattvas or immortals, Guanyin can also appear incognito, as for instance in the tale of "Guanyin and the Rebuked Sister-in-Law," which was retold in Chapter 2 (Exhibit 2).[38] Where a Guanyin tale is not about an apparition or vision of the Bodhisattva herself, it can be about an image or text associated with her.[39]

Below we will have a look at three short tales in which Guanyin appears at the Tidal Sound Cave.[40]

In a twelfth-century inscription (Chapter 6, Exhibit 1) the Prime Minister Shi Hao admonishes later visitors to be patient on their vision-quest. The Mongol general Haladai, however, who visited Mount Putuo about a hundred years later, did not seem to have read the inscription and decided to take harsh measures when he failed to see the Bodhisattva:

In the thirteenth year of the first emperor of the Yuan (1276) when the Grand Councilor Bayan [1237–1295] pacified the Jiangnan region, General Haladai came to visit the [Tidal Sound] Cave, but it was dark and there was nothing to see. He took his bow, nocked an arrow, shot it into the cave and left. When he went aboard his ship suddenly the sea was covered with lotus flowers [and he was unable to leave]. Astonished by this extraordinary event he felt remorse and returned to the cave to pray. Slowly the white robed Bodhisattva appeared with the boy [Sudhana] and passed by gracefully. Thereupon the general commissioned a splendid image and had a shrine hall built on the cave [to house it].[41]

The story of the foreign "barbarian" misbehaving at the cave and his remorse would have appealed to a Chinese audience. There are other tales where misbehavior at the site leads to more or less gentle retribution, but this seems the only case where aggression is directed against the Bodhisattva herself.[42] The fact that Guanyin appears together with Sudhana is not unusual. The faithful who had visions at the Tidal Sound Cave often saw whole ensembles as in the following vivid tale.

In the 21st year of the Yongle reign, on the nineteenth day of the tenth month (1423–11–30), the White Robed Bodhisattva appeared at the Tidal Sound Cave, attended by the Dragon King, the Dragon Girl and the Elder Daquan. In the morning she appeared with opened eyes and a worried expression. At noon her body appeared in a purple hue and she was facing the wall. In the late afternoon Sudhana appeared at the cliff outside and the white-robed, golden-crowned Bodhisattva [was seen] sitting in the red [setting] sun. [The guardian deity] Weituo stood below the sun and arhats gathered in the clouds above the ocean. The next day in the early morning the Bodhisattva appeared again in purple golden hue.[43]

While almost all sightings are dated, at least to the dynasty, sometimes the gazetteers include stories that do not mention who saw the apparition. Such is the case here in an entry for a day in November 1423. It is unusual in that it describes different apparitions at different times of day.

The Dragon King and the Dragon Girl appear often in the iconography of Guanyin; the "Elder Daquan 長者大權," on the other hand, is only rarely part of the ensemble. Known under the names Daquan Xiuli Bodhisattva 大權修利菩薩 or Zhaobao Qilang 招寶七郎, Daquan was a local guardian deity, whose cult seems to have originated in eastern Zhejiang, in the area around Ningbo during the Northern Song. An eighteenth-century encyclopedia says Daquan originated as guardian deity of the Aśoka Temple, but without further study it is difficult to say how reliable this information is.[44] If it were true, one would expect Daquan to have an entry in the seventeenth-century Aśoka Temple Gazetteer, where, however, he is hardly mentioned. The only trace of him in that gazetteer is in a place name (*Daquan dong* 大權洞). A poem written on the cave aptly reflects our lack of information on Daquan: "The ancient cave near the mountain's peak, silent, without dust // Deep within the clouds hides the guardian of the stūpa."[45] Daquan's cult, however, spread to Japan, probably in the thirteenth and fourteenth centuries, where images of Daquan were part of altar ensembles at some Sōtō temples.[46] He is associated with the coast and depicted looking out over the sea, his right hand raised to shade his eyes from the sun. In literature, he appears in at least one Yuan play and is mentioned briefly in the novel *The Water Margin* (*Shuihu Zhuan* 水滸傳). He is practically unknown in Chinese Buddhism today, and modern Buddhist lexicography only gives short and sometimes erroneous information on him.[47] His appearance in the vision above makes the short description curiously authentic; unknown before and obscure after his time, pilgrims could still have expected to see Daquan in the early fifteenth century. The Arhats in conjunction with Guanyin are also a relatively rare motif. They are attested, however, in two fan paintings of the late Ming that show the sixteen Arhats visiting Guanyin at her grotto, which seems modeled on the Tidal Sound Cave.[48]

Contrary to the previous tale, which did not name the observer but gave an exact date of the vision, the following tale of Guanyin's apparition at the Tidal Sound Cave is not dated but names the observer:

> After Mr. Zhang Hanru of Cang Prefecture [near Tianjin] had come to Mount Putuo and paid his respects to the Bodhisattva, he wanted to return, when he saw an old man sweeping outside the [Tidal Sound] Cave. The old man asked him: "You have come a long way. Did you want to see the Bodhisattva?" Zhang said: "I have indeed covered 4000 *li* to come here. If I were able to see the Bodhisattva, I could die without regrets. But how will I be able to see the Bodhisattva?" The old man replied: "If only you pray with deep honesty, there should be something to see." Zhang and his companions, more than ten people, knelt to pray. After a while, they suddenly saw a golden ray at the entrance of the cave. The old man said: "The Bodhisattva has appeared." As the crowd looked intently, they indeed saw the Bodhisattva emerging from the stone walls. But they were only able to discern her in profile and again prayed: "Now that the honored Bodhisattva has appeared, may we behold her in frontal view to pay homage [as well. Thus], after our return, we will be able to fashion a likeness." On that the Bodhisattva turned her back to the cave and faced the ocean [allowing them to see her fully], [standing] only a couple of yards away from them. Her hair was curly and she had high cheekbones and a prominent nose. Her clothes were green. Half of her body remained unseen, hidden by the sea spray. The people joyously prostrated themselves. Suddenly, the apparition retreated into the stone wall and was gone.[49]

About Zhang Hanru 張漢儒 not much is known.[50] The source that is given for this tale in the Wang Hengyan Gazetteer is the *Juyi lu* 居易錄 by

Wang Shizhen 王士禛, which was completed before 1704. The account features the wise and mysterious "old man," a fixture in Chinese stories of the supernatural at least since Sima Qian and widely used in Buddhist and Daoist folklore.[51] In spite of being a trope, the short conversation is credible in the sense that longtime residents and monks of Mount Putuo served as guides and instructed visitors how to interact with the site. It would be interesting to know whether Zhang Hanru and his group came down from Tianjin mainly to visit Mount Putuo or if he was already in Zhejiang for other reasons and his visit was merely an excursion. The dialogue seems to imply the former, but not conclusively so. This is the only tale I found where visitors interact with their vision and tell it to move to get a better view. The promise to create an image of the apparition points to a feedback loop between visions and images that is similar to that between gazetteers and sacred site. Not only did people acknowledge that their visions resembled the images they had seen before, the visions too inform the creation of new images and may have led to iconographic changes or peculiarities.

Exhibit 3: The Miraculous Recovery of Mr. Wang

The reprint of the Wang Hengyan Gazetteer has yet another use for miracle stories: as page filler. Paper was not to be wasted, and traditional Chinese woodblock printing tries to avoid having empty pages in a book. Generally, however, new fascicles begin on the right side of a printing block, i.e., the left page in an opened string-bound book. Thus, if a fascicle ended in the right half of the woodblock, its left side would be empty and would have resulted in an empty right page in the string-bound book. In such cases it was permissible to add a comment or addendum of some kind on the left side to avoid an empty page. In the 1934 edition of the Wang Hengyan Gazetteer, this *horror vacui* was carried over into movable-type printing. In six places an addendum (*fulu* 附錄) was inserted between two fascicles. The addenda had to be short. Whoever was responsible for the reprint chose to insert miracle tales, the last of which is dated 1934. Exhibit 3, which was inserted on page 522, is one of these addenda.[52] The tale became entangled in the gazetteer tradition like a fly caught in resin and preserved in amber. It was not included in the later Fang or the Wang Liansheng gazetteers, doubtless because its contents are not directly connected to Mount Putuo. Although its association with Mount Putuo and its gazetteers is incidental, Exhibit 3 is a good example for the Dream and

Healing Type of the Guanyin miracle story and, being both exceptional and exemplary, deserves to be presented here in full:

> In the days of the Ming dynasty the layman Danning (his personal name was Wang Yingji) always respectfully venerated Guanyin. In 1602 he fell ill and could not even swallow liquid food for seven days. In the ninth month on the night before the new moon [i.e., 1602–10–14], he dreamed that he was riding in a sedan chair along the bank of a great river. Suddenly he toppled over and fell into the water. All kinds of fish and turtles were swimming before his eyes. He thought: "I have often had these for dinner; that's why I have fallen into this calamity." Dizzily, he felt as if someone grasped him under the arms and pulled him out of the water onto the bank. Looking up he saw the sun large in the sky and Guanyin sitting leisurely at the shore. The boy Sudhana, the Dragon Maid, the parrot and the Flask of Pure Water were all there. He touched his clothes—they were completely dry. Gratefully, he prostrated himself.
>
> The Bodhisattva said: "In previous lives you have been a devotee of mine and always venerated me respectfully, therefore I have come to save you. You have been involved in much killing and therefore have contracted this illness. If you can stop the killing, you will quickly get better." Wang said: "This is of long my intention. I earnestly accept this precept now." The Bodhisattva said: "I have a potion for you to drink."
>
> Wang received a cup of some liquid and finished it in one draft. The cup was made as if of glass, luminous throughout. The color of the potion was like gold and jade and it tasted pure and subtle, not as coarse as worldly food. After drinking he thanked the Bodhisattva and awoke suddenly, with the taste of the potion still on his lips. His whole body was covered in sweat. Soon however his fever abated and he felt better. He was able to eat some rice gruel and quickly recovered his spirits. From then on he kept the precept of not killing, and recorded these events in a text "Recording the Miracle of the Intimate Words regarding the Precept against Killing."

Mr. Wang's miraculous cure belongs to an important type of miracle tale: the dream vision.[53] Whether an apparition was seen in waking or in dream was generally of little import in the world of Buddhism. Already in the seventh century the encyclopedia *Fayuan zhulin* 法苑珠林 included a chapter on dreams and their interpretation. It offers a four-fold typology of dreams, the third of which is "Dreams of Celestial Beings" (*tianren meng* 天人夢). While the first two types of dreams are regarded as illusionary and meaningless, "Dreams of Celestial Beings" are considered true: "Here a friendly celestial being appears in a dream and helps the dreamer obtain something good."[54]

The dream vision is paired here with the motif of healing, which too is common in miracle tales. What marks this tale as a Ming dynasty miracle story is mainly the description of Guanyin and her retinue. In pre-Song times miracle tales still describe the Bodhisattva as "a man perhaps twenty feet tall, of beautiful shape and appearance, his body a golden hue."[55] Sudhana, of course, has been associated with Guanyin early on via the *Avataṃsaka Sūtra*, but the full retinue of him together with the Dragon Maid and the parrot developed as a motif only during the Song and Yuan. The ensemble is well established in sutra illustrations during the Ming.[56] The parrot is attested as part of Guanyin worship relatively late and appears in popular literature only since the fifteenth century.[57]

Exhibit 4: Zhu Jin "On Apparitions" (c. 1700)

Somewhat hidden in the fifth fascicle of the Qiu-Zhu Gazetteer is Zhu Jin's essay on the miraculous apparitions of Guanyin.[58] His text is a good example for how literati in late imperial China made sense of the ubiquitous reports of visions or visitations of supernatural beings. His questions reveal a constellation of concerns that is typical for literati culture: Why, if ultimate reality is formless or ineffable, are there apparitions at all? Why do some people see apparitions while others do not? Why do those that see apparitions see different things? Do Confucian sages have visions as well? And if so, why do peasants have them too? Zhu Jin's essay "On Apparitions," begins with the following passage:

> "Apparitions" are also called "numinous resonance." There are cases where there is stimulus (*gan*), but no apparition, but there is never an apparition that appears without stimulus. Seeking to see [supernatural] forms and sounds, is not approved of by the Buddhas. Why then does the Bodhisattva appear in visible form? It is the pinnacle of true compassion, to always guide beings, ferrying them across. What people know is visible form, thus they merely see visible form.
>
> The Bodhisattva's true being, however, is of no [particular] form. It is a form of the formless; it is not manifest, it is a manifestation of the unmanifest. The form of the formless is both form and not-form, the manifestation of the unmanifest is both manifested and without trace.

The Bodhisattva is like the moon, people are like water. They see the Bodhisattva like the water receives the moon. The reflection cannot be called [merely a] reflection, it is indeed the moon, but neither can it be called the moon, because it is truly a reflection. Neither can it be said that the reflection is not a reflection of the moon, or that the moon is without reflection.

The moon shines on human beings: those who have eyes see the moon. The moon shines on earth: where there is water there is a reflection.

Of those who ask the Bodhisattva to appear, some [eventually] see her and some don't. Why is that? This too is like water receiving the moon. If [the receptacle] is clear, it can receive it, if it is muddled, it cannot.[59]

Ganying 感應 is a specific Chinese concept, which has been used by all religious traditions of China. The relationship of the moon, its reflection, and water has been metaphor for the workings of *ganying* since at least the seventh century.[60] Chinese Buddhist scholasticism developed the metaphor of the moon's reflection on still water for *ganying* along the following lines: true reality appears in the quiet mind → like the moon on a silent surface of water → in the same way miraculous visions or effects manifest due to the invocation of a Buddha's or a Bodhisattva's name. In the Putuo gazetteers this metaphor was used well into the twentieth century.[61] Zhu Jin, after a riff on the ineffability of the Bodhisattva's true form, uses it skillfully and then ties it into the semiotics of the characters for the term *ganying* in the Yijing, the *Classic of Changes*:

Of those who receive an apparition after asking to see [the Bodhisattva], there are those which meet [their vision] in a state of no-mind (*wuxin* 無心). Because of being in no-mind they can stimulate (*gan*). The *Classic of Changes* does not say *gan* 感 but *xian* 咸.[62] *Xian* is the kind of stimulus that is produced by no-mind.

Others propitiate an apparition with a faithful mind (*xinxin* 信心). A sutra says: "Faith is the beginning of the path and the mother of merit."[63] Through faith there is stimulus. A sutra also says that the Bodhisattva "well-responds (*shanying* 善應) everywhere."[64] "Well-responds" here means "to appear." How could one doubt this, if there are sutras in which the Buddha firmly said so?

Prime Minister Pei[65] of the Tang dynasty said: "May in the future the learned derive their faith from the Buddha, not from men; may they reach for realization via the root teachings, not via the lesser branches of learning."[66] Ordinary people who do not believe in the Buddha's words, grasp the reflection they have seen, and consider it a view of the highest wisdom. [The state of] no-mind or a faithful mind is like the clarity of water, in their absence things are muddled. Those who consider themselves wise and others foolish, how could they know the depth of their delusion! [. . .][67]

Zhu Jin tries to make sense of the question why *ganying* works for some but not for others. His distinction of a vision grounded in either "no-mind" or "faithful mind" is a reflection of the Chan/Pure Land contrast that was an important feature of the Buddhist landscape in Late Imperial China. The discourse about visions was not uncritical, and Zhu acknowledges the limits of the moon metaphor:

Some say: "When people pray, have an apparition, and then describe what they saw, why do they all come up with different things? Why does not the moon's reflection on water appear differently [to different observers] as well?"

[To this we] say: "The moon has a single form, therefore its reflections all look alike. But when the Buddha's *dharmakāya* manifests itself, how could its sound and form be fixed? The difference in what people see is due to their individual way of affecting (*gan*), not due to a difference in that which responds (*ying*)."[68]

Zhu continues his attempt to connect the miraculous effect of the Buddhist use of *ganying* with that of Chinese naturalism. On the one hand he would like to offer a rational explanation for the Guanyin apparitions, which does not dismiss the experiences as superstitious or illusionary. On the other hand, however, he has no choice but to take recourse to ineffability, be it of the *dharmakāya* or the Confucian-Daoist concept of Heaven, because the power of the stories rest precisely in the fact that they are "miraculous" and cannot be fully explained.[69] Beneath his juggling of Confucian and Buddhist concepts and precedents, Zhu Jin seems acutely aware of this dilemma:

The things produced by Heaven do not have one single form. Some are made hard, some soft, some dry, some moist. Some are light and some are heavy, some are pure, some mixed. Heaven does not cast all things from the same mold. It is not possible to fathom the things produced by Heaven. In the same way how could an ordinary person fathom and understand the many manifestations of the Buddha's *dharmakāya*? When the Confucians talk about Heaven they call it "unfathomable,"[70] when they speak about spirits they say "sagely ones are unknowable."[71] The manifestations of the Buddha are inscrutable [as well]. [. . .] Still countless people do insist to fathom the unfathomable, insist to know the unknowable and think about the inscrutable! But actually they have no clue.[72]

In the following Zhu Jin defends the reality of Buddhist apparitions against the skeptics among his fellow literati. In his most explicit syncretistic move he equates the apparition of Confucian sage-saints (*sheng* 聖) with that of Buddhas and Bodhisattvas:

> Then there are some who say "In as far as apparitions exist at all, they are nothing but illusions. Otherwise why isn't there such a principle for Confucians sages?" Actually, there is. There is the old saying: "[Sitting] one sees [King] Yao on the wall, [eating] one sees [King] Shun in one's soup"[73] Did they not appear in empty space? [They must have, because] how could Yao and Shun have actually been in the wall or the soup? When Confucius studied the zither under Teacher Xiang he saw King Wen, but how could it be that while he played King Wen was actually sitting there? Thus the relationship between the affecting mind and the arising spirit manifests unexpectedly. The same is true for [Confucius] dreaming of the Duke of Zhou. [The Duke of Zhou] appeared in empty space without the slightest hindrance.[74]

What follows is a discussion of a peculiar problem that literati had at popular sites like Mount Putuo. Their class pretensions made it difficult to feel at home among the many less educated pilgrims. Faced with the fact that Guanyin was worshipped by the *hoi polloi,* they had to find a way of experiencing the site that could reconcile their elitist aspirations with popular appeal. Again strategies varied. Zhang Dai, for instance, who visited Mount Putuo in 1638, justly has been called an "ambivalent pilgrim."[75] While he appreciated the curious flair of religious sites, he was impatient with local customs and the often crowded and boisterous reality of religious tourism. Zhu Jin adopts another strategy to address the "cultural gap."[76] His move is to reframe the rusticity of the pilgrims as a form of honest simplicity that in Chinese culture was used as counterweight to the sophistication of ritual and literati life.[77] This allows Zhu to put a positive spin on the perceived ignorance of the average pilgrim and to cast the pilgrim's attitude as more natural and wise than the cherished sophistication of the literati:

> [Again] some say: "Sages might have these [apparitions of spirit beings], but how could an average person be able to have them?" [To this we] say, the Way can certainly bestow understanding and powers to ignorant men and women. Regarding its highest aspect, there is much that even sages do

not know and are not able to do. This does not mean that simpletons surpass the ability of sages, but ignorant men and women too can from time to time experience moments of bliss and clarity. And in their ignorant honesty and constant faith they might do better than a worthy and learned person, who is overly given to doubts and worries. Therefore, when average people pray for an apparition they obtain one. In general, talented people are rare, but average people are many and their thoughts and worries few.

The Way flows throughout Heaven and Earth. Perhaps besides the great sages and worthies only the minds of infants and simpletons can come close to it. Therefore it is said: "Common people every day act according to it without knowing."[78] In their ignorance, their minds are like those of an infant, simple and content. They are like Cūḷapanthaka, a disciple of the Buddha, who attained liberation in spite of being ignorant and dull.[79] Being ignorant certainly does not mean to be apart from the Way.[80]

As in his discussion of *ganying* cited above, Zhu Jin here combines quotes from the *Yijing* with Buddhist tropes. We do not know much about Zhu, but some of his commentaries on Confucian classics have been preserved in the *Siku quanshu*. He also compiled at least one more gazetteer, the Gazetteer of Yongkang County 永康縣志. Zhu concludes his essay considering why supplications are at times not successful.

Some, though they pray for an apparition whole-heartedly, do not obtain a vision. This is like a mirror clouded by one's own breath, like the moon being hidden behind clouds. In this the mind obstructs itself. When praying with a conscious intent, one's sincerity is actually insincere. Worldly people, who do not let themselves sink into emptiness, simply cling to existence, and their vision will be illusionary.[81]

Zhu Jin was concerned with the concept of *ganying* and why and how Guanyin appears to her devotees. His attempts to integrate her appearances into the standards of rationality of his time are a move not too different from our own discourse where we qualify them as "visions" or "religious experiences." One tries to come to terms with the extraordinary by framing it in ordinary terms.

Conclusion

The exhibits above were selected to illustrate the use of foundation legends and miracle tales, the most religious of the genres collected in temple gazetteers. Their presence distinguishes temple gazetteers from official province or county gazetteers, which generally have no comparable sections. Foundation legends and miracle tales explain why a site is considered sacred in a specific, local sense. The emphasis on visions of Guanyin in the Putuo gazetteers is germane. Without Guanyin's presence at Mount Putuo, how could it be the Potalaka?

The two most recent gazetteers—Fang (1995) and Wang (1999)—reflect a hesitation about the status of the religious in the gazetteers. The Fang Gazetteer does not include miracle tales and insists on a secular view of the site. In the Wang Liansheng Gazetteer, on the other hand, miracle tales feature prominently as part of the first chapter. Far from treating them as superstitious anecdotes, Wang duly records supernatural events as recent as 1997.[82] Again, however, change becomes visible in an absence. While Zhu Jin's essay on *ganying* integrates the miracle tales into the religious *imaginaire* of his time, Wang makes no attempt to explain these happenings. Nevertheless, miracle tales have maintained their vitality into the twentieth century, and in the twenty-first century too we can expect pilgrims to meet the Bodhisattva on Mount Putuo.

CHAPTER 4 | Elements of Landscape: Stay, Copy, Move, and Vanish

Although the famous mountains and the great rivers were formed by Heaven and Earth, it is only because of man that they are remembered and venerated.

—TONGXU 通旭 (1696)[1]

IN THE BEGINNING OF a place is a name. Once a site is named, it ceases to be just a location in space and becomes embedded in the larger web of culture and memory. A place without a name cannot be discussed; meanings would not stick. Not only do names allow locations to become meaningful, the very names themselves have meaning: a rock formation becomes "The Stone of Fearlessness"; a cave on the shore is the "Brahma Voice Cave"; a small, single-room hermitage is the "Hermitage of the Fragrant Grove." Names might carry historical or legendary allusions such as "Mei's Peak," or, more prosaically, they might indicate economic functions, as in the case of Mount Putuo's "Tea Mountain."[2] Chinese place names, more so than toponyms in European languages, are often immediately meaningful. "Beijing," the "Northern Capital," can be read literally in a way that "London" or "Berlin" cannot. Because of the pervasive polysemy and homophony of Chinese, place names often have layers of meanings. Most pilgrims, for instance, probably understood Zhenxie's Stone (*zhenxie shi* 真歇石) as a "Stone of True Rest"—they might not have heard about Chan master Zhenxie Qingliao 真歇清了 (1089–1151), who lived at Mount Putuo in the twelfth century. "Mount Mei's Peak" 梅岑山, the earlier name of Putuo Island, is derived from the personal name of the legendary Daoist Mei Fu but might also be read "Plum Tree Peak."

The semantic plenitude tends to obscure the general arbitrariness of the naming process. Even supposedly descriptive names, such as the rock formation "Two Turtles Listen to the Dharma," betray an element of randomness. This was noticed already by the always observant Zhang Dai, who passed those stones in 1638 and remarked: "Heaven playfully creates them, man playfully names them."[3]

How do gazetteers on Buddhist sites present the "mountain" they are ostensibly about? Within most gazetteers a section on topography follows the sections on prefaces and maps. It is constructed as an inventory of landscape and architecture. Hardly more than a list of place names, it glosses them briefly with their location, founding date, and current status. Descriptions lack detail and are usually written in a perfunctory manner, without pretense to style. In the larger, encyclopedic gazetteers, however, the inventory at times morphs into an enthusiastic enumeration of sites. In the Mount Jiuhua Gazetteer (1938), for instance, subtle categorizations maintain distinctions between peaks (*feng* 峯) and ridges (*ling* 嶺), mountain torrents (*jian* 澗) and slower brooks (*xi* 溪), deep lakes (*tan* 潭), and shallow ponds (*chi* 池).[4] Everything is accounted for. The Mount Jiuhua Gazetteer lists fifty-nine peaks, sixteen ridges, fourteen cliffs, twenty-nine rocks, thirteen grottoes, and nine terraces, and these are just the things of stone. The section on buildings, too, is remarkably comprehensive. It remembers more than a hundred monasteries, temples, and hermitages, some abandoned, but many still in use in 1938. Another section lists another hundred buildings that were not directly part of Buddhist monasteries and temples, including Confucian academies, ancestral shrines, Daoist temples, pavilions, and bridges.[5]

At times the compilers added poems to the glosses in order to enliven the dry inventory. This highlights a tension between different modes of description that is peculiar to gazetteers. Generally, the different modes are kept apart and gazetteers divide the labor of landscape description between the *visual*, depicted in maps and images, the *factual*, presented in lists of topological-historical glosses, and the *poetical*, found in the sections on poetry. The bookkeeping mode of the inventory aims to construct the place in encyclopedic enumeration. The poetic mode, on the other hand, breathes life into the names by presenting them in the evocative, poetic language that previous visitors had used to describe the site. The factual and the poetic modes were sometimes used to complement each other, as in the case of the "The Famous Sights of Putuo" *Putuo quansheng* 普陀全勝 (1830). Here the compiler, after a brief gloss, lists poems about the site in lieu of a prose description. Readers who had been to the site would have compared their own impressions with those captured in the poems, while those who had not yet visited could appreciate the poems as such. This design—the inventory of places as anthology—was success-ful; it was taken up in the Wang Hengyan Gazetteer (1924) and even used for a section of the most recent Wang Liansheng Gazetteer (1999).[6]

Another tension that is constitutive for gazetteers is found in the top-ographic sections. In gazetteers the diachrony of history contends with the synchrony of topography. The task of the compiler was to portray an "unmoving vision of a moving world."[7] In the case of Mount Putuo, as we have seen in Chapter 2, place names change often, or at least faster than the places they denote. It would be a mistake, however, to believe that the physical, geological landscape of the island was stable beneath a moving overlay of text and meanings. Even down at the level of geol-ogy, Putuo's outlines have changed considerably over time. What is today the northeastern tip of the island, where the Brahma Voice Cave and the Sudhana Cave are located, was at one time a separate island. The narrow gap between them has since silted up, and in the twentieth century a road was built across what used to be a strait.[8] Another conspicuous change occurred only recently. In the 1990s the western bay of Mount Putuo was filled in by a massive land reclamation project. A straight dam was built that closed off the bay and a stretch of artificial land was created, enlarg-ing the size of the island by almost 10 percent. The new space was used to build housing for the military garrison on Mount Putuo.

Another element of landscape that has changed the look of Mount Putuo considerably is the tree cover, which was absent in centuries when wood was the main material for building, cooking, and heating at the pil-grimage site. The earliest photos of Mount Putuo from the late nineteenth and early twentieth centuries show wide stretches of Mount Putuo bare and deforested, a view that agrees with the woodblock prints of the Zhou Gazetteer (1607).[9] In the 1920s Clara Ho describes the scenery on Mount Putuo: "There is precious little forest on Putuo, only in front of the Baihua Peak [along the way to the Puji Temple] trees grow thickly."[10] Today lush foliage covers the island almost completely; without it Mount Putuo must have appeared very different.

In this chapter I use some of the most prominent sites on Mount Putuo as examples for how textualization could proceed once it had been started by naming. They were chosen partly because of their prominence, but also because they represent different modes or possibilities of how textualiza-tion evolves geographically. I will call these different modes *stay, copy, move*, and *vanish*. A place on Mount Putuo might *stay* where it was cre-ated, it might inspire a structurally similar *copy* of itself, it might *move* to a new location, or it could be abandoned and *vanish* as a place of pilgrimage.

Exhibit 1: Stay—The Tidal Sound Cave

We have seen in the previous chapter how prominently visions of Guanyin at the Tidal Sound Cave have defined Mount Putuo as sacred space throughout its history. Indeed, it is the Tidal Sound Cave together with the Puji Temple that provides a measure of geographic stability within a moving landscape of lesser sites. Whereas other places on the island seem to move about, are established and forgotten again, the numinous cave has been continuously located in the southeast corner of the island. It is possible that its position has shifted slightly, but it will have been along the same stretch of coast, which is still visited by thousands of tourists and pilgrims every year.

The Tidal Sound Cave is a sacred place much in the sense of Eliade's influential definition.[11] Eliade argues that the sacred manifests itself in "hierophanies" at sacred spaces, which is just what we find recorded by the earliest visitors at the grotto. The previous chapter discussed various ways in which apparitions of Guanyin have been recorded in the gazetteers. Another early description is found in the *Fozu tongji* 佛祖統紀 (thirteenth century): "On the island there is the Tidal Sound Cave, [so called because] the tides thrash in and out of the cave with a great roar. In front of the cave there is a stone bridge. Some of the pilgrims who come here and pray sincerely see Guanyin sitting in meditation; some see Sudhana beckoning them; some only see the vase of purity made of green jade; some only see a *kalaviṅka* bird flying and dancing."[12] Many strands converge in the motif of the female saint revealing herself in a grotto. *Kalaviṅka* birds have a beautiful voice and are found in the Pure Land. These birds and the vase of purity are two from a set of auspicious signs.[13] The trope that Guanyin is to be found in a grotto near water entered Chinese Buddhist poetry and art in the early Song dynasty and from there spread to Korea and Japan along the trade routes through Ningbo.[14] The image of Guanyin appearing in a grotto seems to be a Chinese creation without direct precedent in Indian iconography, though in India too Guanyin/Avalokiteśvara was associated with oceanic travel and littoral pilgrimage centers.[15] One inspiration must have been the Daoist idea that it was possible to miraculously encounter (*ganyu* 感遇) supernatural beings in mountain caves.[16] Like the Tidal Sound Cave on Mount Putuo, a "grotto-heaven" (*dongtian* 洞天) is central to many Daoist mountains.[17] The influential "grotto cosmography," which lists ten major and thirty-six minor grotto-heavens, was comprehensively described in the *Dongtian fudi yuedu mingshan ji* 洞天福地嶽瀆名山記

(901 CE), around the time Mount Putuo was founded as a Buddhist site.[18] A comprehensive study of the appearance-in-the-grotto motif, which is impossible here, must also take related littoral cults, like that of Mazu, into account. It moreover deserves comparison with the use of grottoes in Mediterranean religions and in Christianity. In ancient Greece alone we know of more than 130 "grotto-sanctuaries,"[19] and one of Catholicism's most famous visions of the Blessed Virgin took place in a cave near Lourdes. Although relatively recent, Lourdes has had a strong impact on the Catholic sense of sacred space, and "Lourdes grottoes" have been recreated in Catholic spaces worldwide.[20] In effect these are replicas showing Saint Mary in a stone grotto and range in size from a desktop sculpture to a landscaped site.[21] The Tidal Sound Cave too was replicated and miniaturized. The idea occurred to Prime Minister Shi Hao in the thirteenth century, when he decided to recreate the Tidal Sound Cave at a lake close to Ningbo to spare his mother the voyage into the archipelago.[22] The site on the northwest shore of the Dongqian Lake is still in use, today designated as "Little Putuo Scenic Area" (*Xiao putuo jingqu* 小普陀景區).[23] Replication, however, is not what characterizes the Tidal Sound Cave in the context of Mount Putuo. It is better understood as an instance of *stay,* the option not to move, change, or vanish. It may have been recreated elsewhere—as we will see, it was in a sense duplicated even on Mount Putuo—but what distinguishes the Tidal Sound Cave and the Puji Temple is that both their location and their function have been relatively stable when compared to other places on the island. Both sites are labeled on the earliest map of Mount Putuo, and both are mentioned again and again in the sources. Though the Puji Temple was destroyed several times, and pilgrimage to the Tidal Sound Cave was interrupted at times for more than a hundred years, the two sites have always been remembered and revived. They thus survived at (more or less) the same locations where they were established in the tenth century. The Puji Temple and the Tidal Sound Cave are the anchors to which the memory of the whole site is moored.

Exhibit 2: Copy—Fayu Temple and Brahma Voice Cave

Over the centuries the Buddhist settlement of Mount Putuo proceeded from south to north. All early sources agree that at least three places existed in the south of the island during the Song and Yuan dynasties: a small harbor, the Tidal Sound Cave, and the Puji Temple. The fourteenth-century painting *Budaluo shengjing* (see Chapter 2, Exhibit 1) seems to show a large number of smaller sites all over the island, but the map is distorted and in fact only depicts the southeastern part of the island. With the founding of the Fayu Temple in the 1580s, the dynamics of the island's geography changed considerably.[24] As mentioned in the Introduction, the competition for visitors and patronage between the Puji and the Fayu Temple is visible in the edition history of some gazetteers. The Fayu Temple was originally founded as alternative to the Puji Temple. This becomes evident in a story surrounding the monks Dazhi and Zhenbiao, both key figures in the late Ming revival of Mount Putuo. The story clarifies why the Fayu Temple was created and why it quickly attracted support.

Dazhi Zhirong 大智直融 (1524–1592), the *de facto* founder of the Fayu Temple, had a special connection with the group of literati around Hou Jigao and Tu Long who were responsible for the first Ming gazetteer. He arrived at Mount Putuo in 1580 and was involved in a confrontation that saw the judge Long Defu 龍德孚 (1531–1602) take strong action against the monk Zhenbiao 真表, who in 1578 had become abbot of the Puji Temple. Long Defu was sympathetic toward Buddhism and evidently gave his friend Tu Long a firsthand account of what happened.[25]

In his retelling, Tu contrasts the behavior of the newly arrived Dazhi with that of Zhenbiao, who had been in charge of the main temple for some time. According to Tu, Dazhi strictly adhered to the Vinaya rules and had gained a large number of followers. The abbot Zhenbiao, on the other hand, was said to be arrogant and corrupt. He was accused of breaking the precepts by drinking wine and eating meat and handing out heavy-handed punishment for minor offenses by others. In 1582 someone sued him before the provincial authorities, and Long Defu was dispatched to investigate the matter. Long divided the temple property and reorganized its administration in order to diminish Zhenbiao's influence.

Having dealt with the allegations against Zhenbiao, Long Defu decided to take further measures. He burned a copy of the Lotus Sutra, had the monks kneel on the ashes, and made them vow not to repeat their transgressions. After this scandalous measure he suddenly felt unwell and "developed a painful mark on his chest." The account then shifts into a different register. As Long swooned, he found himself before a judge in the underworld. He was informed that his Buddhist sympathies did not count in his favor, but on the contrary "if someone who upholds the Way, harms the Way [instead], he is to be punished especially hard." Long Defu was condemned to serve as "Three-Stone-Ox Country Official," a position that he refused to fill. While Long's mind lingered in the netherworld, humiliated by a *déclassé* job offering, Dazhi performed rites of repentance in the waking world and even vowed to take on the guilt that resulted from the burning of the scripture. After ten days Long saw a white light and returned to the world of the living. In the following days Dazhi used acupressure to treat the mark on his chest. Dazhi's assistance was appreciated not only by Long Defu himself but also by his friends Tu Long, Hou Jigao, and a number of other literati. Long Defu wrote a poem expressing his gratitude, and Tu, who had been informed about Long's sickness and had worried about his friend, later wrote a stele inscription praising Dazhi.[26]

The Zhou Gazetteer (1607) and all following gazetteers have omitted this account. As we saw in Chapter 1 (Exhibit 3), Zhou Yingbin had reason to portray Mount Putuo as an orthodox site deserving of imperial support. Moreover, gazetteer literature on principle does not mention events that could reflect negatively on the site.[27] Nevertheless, the story has survived and now illustrates why the Fayu Temple so quickly developed as an alternative to the Puji and why it was so successful among the local literati. In 1599 the court dispatched the eunuch Zhao Yong 趙永 to gift a valuable copy of the Buddhist canon to the Fayu Temple, and in 1606 the Fayu Temple gained one of the coveted imperial gate plaques, legitimizing its national status and protecting it from encroachment. Thus only twenty-five years after its foundation, the Fayu Temple was on an equal footing with the Puji Temple. Still, one disadvantage remained: it lacked a numinous site. Geographically, it was outside the established pilgrimage round consisting of the harbor area, the Puji Temple, and the Tidal Sound Cave. Although some visitors would have enjoyed a stroll along the scenic "Beach of a Thousand Steps," there was no religious reason to go north to visit the Fayu Temple. In response to this need, the Brahma Voice Cave 梵音洞 at the northeastern shore of the island started to be used in parallel to the Tidal Sound Cave. Like "Tidal Sound," "Brahma Voice" (*brahmasusvara*) is a term taken from the Lotus Sutra where it describes the sound of a Buddha's voice preaching the Dharma. Like "Tidal Sound," "Brahma Voice" expands a metaphor from the Lotus Sutra to the sound of waves rushing into a narrow cave. Thus, already in its naming, the Brahma Voice Cave is a structural parallel to the Tidal Sound Cave. Its name unites textual reference (to the Lotus Sutra) with elements of doctrine (the special quality of Buddha's voice) and landscape (the grotto).

The Brahma Voice Cave is not yet mentioned in the Zhou Gazetteer of 1607, but a passage in Zhang Dai's travelogue indicates that by 1638 it was in competition with the Tidal Sound Cave. During his visit, Zhang Dai asked a monk at the Tidal Sound Cave if he had ever seen Guanyin himself. The monk answered that after the bridge had collapsed in a storm, the Bodhisattva had moved to the Brahma Voice Cave in the northeast of the island. Zhang, never much impressed with sacred sites, remarks "I did not dare to laugh out loud and quickly took my leave."[28] Some sixty years later the Brahma Voice Cave was well established, and the Qiu-Zhu Gazetteer contains a large number of poems and miracle tales associated with it.[29]

The early seventeenth-century duplication of the Tidal Sound Cave as Brahma Voice Cave is an example of *copying* or replicating the structure of one site elsewhere. Once a part of the landscape is textualized in a web of references to the scriptural tradition, the constellation can be copied in similar fashion elsewhere. The Brahma Voice Cave is located only somewhat further away from the Fayu Temple than the Tidal Sound Cave is from the Puji Temple. Both in location and function it is to the Fayu Temple what the Tidal Sound Cave is to the Puji. On Mount Putuo and elsewhere this type of self-similar reduplication existed as a possible mechanism by which the elements in the landscape of the larger site evolved.

This notion of copying is related to the idea of "*translatio loci*" proposed by Lothar Ledderose in a recent essay.[30] Ledderose has coined the term to describe the translation of Indian Buddhist places into Chinese geography. His example is the *translatio loci* of Vulture Peak (*Gṛdhrakūṭa*) to Mount Gang 崗山 in Shandong. As on Mount Putuo, sites on Mount Gang are modeled on Indian places as they appear in Buddhist texts. At Mount Gang too elements of the landscape are textualized by naming or by inscription. The concept of *translatio loci* assumes a stronger form of identification than I propose for the structural copying that I see at work at Mount Putuo, but it points to the same mechanism. A place is endowed with meaning through replication rather than invention. In a *translatio loci*, the place is assumed to be the "same" place, in the same way as a translation is assumed to be the "same" text as the original. The Brahma Voice Cave, on the other hand, does not pretend to *be* the Tidal Sound Cave in the way that Mount Putuo *is* Mount Potalaka. However, both the textual connection (via the Lotus Sutra) as well as the geographical and functional parallels leave little doubt that the Brahma Voice Cave was modeled on the Tidal Sound Cave.

Mount Putuo itself is not only a *translatio loci* (the translation of a Buddhist site from India to China) but at the same time the result of structural copying of another similar site in China. The actual Indian site mentioned by Xuanzang never figures largely in the Chinese imagination of Indian Buddhist geography as did, e.g., Lumbini or Sarnath, both of which were visited by a number of Chinese monks. On the other hand, Raoul Birnbaum and James Hargett have convincingly argued that the creation of Mount Putuo and Mount Emei was modeled on Mount Wutai.[31] As with Mount Putuo, the textualization of Mount Wutai is mainly based on the *Avataṃsaka sūtra*, which names Mount Wutai (*aka* Qingliang Shan 清涼山) as the abode of Mañjuśrī.[32] The *translatio loci* of Mount Wutai in the fifth and sixth centuries was paradigmatic and inspired the development of other centers. Once Mount Wutai had been established as the preeminent Buddhist pilgrimage center during the early Tang, other places could assume similar roles in Chinese Buddhist geography.[33] The structural parallels between Mount Wutai and Mount Putuo are manifold. In a recent book on Mount Wutai, Mary A. Cartelli outlines five characteristics of sacred mountains in Chinese Buddhism. The mountain is said to be marked by the presence of a Bodhisattva, who has taken residence (1), in a unique geographical location and landscape (2), on which a variety of numinous sites are projected (3). Visitors and pilgrims can experience extraordinary natural and supernatural phenomena (4), and they have to journey to the site because it is remote from ordinary society (5).[34] All these attributes apply to Mount Putuo.

At Mount Putuo itself the move to create self-similar copies is evident on all levels. In the early twentieth century, for instance, a small islet southeast of Putuo Island was incorporated into the larger ensemble of Mount Putuo.[35] By giving it the name *Luojia shan* 洛迦山 (an alternative abbreviation of the Chinese for Potalaka ([*Putuo*]*luojia shan*)) it is effectively cast as a smaller version of the main island of Mount Putuo (*Putuo[luojia] shan*). Equipped with a lighthouse, it is these days much promoted by the tourism industry—"A visit to Mount Putuo is incomplete without a visit to Mount Luojia!"—and ferries run twice a day from Mount Putuo.

Once a site is successfully established, it can be copied, or rather imitated, elsewhere. The duplicate site can take the same name, or a name doctrinally connected with the name of the original site, or it might merely be connected by geographic similarity or functional equivalence. For Mount Putuo the process is relevant both on the level of the mountain as a whole as well as in the creation of the places that are part of it. The Brahma Voice Cave and the Fayu Temple echo the relationship of the Tidal Sound Cave and the Puji Temple, just as Mount Luojia's dependence next to Mount Putuo echoes Mount Putuo's dependence on the larger island of Zhoushan. The self-referential replication of structures increases the complexity of the site, which is, as I have argued in the introduction, characteristic for the process of textualization. *Copy* in the sense described above is in the main a semiotic, textual operation, even if it results in physical structures. The other operations discussed in this chapter too rely on and can only be observed in the presence of text. If a sacred site is to *stay* and persist, it needs the constant retelling of its religious meanings, and we only know it has *moved* or *vanished* because there remains some memory that it was once otherwise. As Zhang Dai said in his travelogue of 1638: "If no one goes on about it, a place won't go on."[36]

Exhibit 3: Move and Vanish—The Sudhana Cave

Sacred sites generally do not move well. While a pub can easily be reopened in a different location, sacred sites, legitimized by a religious explanation of their origin, have a specific reason for being just where they are. Moving them compromises their raison d'être. There are sacred places that are only instantiated temporarily through a ritual—in Buddhism, for example, the space that is used for the ordination ceremony. Other sacred sites derive their prominence from sacred objects. Sites in Catholicism and Buddhism, for example, might be famous on account of their relics, which can be moved or lost.[37] And movement is indeed inevitable, especially within larger pilgrimage sites such as our mountain, even where it is not deemed desirable.[38] On Mount Putuo religious meaning is tied not to relics or to a particular school affiliation but to landscape features.

Among these features is Mount Putuo's alleged remoteness—far enough to suggest a trying journey but close enough to succeed in it. There is also the scenic beauty of the mountainous island itself, its temples set in secluded valleys but easily accessible. And, of course, there are the numinous caves where Guanyin might appear to the pilgrim. Nevertheless, change always seeps in, and places are moved or dissolved for some reason or other. Contrary to *stay*, in which recorded memory and religious intuition are aligned, in the case of *move* and *vanish*, the record-keeping of the gazetteers works against the grain of religious sensibility and reveals a subversive aspect. Once a sacred site has moved, the move must either be explained or forgotten. In the gazetteers it remains stubbornly on record.

As mentioned in Chapter 2 (Exhibit 1), even the heavy Pantuo Rock was probably "moved" after the Yuan dynasty—i.e., the original site was lost and the current site took on its name. Its earliest description is found in the Sheng Gazetteer: "The Pantuo Rock is flat and wide; more than a hundred people can sit on it. At day break [it is said] one can see Japan in the distance. Emitting the five colors, the huge wheel [of the sun] emerges from the ocean. A splendid sight indeed!"[39] Based on this and earlier poems it seems clear that the site used to be oriented eastward. The current site, however, looks out over the sea to the west of Mount Putuo. The move must have taken place in the hiatus between the Yuan and the revival of the site in late Ming, as the Hou-Tu Gazetteer shows the Pantuo Rock at its present location. The Yuan painting might not be drawn reliably enough to decide the case but to assume a move would also explain the change of the stone's use from viewing the dawn to viewing the sunset.

Another example for *move* on Mount Putuo is that of the Sudhana Cave (*Shancai dong* 善財洞). The fact is obscured in the older gazetteers as well as in the current tourist brochures—after all a cave is not supposed to move—but the more recent gazetteers do remember it.[40] On the Yuan painting, as well as on Hou Jigao's maps, the Sudhana Cave is shown close by and to the west of the Tidal Sound Cave. To have a cave for Sudhana near the cave where Guanyin appears is only logical; after all, Mount Putuo is where they meet according to the *Avataṃsaka Sūtra*. The textual record too has the Sudhana Cave as adjacent to the Tidal Sound Cave until the late Ming.[41] According to today's maps, however, the Sudhana Cave is located in the northeast of the island near the Brahma Voice Cave. It is not even on the shore. Instead at a deep grotto, pilgrims pray at a shallow cave, some 13 feet deep.

The Sudhana Cave was obviously "moved" to the northern part of the island near the Brahma Voice Cave, which as a parallel to the Tidal Sound Cave was in need of a supporting, smaller Sudhana Cave. The name of the original Sudhana Cave was changed gradually to Dragon Girl Cave (*Longnü dong* 龍女洞). Hou Jigao still refers to the grotto as Sudhana Cave in his travelogue, but elsewhere in the Hou-Tu Gazetteer the cave to the right of the Tidal Sound Cave is already called Dragon Girl Cave. Tu Long is aware of this as he remarks that "in the old gazetteer the Dragon Girl Cave is called Sudhana Cave."[42] Indeed, the "old" Sheng Gazetteer does not mention a Dragon Girl Cave at all.

The triad of Guanyin, the Dragon Girl, and Sudhana is attested since the twelfth century.[43] The iconographic association of the Dragon Girl with Guanyin has become increasingly popular after the Yuan, in the fifteenth and sixteenth centuries, while the connection with Sudhana became less relevant. In China and Japan the figure of the dragon king's daughter was a literary trope independent of Buddhism, and the motif has inspired countless variations.[44] In conjunction with the legend of the girl heroine Miaoshan and the presence of a large body of stories about shape-changing snake-, fox-, and ghost-women, it is not surprising that the Dragon Girl eclipsed Sudhana in Late Imperial China. By the eighteenth century the popular precious scroll (*baojuan* 寶卷) genre placed the Dragon Girl firmly at the Tidal Sound Cave. According to the *Precious Scroll of Good-in-Talent and Dragon Girl*, Guanyin tamed the Dragon Girl and took her "to the Southern Sea so she could cultivate perfection in the Roaring Tides Cave."[45]

Thus the gazetteers remember what the site wants to forget: the name change from Sudhana Cave to Dragon Girl Cave. In the late sixteenth century Mei Kui 梅魁 (*jinshi* 1568) wrote a poem titled "The Cave of Sudhana and the Dragon Girl" (*Shancai Longnü dong*善財龍女洞).[46] On this the Wang Hengyan Gazetteer comments: "Various records have this as 'Sudhana Cave,' but the Xu and the Qin Gazetteers call it only 'Dragon Girl Cave,' which is actually the same site. In any case, it is a place with numinous traces of the Bodhisattva; how men name it is not all that important."[47]

Today, visitors are not encouraged to look for other caves near the Tidal Sound Cave. During the reconstruction of the Purple Bamboo Hermitage in the 1990s, the opening of the Dragon Girl Cave was filled up with concrete.[48] The Dragon Girl Cave has, for now, vanished. And in fact many of the minor sites that are recorded in the gazetteers are gone and were often already gone when the gazetteers were compiled. Even structures that were at one time deeply embedded in the history of the site were lost, such as the Shrine to the Three Masters that had once commemorated the rebuilding of the Puji Temple (see Chapter 7, Exhibit 2). Of the eighty sites labeled on the Yuan dynasty *Budaluo shengjing* painting (see Chapter 2, Exhibit 1), virtually none have survived under the names they once had except for the Tidal Sound Cave.

Thus places, their names, and their memories are often more transient than their creators hope. Only thirty years after Mount Putuo was reopened in the late Ming, the Zhou Gazetteer already remarks for eight sites: "now abandoned" (*jinfei* 今廢).

Conclusion

Stay, copy, move, and *vanish* are modes in which numinous sites have been emplaced into and displaced from the particular geography of Mount Putuo Island. The list is not supposed to be exhaustive. Still other terms might be applied to the dynamics of sacred sites, such as *interruption* (a temple is destroyed by fire and rebuilt), *repurposing* (a hermitage is turned into a hotel), or *name change* (cf. the changing names of the Prince's Stūpa (Chapter 2, Exhibit 1)). Another lacuna should be mentioned here: the lack of any sustained discourse on the role of architecture at Mount Putuo in the gazetteers. In all the many genres collected in gazetteers, there is little room for that of architecture. As Lindsay Jones has pointed out: "Privileging the written word [. . .] both solves and creates problems for the interpretation of sacred architecture."[49] The gazetteer tradition conflates landscape and architecture in that it does not *structurally* distinguish between scenic sights (*xingsheng* 形勝) and buildings. The larger and smaller temple buildings (*fancha* 梵剎, *jinglan* 精藍) are listed and glossed in the same way as caves, mountains, and rock formations. The approach is that of inventory taking. While chapters on poetry reflect an aesthetic appreciation of the site and chapters on miracle tales reflect religious interest, architecture is accounted for in the mode of bookkeeping. Larger temples are often itemized as an ensemble of smaller buildings, preceded by a short section on their history and imperial donations. The compilers of the gazetteers were interested in the relationship between Confucianism and Buddhism (see Chapter 1, Exhibit 4) and perhaps even the supernatural (see Chapter 3, Exhibit 4) but not, apparently, in architecture. Although they occasionally contain ground plans of temples, an architectural perspective is otherwise absent from the gazetteers.[50] Temples were built to house gods, people, objects, and the rituals of their interaction, both sacred and mundane. These functional dimensions and their relationship with architectural space are foreshortened in the kind of textualization that we encounter in gazetteers. From today's perspective this seems a blind spot, and, as if to rectify it, the first modern, comprehensive description of Mount Putuo was done by an architect who was deeply fascinated with the construction and layout of the temples.[51]

Although traditional gazetteers rarely pay attention to architecture, they do generally mention who was responsible for the construction of a building. They privilege the memory of people who were involved with a site, especially those who contributed to its prosperity. The dynamics of this aspect of memory will be the focus of the following chapter.

CHAPTER 5 | People, Biographies

A first-order observer looks at the differences between humans
and their various fortunes and asks about justice. Second-order
observation can observe and describe that and how society
regulates itself, which positions it assigns to persons, and how these
assignments are being justified.

—NIKLAS LUHMANN[1]

BUDDHIST TEMPLE GAZETTEERS REMEMBER people in a variety of ways.
Their names appear in lists and lineages, in commemorative inscriptions, and in biographies.[2] By the time gazetteers became fashionable in
the Ming dynasty, these genres had already been in use for more than a
thousand years. Simple lists of names with short remarks—abbots and
their period of office, for instance—are related to annals and arranged
chronologically. Somewhat more complex, lineage records (*zongpu*
宗譜) are organized by generation, and student–teacher relationships
are modeled as genealogy. Inclusion and exclusion in lineages was an
important matter for Buddhists in late imperial China, as membership
in a prestigious lineage brought status and sacerdotal power. *Zhuan* 傳-
type biographies, on the other hand, look at individuals largely outside
the context of lineage.[3] With the rise of Chan and Pure Land Buddhism,
the *zhuan* genre was eclipsed. Eminent Chan monks were most often
remembered by collections of their "recorded sayings" (*yulu* 語錄),
rather than in a *zhuan*.[4] The biographies of monks and laypeople in
temple gazetteers are therefore rarely titled *zhuan* and are often a hybrid
of *zhuan* and *yulu*.

Typically, biographical information takes up between 10 and 30 percent of the page volume of a gazetteer.[5] Some compilers were more interested in biography than others, but biographical information is always part of a gazetteer. The focus, however, is often limited to the relationship of a person with the site. Biographies in gazetteers rarely attempt to be comprehensive. Biographical information is not only contained in chapters on monks or benefactors but also appears in other sections, especially those on stūpa and stele inscriptions. The biographical sections usually appear between the topographic description of the site and the sections with literary texts. Thus the lives, very sensibly, link the landscape with literature.

One problem for the compilers was how to categorize the people associated with the site. Alongside Buddhist monks (nuns appear only rarely), there were of course laypeople and patrons (*hufa* 護法), but at sites with a Daoist presence room is made for Daoist practitioners as well. The gazetteer of Mount Emei (1933), for instance, includes biographic entries for immortals (*xian* 仙), hermits (*yin* 隱), and famous visitors or short-term residents (*liuyu* 流寓).[6] The encyclopedic gazetteer of Mount Tiantai (1894 [1601]) has entries for 26 "saintly" or miracle-working monks (*shengseng* 聖僧), the first 17 Tiantai patriarchs (*zushi* 祖師), and 131 eminent monks (*gaoseng* 高僧). As one of the most ecumenical gazetteers, it mirrors these different tiers in the biographies of non-Buddhists and lists 36 Daoist immortals (*shenxian* 神僊), 37 Daoist practitioners (*daoshi* 道士), and 60 hermits (*yinshi* 隱士).[7]

The three exhibits here illustrate different ways in which people were commemorated in gazetteers. As a common theme, each reveals a different facet of the early Qing revival of Mount Putuo. Exhibit 1 highlights the influence of the Chan lineage discourse. It shows how and why Chaoyin Tongxu 潮音通旭 (1649–1698) recast the role of Zhenxie Qingliao 真歇清了 (1088–1151) in the history of Mount Putuo by including him in the Chan lineage narrative. Exhibit 2 discusses the role of local military officials and how they were remembered. The support of military officials turns out to have been crucial for the various revivals and maintenance of Mount Putuo during the Ming and Qing. Exhibit 3 is about the memory of imperial patronage in conjunction with biography. It illustrates how abbots were remembered as recipients of imperial favor in a list of "donations by the imperial court" (*banci* 頒賜). An association with the court that provided funds and protection was obviously important for institutional Buddhism, and this is reflected in the way successful abbots were portrayed in the gazetteers.

Exhibit 1: Zhenxie Qingliao (1088–1151) as First Abbot of Mount Putuo

In the twelfth century, at a time when Chan was a vibrant force in Chinese Buddhism, Zhenxie Qingliao 真歇清了 was a major figure in the newly revived Caodong lineage.[8] The way Qingliao was remembered in the Putuo gazetteers of the Qing dynasty reflects subtle changes in the way Chinese Buddhists conceived of the site. The past of Mount Putuo, a site not originally tied to any particular school, was recast in terms of Chan lineages. This process started during the early Qing and continued into the nineteenth century.

Born in Sichuan, Qingliao traveled far and wide and during his lifetime held important abbotships at various temples in Nanjing, Fujian, and the Ningbo region. At the center of one of the most important debates within the Chan School, he was attacked by his contemporary Dahui Zonggao 大慧宗杲 (1089–1163) about the correct way to practice meditation.[9] Some generations later his lineage was transmitted to Japan by Dōgen and became a constitutive element in the formation of the Japanese Sōtō School. Qingliao was not bound to any particular teaching or corpus of texts, and there is evidence that he engaged with Pure Land teachings. The late Ming Pure Land master Zhuhong even claims that Qingliao preached Pure Land teachings while he was on Mount Putuo.[10]

The earliest sources about Qingliao's life are his "recorded sayings" and the funerary inscription for his commemoration stūpa (1156 CE).[11] The inscription briefly mentions his visit to Mount Putuo in 1128. It is said that during his two-year stay he persuaded the fishermen on the island, more than seven hundred households, to give up their trade, "thus every day innumerable lives were saved."[12] The impact of Qingliao's stay on the island is also evident from an entry in the Sheng Gazetteer:

> In 1131 the Chan Master [Qing]liao came south from the Changlu Temple [near Nanjing], crossed the sea and built himself a hut in the mountains. He called it "Secluded by the Ocean." All the outstanding talents of the Chan School came to rely on him. The regional [authorities] petitioned the court and [the school affiliation of the Puji Temple] was changed [by imperial decree] from "Vinaya" to "Chan."[13]

The designation "Vinaya" meant simply that a temple did not have any particular sectarian affiliation.[14] During the Northern Song many unaffiliated temples were turned into "Chan temples." In the Ningbo region, two other important Buddhist centers, the Tiantong Temple and the Aśoka Temple, had been assigned to the Chan School earlier (in 1007 and 1008, respectively). The change meant, in principle, that henceforth the abbot had to be part of a Chan lineage and that previous abbots were from now on venerated in a "patriarch hall" (zutang 祖堂).[15] This practice was also claimed for the Puji Temple. In the late Ming the Hou-Tu Gazetteer says: "From [Qingliao] onwards, those who came and took up office [at Puji Temple] all were endowed with the Treasury of the True Dharma Eye of the Caoxi School."[16] Thus Qingliao is remembered in the gazetteers as the first abbot of Puji Temple; in fact, he is the first named monk associated with the island since Egaku. However, though Qingliao is present in toponyms ("Zhenxie's Hermitage," "Zhenxie's Stone"), the compilers of the two Ming gazetteers did not collect any biographical information on him beyond what was known to the Sheng Gazetteer.

In the Qing the biography of Qingliao became more important for the gazetteer tradition. The compilers of the Qiu-Zhu Gazetteer did not quite agree with the Ming claim that Puji Temple had been resurrected in the Wanli period as a Chan temple. In their view, it was only in the late seventeenth century that the Chan lineage was reestablished there. The person credited with the reintroduction of the Chan lineage is Chaoyin Tongxu 潮音通旭 (1649–1698), who served as abbot of Puji Temple from 1690 to 1698. Tongxu is the author of the "Record of the Lineage of Patriarchs on Mount Putuo " (1696), in which he collects information on eighteen Chan lineage members associated with Putuo, starting with Qingliao.[17] In the preface he admits that there was no uninterrupted presence of "patriarchs" on the island and deplores the "more than a hundred years" during the Ming when the "Dharma drum fell silent."[18] The late Ming revival of Mount Putuo had reestablished Mount Putuo as a pilgrimage center, but in the eyes of Tongxu the stewardship of the site had not been sufficiently tied to the Chan School. The "Record of how Master Chaoyin Rebuilt Putuo Temple" says: "In the three hundred and fifty or sixty years after [Zhufang Dao-] Lian [1346–1409], i.e. from the Yongle era until now, the customs of the [Chan] school were not known [on Mount Putuo]."[19]

For all we know, Tongxu's assessment was correct. The Yuan and Ming gazetteers contain indeed little that connects Mount Putuo to the Chan School in particular. Although the Puji Temple was a Chan temple in name, the characteristic practices of Chan monasticism are not attested. There is, for instance, no indication that a patriarch hall, or a cult around the portraits of former abbots, existed at either the Puji or the Fayu Temple before the Qing revival of Mount Putuo.[20] The current patriarch halls of the Puji and Fayu temples were built only under Tongxu in 1692.[21] Tongxu's histo-riographic emphasis on Qingliao as Chan lineage holder was shared by the compilers of the Qiu-Zhu Gazetteer. Consequently there is an emphasis on Zhenxie Qingliao as the first abbot of the Puji Temple. His biography in the Qiu-Zhu Gazetteer was copied—abridged and slightly edited—from Tongxu's "Record of the Lineage of Patriarchs on Mount Putuo."

Chan Master Zhenxie had the taboo name Qingliao.[22] He was the son of a family in Shu [Sichuan] named Yong. Endowed with intelligence from birth, he was handsome and his face showed serenity and depth of mind. Once he found Buddhism he cherished it and never let go of it again. At eleven he became a novice under Qingjun in the Shengguo Temple [in Sichuan]. After seven years he [successfully] tested in the Lotus Sutra [track of the monastic examinations] and was allowed to receive [full] ordination. Listening to the lectures during the ordination ceremony he heard about the deep and dif-ficult aspects of the sutras and treatises. He found that language would not, in the end, allow him to understand them. Thereupon he left Sichuan and came to Hubei, where he begged Danxia Zichun [to instruct him]. Zichun asked him: "Where were you in the empty eon [between the end of the pre-vious world and the beginning of this one]?" As Zhenxie wanted to answer, Zichun hit him and Zhenxie understood what mattered. The next day Zichun ascended the hall and said: "The sun shines on the single verdant peak, the moon on the cold waters of the little brook. The profound cases of the patri-archs, how could they be kept in a small mind?" Zhenxie stepped forward and said: "Who do you think you are kidding?" [Zichun] said: "Just try to answer it!" Zhenxie remained silent for a long time. Zichun said: "I will say you caught a glimpse of it."

[After that] Zhenxie left and went north to Mount Wutai and Kaifeng, [then back] south to the Yangzi river. There he went to study with Changlu Zuzhao (1057–1124). In 1131 he left Changlu's Temple [where he had become abbot], traveled south, and crossed the ocean to Mount Putuo. He built a hut deep in the mountains and called it "Secluded Place by the Sea." All the outstanding talent of the Chan School came to follow him. The regional [authorities] petitioned the court and [the school affiliation of the Puji Temple] was changed [by imperial decree] from "Vinaya" to "Chan." At that time there were more than seven hundred families on the island who were fishermen. Once they heard the Dharma, they aban-doned their boats [and changed their livelihood], thus every day innu-merable lives were saved. Later Zhenxie served as abbot at the Guoqing Temple, the Xuefeng Temple, the Aśoka Temple, the Longxiang Temple, the Xiangqing Temple, and the Shuangjing Temple. He taught everybody wherever he went[23], and received five imperial missives. He ordained more than four hundred disciples and had more than thirty Dharma heirs. There are two collections of his "Recorded Sayings" of several fascicles each. The Chan School at this mountain [Mount Putuo] started with him, and he is commonly considered the first to have preached the Dharma here.[24]

This late seventeenth-century version of Qingliao's biography does not add anything about his activities on Mount Putuo beyond what was already known in the fourteenth century. What it does add to previous accounts is the emphasis on Qingliao as a Chan master. Tongxu aims to embed Mount Putuo in the Chan lineage narrative, because lineage had again become a major concern in the seventeenth century.[25] Tongxu's presentation of Qingliao was successful and was copied almost verbatim in all later gazetteers. In the early twentieth century, however, Wang Hengyan picked up on the intrusion of the lineage discourse and included a critical note:

> To promote the lineage and expound the precepts, these two are the main pillars of Buddhism. The realization of the Way is Chan, maintaining the Way is the precepts. If those who study Buddhism wanted to attain meditative concentration and wisdom without keeping the precepts, it would be just as if we Confucians were to hope to receive the transmission of the Way without exertion and practice. If the precepts are not kept pure, how could there be enlightenment in meditation? Thus those who propagate the Dharma give equal importance to precepts and meditation.
>
> [. . .] Zhenxie [Qingliao] is considered the first teacher at Mount Putuo, but did he belong to the Chan School? [. . .] He said: "The Buddhas and Patriarchs, whether in the 'Teaching' School or in the Chan School, all practiced Pure Land and returned to the single source." From this we can know that he was practicing both Chan and Pure Land, the gradual as well as the sudden.[26]

Wang Hengyan was eager to establish a balance between Pure Land and Chan, not least because he compiled his gazetteer under the patronage of Yinguang, an influential Pure Land teacher. All in all, the gazetteers of the twentieth century portray the site in relatively neutral terms. In them Mount Putuo is again first and foremost a pilgrimage destination, not a Chan, Tiantai, or Pure Land monastery.[27]

Exhibit 2: Huang Dalai (d. 1690) and Lan Li (1649–1720) as Patrons of the Early Qing Revival

In Chapter 1 (Exhibit 3) we saw how Mount Putuo was revived in the late Ming by an alliance of clerics, eunuchs, palace women, military officials, and local literati. The members of that motley coalition convinced the Wanli emperor to support the site throughout his long reign (1572–1620). This pattern was repeated with variations about a century later, during the Kangxi era (1661–1722). By then, eunuchs played a much diminished role at court, and Qing palace women were less associated with the support of Chinese Buddhism. The Manchu emperors themselves, on the other hand, took a more proactive, personal role in shaping religious policy than their predecessors in the Ming. Susan Naquin has called this "strong interest in the overlapping zones of what we call religion and government [. . .] characteristically Qing."[28] Kangxi's role in the early Qing revival of Mount Putuo is a case in point.

In this and the next exhibit, and again in Exhibit 3 of Chapter 6, Kangxi will be shown as a supporter of Mount Putuo. It should be remembered, however, that the decline that preceded the revival also took place under Kangxi. For the powerful emperors of the seventeenth and eighteenth centuries, religion was only one vector of control. When strategic considerations made another forced evacuation of the Zhoushan archipelago advisable in 1671, Kangxi, still only seventeen, used the tried-and-proven policy of an "ocean embargo" (*haijin* 海禁). Island dwellers were forced to relocate to the mainland and coastal trade was prohibited. As in the late fourteenth and the early sixteenth centuries, control of the archipelago became too expensive, and the outright interdiction of all trade was a relatively simple, if temporary, solution. This time the disruption of the official maritime trade of Zhejiang and Fujian by unregulated trade was due not only to Chinese and Japanese bands, as by now Dutch and Spanish colonialist merchant fleets too had entered the fray. Kangxi was preoccupied at the time with the Revolt of the Three Feudatories (1673–1681) in the southwest, and he and his generals did not want to divert forces to the comparatively harmless pirate incursions. However, having learned from the inept handling of the prolonged *haijin* under the Ming one hundred years earlier, he never intended the *haijin* of 1671–1684 as a permanent solution.

Nevertheless, in 1671 the monks of Mount Putuo, including Tongxu, were moved to temples in the Ningbo region and the temple buildings left open to plunder and decay. Many must have feared another prolonged interruption for the pilgrimage site, but this time the *haijin* was lifted and Mount Putuo reopened only thirteen years later. The site, however, had suffered greatly, and both the Puji and the Fayu Temple were largely in ruins. Again as in the late Ming, Mount Putuo recovered steadily, and thirty-five years later the two main temples and a host of smaller sites had been rebuilt or newly created. Both major temples had received imperial stele inscriptions, Mount Putuo had gained a tax exemption for its landholdings, and, of course, new gazetteers had been produced. The cliques of monks, military men, and literati that had made this possible are represented in the pages of the Qiu-Zhu and the Xu gazetteers. Like their Ming predecessors, they knew each other well, exchanged poems, wrote prefaces and inscriptions, and built memorial shrines for one another.

In this exhibit we will look at the involvement of military officials in the early Qing revival of Mount Putuo. We will focus on two Regional Commanders of Dinghai (*Dinghai zongbing* 定海總兵), Huang Dalai 黃大來 (d. 1690) and Lan Li 藍理 (1649–1720), who made important contributions to the recovery of Mount Putuo in the years after the Kangxi *haijin*. Both were part of a larger network of military supporters, who ushered in a long period of prosperity that would last until the early nineteenth century. Besides Huang and Lan the Provincial Military Commander Chen Shikai 陳世凱 (?–1689) and another Regional Commander of Dinghai, Shi Shibiao 施世驃 (1667–1721), patronized the site. All of them were remembered on Mount Putuo with shrines, and their contributions were praised in the gazetteers.

Not much is known about Huang Dalai, but in the gazetteers he is credited for bringing the blight of Mount Putuo after the *haijin* to the attention of the Kangxi emperor. His contact with Kangxi was later embellished with a Guanyin legend. The story goes:

In spring of 1689 his Highness [the Kangxi emperor] was on the way back from Yuling [a station on his second Southern Tour]. He rowed alone [on the river] in his small barge with a dragon as figurehead. When they arrived at Jiaxing, passing under the bridges, he suddenly saw an old woman alone in a boat, a bright red flower pinned to her hair. He steered towards her and asked: "What boat is this?" The old woman said: "A fishing boat." His Highness asked: "Are there any fish?" The old woman replied: "There are; do you wish to buy some?" With these words, she left without looking back, and no one could make out where she had gone. Huang Dalai, the Regional Commander of Dinghai, who traveled behind the imperial barge, saw his Highness talking to the old woman. Alarmed, he quickly grasped his oars and pulled forward. When the emperor asked who he was, Huang answered: "Your minister is the Regional Commander of Dinghai, Huang Dalai" Thereupon the emperor asked Dalai about the situation in the Zhoushan [archipelago under his command]. Dalai used his audience to describe the matter of Mount Putuo in some detail. The next day Dalai was called before the emperor, and given a thousand taels of silver for the reconstruction of the temples on Mount Putuo.[29]

Huang took the funds to Mount Putuo and had started to supervise the reconstruction efforts when he died in 1690. For his efforts the monastic community rewarded him with a memorial shrine (ci 祠), where his spirit tablet would have received prayers akin to those used in ancestral rites. An "Inscription for the Memorial Shrine of Master Huang" by Huang's contemporary Zheng Liang 鄭梁 (1637–1713) is contained in the gazetteers.[30] Zheng was a student of the famous historian Huang Zongxi and accordingly begins his essay with an excursion about the origin of "living" memorial shrines to people who were still alive (sheng ci 生祠). According to Zheng, Huang Dalai

> . . . believed in the Way and venerated the Buddha. He pitied Putuo, regarding it as the place where the Bodhisattva [Guanyin] appears. Now the coastal frontier has been reopened and the ocean pacified. The famous monasteries of the nation are all appreciated and supported. However, the site where the numinous power of the Bodhisattva manifests was still neglected. One or two monks were shouting out to each other, clanging the gong and banging the drum amidst a barren waste. He was greatly grieved by this. [. . .] When the opportunity arose and the emperor asked him, he used the chance to bring [the situation of Mount Putuo] to his attention. The emperor granted his wish, provided funds and dispatched them with a courtier and guards. Mount Putuo was to be splendidly rebuilt. The Master had just begun with various reconstruction projects, to rebuild the famous temples in great style, when he fell ill and died in office the following year. The day he died, soldiers and peasants all mourned him as if he was their own kin. In particular, the more than a thousand monks on the island felt the loss and will always remember him.[31]

The inscription for Huang Dalai was requested by the abbot of Puji Temple, Chaoyin Tongxu, whom we have met as the author of the "Record of the Lineage of Patriarchs on Mount Putuo." Tongxu had reason to be grateful to Huang. Kangxi's generous donation of 1689 had indeed made a difference. It allowed Commander Huang and the Sangha administrators on Mount Putuo to rebuild the Puji and repair the Fayu Temple and other buildings. In 1690, the year of Huang's untimely death, his successor Lan Li invited Tongxu back to the island to take charge of the Puji Temple. Tongxu had resided on Mount Putuo before, but his appointment by Lan Li gave him additional power. As soon as Tongxu returned to Putuo in 1690, he petitioned Lan Li to again define the Puji as a Chan lineage temple.[32]

Lan Li was born in Fujian and as a young man had participated in the campaign to incorporate Taiwan into the Qing empire. During the course of the campaign, his military skills came to the attention of the commanding Admiral Shi Lang 施琅 (1621–1696).[33] Lan Li rose quickly through the ranks. When he became Regional Commander of Dinghai, in charge of all military matters in the Zhoushan archipelago, he strongly supported the reconstruction of Mount Putuo. For this Lan was commemorated at the site itself. Already in his lifetime, a grateful community built two shrines for him—one at the Puji, and another at the Fayu Temple. In 1697, the monks asked the Ningbo calligrapher and historian Jiang Chenying 姜宸英 (1628–1699) to write an inscription for these shrines.[34] Not surprisingly, Jiang's account heaps lavish praise on Lan, whose "untiring efforts" seemed "unprecedented." The eulogy also contains details of his patronage, for instance, Lan donated the heartwood of large trees from his own estate for the rebuilding. This type of wood was expensive to come by but necessary for the construction of temple pillars and beams. The stems were "rafted and shipped across the ocean," and we can assume that Lan used military resources to do so. After all, the emperor had by his own donation endorsed the rebuilding of the site. Moreover, unlike the late Ming, this time around the revival did not encounter any serious opposition, and the patrons did not have to justify their support.[35]

The early Qing revival of Mount Putuo was strongly supported by local military officials, who requested funds from the central government and used their own resources for reconstruction. The basis for this, as in the Ming, was the cordial personal relationship between leading members of the Sangha and the military. When Lan was transferred to a new post in Shandong, he left his coat behind at the Fayu Temple as a gesture of protection and patronage. The coat was enshrined by the abbot Xingtong 性統 (1661–1717), who, like Tongxu, was an able administrator. Xingtong's account of Lan's departure gives an idea of how important Lan's support must have been for the temples on Mount Putuo:

In 1690, the Great Principal Marquis[36] Master Lan was transferred from Xuanhua to command Dinghai. As soon as he arrived, wishing to pray for the well-being of the empire, he ascended Mount Putuo. Amid the over-grown paths and the piles of rubble, he munificently decided to rebuild the place. In the twelve years of his tenure in office he has fully devoted his efforts to this end against all obstacles. The halls were splendidly rebuilt, again rising into the clouds. He diligently arranged for donations from the court and the bestowal of an imperial plaque [for the gate]. As for his administration of Dinghai, he opened up new farmland, dredged rivers and lakes, established an office for overseas trade, maintained discipline in the army and kept peace among the peasants. He was respected by everyone in the county for his brilliant achievements. This year he has been transferred to Tianjin. Before he left he came to the [Fayu] Temple to take leave of the Bodhisattva. After lingering for quite a while, he left his coat as a token of remembrance.

Long ago Han Yu (768–824) asked Master Lingshan Dadian (732–824) about the Way, and [he too] left his coat to guard the temple. Later Zhou Dunyi (1017–1073) saw the "Pavilion of the Coat Left Behind" and said "Should you want to know what Dadian was like, just take a look at [Han Yu's] letters and his coat." Master Lan's contributions are by far greater than Han Yu's, but our attainment does not measure up to that of Dadian. We can only blame ourselves for this discrepancy. Nevertheless, "looking at the thing, one fondly remembers the owner," who will thus guard us for a thousand years. This is indeed a cause for happiness for me. To express this I have established this "Hall for the Coat Left Behind."[37]

Lan's successor in the office of Regional Commander of Dinghai was Shi Shibiao 施世驃 (1667–1721). As soon as he arrived in Zhoushan in 1701, he visited Mount Putuo, chatted with the abbots of the Puji and the Fayu Temple, and reminisced about Lan's good works.[38] Shi Shibiao must have known Lan Li quite well. Shi was the son of Shi Lang, who had first pro-moted Lan after the conquest of Taiwan. Like Lan, Shi Shibiao appears prominently on the pages of the Qiu-Zhu Gazetteer, and both men con-tributed prefaces to the compilation. They were central actors in the clique of Mount Putuo supporters in the military, a group that included Huang Dalai, Chen Shikai 陳世凱 (d. 1689), Tu Cuizhong 屠粹忠 (1634–1706), Zhang Jie 張杰 (active in Dinghai 1646), and others.[39]

The agency of military officials in the local patronage of Buddhism is not well understood so far, but it deserves more attention. In the case of Mount Putuo we find that in the late Ming and in the early Qing, sup-port from military officials was crucial for the reconstruction efforts. The logistics and manpower of the military network enabled them to move building supplies, organize repair works, and prevent encroachment on temple land by the peasantry or the local gentry. Like Hou Jigao a century before, Huang Dalai, Lan Li, and others actively contributed to the reconstruction of the site and the production of a gazetteer to commemorate its revival.

Exhibit 3: Yitang Xinming (1655–1745) and Bie'an Xingtong (1661–1717) as Favored by the Kangxi Emperor

The early Qing revival of Mount Putuo was made possible because capable leaders within the Sangha and supportive members of the military were able to solicit imperial support. As we have seen in the previous exhibit, military officials brought Mount Putuo to the attention of the Kangxi emperor and assisted with the rebuilding of the infrastructure that was needed to accommodate monks and visitors. While donations from pilgrims usually generated enough income to support the monks, only the court was able to bestow official recognition and protection for Mount Putuo. According to the gazetteers, it was the skillfulness of the abbots representing Mount Putuo in court audiences that maintained imperial patronage, under Kangxi and Yongzheng.

From 1696 to 1717, the monks Yitang Xinming 繹堂心明 and Bie'an Xingtong 別庵性統 were the recipients of a long list of gifts from Kangxi. Imperial gifts and emissaries were often listed prominently in a special section of the temple gazetteers.[40] Examples from the lists in the Qiu-Zhu and Xu gazetteers[41] include:

1696: The Puji and the Fayu Temple each receive one scroll with the Diamond Sutra copied out by the emperor himself.

1699: On his third Southern Tour the emperor sends emissaries with more copies of the Diamond Sutra and a thousand tael of gold. The two abbots, Xingtong and Minghu 明忠, are invited to follow the emissaries back and are granted an audience.[42] Kangxi writes gate plaques (e 額) for the Puji Temple ("Gathering Souls for Universal Salvation" 普濟羣靈 and "Tidal Sound Cave" 潮音洞) and the Fayu Temple ("Dharma Rain of Heavenly Flowers" 天花法雨 and "Brahma Voice Cave" 梵音洞). The Empress Dowager gives Xingtong a rosary.[43] Kangxi orders 120,000 glazed roof-tiles from the former imperial palace in Nanjing to be moved to Mount Putuo to cover the roofs of the main halls of the two temples.

The bestowal of imperial gate plaques for the temples and the two caves was of great significance. Gate plaques were highly coveted as they implied imperial recognition and provided a measure of protection from encroachment.[44] Mount Putuo had received imperial gate plaques in the Song, Yuan, and Ming dynasties, and for Kangxi to follow the precedent was crucial for the early Qing revival. It was Kangxi's policy to treat both temples equally. Equal recognition was especially important for the Fayu Temple, which had been founded so much later than Puji (see Chapter 4, Exhibit 2). That the Fayu was able to preserve the status it had gained in the late Ming through the early Qing revival was mainly due to the successful management of Bie'an Xingtong. Xingtong made a good impression not only on the emperor but also on other court members, such as the empress dowager. He was born in Sichuan and had traveled widely before taking up residence on Mount Putuo. As he was not a native of the Ningbo region, he could not rely on a clan network to gain patronage. Like Tongxu he wrote works on the history of Buddhism while leaving his own traces in it. Xingtong too was member of a lineage. In Chapter 1 we met him asking Yang Yongjian for an inscription in memory of his master, Sanshan Denglai. On other occasions he himself wrote inscriptions for members of his lineage.[45] By all accounts Xingtong was an able administrator and networker, who could hold his own during an audience with the emperor.

The use of calligraphy as an instrument of rulership is a constant in imperial China and well attested for the Qing as well as for the modern period.[46] Kangxi often performed his writing as a semi-public event, and it is possible that the calligraphy given to Xingtong and Minghu was written on the spot during the audience.[47]

While Kangxi made gifts of his calligraphy on many occasions, the transfer of the expensive and prestigious roof tiles from the former imperial palace to the temples of Mount Putuo is a rare gesture. It went beyond the many courteous displays of patronage that Kangxi made throughout his reign but, as so often with Kangxi, was nevertheless carefully calibrated. Using the palace built by the founder of the Ming to support a sacred site was not only an elegant way to dismantle remnants of the early Ming but also subtly ironic: in the late fourteenth century Ming Taizu's policies caused Mount Putuo to be destroyed and abandoned, and now the tiles of his palace were used to cover the roofs of the Puji and the Fayu Temples. Still another factor that must have influenced Kangxi's decision to support the site was the strategic importance of the Zhoushan archipelago. Here one of the Ming pretenders had fought his retreat in the 1640s and 1650s, and Kangxi himself had been forced on the defensive by pirate incursions in the 1660s and 1670s. The resurgence of Mount Putuo as pilgrimage site after the lifting of the *haijin* in 1684 proved that he had brought the eastern seaboard under control. Thus his support of Mount Putuo both consolidated and celebrated his rule over the southeast.

1703: On his fourth Southern Tour Kangxi sends emissaries with gifts to Putuo. Abbot Xingtong and representatives of the Puji Temple, including Xinming, are invited for an audience.[48] Kangxi writes two characters in honor of Xingtong's mother. Kangxi asks Xingtong to compose a poem *ad hoc*, which he then writes out for him. The crown prince and other members of the court give money and calligraphy.[49]

Court culture likes precedent, and the protocol of the Southern Tour of 1703 resembles that of 1699. Kangxi seemed to have taken a liking to Xingtong, who is again singled out for special favors. The records imply that it was Xingtong's skill in composing impromptu poetry that pleased the emperor. This time around, Xinming too seems to have caught the emperor's attention and was invited back to Beijing as part of the entourage. Yitang Xinming was a disciple of Tongxu. He had been offered the abbotship of the Puji Temple after Tongxu's death in 1698 but politely declined in favor of his elder "brothers" in Tongxu's Dharma lineage, Guxin Minghu 古心明恝 and Zixiu Mingguo 自修明果. In what seemed to have been a gentleman's agreement, Minghu and Mingguo each held the abbotship for three years, while Xinming was in charge of day-to-day affairs. Only in 1704 did Xinming become abbot in name as well, and served in that office for fifteen years. The connections he had made during this journey to the capital must have further strengthened his position on the island, as his appointment occurred soon after his return from Beijing. Xinming's long and illustrious career thus spanned the decline and revival of Mount Putuo in the early Qing and the reign of three emperors.[50]

Xinming belonged to the influential Shao clan of Ningbo, which had produced a number of government officials in the late Ming and Qing. Members of the clan had contributed prefaces and poems to the Putuo Gazetteers since the late Ming, and their influence and support contributed to the dynamism of Xinming's abbotship.[51] The texts portray him as a strong and active personality, who at thirteen refused to marry and, against the wishes of his family, went to Mount Putuo to become a novice under Tongxu. When the monks of Mount Putuo were moved inland during the *haijin* in 1671, he followed them back to the mainland.

There his powerful clan exerted pressure on local officials to have him returned home. Tongxu asked him to be "filial," that is to go back and bide his time. Soon after Xinming's mother passed away, an uncle was bitten by a rabid dog and died. It seemed that bad luck had been brought on by the clan elders because they had kept Xinming from ordination. They soon relented—Xinming was ordained, following Tongxu back to Mount Putuo and assisting him in reestablishing the site.[52]

Winter 1704/05: Kangxi writes the stele inscriptions for the Fayu and the Puji Temple, and gate plaques for some smaller buildings on Mount Putuo. He challenges Xingtong to compose a poem on a given theme. Xingtong succeeds and is given more imperial calligraphy.

Spring 1705: The inscriptions are sent to Mount Putuo. Kangxi gives two copies of the Heart Sutra to Xingtong and one to Xinming. Both receive a stūpa painted with the characters of the Heart Sutra.[53]

1707: Kangxi sends a ginseng root to Xingtong, which he shares with Xinming and other monks on Putuo. Kangxi writes a short calligraphy for Xinming.

Kangxi's inscriptions written in Beijing during the winter of 1704 stood in front of the temples for some 260 years before they were destroyed in the Cultural Revolution. (They will be discussed in more detail as the third exhibit in Chapter 6.) The anecdote about sharing the imperial ginseng gives us a rare glimpse into the relationship of Xingtong and Xinming. With the sources we have it is difficult to gauge how well they actually got along, but the sharing of ginseng points to a harmonious and perhaps even cordial relationship. While for the late Ming revival the gazetteers preserve traces of communal friction (see Chapter 4, Exhibit 2), the community elders during the early Qing revival seem to have gotten along well.

1709: In spring the court sends emissaries with gifts for both temples to Mount Putuo. In summer Xinming "reports" to Gu Wenxing 顧問行 at Jehol to tell him about the Fahua Building.[54]

The year 1709 was an important one for Mount Putuo. Both Xinming and Xingtong followed the emissaries back to the capital, and from there they went to the imperial summer residence at Jehol (today's Chengde). The eunuch official Gu Wenxing was one of three emissaries that Kangxi had sent to Mount Putuo in 1699 to conduct prayers for the well-being of the empire and (implicitly) to see what was happening there and whether the island deserved support. Gu was thus acquainted with Xingtong and Xinming as well as with the architecture and landscape of the island. Xinming reported to Gu, because Gu had sponsored the (re-)construction of the three-storied Fahua Building, which later was turned into a memorial shrine for him. Gu's involvement shows that Mount Putuo was popular not only with the emperor but that other members of court too supported the site.

This was fortunate for Xinming and Xingtong, because they had come to the capital for a reason. Due to a shortage, rice shipments were not allowed to leave the coastal areas and the abbots had to petition their friends at court to allow rice for the island to be exempted from the shipping ban. In this context we learn how many monks lived on the island in 1709 and how much food was needed to maintain the community. The abbots explained that they were responsible for 666 monks, each in need of two handfuls of rice a day. This amounted to 2,397 piculs and six ladles of rice (c. 143 tons) per year.[55] Fortunately, their request was granted, and the rice headed for Mount Putuo through the estuaries of Hangzhou Bay was cleared by the authorities.

> 1710: Kangxi gifts a precious seal and a set of the Buddhist canon to the Puji Temple.

> 1713: First month: On the occasion of Kangxi's sixtieth birthday, Xingtong and Xinming go to Beijing to congratulate him and both receive a purple robe. Their five attendant monks receive red robes. The next month they receive gifts of ginseng.

Gifting the Buddhist canon to an institution was obviously an important sign of imperial patronage. During the Ming the Wanli emperor and his mother donated over one hundred sets of the Tripiṭaka to monasteries. The canon, on Putuo and elsewhere, was mainly treated as an object of veneration and only secondarily as a repository of texts. It was in principle accessible to monks, who wished to study the sacred texts in earnest, but in Chinese Buddhism monastic education developed very differently from Tibet, where talented monks were trained systematically in scriptural study. Nevertheless, the Mount Putuo library was kept in good repair. The French missionary Évariste Régis Huc, who visited Mount Putuo in the 1840s, reports:

> The large monasteries of Putuo, where formerly monks congregated in large numbers, are almost completely abandoned to legions of rats and to huge

spiders, which spin their webs peacefully in the deserted rooms. The most proper and best preserved place was the library. The monk charged with its upkeep allowed us to visit. We found it much inferior to the ones we have seen in Tartary and Tibet. It nevertheless had about eight thousand volumes, wrapped in yellow fabric, exactly labeled and orderly arranged in cases, which lined the walls of the large hall.[56]

While the canon was still well preserved by mid-century, Kangxi's gift of tiles has fared less well. Again Huc:

> This temple [Puji], the construction and ornamentation of which must have consumed great sums, is now in total disrepair. The roofs covered with golden glazed tiles, have holes in several places, such that when it rains, the water falls on the head of the poor idols, which seem more in need of an umbrella than of the incense that burns at their feet.[57]

In addition to material gifts such as money, roofing material, steles, plaques, calligraphy, and the occasional ginseng root, Kangxi also bestowed a special, highly coveted favor on Xinming that only the emperor could grant. Since the 1690s, and increasingly in his later reign, the Kangxi emperor made changes in the memorial system that opened up direct lines of communication for him.[58] Selected individuals were allowed to send secret palace memorials (*zouzhe* 奏摺) to him, bypassing the bureaucracy of ministries and the Grand Secretariat. At times this privilege was also extended to monks.[59] The first to use the palace memorial were bondservants associated with the imperial household department, such as the textile commissioners Cao Yin 曹寅 and Sun Wencheng 孫文成.[60] We know that both Cao and Sun had visited Mount Putuo in 1708, when they delivered a gift of two statues from the emperor.[61] Moreover, Sun was involved in ensuring its exemption from paying tax on its landholdings in the negotiations between 1717 and 1719. It appears that Sun Wencheng, like Gu Wenxing, was a friend of Mount Putuo at court, who had the ear of Kangxi. Moreover, it seems that Xinming was given permission to submit secret palace memorials during his stay in Beijing in 1703. This direct contact with the emperor was unprecedented for the monastic establishment of Mount Putuo. Xinming made good use of it. Between 1703 and 1720 he submitted thirteen memorials, mostly to thank the emperor for his favors, but also to elicit some.[62]

In the context of Kangxi's "personal government,"[63] and supported by military and civil administrators, talented monastics like Xingtong and Xinming were able to gain direct access to the emperor and receive the highest level of imperial support. The prominence of Xingtong and Xinming in the Qing Putuo gazetteers is a reflection of their success at soliciting this support. Their traces in the gazetteers show them embedded in a network of official relationships. Each also managed to train a cohort of students who extended their influence far into China's "long eighteenth century."

Conclusion

In Exhibit 1 we have seen how, during the early Qing revival of Mount Putuo, the biography of Zhenxie Qingliao was used to embed Mount Putuo in the Chan lineage discourse. This was mainly a monastic concern, as power within the monastic community derived to some degree from one's position in a prominent line of Dharma transmission. Exhibit 2 explored how the regional military establishment of the early Qing was, as it had been during the late Ming, an important link between the local and national levels of patronage. Less concerned with lineage, it supported the sacred site for its own religious reasons. The final exhibit highlighted the contacts of two prominent abbots with the Kangxi court. The national influence of Mount Putuo's representatives was never greater than in the early years of the eighteenth century when the mighty Kangxi and Yongzheng emperors extended their favors to the site.

My reliance on gazetteers, here as in other chapters, reveals a temporal bias toward events and figures of the Ming and Qing. Very probably the Song and the Yuan saw their share of interesting characters, and the site as a whole was probably more international, with ships from Korea and Japan stopping regularly on their way from and to Ningbo. Back then, the international fame of Mount Putuo was put to diplomatic use at least once when the Yuan government dispatched the abbot Yishan Yining 一山一寧 (1247–1317) as goodwill ambassador to Japan.[64] Yishan became a key figure in the Buddhist exchanges of his time and had an illustrious career in Kamakura Japan. With his involvement in Buddhist politics and his many Japanese students, some of whom in turn visited China, his *vita* should have been of interest for compilers of a Mount Putuo gazetteer.

The gazetteer format, however, is not overly invested in biography, and Yishan is mentioned only in passing.

Biography tends to unify historical narrative. In the "great men" version of history, events are caused by the actions of heroic individuals around whom the world unfolds. In the temple gazetteers, where text is arranged by genre, biography loses its privilege. Gazetteers document the textualization of a sacred site in many different genres: prefaces, maps, miracle stories, poems, inscriptions, essays, *and also* biography. Information about a single figure is often scattered across different chapters, and at times even important actors do not have their own biographies. Thus, in their own disjunctive and encyclopedic manner, gazetteers deny biography its power to provide a single viewpoint from which to observe events and explain their causes. In this sense biography resides uneasily within the gazetteers. The next chapter, on the other hand, will showcase a genre that fits only all too well into the edifice of compilation.

CHAPTER 6 | Inscriptions

Since for my purpose the inscriptions were indispensable, I thought
I would dare to bring the translations.

—ERNST BOERSCHMANN (1911)[1]

MORE TIGHTLY BOUND TO place than any other form of text, inscriptions
are in a way the epitome of textualization. We have described textualization as the feedback loop between place and text and often observed
how meanings associated with a locale are encoded in texts. Inscriptions
are part of the countermove: the text reaching out into place and literally turning the site itself into text. Gazetteers encode information about
a site in a way that is largely independent of its locale. If all we had
were its gazetteers, the actual pilgrimage site of Mount Putuo might have
never existed, like Tao Yuanming's Peach Blossom Spring or Tolkien's
Middle Earth. Against that, epigraphy is bound to the material reality of
the site: it is part of the site itself. While all texts are self-referential to a
degree, inscriptions, by force of topography, always also commemorate
themselves.

Epigraphy is inherently public in nature. Public does not necessarily
mean accessible, however. Both at the Puji and the Fayu temples some
imperial inscriptions were kept in special halls (*yubei tang* 御碑堂).[2]
Moreover, the formal register of stele inscriptions often demanded a
high degree of literacy. The function of such inscriptions, at sacred as
well as at secular sites, has often been to embed the site in the prevailing
system of political control. Because of the persistent, normative idea of
a "center" from which power devolves to a "periphery," Chinese sacred
sites tend to give pride of place to inscriptions that connect it with the

imperial center. Other inscriptions serve to commemorate events and persons that were associated with the place, or they reproduce, for a variety of reasons, sacred texts. It is helpful to distinguish between the generally shorter, exclamatory rock inscriptions (*moya* 摩崖), which were often prized for their calligraphy, and the longer stele inscriptions (*bei* 碑, or *beiming* 碑銘) that often record events of political and legal importance for the site.[3] Another common genre of Chinese epigraphy, tomb inscriptions (*muzhiming* 墓志銘), is often represented at Buddhist sites in the form of *stūpa* inscriptions (*taming* 塔銘).

As all sites have at least some inscriptions, almost all gazetteers have sections dedicated to them.[4] The distribution and makeup of these sections is, however, less consistent than that of the other genres we find in gazetteers. At times gazetteers, mirroring their sites, place imperial inscriptions and edicts at the very beginning, with section titles such as "heavenly proclamation" (*tianzhang* 天章) or "imperial autograph" (*chenhan* 宸翰). Tomb and stūpa inscriptions are at times appended to the sections on biography, as they generally contain biographical information.[5] Often inscriptions are grouped in their own section (*beiming* 碑銘, a.o.), but sometimes they are included in the chapter on patronage.[6] In general, the gazetteers of smaller temple sites, such as the Hanshan Temple in Suzhou, or the Huiyin Temple in Hangzhou, pay more attention to their steles, lost or extant. The gazetteers of larger sites focus instead on the topography of the many temples and other sites of the "mountain."

That the four exhibits below are all stele inscriptions should not detract from the importance of the *moya*. Many, probably most, pilgrims would not have been able to read the stylized idiom of the longer stele texts, but all would have experienced the emblematic force of the *moya* on their visit. Beginning with the Qiu-Zhu Gazetteer (Fasc. 10, p. 14b) the Putuo gazetteers record the most famous *moya* and comment on their calligraphy. The Wang Liansheng Gazetteer lists more than 180 extant *moya* at different sites all over the island for 1999. Forty more are known to be lost, mostly due to the Cultural Revolution, during which many inscriptions were erased, damaged, or overwritten with political slogans.[7]

If its attribution is correct, the oldest extant *moya* are the characters "Zhenxie's Spring" (*zhenxie quan* 真歇泉). They are ascribed to Shi Hao 史浩 (1106–1194), who also wrote the oldest known inscription, discussed in Exhibit 1.[8] The most famous *moya* is perhaps the large four-character inscription "Buddha Land between Sea and Sky" (*haitian foguo* 海天佛國) on the path from the Fayu to the Huiji Temple on Foding mountain (Figure 6.1).[9] The calligraphy is that of General Hou Jigao, whom we

FIGURE 6.1 *Moya* in the calligraphy of Hou Jigao—"Buddha Land between Sea and Sky" (*haitian foguo* 海天佛國)

have met in Chapter 1 and whose journey to Mount Putuo we will discuss in Chapter 8.

In his study of literati perspectives on Buddhism in the Tang and Song, Mark Halperin has distinguished between "two idioms, the devotional and the apologetic."[10] For the study of inscriptions this is an important dimension that complements the pro-Buddhist/anti-Buddhist spectrum on which literati pronouncements on the subject can be positioned in general. Literati who were strongly opposed to Buddhism did not write inscriptions for Buddhist sites at all. Literati who were sympathetic or at least tolerant toward Buddhism could do so in different modes. Outing themselves as sympathetic toward Buddhism, or even as devout Buddhists, writers like Bo Juyi 白居易, Liu Zongyuan 柳宗元, Su Shi 蘇軾, Huang Tingjian 黃庭監, and less well-known figures such as Hou Jigao and Tu Long positioned themselves at varying degrees of distance to local Buddhist communities. The register of their pronouncements was influenced by occasion and audience and might have changed over their lifetime.

The four exhibits here were chosen to suggest a development. My thesis is that before the Ming, government officials were overall free to voice sympathy for Buddhism, whereas in late imperial China and during the Republican period their rhetoric was muted, as expressing strong admiration for Buddhism had become problematic for office holders. Accordingly, the first inscription, by Shi Hao of the Song dynasty, belongs to the devotional mode of expression. The second, by Zhou Yingbin 周應賓 (Chapter 1), is apologetic only in the sense that the author felt compelled to justify why Buddhism is still around at all, not in the sense that he defends a personal belief in it. In the third exhibit, the Kangxi emperor uses devotional tropes in his poetic address to Mount Putuo while appropriating its symbolic power into the larger unity of the Manchu empire. The emperor was free to praise Buddhism as much as he liked. Moreover, it was in his interest to cultivate other discourses as a counterweight to the Confucianism of his Chinese officials. Exhibit 4 is by Sun Yat-sen, the "Father of the Nation," who as Christian was surprised by his vision at a Buddhist site.

The series also suggests a trend away from the devotional to a more administrative and/or touristic mode; a pattern similar to that which we have observed with the visual representation of Mount Putuo in Chapter 2. Although the sample is small and impressionistic, I propose that it reflects a wider shift in the rhetoric of scholar-officials toward Buddhism. It should be remembered, however, that the story of inscription does not end here. The inscriptions of the last thirty years are again devotional, and their authors are no longer scholar-officials but Buddhist laypeople newly empowered to leave their mark in stone.[11]

Exhibit 1: Shi Hao's Verse Inscription on a Vision of Guanyin (1148 CE)

Among the earliest inscriptions preserved in the Mount Putuo gazetteers is that left by Shi Hao 史浩 (1106–1194), who visited the island in April 1148.[12] Shi Hao of Ningbo had passed his *jinshi* exam only three years before and was in the early stages of a successful career in government, which would see him rise to the lofty heights of Grand Councilor or Prime Minister, the top ranking official in the empire. As well as being one of the most influential politicians in the twelfth century, Shi Hao was involved with Buddhist sites throughout his life.[13] His mother was a regular visitor to Mount Putuo, traveling there every year. When her eyesight failed and the journey became too arduous, Shi Hao built a miniature Putuo Cave near the Xiayu Temple 霞嶼寺. The temple was (and still is) located on an artificial island on Lake Dongqian, on the outskirts of Ningbo, which allowed for safe visits by the aging matriarch.[14] Shi Hao was actively engaged with the Buddhist world, and his encounters with Buddhist masters are remembered elsewhere in Buddhist historiography, e.g., the *Bu xu gaoseng zhuan* 補續高僧傳.[15] The thirteenth-century historian Zhipan even opined that Shi Hao's peaceful policy approach toward the Jurchen was a result of his contact with Buddhism and more specifically his journey to Mount Putuo.[16]

Financial support of monasteries was a matter of course for many wealthy laypeople.[17] The Wang Liansheng Gazetteer (p. 723) includes an early fundraising appeal by Shi Hao for the repair of Puji Temple, in which Shi urges his peers in the local gentry that "more than 3000 strings of cash are needed to restore the main hall. If the wealthy donors could unite as one family and the abbot and monks do their part, indeed the four communities of monastics and laypeople will be able to create good karma." The stone on which Shi Hao's inscription was inscribed is long lost, but its text survives in the gazetteers. It consists of a eulogy to Guanyin and a prose preface, which describes his visit to the Tidal Sound Cave. Shi Hao was determined to see the Bodhisattva. When he was not able to see Guanyin in the morning, he tried his luck again in the afternoon:

On April 12th, 1148, Cheng Xiufu of Poyang and [I,] Shi Hao of Siming, set out from Shenjiamen. The wind filled our sails and we soon arrived [at Mount Putuo]. The next morning, we went to the Tidal Sound Cave to pay our respects to the Bodhisattva Guanyin. Everything was quiet and we saw nothing.

We burned incense and boiled some tea, but only [saw some] blossoms floating in our cups. We returned to the temple, and after lunch discussed with the Abbot Lan how Mañjuśri [in the *Śūraṅgama Sūtra*] came to choose the [practice of] perfection, and how the young man [Sudhana in the *Avataṃsaka Sūtra*] entered the Dharma-world. In the afternoon, we went again to the cave and prostrated ourselves on the little stone bridge. We strained our eyes and peered into the cave, but saw only rocks piled in random heaps.

As we got ready to return a monk said: "At the top of the cliff is an opening from which you can peak in." Having climbed up to the top we looked into the cave and the auspicious image suddenly appeared. It was of golden hue, radiant, and we could clearly make out the eyes and eyebrows. We both beheld the same scene, but only I saw that her teeth were white like jade.

Filled with joy we prostrated ourselves and left. Before taking the boat back to Yongdong, afraid that this event might be forgotten, I write this on a cliff [and have it inscribed onto the stone]. Reading this, I hope, future visitors will persevere and not give up if they do not see anything on their first visit [to the cave].[18]

An abbreviated version of this story was included in the Sheng Gazetteer, which also mentions that Shi Hao "wrote [his eulogy] on a stone cliff, wishing to encourage those who came after not to give up, if they do not see [Guanyin] right away."[19]

According to the Wang Liansheng Gazetteer there are sixty-eight extant steles.[20] Of another thirty-three the text remains, while the stele itself has been lost. That the text of Shi Hao's eulogy (*zan* 贊) survived its stone is partly due to the prominence of the author and partly because it was deemed a paradigmatic expression of the vision quest at the Tidal Sound Cave.

I bow to the Great Bodhisattva Guanyin of Mount Putuo
who in thirty-two miraculous manifestations bestows good fortune
   on men and gods,
the sun of [her] wisdom shines broadly and perfectly illuminates
   every unlit nook.
Long have we cultivated a karmic connection with the Bodhisattva;
since ancient times the Bodhisattva has been able to discern our
   every little deed.
Now we are fortunate that our boat came to this gem of a place,[21]

[guided hither by] the beautiful landscape's sagely breeze [across] the sea that lay clear like a mirror.

Leaving Dongqin shore[22] in the morning we swiftly arrived at the lotus palace.

After the monks had finished their meals and washed their bowls, we set out together to see the distant mountain roads.

On the stone bridge spanning across huge breakers we cowered, chilled to the bone,

myself, a worldly man, now in the company of virtuous monks.

Together we recited the secret verses,[23] again and again calling our teacher's name [- "Guanyin"].

Then our eyes were permitted to behold the light of compassion and suddenly [her] purple-golden form,

sitting cross-legged and at ease in the opening of the grotto,

was revealed through the spray and mist. For a long time we knelt.

All who were with us, old and young, saw the miraculous image manifest,

and sighed and praised in joy that which they had never seen before.

I reckoned among those present were many that had much good karma.

Respectfully approaching our teacher at dusk,[24] our prayers were answered [immediately] like an echo;

having repented our wrongs, we were allowed to see the Tathāgata.

Together we offered incense with great sincerity as we laid out another daily offering.

If even our past good deeds could bring us such auspicious fortune,

we now vow to strive that our future acts too may be forever remembered by the Tathāgata.

This floating life is but a dream, where [else] is one taught[25] how to regulate one's life?

Abstaining from killing we eat a vegetarian diet, and read widely in the Buddhist scriptures.

Every moment is precious indeed, one really should abide in seclusion [on Mount Putuo].

Manning the raft of wisdom, again and again ascending to the shore of awakening,

to help those living beings still lost in the sea of suffering, to let them know the ford.

Let us aim high and aspire to meet the Buddha—life after life.[26]

With this eulogy Shi Hao is writing—in both form and content—firmly within the devotional mode of Buddhist inscriptions that in his time, when Neo-Confucianism had not yet achieved ideological hegemony, was still available to scholar officials. We have similar literati accounts of visions for other sites, such as Zhang Shangying's vision of Mañjuśrī on Mount Wutai,[27] and for other times, as we will see below in Exhibit 4.

Not everyone had the option of composing an inscription on stone and having it cut by artisans. For his brushwork to be preserved the visitor had to possess political power or literary prominence. The preface remarks that Shi Hao was entertained by the abbot. As a *jinshi* and an official this was customary, and the same courtesy was extended to Commander Hou Jigao some 450 years later. What is notable about Shi Hao's piece in the context of this series of exhibits is his piety and the fact that he feels no need to justify himself as a Buddhist lay person. For scholar officials this mode of expression became rare in late imperial times. Based on the texts in the Mount Putuo gazetteers, it seems that, due to the Neo-Confucian demand of stricter adherence to a Confucian identity, texts by officials in the Ming and Qing tend to be more defensive or apologetic when discussing Buddhism. The next exhibit is an example for how the tone had changed in the late Ming.

Exhibit 2: Zhou Yingbin's Inscription for the "Three Masters of the Inner Palace" (c. 1607)

As with the previous inscription, the stele for this laudatory text by Zhou Yingbin originally stood near the Puji Temple and is now lost. In the text, Zhou commemorates three eunuch palace officials who played an important role in the revival of Mount Putuo. In particular it describes the deeds of Zhang Sui 張隨, who was sent to Putuo to supervise the rebuilding of Puji Temple after the fire of 1598. The inscription is at the end of a cluster of texts pertaining to the revival of the site in the Wanli period, the politics of which have been described in Chapter 1. It concludes the victory of the "pro-Putuo" faction that wanted to see the site restored. It is of particular interest as it highlights the crucial role eunuchs played in the patronage of Buddhist institutions in the Ming. Again and again eunuchs appear as patrons of temple construction or reconstruction[28] or were charged with rebuilding temples in the name of the emperor. However, as Susan Naquin notes: "When eunuchs were appointed by emperors and empresses to take charge of construction projects—as they often were—it is difficult to disentangle them from their imperial masters and mistresses and not always obvious where the initiative came from."[29]

One of the reasons for the interest of eunuchs in Buddhism was that Buddhist ideas and rituals surrounding the afterlife would have been more attractive to them than the other available options. To be ritually remembered after death was generally seen as desirable in traditional China, but in Buddhist lore appropriate ritual remembrance was not bound to either ancestor worship or physical integrity of the corpse. During the Ming wealthy eunuchs were able to provide for their posthumous future by endowing "tomb temples" (*fensi* 墳寺), often close to Beijing.[30] On Mount Putuo too there used to be a memorial shrine (*ci* 祠) for a group of palace eunuchs who had supported its late Ming revival. The "Memorial Shrine for the Three Masters" (*Sangong ci* 三公祠) was built to commemorate Zhang Sui 張隨, Dang Li 党禮, and Ma Qian 馬謙. By 1705 the shrine was called the "Memorial Shrine for the Four Inspectors" (*Sijian ci* 四監祠) because Zhang's assistant Wang Chen 王臣 had become enshrined there as well. *Ci* is also the term for an ancestral temple. As we have seen in the previous chapter, the construction of memorial shrines was in no way limited to eunuchs, but being commemorated in a memorial shrine at a Buddhist temple would have been an attractive prospect for Zhang Sui and his colleagues, who had no descendants of their own to conduct ancestral rites.

Zhou's commemorative inscription for Zhang Sui is first transcribed in the Qiu-Zhu Gazetteer (Fasc. 11, pp. 14b–16a).[31] It was inscribed on a stele, which stood originally in the "Memorial Shrine for the Three Masters" but is now lost. The shrine still existed in 1832 when the Qin Gazetteer was compiled but was abandoned later in the nineteenth century. In 1915 the abbot Liaoyu 了餘 (1864–1924) built another hall on its ruins.[32] Below is the text translated from the version preserved in the Qiu-Zhu Gazetteer:

Stele Inscription for the Newly Built Memorial Shrine for the Three Masters from the Inner Palace

The strings that fasten the caps and clothes [of officials, bind] unlike the spells of sorcerers. The constant application of penal justice is not like a furious outburst. Humans have a tendency to be wild and ferocious, but the laws of the realm cannot always keep them in check. Making use of the teaching of the Bodhisattva, it is possible to awe them and give them guidance. Often thereby their evil intentions can be destroyed and good thoughts fostered instead. This is why the followers of [the teachings from] the Western Regions have never been done away with. This is why Putuo of the Southern Sea, although it has seen several cycles of destruction and revival, is still here.

In Wanli 27 [1599 CE] the court sent messengers to bestow the Buddhist Canon on each of the famous mountains, among them Mount Putuo. At that time the god of fire had completely burned down the [Puji] temple, and the site that was once famous throughout the world, was densely overgrown with grass. When this was brought to his attention, his Majesty [the Wanli emperor] dispatched the Palace Eunuch Master Zhang [Sui] Yaquan from the Directorate for Imperial Accouterments, with several thousand *tael* of silver, to oversee the reconstruction of the site.

The Master was by nature wise and reasonable, and he fulfilled his duties firmly and resolutely. He was well read in the Buddhist scriptures and a skilled calligrapher who used to work for the Chinese Buddhist Palace Press.[33] Whenever the emperor ordered rites for the well-being of the country, Zhang would [in preparation] always eat vegetarian, refrain from alcohol, and scrupulously keep all precepts. Thus the emperor was convinced he was the right man and assigned the duty [to repair the temple to him].

The Master stayed on his assignment [at Mount Putuo] for four years, carrying out his orders [consistently] as if it was but a single day. He joined the morning and evening recitations [at the Fayu Temple], and quietly and contently kept to himself. He never got involved in worldly matters. He did not receive any of the messengers that the local elite sent him [that could involve him in local politics], but instead dedicated all his skill and energy to [rebuilding] the [Puji] temple.

There were several hundred monks that belonged to the temples. The master assigned duties in the management of the temple to the older and more accomplished ones. For the young and bright ones he hired teachers to instruct them in the scriptures of their tradition.

In the temples of the Bodhisattva on Mount Putuo "dragons and snakes" lived together. At times there were corrupt fellows who staked out monopolies and schemed for their own profit, against the rules of the monastic order. Their superiors were weak, and did not know what to do. However, as soon as the Master stepped down from his carriage they fled like rats.

Once the island and its temples had been put in order and the reestablishment [of the Puji Temple] was complete, he invited a large number of Confucian gentlemen to compile a gazetteer and thus create a lasting record. All this was due to the Master's efforts.

Later he again received an imperial order to go to the Southern Sea to convey an imperial stele inscription and to perform the rites to inform the local earth-god that the project has been successfully completed.

Besides him there was Palace Eunuch Dang from the Directorate of the Imperial Horses, who protected the inner palace, and [having been dispatched to Mount Putuo] reported the progress to the emperor. He also donated one thousand taels of silver to help the project. The Palace Eunuch Ma from the Directorate of Palace Eunuchs also played a part in these works.

When the island could be settled,[34] and the various works were completed, the monks of the temple erected a memorial shrine with three rooms behind the temple, and prayed for the three masters.

This shows that the saying "there is no merit that is not rewarded" is right. Myself, of little skill, each time I ascend the peaks of Mount Putuo, I am deeply moved by the fact that the restoration of the temple precinct was not merely due to the numinous power of the Bodhisattva and the virtue of our Emperor, but also due to the hard work of the three masters. Therefore I write this commemoration as the monks of the temple have requested.

Master Zhang's personal name was Sui. He was from Wen'an County in Tianshun Prefecture. Master Dang's personal name was Li. He was from Huayin City in Shaanxi. Master Ma's personal name was Qian.[35] He was from Shenzhou City in Zhending.

Written in the year Dingwei of the Wanli reign, in the month of mid-autumn (1607–09–21 to 1607–10–20) by Zhou Yingbin of Siming. Stele erected by the monk Rujiong of Putuo Temple.

([Postscript in the Qiu-Zhu Gazetteer:] The "Three Masters' Shrine" is now called the "Four Eunuchs' Shrine." In it are four images. In addition to Zhang, Dang, and Ma, there is one of Wang Chen. Chen was sent on imperial orders together with [Zhang] Sui. But only Sui served in the inner palace, and therefore Chen was not mentioned in the [above] text. Chen was Sui's subordinate and together with him oversaw the reconstruction of the temple. Due to his long dedicated effort he [too] has [since] been enshrined with the others.)[36]

That Zhou Yingbin, vice minister in the Ministry of Rites, wrote a stele inscription in honor of Zhang, Dang, and Ma reminds us of the fact that in spite of the general antagonism between Confucian officials and palace eunuchs, coalitions were always possible. The rationale he gives for the continued survival of Buddhism—that, more so than laws, it is able to tame our "evil instincts"—is typical for the late Ming. It goes beyond the apologetic mode that Halperin has identified in Tang and Song inscriptions. Zhou's implied question, "Why is Buddhism still around at all?" makes sense only after the decline of institutional Buddhism in the early and mid-Ming. That Confucian government officials in the late

Ming had to explain why "the followers of the [teachings from the] West [i.e., Buddhists] have never been done away with," shows to what degree Buddhism had become a curiosity in their eyes, or at least their rhetoric. In Zhou's account neither the numinous workings of Guanyin nor the monastic establishment plays an important role, and the latter, if anything, is a bother. His wording ("followers of the [teachings from the] West" 西方之徒, "dragons and snakes" 龍蛇) shows only minimal respect for the Sangha, and his comparison of some "corrupt fellows" with rats is quite drastic considering they were monks. Tellingly, his inscription is not included in the Wang Hengyan Gazetteer (1924), which attempted, after several "official" gazetteers, to shift the emphasis back toward a Buddhist perspective. Zhou's rhetoric is neither devotional nor apologetic but instead forcefully asserts the right of the court to intervene in, to maintain, and to approve of religious activity. Nevertheless, his eulogy and the shrine to the three eunuchs stood near the main temple for more than three hundred years.

Exhibit 3: Kangxi's Inscription "For the Fayu Temple on Mount Putuo in the Southern Sea" (1704)

In Chapter 5 we met some of the actors associated with the "early Qing revival of Mount Putuo" that took place in the late seventeenth and early eighteenth centuries. The site was destroyed in the 1660s and 1670s mainly because of the inability of the central government to keep the peace in the archipelago. Maritime traffic was disrupted, and piracy made pilgrimage difficult and at times impossible. However, compared to the long hiatus in the Ming when Mount Putuo had been abandoned for several generations, the seventeenth-century problems were but a short interlude.

As described in Chapter 5, Xingtong and Xinming successfully petitioned Kangxi for imperial name plaques in 1699. Five years later, the two abbots stayed in the capital and received imperial stele inscriptions for their temples. The text of both inscriptions was first included in the Xu Gazetteer of 1739.[37] The one for the Fayu Temple is listed first, perhaps because the Xu Gazetteer had been sponsored by this temple, but also perhaps because it was written some weeks before the inscription for the Puji Temple. The tone of the Puji inscription is more personal. The emperor concedes his lack of erudition in Buddhist scriptures, because "from childhood on I [Kangxi] studied the [Confucian] classics and the history books, to train myself in politics and rulership. I have not studied the golden sutra leafs on the meaning of emptiness."[38] His lack of reading did not keep him from patronizing Buddhism, and in the Putuo steles he records his support for the site, which was, as we have seen in the previous chapter, considerable. Kangxi's appropriation of merit is in line with the imperial ideology that sees itself as the exclusive agency that initiates and sustains public works. There is no reason to doubt that donations by the court played an important part in the revival of the site, but it should be remembered that the long-term support for the monastic establishments on Mount Putuo (as well as elsewhere) came from many smaller contributions by laypeople. Kangxi's stele text, nevertheless, integrates the changing fortunes of Mount Putuo skillfully and poetically in the context of imperial patronage:

I have heard that the [teachings of the] perfect, miraculous appearances are a true source of wisdom.

[They are like the] "golden rope that lines the road to enlightenment"[39] and the great earth is witness to the wisdom of awakening.

Listening to the sounds of the tide on the jade-green sea, the sand forever[40] resounds with the voice of salvation.

[After the raids and the fire] the temples are rebuilt, and the sea will forever be peaceful.

The Fayu Temple is the second temple of the Bodhisattva on Mount Putuo of the Southern Seas.

A Buddha Land among the famous mountains, a boat of compassion on the great sea—its green mountains touch the clouds, their height almost reaching the Brahma heavens, while the sun bathes in the ocean waves, auspiciously opening up a Pure Land.

[Mount Putuo is] a mighty pillar of the sky, a famous site of China, from which one might reach the three islands [of the immortals];[41] its miraculous events are recorded in gazetteers.

Through the turbulent upheavals [of recent decades], its mountains and rivers became deserted. Monks and lay followers dispersed like clouds, the ashes of the Buddha Halls blowing in the wind.

Now, however, we have steered steadily into this "Bright Peace of Qing,"[42] and the waves of unrest have been smoothed; both on land and on sea one can now visit numinous sites and take the precepts.

Imperial funds were sent to rebuilt the abode of the King of Emptiness [, the Buddha].

Workers were gathered, and an auspicious time chosen. Untiringly [the workers] lived in straw huts [during the construction].

The foundations were laid, without using drums [forcing a rhythm on the workers].

The pearly halls [of the temples are now] decked with tiles [like the palace of the Dragon King below the sea], and contain the holy waters [of mercy] within their vastness.[43]

Leviathans are its pillars and giant turtles serve as roof beams, awakening those who are misguided to the right ford.

Seated on the blue lotus is the precious image, perfect in its radiant halo, in the purple bamboo in Jeta's grove; majestic in every tiny detail,

its gaze [emits] the universal radiance of the clouds of compassion, and bestows the pleasant words of the Dharma.

On sea the numinous power manifests, and the God of Water protects the Dharma.

Like clouds piled high by the wind come the boats of countless foreign realms.

This shore welcomes them, and is itself a raft for all.

By [the Bodhisattva's] greatness, may [my mother] the empress dowager live long amidst us on high, and by [the Bodhisattva's] compassion, may the common people below enjoy good fortune.

Thus, even beyond the reach of the sandalwood fragrance, there will be regions where humaneness and long-life are established, all suffused with the merciful light of the water moon [Guanyin].

This is carved as a declaration to all.

Written in winter, the eleventh month of the year Kangxi 43 [1704–12–11][44]

Throughout the text the Kangxi emperor alludes to motifs from the Chinese Buddhist *imaginaire* and blends them with the imperial discourse of rulership. The "boats of countless foreign realms" coming to Mount Putuo acknowledge its strategic location on the shipping lanes, before the island itself is compared to a "raft" that carries sentient beings to the other shore. In the last line of the inscription proper, the "[reach of] the sandalwood fragrance" might allude to India. In this case the other "regions" could refer to Mount Putuo alone, but more likely the line reconfirms what was said in the previous sentence and expresses the hope that Mount Putuo will have a positive influence on China. The final metaphor of the "water moon light" alludes of course to Guanyin in her manifestation as "Water Moon Guanyin," considered as the "first truly Chinese" Guanyin image.[45] The metaphor also evokes the ubiquitous reach of the numinous as the same moon is reflected fully in every single drop of water. The last lines therefore express Kangxi's hope that the grace of the Bodhisattva will spread to all corners of the empire, and that his support of Mount Putuo will bring fortune to his immediate family as well as his people.

The stele was destroyed in the Cultural Revolution, as was its pendant that stood at the Puji Temple. While the Puji Temple stele was recarved after a rubbing in 1984, the Kangxi Fayu Temple stele is (for now) lost.[46] The imperial steles crowned by dragons that are on prominent display at the site today are not those of Kangxi, but were issued by his son the Yongzheng emperor, who imitated his father in many ways. The Yongzheng emperor too donated large sums for renovation work on the two temples, which took place during 1731–1733. On February 18, 1734 he composed two letters to commemorate his kindness. These texts, which explicitly reference the precedent of the Kangxi inscriptions, were carved on steles and erected at the Puji and the Fayu temples. Their texts too, of course, were included in all later gazetteers.[47]

Exhibit 4: Sun Yat-sen: "An Unexpected Event on Mount Putuo" (1916)

Erected in 1995, the stele for this text is located in the front yard of the Willow Twig Hermitage (Yangzhi An 楊枝庵), near the Fayu Temple. It bears a short note written by Sun Yat-sen (1866–1925) in the summer of 1916 on the occasion of his visit to Mount Putuo.[48] This text differs from our previous three exhibits in that the text was not originally composed as an inscription but only later appropriated as such. It is obviously in the interest of the site to show that Sun Yat-sen had an epiphany there, even if it was not at the Tidal Sound Cave and not about Guanyin. Sun's account is in many ways an interesting document that shows how little the mechanism of visits to Mount Putuo has changed over the centuries. His visit, or at least his account of it, shares many features with that of Shi Hao (1148), Hou Jigao (1589), and others. Like them, Sun went as part of a larger group and diligently names his companions. Like Hou Jigao his visit is portrayed as part of a tour with military purpose. The main storyline follows what we know of Shi's and Hou's visits: the group is entertained by the abbot and does some sightseeing before experiencing a numinous vision (or bemoaning the lack of one in the case of Hou Jigao). The accounts usually conclude with a few sentences reflecting on the site or the return journey. Sun's *You putuo zhi qi* 遊普陀誌奇, despite being our most recent example, poses the greatest textual difficulties as it appears in print, online, and even on the stele itself with numerous spelling mistakes.[49] The versions circulating on the Internet are a good example of how unreliable online versions can often be. But here is Sun Yat-sen's account of his visit:

When I was inspecting the military harbors of Xiangshan and Zhoushan I also visited Mount Putuo. With me went Mr. Hu Hanmin, Mr. Deng Mengshuo, Mr. Zhou Peizhen, Mr. Zhu Zhuozhang, and the secretary of the Civil Affairs Bureau of Zhejiang, Mr. Chen Qubing. We went on the warship *Jiankang* under captain Ren Guangyu. When we arrived on Mount Putuo, it was already afternoon. We went ashore together and met the monk Daojie[50] from the Fayuan Temple in Beijing, who led us to the guest quarters of Puji Temple. There the abbot Liaoyu[51] arranged for some bamboo carriages.[52] With that we set out [for a tour of the island]. Along the way there were many numinous stone formations. On the sandy ground the forest grew only sparsely, beckoning the traveler, and for a long time we moved along the meandering ways going up and down [over the hills]. Having ascended to the sky lantern platform on Mount Foding, we had a vast view and I lingered alone there for a while pacing up and down before returning to the Huiji Temple. On the way I saw a vision in the distance. In front of the temple, somewhat hazily, I saw a tall and imposing archway, decorated with wreaths of rare flowers and banners dancing in the wind. Strangely, there were several dozens of monks looking like they were ready to welcome a guest. I was astounded by how splendid they looked and how fast they proceeded.[53] As [their procession] winded along and drew nearer, I gradually saw something bright. In their midst there was a big wheel, spinning at great speed, though it was impossible to make out what it was made of or what force moved it. I wanted to ask them, but all of a sudden they vanished without trace, and I was already past the spot [where I had seen them].

After this I entered Huiji Temple and urgently asked my companions about the matter, but no one else had seen it, so I concluded it could only have been a miracle. I never think about miracles or the fantastic, and I still do not fully understand what I saw there. Thinking back to that moment on Mount Foding, as I gazed above and below it was as if I could see the whole universe and hold it in my hands. Between the azure sky and the white-crested waves, gazing across the green mountains, it was as if I had never seen a sight more pure in my whole life. The ear has heard the Sound of the Tide, the heart contains the Ocean Seal. Indeed our physical existence is insubstantial like a shadow and thus shapes and thoughts arise and vanish in it. The spiritual nature of this place affects one's inner being.

After we left Mount Foding, we passed by Fayu Temple, where the sounds of the evening bell and drum hurried us along to the Brahma Voice Cave. The evening colors were now deepening and we returned to the Puji Temple for dinner. [The monks] Yuliao and Daojie were expounding the principles of Buddhism and it was both relaxing and inspiring to chat with them.

Above we have outlined some features that Sun's text shares with earlier accounts. In some ways, however, Sun's text is exceptional. Especially that his vision is *unexpected* for him is unprecedented. He sounds almost embarrassed about his experience, which his companions are unable to confirm. Already the move to seek immediate corroboration is a sign of different times. Through most of its history people went to Mount Putuo because they *expected* to see something, but they did not expect to see the same as their fellow travelers.[54] Sun, as a Christian convert, seems surprised about his Buddhist vision. In his late teens Sun stayed in Hawaii, where he desired to be baptized so fervently that he broke with his traditionalist brother. In the end he returned to China, forgoing his brother's support, which might have afforded him a university education. Back in his home village he desecrated the images in the local temple before moving to Hong Kong, where he was baptized in 1884.[55] His surprise in seeing a vision of a Dharma wheel is understandable. Although his wording makes efforts in the Buddhist register by using metaphors such as "Tidal Sound" and "Ocean Seal," the tenor of his text leaves no doubt that he is not a Buddhist layman on pilgrimage. He explains his vision as a product of a generic spiritual essence of the scenic site. Guanyin, who, as we have seen in Chapter 3, was seen in most visions and is mentioned in most other inscriptions, was not part of Sun's experience. This makes his inscription unique. In another sense, however, the brand-new stele of 1995 closes the cycle: at the end of the twentieth century a religious vision by an influential politicians is again inscribed at Mount Putuo. Like those of Prime Minister Shi Hao in the twelfth century, Sun Yat-sen's words were deemed important enough to carve in stone.

Conclusion

Our tour of inscriptions from Prime Minister Shi Hao, via Vice Minister of Rites Zhou Yingbin, and the almighty Kangxi Emperor, and finally to the skeptical "Father of the Nation," has shown that the smooth surfaces are inscribed with very different attitudes and motives. In the account of Shi Hao's visit there is nothing to indicate that his attitude was different from that of any other pious Buddhist who cherished his vision of Guanyin. In the twelfth century, this kind of unapologetic devotion on the part of a high-ranking politician was still easily possible. Almost five hundred years later the picture had changed. Zhou Yingbin's stele was embedded in the complicated debate that surrounded the reopening of Mount Putuo, and his praise of Zhang Sui and the other eunuchs was at least in part a favor for a political ally. The text betrays Zhou's skepticism about the Sangha's ability to manage itself. As is evident from his preface to the gazetteer that bears his name, he does not consider himself a Buddhist (Chapter 2, Exhibit 3). The panegyric voice of Kangxi, a hundred years after Zhou, appears on the surface more generous toward Buddhism. Beneath the rhetoric, however, one can sense the unyielding determination to integrate another site into the "Peace of the Qing." Still another two hundred years later, more pedestrian and via muddled sources, comes Sun Yat-sen in style. That the carved version of his inscription has textual errors is symptomatic of the relationship between politics and Buddhism in China during the twentieth century, which has never found a mutually agreeable code. Neither in Republican nor in Maoist or post-Maoist China was there time to find a stable idiom that would allow politicians to create inscriptions that do not seem comical or that can be viewed without cynicism. Still, then as now, the Buddhists on Mount Putuo have taken shelter under the words of the mighty in hope for a continuity that was always precarious.

CHAPTER 7 | The Poetic Landscape of Mount Putuo

It therefore makes sense from where we have positioned ourselves in
a philosophy of literature and poetry to say that we "write a room,"
"read a room," or "read a house."

—GASTON BACHELARD[1]

ONE ASPECT OF MOUNT Putuo's textualization, the feedback loop between
texts and the experience of landscape, is especially obvious in the case of
poetry. Visitors often perceived the site through the lens of poems they
had read before coming to the island. When Clara Ho describes her visit
to Mount Putuo in 1934, she extensively quotes poems in support of her
observations, her experience of the site mediated by poetry.[2] Thus the
memory of poetry played a central role in the aesthetic appreciation of the
site and in turn stimulated the production (*poïesis*) of new poems. The visitors' urge to leave a poem could at times even turn into a nuisance. In the
early twentieth century administrators on Mount Putuo felt compelled to
point out: "For erudite guests, who come and compose a poem, the monks
are instructed to provide writing material. Kindly do not to write poems on
the walls. All such writing will be quickly removed."[3]

It is difficult to overestimate the importance of poetry for Chinese literati culture. Because of the *Shijing*, the Classic of Poetry, poems were
a respected part of classical education since its very beginning. During
the Tang and Song and again in the Qing after 1756, the composition of
shi- and *fu*-style poetry was part of the civil examinations.[4] Every literatus
would not only be able to read poetry but was also expected to be able to
compose at least the occasional verse. More so than in Europe, in China,

as well as in Korea and Japan, poetry was the medium in which aesthetic judgments and moods could be communicated in a way that was both standardized and ad hoc. Especially *shi*-style poetry, with its regulated but still flexible rhyme and meter, proved to be an immensely successful genre.[5] People from different parts of China, speaking different forms of Chinese, could communicate personal, situational sentiments in a *shi* poem, safely mediated through common motifs and prosody. Poems also feature prominently in Chinese novels and dramas, as part of the structure (e.g., as chapter opening or summary), as part of the plot, or as spoken by the protagonists. Moreover, at least during the late Ming and Qing, poetry was also a rare cultural expression that was widely shared by men and women.[6]

The corpus of poetry, especially for later imperial China, is therefore enormous. While there are "complete" collections of the extant poetry of the Tang (c. 50,000 poems) and the Song (c. 200,000 poems), there is no "*Quan Ming Shi* 全明詩"—no "Complete Collection of Ming Dynasty Poetry." Estimates reckon that more than one million poems of the Ming and Qing have survived in thousands of collections, most of them *shi* poems.[7]

It is therefore not surprising that, while only a few visitors left prose impressions of their journey, we have many poems that were written before, during, and after visits to Mount Putuo. Poems often fill a sizable part of the gazetteers, and their number usually dwarfs all other *belles-lettres* writing. More than half of the Hou-Tu Gazetteer, almost 40 percent of the Mount Huangbo Gazetteer, and some 30 percent of the Huiyin Temple Gazetteer consist of poetry.[8] In the 1643 gazetteer of Quanzhou's Kaiyuan Temple, which contains relatively few poems, the compiler laments that he couldn't find more poems in his sources.[9] In 1757 the Aśoka Temple Gazetteer of 1612 received a supplement, which consisted entirely of literary texts, most of them poems. Poems are of limited value to the historian as they contain very little historical information, but they were clearly highly valued by the gazetteer compilers and their readership. For the literati reader the tapestry of poems conveyed a sentimental map of the place that we have trouble to fully appreciate today.

The most comprehensive modern anthology of poems on Mount Putuo (Wang 2008) contains 1,572 poems by 593 authors,[10] and even given Wang's liberal inclusion policy the collection is not complete.[11] The *shi* that Wang, and many gazetteers, anthologize as the earliest poem—Wang Bo's 王勃 (649–676) eulogy on Guanyin with preface—is one of the first instances of the legendary Mount Potalaka appearing in literati culture, but it is not about Mount Putuo in Zhejiang. It is rather a reminder that the idea of Guanyin's abode was present among the literati already in the early Tang, two centuries before the island site of Mount Putuo started its rise to prominence. To include Wang Bo's poem on the Potalaka of the *Avataṃsaka Sūtra*, as some gazetteers have done, blurs the borders between the religious *imaginaire* and the actual site, which is of course exactly what textualization is about. As Chinese landscape painting, travel poetry blends the real-life experience with its mix of inconveniences and comforts with that of a transcendent, poetic landscape.

In recent years Tian (2011) and Cartelli (2013) have proved that it is possible to convey the Chinese poetic experience of travel, landscape, and scenery in English.[12] Nevertheless, poetic conventions are among the more difficult aspects of culture to present in translation.

Benjamin Elman has remarked that the Chinese education and examination system did not aim at a "reading" but a "writing elite."[13] Not only, therefore, is the translation of poetry generally more lossy than that of prose, but the lack of a shared cultural context of production, in which most readers are also potential writers, is a greater handicap that it may seem. Even in China today *shi* poetry is now generally seen as something of the past, and, as elsewhere, readers and writers have parted ways. The price for near universal literacy is that certain aspects of elite culture, such as a stable canon, or widely shared poetic forms, fall away. After literary Chinese was replaced by the vernacular in the first half of the twentieth century, *shi* poetry lost much of its status as a *lingua franca* of aesthetic appreciation, and visitors to the site today are more likely to record their journey in a blog entry or a Weibo tweet than in a poem.

Somewhat against the odds, therefore, this chapter attempts to showcase some examples of the poetic culture regarding Mount Putuo. First, we take a look how Mount Putuo was described by a Confucian scholar in the early fourteenth century. Exhibit 2, Tu Long's cycle of poems titled "Twelve Famous Views," shows how the island was perceived as a landscape of scenic sites in the late Ming. Exhibit 3 is again by Zhou Yingbin, whom we have met before in Chapters 1 and 6. Zhou here appears with a different, more personal voice, and only here, in the poetry section, do his kinship ties become obvious and further clarify his ambivalent role in the production of the gazetteer that bears his name. Exhibit 4 returns to poems that are associated with sites and presents a different set of "Twelve Views." Selected from poems of an early nineteenth-century anthology, they showcase the wide spectrum of Mount Putuo poetry that visitors employed to casually record their impression of a place.

Exhibit 1: Three Poems by Wu Lai (c. 1324)

When Tu Long compiled the Hou-Tu Gazetteer, he included a number of works by the Yuan scholar Wu Lai 吳萊 (1297–1340). Among them were ancient style, rhyming *shi*-poems, which were written on the occasion of Wu Lai's visit to Putuo in 1324.[14] Wu Lai is the author of one of the earliest notes about Mount Putuo, the *Yongdong shanshui guji ji* 甬東山水古蹟記, which Zhang Dai considered the most interesting record from the time before the suppression of Mount Putuo in the early Ming.[15] Born in Zhejiang, Wu was obviously interested in the island, though he was not drawn to it as a sacred Buddhist site. He rather appreciated the island within the poetic repertoire that was available to describe a scenic landscape. Below are three poems from a set titled "Setting out one evening eastwards across the sea to find the Tidal Sound Cave on Mount Meicen, climb the Pantuo Rock and watch the sun rise" 夕泛海東尋梅岑山觀音洞登磐陀石望日出詩.

Poem 1:
山月出天末 水面生晚寒
扁舟劃然往 萬頃相渺漫
星河自搖撼 島嶼青屈盤
遠應壺嶠接 深已雲夢吞
蟠木繫予纜 扶桑緌我冠
寸心役兩目 少試鯨魚竿

The mountain moon rises from the end of sky // from the surface of
    the water the evening cool
Rowing the small boat ahead // amidst vast, empty spaces
The milky-way itself seems to sway // as we meander among green
    isles[16]
far away—touching on the islands of the immortals // so deep—it
    could devour all the lakes of Yunmeng[17]
I'll moor my boat at [a] Panmu [tree / Mountain] // tie my cap to [a]
    Fusang [tree / Island][18]
My single heart directs my pair of eyes // let's try and fish for whales!

Poem 2:
起尋千步沙 穹石塞行路
怒濤所搣擊 徒以頑險故
卓哉梅子眞 與世良不遇

上書空雪衣 燒藥迺煙樹
玄螭時側行 縞鶴一迴顧
從之招羨門 滄海晝多霧

We rise [in the morning] to look for the Beach of a Thousand-Steps
    // huge boulders block the way.
The angry waves pound the shore // through the rugged reefs.
Ah, the great Mei Zizhen // who has long since left this world of men,
writing his memorials into the void [here] he walked, clad in snow //
    concocting elixirs until the smoke from his fires filled the forest.
The black dragon always at his side // and the white crane watching
    over him,
I wish to follow him to visit the immortal Xian Men[19] // but in the
    morning the sea is covered with mist.

Poem 3:
茫茫瀛海閒 海岸此孤絕
飛泉亂垂纓 險洞森削鐵
天香固遠聞 梵相俄一瞥
魚龍互圍繞 山鬼驚變滅
舟航來旅遊 鐘磬聚禪悅
笑撚小白華 秋潮落如雪

Out from the vast ocean // The shores [of Mount Putuo] rise in peace-
    ful seclusion
its waterfalls drifting wildly like tassels from a cap // deep caves [the
    mountain ranges] dark and serrated
From far one can smell the incense in the air // at times here one can
    glimpse the Bodhisattva
Encircled [and protected is she] by sea dragons, // [all malevolent]
    mountain spirits have fled and vanished.
Traveled hither in our boats // we meditate among the bells and chimes
with a smile turning a little white flower // while the spray of the
    autumn tides falls like snow

Wu Lai was trained as a historian and scholar of the classics. He left
government office early to pursue a life in (relative) seclusion. Among
his students was the famous Song Lian 宋濂, advisor to the first Ming
emperor, who played an important role in the Yuan–Ming transition. Wu's
poetic description of his visit to Mount Putuo is less concerned with the

Buddhist semantics of the site than Tu Long's set. His first poem ties Mount Putuo (or Meicen as he calls it) into the classical, legendary geography of the archipelago. He depicts his nightly journey in the spirit of the type of poetry called "roaming in transcendence" (*youxian* 游仙).[20] The second poem evokes the recluse Mei Fu and the immortal Xian Men, who were said to have been active in this region. Only poem No. 3 turns to the Buddhist dimensions of the site and mentions the visions at the Tidal Sound Cave and some other Buddhist tropes. It does so, however, in the most distant of terms: visitors might "catch a short glimpse" of a "Buddhist image." The "little white flower" in the last line is a *double entendre* alluding to two invented traditions. First it points to the legend of the first transmission of the Chan School from Shakyamuni to Mahākāśyapa; second, to the alleged meaning of Potalaka in Chinese.[21]

As a historian Wu Lai saw his native region in terms of native Chinese imagery rather than in those of Buddhism, which he deemed a foreign import. In his poetry Wu Lai evokes the legendary Daoist antecedents of the region, in spite of the fact that there was very little evidence for a Daoist presence on Mount Putuo either before or after the arrival of Buddhism there.[22] References to Daoist recluses such as An Qisheng, Mei Fu, and Xian Mengao and the mystical geography of the Penglai Islands continued to appear frequently in the poetic depictions of Mount Putuo.

Exhibit 2: Tu Long's "Twelve Famous Views of Mount Putuo" (c. 1589)

In 1925 Lu Xun was both sad and amused to hear that the Leifeng Pagoda, one of the "Ten Famous Sights of the West Lake," had collapsed: sad, because the destruction served "no purpose" and was merely brought about by people looting bricks; amused, because the fall of the pagoda upset what he called the "ten sights disease." Lu felt that the custom of grouping famous sights in sets of ten or eight was a nuisance that had reached "epidemic proportions in the Qing dynasty." "Look through any county gazetteer, and you will find that the district has ten sights."[23]

Grouping famous views of a region into sets was a result of the growing appreciation of local culture since the Song dynasty. Sets of famous spots gave travelers a route not unlike the routes of shrines one was supposed to visit on a pilgrimage. The sets thus gave structure to a journey and its memory. In modern tourism a sizable segment of the market seems to cater to tourists who do not want to be simply tourists. Going to places "unspoiled" by tourism is highly valued. The mindset with which tourist-pilgrims undertook scenic travel in late imperial China was almost never concerned with the "new." Explorers like Zheng He 鄭和 (1371–1433) and Xu Xiake 徐霞客 (1587–1641) were rare figures, and most people were content to see what they had read or heard about a site before. It was good enough that the site was new to them. By grouping places into sets of famous sights, local culture created a grid both for visitors suggesting what to visit as well as for poets suggesting what to write about.

In the texts of the Song and Yuan dynasties, Mount Putuo was perceived mainly as a religious site as well as an important landing place for envoys and embassies. In the Ming and Qing another aspect became prominent: the island began to be appreciated more and more as a scenic site. In his gazetteer of 1590, Tu Long 屠隆 (1543–1605) included no less than five poem-cycles on "Twelve Sights of Mount Putuo," written by Wang Shouren 王守仁 (1472–1529) (Ch. 5, p. 7), Long Defu 龍德孚 (1531–1602) (Ch. 5, p. 20), Wang Shike 王世科 (d.u., fl.1544–1577) (Ch. 5, p. 35), Guan Daxun 管大勳 (*jinshi* 1565) (Ch. 5, p. 40), and himself (Ch. 6, p. 13). The presence of Wang Shouren or Wang Yangming, the eminent philosopher, is surprising; if the famous Wang Yangming had made a visit to Mount Putuo, his poems should appear prominently in all gazetteers. However, the Huo-Tu Gazetteer already made clear that the attribution to Wang Yangming is spurious,[24] and the set was not included in any of the later editions, nor is it part of Wang Yangming's collected works.[25] Although Long Defu, Wang Shike, Guan Daxun, and Tu Long knew each other well and their sets originated very likely on a shared occasion, only the sets of Tu Long and Long Defu were eventually carried forward in the gazetteers. Wang Shike's and Guan Daxun's sets were forgotten and are not even contained in the comprehensive collection by Wang Liansheng (Wang 2008), another reminder of how lossy textualization is.

The decision to include all five sets of twelve poems each was made by Tu Long. A native of the Ningbo region, Tu Long is an interesting, if understudied, author.[26] Having gained his *jinshi* degree in 1577, his official career came to an ignominious end in 1584, when he was accused of having an affair with a married woman. After exiting government service he lived off his skills as a writer, and the Hou-Tu Gazetteer is one of the projects he took on to keep afloat. Tu Long gained fame for his poems and plays and was a renown calligrapher. He was a friend and sometime neighbor of Wang Shizhen, the influential *arbiter elegantiarum* of the late Ming, who considered Tu Long to be one of the "Five Lesser Masters" (*wumozi* 五末子) of his time—a ranking that translates perhaps to "second-rate, but first-class second-rate." Thus Tu lived at the center of late Ming literary culture and was in many ways a typical Zhejiang literatus. He recorded his sophisticated tastes in a compendium (*Kaopan yushi* 考槃餘事 "Lingering on Superfluous Things"), which describes the world of things that these erudite men inhabited.[27] More so than most of his peers, however, his interests went beyond the confines of Confucianism, and he was an outspoken supporter of Buddhism. Timothy Brook has called him the Ningbo "county figure most associated with the patronage of Buddhist institutions, ... not just in Yin [Ningbo], but nationally."[28] This is corroborated by the fact that he is mentioned in no less than twenty-six temple gazetteers.[29] He called himself a "disciple of the Buddha" (*fodizi* 佛弟子)[30] and wrote a comprehensive apologetic—the *Fofa jintang lu* 佛法金湯錄—against Neo-Confucian criticism of Buddhism. The first chapter contains a detailed refutation of seventeen different arguments that Han Yu and the Neo-Confucians had forwarded against Buddhism.[31] Chapters two and three contain a collection of 146 notes on Buddhist terms, reflecting Tu's understanding of issues ranging from death and meditation to the difference between immortals and Buddhas. The preface to the *Fofa jintang lu* by the monk Zhenyi 真一 is dated to 1602. It was written on Mount Putuo, an indication that Tu Long stayed in touch with the monastics of Mount Putuo, long after he had compiled the Putuo Gazetteer in 1588/89.[32]

Doubtless it was Tu Long's sympathy toward Buddhism as well as his literary skills that caused Hou Jigao to charge him with the compilation of their gazetteer. As Tu Long was well established in the regional literary scene, it was easy for him to collect or request poems about Mount Putuo from his friends in the Ningbo area. Most of these men would have heard of and even visited Mount Putuo. Many would have been pleased to see the ancient site revived, and it was the circle of Tu Long's friends that came up with the first set of twelve scenic spots for Mount Putuo.[33]

Below is a translation of Tu Long's own set, which he humbly arranged in the gazetteer after those of his friends.[34] The cycle consists of heptasyllabic quatrains (*qijue* 七絕). The rhyme (at least in Tu's southern diction) is on the first two lines and the last (AAxA), which is typical for this type of *shi*-poem.[35]

1. Spring Morning in Plum Bay 梅灣春曉
梅尉丹爐火不溫 踈枝淡月島烟昏
只愁海叟吹龍笛 擪落羅浮萬樹魂

Mei Fu's cinnabar oven has gone out // through the sparse trees: the
    pale moon and the island in morning mist,
in sorrow an old man plays the flute //—the tune breaks off and [falls
    like those blossoms] of Mount Luofu's [plum] trees spirit[-white][36]

2. Morning Mist on Tea Mountain 茶山夙霧
龍宮蛟室霧絪縕 幾樹珊瑚認未真
雪裏頹霞高十丈 紅綃恐是獻珠人

The sea [below] vague in the reddish morning mists: // how many
    coral trees?
Among the snowy peaks the carmine clouds are piling high // the
    Dragon Girl's red silk?[37]

3. Tidal Sounds in the Old Cave 古洞潮音
海濤飛雪復春雲 寶殿疎鐘入夜分
潮自砰鍧僧自定 悟來原不是聲聞

Ocean tides and flying snow pound the clouds // the slow sounding
    of the temple bell rings through the night
The waves naturally break on the shore—whoosh—the monks natu-
    rally attain concentration // their enlightenment, however, is not
    that of the "hearers"[38]

4. The Cool Waters of Turtle Lake[39] 龜潭寒碧
清江使者夢賓賓 五兆空嗟朽甲靈
豈是來遊蓮葉上 水天凉冷月痕青

The ambassador [turtle] to Clear-Water[40] as seen in a dream, darkly;
    // drilling and mumbling the fortune-tellers destroy its carapace
Could it have come to be reborn on these lotus leafs? // Water
    and sky are cold and clear beneath the green-blue shadows of
    the moon

5. Clarity at the Gate of Heaven[41] 天門清梵
野衲齊繙貝葉書 磬聲遙度暮沙虛
神龍聽法妖蛟舞 親見如來金臂舒

The monks leaf through the Buddhist scriptures, // The sound of the
    temple chime rings across the evening and the empty beach
Mighty dragons listen to the Dharma,[42] the lesser spirits dance, // with
    their own eyes they see the Tathāgata extending his golden arms

6. Sunrise at the Pantuo Rock 磐陀曉日
黃烟黑霧罩潺湲 忽破天昏海色殷
誰駕火輪推雪浪 赤光如矢射千山

Yellow-black the mists cover the sluggish water // Suddenly the
   overcast sky breaks open: the sea turns dark red
Who rides the wheel of fire through the snow-white crested tide? //
   Its red rays like arrows piercing a thousand peaks

7. The Thousand Step Beach 千步金沙
黃如金屑軟如苔 曾步空王寶筏來
九品池中鋪作地 祇疑赤腳踏蓮臺

Yellow like bits of gold, soft like moss // where once the King of
   Emptiness stepped off the precious raft[43]
Like on a piece of land in the pond of the nine grades[44] // have we
   ascended here barefoot on the lotus dais?

8. Crossing the Lian[hua] Sea at Noon 蓮洋午渡
波上芙蕖盡著花 香船蕩槳渡輕沙
珠林只在琉璃界 半壁紅光見海霞

The waves are filled with lotus blossoms // where the fragrant ferry
   is rowed across the shallow sands
there is a Pearl Grove in this Beryl World[45] // on one face of the cliff
   reddish light reveals the sunset clouds on sea

9. Incense Censer [Island][46] in Green Haze 香爐翠靄
博山突兀海孤懸 日對軍持大士前
不用栴檀燃佛火 曉來嵐氣自生烟

[Shaped] steep and tall, like [a] Mount Bo [censer][47], suspended
   lonely in the sea, // by day-light like the vase before the Bodhisattva
[Here] one does not have to burn sandal wood for the Buddha: // when
   the morning comes, the mountain breeze brings its own billows

10. Begging Bowl[48] in the Vastness 鉢盂鴻灝
應器東行大眾從 遍施香飯說禪宗
更看一酌滄溟竭 此物由來制毒龍

Following the vessel east, the masses came // everywhere rice and
   incense is donated, Chan teachings are explained

Again there is a cup that can exhaust the sea // the same that once had
   tamed the evil dragon

11. The Light-Tower on Luojia [Island]⁴⁹ 洛伽燈火
熒熒一點照迷津 光奪須彌日月輪
萬刦靈明應不滅 五燈傳後與何人

The twinkling little light shines for those who have lost their way //
   [to them] more brilliant than sun and moon [on their way around]
   Mount Sumeru
The numinous light of wisdom⁵⁰ of ten-thousand eons has hardly
   been extinguished // but to whom has the lineage of the five
   Lamp[-histories] now passed?

12. Tea in the Silent Abode 靜室茶烟
蕭蕭古寺白烟生 童子烹茶煮石鐺
門外不知飄急雪 海天低與凍雲平

Cold and quiet lies the old temple, white steam rises // from the
   ceramic kettle as my boy brews tea
Outside the gate the snow who knows how fierce // sea and sky lie
   low, flat beneath the frozen clouds

Although each of the quatrains can stand on its own, the cycle was to be
read as the record of a visit. After arriving by boat in Plum Bay, the way to
the Puji Temple leads through tea plantations (poems 1 and 2). The next station is the Tidal Sound Cave (No. 3). Then follow poems on other sites on
the island, including the Pantuo Rock and the Thousand Step Beach (Nos.
4–7), before, with poem No. 8, Tu Long embarks on a series of visits to
smaller islands (Nos. 9–11). This seemed to have been a common practice
that was also described by Hou Jigao in his travelogue (Chapter 8, Exhibit
2). The closing quatrain of the series brings the scene back to the main island
and shows the travelers at rest. In this way the poem allows for armchair
traveling in a way similar to the images of the "Twelve Views of Mount
Putuo" (Chapter 2, Exhibit 3), which were created in reaction to the poem
cycle.

Exhibit 3: Zhou Yingbin's Poem for Abbot Rujiong (1607)

The following poem was written by a literatus and dedicated to a
Buddhist monk. Zhou Yingbin lent his name to the Zhou Gazetteer

that was compiled in the wake of the debate around the reconstruction of Mount Putuo in the early seventeenth century. As we have seen in Chapters 1 and 6, Zhou patronized Buddhism reliably, while foregrounding the politically orthodox dimension of his support. Judging from his writings, he was not especially interested in Buddhism as such, but he clearly took an interest in how Mount Putuo was administered.[51] A look at his family network at once clarifies why he lent his support to the faction of the empress dowager that supported Mount Putuo. The Zhou clan was based in Ningbo and flourished in the late Ming. Zhou Yingbin was one of eight brothers, which included at least one more office holder. His younger brother Zhou Yingzhi 周應治 (1556–?) passed his *jinshi* exam in 1580 (three years before his elder brother), and Yingzhi too held office, though not quite as high in rank as Yingbin, who as vice minister of rites held an influential position in the capital. Yingzhi and another younger brother, Zhou Yingchen 周應宸, both contributed poems on Mount Putuo to the Zhou Gazetteer and their works are in a much more Buddhist register than their brother's. One of Zhou Yingchen's poems even criticizes the orthodox Confucian attitude against Buddhism: "For Confucians to proclaim themselves Buddhists is strictly forbidden // they might donate money, but are stingy with themselves."[52] As it turns out, Zhou Yingbin's family was tied into the Ningbo scene of Buddhist laypeople and monks, and he must have been personally acquainted with many of them.[53] All three of his own poems that were included in "his" gazetteer are dedicated to monks. Below is the one titled "Dedicated on the occasion of the rebuilding of the Temple on Mount Putuo and the Abbot Master [Ru] jiong answering the imperial summons to become Buddhist patriarch" 普陀山寺鼎新, 住持迥公爰拜左善世之命, 賦此爲贈.[54]

紺宮崒嵂海中開 更有東林大辯才
祇舍界分成淨土 昆池刦盡識餘灰
鍾聲遠振黿鼉窟 幢影髙懸日月臺
何幸聖皇知宿德 紫衣降自九重來

The temples and the high mountains amidst the sea // now have an
   exegete great [like Huiyuan of the] Donglin temple [on Mount
   Lu]
The holy site of the Jetavana has turned into a Pure Land, // at the
   bottom of Lake Kunming one finds the left-over ashes [of the
   previous world]

The sound of your temple bells reverberates deeply into the caves of
the sea monsters // the shadow of your prayer flags stretch high
above the altars of the sun and moon
How fortunate that our holy emperor recognized your virtue, // and
the court bestowed the purple robe [on you]

At first glance the poem seems but a generous congratulation to Rujiong's
promotion as "World Benefactor of the Left" 左善世, the highest ranking
cleric in the realm.[55] As previous dynasties, the Ming had institutionalized
religious administration and created a structure of monastic offices that, at
least nominally, were responsible for the control of Buddhist and Daoist
institutions throughout the empire. A relatively small number of monks
were appointed to these offices to interface between the government and
the local and regional religious institutions. These offices, however, were
part of the Ministry of Rites, and we can assume that Zhou Yingbin as vice
minister of rites was to some degree responsible for Rujiong's promotion.
In effect, the poem should therefore be read as a superior's congratulation
to his new hire.

Not surprisingly, the boss was well acquainted with the history of
Mount Putuo. The second couplet contains a thoughtful allusion to a story
related in chapter thirteen of the *Soushen ji* 搜神記, a fourth-century collection of tales on supernatural phenomena. Legend has it that in 122 BCE,
Emperor Han Wudi ordered a large lake to be excavated near Chang'an as
reservoir and training ground for his navy. Digging deep into the ground,
the workers found a layer of ash, which no one was able to explain at that
time. Some three hundred years later a monk from "the western regions"
was asked about this and answered that the ash was a remainder of the
last conflagration of the world at the end of the last eon. Thus, in this
relatively obscure allusion, Zhou points both to the fire that destroyed the
Puji Temple in 1598 and, one layer deeper, to the suppression of the site
during the early and mid-Ming. With Rujiong's ascension to court office
Mount Putuo's revival "from the ashes" was secured for the foreseeable
future. As this reestablishment of Mount Putuo was gained against considerable resistance by more conservative factions at court, Zhou's rhetoric
is pitched to assuage the conflict by foregrounding the role of imperial
control in the running of the empire. As a vice minister, Zhou needed to be
seen as impartial in his official pronouncements. However, his decision to
rebuild the Puji Temple and keep Mount Putuo open for pilgrims was in
line with his relaxed personal attitude toward Buddhism and the perhaps
even more pro-Buddhist proclivities of some of his brothers.

Exhibit 4: The Twelve Views in Zhu Defeng's "The Famous Sights of Putuo" (1830)

Writing poetry while traveling was part of the cultural repertoire of a literatus, as taking a selfie is for cell phone owners today. The importance of poetry declined in the twentieth century, when Chinese was written increasingly in the vernacular and the custom to describe landscape in *shi*-poems went out of fashion. For Mount Putuo this change is epitomized by the difference between two short guidebooks that were published some hundred years apart: Zhu Defeng's 祝德風 *The Famous Sights of Putuo* (*Putuo quansheng* 普陀全勝) (1830) and Shi Chenkong's 釋塵空 *Small Gazetteer of Mount Putuo* (*Putuo shan xiao zhi* 普陀山小志) (1948).

The *Complete Sights* is an anthology of poems arranged by location. In the *Complete Sights* actual and armchair travelers alike move on Mount Putuo as a poetic space, appreciating, as it were, the appreciation of previous travelers. The *Small Gazetteer,* compiled and largely written by the monk Chenkong (1908–1979), is a more prosaic affair. It was published during the civil war, only one year before the younger monks on Mount Putuo were pressed into army service by the fleeing Nationalist army.[56] In his introduction Chenkong emphasizes how well the various temples are organized along Buddhist principles and how the markets are forbidden to sell meat or alcohol.[57] The *Small Gazetteer* of 1948 contains only a small number of poems, because it was written as a guide book for an emerging new audience that did not consist of literati—a Republican audience that failed to come after the Communist victory in 1949. When tourists and pilgrims returned to the island in the eighties, delayed by thirty years of Communist rule, the descriptions that Chenkong had offered in his *Small Gazetteers* were outdated.

Complete Sights, on the other hand, consists of little else but poems. It begins with poems on the "Twelve Views," because, as Zhu Defeng explains, "if one wants to contemplate the famous sights of the West Lake [in Hangzhou], one must first resort to the 'Ten Views,' if one wants to contemplate the famous sights of the Yunqi Temple [near Hangzhou] one must first go for the '48 Views.' In our case, describing Mount Putuo, we should therefore first list the 'Twelve Views.'"[58]

Zhu's "Twelve Views" are not identical with the sites described in Tu Long's poem cycle translated above. Zhu rather follows the pictorial representation of the "Twelve Views of Putuo," which had appeared first in the Qiu-Zhu Gazetteer (see Chapter 2, Exhibit 3). The "Twelve Views" thus started out in poetry, then inspired the illustrations of the Qiu-Zhu

PT Gazetteer. The set of sites defined by the illustrations became in turn the matrix for Zhu Defeng's anthology of poems about Mount Putuo. Such back and forth between genres is facilitated by the gazetteer format, which archives them next to each other in one container without stylistic leveling by the editor. Zhu Defeng has collected between five to ten poems for each of the twelve sites. Below I have selected one poem for each location in order to illustrate how literati visitors expressed their experiences on Mount Putuo.

1. The Buddha chooses the Mountain (by Qiu Lian 裘璉 (1644–1729))
海外奇峰翠入天 峯頭朵朵削青蓮
名山如此不肯去 成佛應居靈運前

Out at sea the marvelous peaks reach greenly into the sky // their
   summits cluster silently like blue lotus
Indeed one "does not want to leave" this famous mountain // Better
   "become a Buddha before [Xie] Lingyun"

Writers of landscape poetry had different options to present their content, moving on a spectrum of heavy to light intertextuality. At one end of the spectrum the verse relies heavily on allusions to other poems or "traditional stories" (*diangu* 典故) and privileges the experience of a place as mediated by cultural memory.[59] By reaching out to what happened at the same place before, via stories or allusions to similar sites, the place is experienced in a network of connotations. In the words of the otherwise unknown Zhou Xuelu 周學魯 in poem No. 7 below, "past and present seem to meet." Of the poems selected here Nos. 1, 2, 7, 11, and 12 rely on the reader to be able to decode the allusion in order to fully appreciate the poem. Without knowing the story the lines make little sense.

Another form of intertextuality, employed in poems Nos. 5 and 6 below, is to quote other texts directly. These textual "echoes" are generally not attributed, but then originality was neither asserted nor assumed. The reader might sense that a passage is "on loan" but can understand the passage well enough without knowing its origin.

At the other end of the spectrum, the author could choose to express a momentary, private experience with only minimal references to other texts (below Nos. 3, 4, 8, 9, and 10). This type of poem is more accessible and resembles to a degree the snapshot image that tourists take at a site. By encoding the experience of the visit in a poem, the author creates a memory of "me at site X" and to read these poems is not unlike browsing through someone's holiday photo album.

In the poem above, Qiu Lian, one of the compilers of the Qiu-Zhu Gazetteer, draws on a relatively obscure story about the famous poet Xie Lingyun 謝靈運 (385–433). Xie reputedly said to his nemesis Meng Kai 孟凱, the pious governor of the Shaoxing region: "You might ascend to heaven before me, but will become a Buddha only after me."[60] The topos of attaining Buddhahood "earlier" than Xie Lingyun was used before, and Qiu Lian here echos a line in a poem of the eminent Song poet Liu Kezhuang 劉克莊 (1187–1269).[61]

2. Guanyin appears to the rebuked Sister-in-Law (by Ziyong Chengru 子雍成如 (1647–? (after 1701))[62])

原性蓬胎化女身 短姑踏得豈常人
別開一景輝天地 自有風光處處春

The original nature manifested and became a woman // how could a normal person have stepped [on the magically appearing stones] and reached [the boat at] Duangu [Pier]?
And opened up another world: bright // with scenic beauty and everywhere spring

This is one of the few poems in Zhu Defeng's anthology that was written by a nun. We know more about Ziyong because she is one of the few seventeenth-century nuns for whom we have a collection of "Recorded Sayings" (*yulu* 語錄).[63] Ziyong's "Recorded Sayings" contain more of her excellent poetry, not, however, the poem above, in which she comments on the Duangu Pier and the legend of the Scolded Sister-in-Law (told in Chapter 3). Ziyong was one of a number of illustrious nuns who were part of the seventeenth-century revival of the Linji school.[64] In the 1690s, Abbess Ziyong left her monastery in Beijing to journey south to the Jiangnan region. We know that she visited Mount Jiuhua, and, from the poem above, she must have also stopped by Mount Putuo. Though nuns did not play a visible part in the establishment of Mount Putuo and no convent existed there before the twentieth century, it would have been an obvious place to visit on a pilgrimage.

3. The Tidal Sound and the Brahma Voice Caves (by Zhu Defeng 祝德風 (fl. 1830))

紫竹林中響怒濤 息心專視不知勞
凡夫到此凡心寂 況見靈山眼界高

In the purple bamboo grove sound the angry breakers // the heart, at
    rest and mindful, forgets its wariness
A worldly man comes here, his worldly heart is calmed // more so
    glancing at the sacred mountain - higher than the eyes can see

After grouping five to ten poems on one of the "Twelve Views," Zhu
Defeng always adds a (modest) poem of his own.

4. The Golden Thousand-Step Beach (by Li Qilong 李起隆)
午夜波濤去復臨 幾番淘汰見眞心
恆河無數雖云闊 不及滄涯步步金

Day and night the waves come and go // how often until [our errors]
    are washed away, until we see the true mind?
The countless [grains of sand on] the Ganges, said to be so vast // are
    fewer than those on the ocean shore - each step on gold

The "grains of sand on the shores of the Ganges" are a widely understood
metaphor for a vast, unknowable amount. Like Mount Putuo itself the
metaphor is an Indian import, but by the time of the Ming and Qing it had
lost its exotic overtones. There is nothing that implies "foreignness" in the
writings of Qing dynasty visitors.

5. Waves of clouds at Peak Hua (by Chen Chenhai 陳辰海)
普陀最高處 厥名曰華頂
已證上上乘 無上無等等

The highest point on Mount Putuo // is called Huading
having reached the highest vehicle // there is nothing higher,
    nothing equal

6. On Guangxi Peak after snowfall (by Tu Zhuo 屠倬)
心境真開闊 悠然見太虛
光熙峯上立 不動自如如

It truly is mind-opening // to look out on the empty vastness
standing on Guangxi peak // unmoving, just being oneself

Poem No. 5 ends with a line that is consciously "Buddhist-sounding"
but for a witty or even slightly comical effect, especially when recited.
It closely echoes a passage in the *Ratnakūṭa Sūtra*.[65] Poem No. 6 is even

more conventional. Its last line is copied, perhaps unconsciously, from a poem by Hanshan Deqing.[66]

7. The Immortal's Well at Mei's Peak (by Zhou Xuelu 周學魯)

隱者亦紛綸 傳名有幾人
今看岑下井 隔世怳相親

Recluses there were many // few the names that are remembered
Looking at the well below [Mei-]cen peak // it appears that past and
    present meet

The recluse alluded to here is of course Mei Fu, the legendary Daoist master.

8. The numinous Fahua Cave (by Gu Guang 顧光)

壘嶂層巒裏 陰森不可攀
安能身有翼 飛遍白雲灣

Huge cliffs folded into the mountain // hidden groves beyond
    our reach
I wish I had wings // and could fly—into the bay of white clouds

9. The morning sun rises from the ocean (by Zhang Bing 張炳)

紅日浴咸池 山房來鵲時
支節偏早起 老眼望迷離

The reddish sun bathes in the briny pond // the magpies come out of
    their mountain homes
My arms and legs are stiff - got up too early // my old eyes gaze
    out hazily

10. Listening to the bell near Baotuo Stūpa
    (by Shen Shuhua 沈舒華)

浮生擾擾欲何之 一杆鐘聲夢醒時
塔下經行真自在 耳根已許破愚癡

This floating life—so filled with troubles! What is one to do? // One
    bell stroke and I wake as if from a dream
Walking carefree beneath the stūpa // it seems my hearing has broken
    through my ignorance

Similar to poems 8 and 9, poem No. 10 presents the personal experience the author had at the site in a relatively immediate fashion. In line with the sites they describe, No. 9 focuses on sight, No. 10 on hearing. Both are in a relaxed way self-deprecatory, but while Zhang Bing is lightheartedly resigned to his blurred vision, Shen Shuhua is impressed with his good time on hearing the evening bell.

11. Sunset at the Pantuo Rock (by Ping Guan 平觀)

我愛磐陀石 曾親大士容
至今春草碧 一朵翠芙蓉

I like the Pantuo Rock // here one could once behold the Bodhisattva
now on the light green grass of spring // - the dark green of the
    hibiscus tree

According to the *Avataṃsaka Sūtra*, the Pantuo Rock is the spot where Sudhana first met Guanyin. The poem is another example of how this type of poetry works. In cultural memory a tale is associated with a place. And just as the past is seen there in the present, the experience of the present is colored by the past.

12. Watching the moon in the Lotus Pond (by Hanshan Deqing 憨山德清 (1546–1623))

我來蓮花池 瑩然見夜月
無始到於今 用之而不竭
指月在自然 拈花不可說
人間六月香 金臺開不絕
下品勝天堂 彼國真樂極
上品而上生 花開早見佛
所以日牧牧 盼望此一席

I came to the Lotus Pond // to see the evening moon shine
From beginningless time until now // [moon light can indeed be]
    "used without ever being depleted"[67]
Pointing freely to the moon // turning a flower in one's fingers —it
    cannot be explained
Within this human world, amidst the scents of June // the golden dais
    opens without end
[Even] the lower types [achieve rebirth] surpassing the heavenly abodes
    [of this world] // into that realm which truly is a land of supreme bliss

Those of high achievement are born higher still[68] // they see the
   Buddha as soon as their flower opens
Practicing day by day // let us aspire to reach that very spot

This is the only poem in this exhibit that is not a *shi*-poem, and one of the
few that convey an actual religious concern. The attribution of the unregulated *ji* 偈 verse to the famous Hanshan Deqing is somewhat doubtful,
and it is not contained in the main collection of his writing, but by tone
and subject it could well be his. Starting out with Chan images ("pointing
to the moon" and "turning the flower"), Deqing, again uniquely in this
series, uses Pure Land imagery to describe the site. His imagery fuses the
lotus pond in front of the Puji Temple with the lotus pond in Amitabha's
Pure Land, which is described in the *Guan wuliang shou jing* (T.365). The
souls (for lack of a better word) enter the Pure Land by being reborn into
closed lotus blossoms on this pond. After some time they open to reveal
Sukhāvati, the Land of Bliss, in all its glory. The "golden dais" that "opens
without end" probably points to the golden lotus on which the Buddha
preaches the Dharma. The "spot" or "seat" in the last line is the front-row
seat close to the preaching Buddha that Pure Land Buddhists aspired to.
Deqing's poem depicts the site through the lens of the religious *imaginaire*
of Pure Land Buddhism, which is otherwise not especially prominent on
either the site or in its textual record.[69]

Conclusion

The four exhibits above highlight the role poetry played in the textual
weave around Mount Putuo. They reveal a spectrum that runs from the
intricate poetry cycle of Tu Long to situational doggerels dashed off by
visitors. Notwithstanding Mount Putuo's Buddhist identity, they reflect
both secular and religious concerns and contain a rich dose of Daoist imagery. Poems written by monastic authors are generally more Buddhist in
tone. In the largest collection of poems about Mount Putuo (Wang 2008),
about a third of the authors are Buddhist monks and nuns.[70] Many of their
poems, however, are extracted from their "Recorded Sayings" (*yulu* 語錄)
and were rarely included in the gazetteers.[71] Still, poet-monks were part of
the gazetteer tradition since the Sheng Gazetteer (1361), which contains
a poem of Sheng Ximing's contemporary Laifu 來復 (1319–1391). Laifu
had served as abbot in Ningbo before taking up the prestigious abbotship
of the Lingyin Temple in Hangzhou. In a farewell poem to a fellow monk

going on pilgrimage to Mount Putuo, Laifu the poet-monk reminds his friend to transcend "words and sentences" on his journey:

一文中現無盡身 一句中含無盡義
一文一句妙難思 了心證入三摩地
是身非相空名模 蓮花舌滴香醍醐
見超文句會真說 普門有路昇天衢

Endless forms within one word // Countless meanings within one
    sentence
Words and sentences are difficult to understand // The clear mind
    enters *samādhi*
There forms lose their characteristics, names and patterns are emp-
    tied // From the Lotus drips the fragrant nectar of true nature
Seeing beyond words and sentences one meets the real teaching //
    Through the Universal Gate the road leads up to heaven

With the founding of the Ming, Laifu was called to the capital and, like Rujiong in Exhibit 3, received the purple robe and was made part of the official clerical hierarchy. Laifu lived in more perilous times, however. The founder of the Ming, the Hongwu emperor, at first complimented him on his poetry, but later, during Hongwu's long descent into paranoia, a line of Laifu's poetry was perceived as criticism, and Hongwu had him executed in 1391. In spite of his trust that language can be transcended, Laifu was trapped by it.

CHAPTER 8 | Travelers and Pilgrims

AS WITH THE OTHER sacred mountains of Chinese Buddhism, Mount Putuo is first of all a destination. In a seminal essay on pilgrimage, Victor Turner remarks on the "peripherality of pilgrimage sites," the fact that pilgrimage sites are rarely located in the socio-political centers of a polity.[1] The very idea of pilgrimage implies a journey away from familiar, secular environments to numinous, religious places. However, people traveled to religious sites for a variety of reasons—a temporary escape from domestic structures, a desire for *communitas,* an experience of liminality, the creation of merit, or to pray for help. Their motivation might be strong or weak, simple or complex, unambiguous or contradictory. Contemporary distinctions between tourist and pilgrim, or traveler and tourist, that try to delineate these motivations can be mapped back onto history only with great difficulty.[2]

In China both Daoist and Buddhist pilgrimages have been closely associated with the cults surrounding "sacred mountains."[3] Mount Putuo, like Mount Wutai, Mount Emei, and Mount Jiuhua, attracted large numbers of pilgrims for many centuries. The economy of these sites relied heavily on pilgrimage, and we have seen how the Buddhist establishments on Mount Putuo quickly declined once political circumstances prevented travel to the island. In spite of the dependence on pilgrims, pilgrimage is something of a "blind spot" in the gazetteers. They offer only an indirect and veiled picture of pilgrimage, as the literati writers were not interested in documenting the pilgrimage streams or trying to understand the site from the perspective of less educated visitors, who visited the island in organized pilgrimage groups. Both in poetry and prose gazetteers stay within the limits of literati discourse.

In the previous chapter we saw how poetry was used to record the experience of the site. This chapter is about how travel and pilgrimage to the island was told in prose, especially in the genre of the travelogue (*youji* 遊記).[4] It is no coincidence that the rise of the local gazetteer in the Ming coincided with the growing use of travelogues. The interest in local sites and their history and an appreciation of scenic landscape fueled literati travel as well as the production of travelogues. The motivation for literati travelers was hardly ever purely religious, and sightseeing was an important, often perhaps the only, reason for their journeys to Buddhist and Daoist sites. We know that they moved among crowds of pilgrims, who came to the sacred site on organized tours to "offer incense" (*jinxiang* 進香), but we do not have first-hand accounts by these pilgrims until the twentieth century.

Some Confucians were opposed to a Buddhist presence at "their" scenic spots in principle. In his "Notes on Mount Wutai" Gu Yanwu 顧炎武 (1613–1682) includes some strident criticism of the clergy there, to the point of endorsing Han Yu's dictum to "Return [the monks] to laylife, burn their books, and appropriate their dwellings!"[5] His contemporary, the poet Shi Runzhang 施閏章 (1618–1683), on the other hand, did not seem to mind the presence of monks at Mount Jiuhua. He too, however, was not interested in conversing with them but rather wished to commune with his Tang dynasty colleagues, who had stayed at Jiuhua nine hundred years earlier.[6] Zhang Dai 張岱 (1579–1679), who left records of his trips to Mount Taishan and Mount Putuo, was never much concerned about the religious context of either site. If anything, the large number of religiously motivated pilgrims, where mentioned at all, were a nuisance to him.[7] Most of these pilgrims would have been women, who rarely wrote in the travelogue genre. In this the Chinese sources differ from those we have for Japan, where the diaries and novels written by Heian court ladies afford us a better picture of what it was like to travel to sacred sites as a women.[8]

In this chapter we will use the term travelogue liberally to apply to all first-person reports of travelers to Putuo. For the time before the twentieth century, the gazetteers include the following travelogues describing journeys to Mount Putuo:

1. Section *Meicen* 梅岑 in Fasc. 34 of *Xuanhe fengshi gaoli tujing* 宣和奉使高麗圖經, by Xu Jing 徐兢 (1091–1153). Arrived on Putuo in the fifth month of Xuanhe 5 (1123-06-28) on his way to Korea. First included in the Wang Liansheng Gazetteer (p. 681).

2. Untitled, by Shi Hao 史浩 (1106–1194). Journey in the third month of Shaoxing 18 (1148–03–29 to 04–26). First included in the Hou-Tu Gazetteer (Fasc. 4, p. 3b).

3. *Yongdong shanshui guji ji* 甬東山水古蹟記, by Wu Lai 吳萊 (1297–1340). Journey in the sixth month of *Taiding* 1 (1324–06–30 to 07–29). First included in the Hou-Tu Gazetteer (Fasc. 3, p. 1).

4. *Changguo zhou Baotuo si ji* 昌國州寶陀寺記, by Liu Geng 劉賡 (1248–1329). Mentions three journeys in the spring of 1298, 1299, and 1300. First included in the Hou-Tu Gazetteer (Fasc. 3, p. 15).

5. *You Butuoluojiashan ji* 遊補陀洛迦山記, by Hou Jigao 侯繼高, 1589. Describes a journey to Putuo in 1588. First included in the Hou-Tu Gazetteer (Fasc. 3, p. 5).

6. *Butuoluojiashan ji* 補陀洛迦山記, by Tu Long 屠隆. First included in the Hou-Tu Gazetteer (Fasc. 3, p. 11).

7. *Duhai jishi* 渡海記事, by Yin Yingyuan 尹應元 (d.u.). Arrived on Putuo 1603–06–23. First included in the Zhou Gazetteer (p. 377).

8. *You Butuo ji* 遊補陀記, by Lu Bao 陸寶. Stayed for seven days in the second month Wanli 45 (CE 1617–03–20 to 1617–03–27). First included in the Qiu-Zhu Gazetteer (Fasc. 11, p. 29).

9. *Putuo* 普陀, by Zhu Guozhen 朱國禎. Traveled to Mount Putuo in early June 1617. First included (partially) in the Wang Liansheng Gazetteer. Complete text in his *xiaopin* collection *Yongchuang xiaopin* 湧幢小品 (Zhu 1619 [1991]: Fasc. 26, p. 10ff.).

10. *Haizhi* 海志, by Zhang Dai 張岱. Traveled to Putuo in late March, early April 1638. First included (partially) in the Wang Liansheng Gazetteer. Complete text in his *xiaopin* collection *Yuanhuan wenji* 瑯嬛文集 (Zhang Dai 1638 [1935]: 44–53).

11. *Li Nanhai Butuoluojiashan ji* 禮南海補陀洛迦山記, by Shi Shibiao 施世驃. Traveled to Putuo in autumn-winter 1701. First included in the Xu Gazetteer (Fasc. 15, p. 8).

12. *Duhai zhuli ji* 渡海祝釐記 by Lao Zhibian 勞之辨 (1639–1714) Written in 1714. Traveled to Putuo 1713–03–11 to 16. First included in the Qiu Gazetteer (Fasc. 12, p.47bff).

After 1714 it seems no more prose travelogues were written until the end of the nineteenth century. Neither the Qin Gazetteer (1832) nor the Wang Hengyan Gazetteer (1924) adds any new texts in this category. In the Wang Liansheng Gazetteer (1999) the next travelogue is dated 1898, after which follow a number of twentieth-century accounts. Although we have plenty of poems for the eighteenth and nineteenth centuries that were written on trips to Putuo, there is a strange lacuna of travelogues for almost two hundred years. As if to make up for the lack of travelogues by Chinese visitors, there are a number of accounts by Western travelers for the nineteenth century. In the nineteenth century quite a few foreigners visited Mount Putuo. Close to the treaty port Ningbo, even closer to Zhoushan, which the British occupied during 1840–1846, and later connected via steamer to Shanghai, it became a destination for colonial recreation.[9]

The absence of Chinese travelogues might be an indication that Mount Putuo in the late eighteenth and nineteenth centuries had lost its luster for the literati traveler. Other pilgrimage sites came into fashion and competed with Mount Putuo. This is suggested by the relatively large number of pilgrimage routes for Mount Jiuhua in Anhui and Mount Tiantai in Zhejiang that are listed in Xianchang's guidebook (1826) (see Exhibit 3). Moreover, with the westward expansion of the empire under the Qing, previously remote mountains like Wutai and Emei had become more accessible. Nevertheless, the lack of literati travelogues between 1717 and 1898 is remarkable.

In the following, we will explore three works that showcase travel to Mount Putuo in the Song, Ming, and Qing dynasties. Exhibit 1 presents the earliest dated prose account of a journey to Mount Putuo. Xu Jing's short note should be read in conjunction with the contemporary report by Zhang Bangji that was translated in the introduction. Exhibit 2, the centerpiece of this chapter, explores the travelogue of Commander Hou Jigao, whom we have already met in Chapter 1 (Exhibit 3). Hou's travelogue shows Mount Putuo in the late Ming at a crucial juncture, as it was being reestablished after 150 years of abandonment. Exhibit 3 is not a travelogue in the narrow sense but belongs to the genre of route books. It is significant in that it was written by a monk for his fellow monastics and provides a rare glimpse into the world of monastic travel. Like women, monastics generally wrote poetry not travelogues. Nevertheless, monks did travel to sacred sites, and Xiancheng's "Knowing the Paths of Pilgrimage" (1826) speaks of their concerns.

Exhibit 1: Xu Jing's "Route Book of the Embassy Sent to Koryŏ in the Xuanhe Era" (1123)

The earliest record of a journey to Mount Putuo is part of a twelfth-century travelogue by Xu Jing 徐兢 (1091–1153), the "Route Book of the Embassy Sent to Koryŏ in the Xuanhe Era" (*Xuanhe fengshi gaoli tujing* 宣和奉使高麗圖經).[10] In 1123 Xu Jing took part in the last Northern Song embassy to the Koryŏ court. The closer and safer northern route had already been blocked by the Liao, and the embassy had to take the "southern" way via Ningbo crossing the ocean northeast to Korea. The embassy left Ningbo on June 18, 1123, and arrived in Korea on July 7. Xu Jing's short account of his stay at Putuo is an important source as it shows the site at a relatively early stage in its development.

> On June 28th 1123 there was a strong wind from the northwest [making the northward course difficult] and the ambassador led the three ranks of the embassy[11] ashore on Mount Meicen. Tradition says that Master Mei Zhenxi lived here as a hermit. Traces of his steps can still be found on the Stone Bridge.[12]

Like in most Song and Yuan dynasty texts, Mount Putuo is still called Mount Meicen. The mention of a stone bridge and the imprint of footsteps are revealing. It is a faint echo of the—in the case of Mount Putuo largely unknown—process by which Buddhism appropriated the island as a religious site and endowed it with a distinctly Buddhist identity. Footprints of deities and saints are of course a common icon at sacred sites worldwide.[13] And while Mei Zhenxi's footsteps were dropped from future narratives and are no longer part of the site, footsteps in stone remain. Visitors today can visit a site called Guanyin Leap (*Guanyin tiao* 觀音跳), a large boulder near the Tidal Sound Cave where the Bodhisattva left her footprint on a rock when she leaped from Putuo to the neighboring Luojia island. Xu Jing's account continues:

> In the deep forest at the foot of a mountain there is the Puji Temple that was built in the Southern Liang dynasty.[14] The shrine hall had a Guanyin statue of numinous power that was once brought by a Silla merchant coming from Mount Wutai, who had the image carved, because he wanted to take it back to his country. When he set out to sea, the boat got stuck on a reef and would not advance until he left the image on the shore [of Mount Putuo]. A monk from the temple enshrined it in the main hall and from that time on, whenever the crew of a ship on an oversea voyage came here to pray for good luck [for the crossing] their prayers were always heard.
>
> Under the house of Qian of Wuyue (907–978) the image was brought to the Kaiyuan Temple in the city [on the mainland]. The image venerated today on Meicen was carved later. In the Chongning reign (1102–1107) [of our dynasty] ambassadors [to Korea] obtained permission by the court to present the temple with a new door plaque, monastic robes for the new year and other clothes.

According to ritual the ambassadors must pray here for the emperor's longevity. During that night's evening recitation the monks intoned their prayers with great seriousness. All the people of the embassy bowed in deep reverence. When midnight came and the stars shone brightly, a wind agitated the banners. People said happily: "The wind has turned and is blowing from the south!"

The passage once more illustrates the role of Mount Putuo in the international trade around the Ningbo region. In the Song all embassy traffic between China and Korea went through Ningbo, because the overland route was *de facto* closed after the founding of the Khitan Empire (907–1125). Traffic to and from Japan too went through Ningbo during the Song and, exclusively so, during the Ming. As Xu's account shows, in 1123 it was established practice for embassy members to conduct rituals at Puji Temple. We can assume that both incoming and outgoing ships from China, Japan, and Korea stopped at Mount Putuo for religious reasons. Many important figures in the history of Sino-Japanese Buddhist exchanges passed through the region. Saichō 最澄 (766–822) and Kūkai 空海 (774–835) arrived through Ningbo before Mount Putuo was founded, but Jōjin 成尋 (1011–1081), Kaikaku 戒覚 (d.u.), Chōnen 奝然 (938–1016), Eisai 栄西 (1141–1215), Shunjō 俊芿 (1166–1227), Tankai 湛海 (1181– c. 1255), Dōgen 道元 (1200–1253), and many others must have been aware of Mount Putuo as a site sacred to Guanyin.[15] They arrived at Mingzhou mostly on merchant ships to study Buddhism in China. On their return, like Egaku, they carried images and scriptures. While in the foundation legend Egaku's Guanyin image "did not want to leave" and forced him to leave it behind on Mount Putuo, later generations had better luck. According to Isao Nishitani two statues—the famous Yang Guifei Guanyin and an image of Somachattra—were originally enshrined at Mount Putuo before being brought to Japan in 1230 by the student-monk Tankai.[16] This would make them the two oldest surviving ritual icons of Mount Putuo.

Exhibit 2: Hou Jigao's "An Account of a Journey to Mount Putuo" (1588)

Commander Hou Jigao's 侯繼高 (1533–1602) "Account of a Journey to Mount Putuo" (*You Butuoluojia shan ji* 遊補陀洛伽山記) is exceptional among the travelogues in that Hou was very much sympathetic toward

Buddhism. As a military official he was not bound by Confucian orthodoxy to the same degree as his colleagues in the civil administration.

Hou Jigao came from an illustrious family of military officials that for
several generations had been in charge of the Jinshan 金山 coastal region
near Shanghai.[17] He was a seventh-generation descendant of Hou Lin 侯林,
who took part in Zhu Yuanzhang's uprising, which resulted in the fall of
the Yuan and made Zhu Yuanzhang the first emperor of the Ming. For his
services Hou Lin was rewarded with the title of Assistant Commander
(Rank 4a) in 1379.[18] Military office being hereditary in the Ming, his male
descendants all held military positions, some with distinction, such as
Hou Jigao. Hou Jigao's patriotic rhetoric in both his postscript (Chapter 1,
Exhibit 3) and his travelogue is thus not merely rhetorical but an intrinsic
part of his family history.

As a young man, Hou Jigao took part in the campaigns against the so-
called "Japanese Pirates" (*wokou* 倭寇), who are mentioned several times
in the account below. He fought under Qi Jiguang 戚繼光 (1528–1588),
one of most effective and successful Ming generals, and who might have
been his role model. Like Qi Jiguang, who wrote poetry and essays as
well as military treatises, Hou was not only a successful general but also a
man of letters. Apart from his role in the edition of the first Ming dynasty
gazetteer, he is the author of some of Mount Putuo's most emblematic
inscriptions, from the large "*Tianhai Foguo* 天海佛國" to the eulogy on
the engraved Guanyin image kept in the Yangzhi Temple. In addition to
the texts preserved in the Hou-Tu Gazetteer, two more of his works have
survived. The "Report on the Defenses of Zhejiang" (*Quanzhe bingzhi*
全浙兵制) (1593) describes the coastal defenses in great detail, down to
the price of nails needed to build ships. The other work, "An Account
of the Customs of Japan" (*Riben fengtu ji* 日本風土記), is the most
important Ming dynasty ethnograph of Japan. It offers a concise and well
researched account of Japan, including a Japanese reader and an illustrated
description of Shōgi 将棋 rules.[19] The *Riben fengtu ji* shows the powerful
Commander as a rather gentle, curious person, who carefully and playfully collects what is essentially strategic information. Hou's career was
by all accounts successful—at one point he was ranked 2a in the hierarchy
of imperial bureaucracy. He fought in battles against pirates into his six-
ties and, perhaps more difficult, survived an impeachment attempt in 1591
without major damage to his career.[20] "An Account of a Journey to Mount
Putuo" was written some days after his second journey to the island in
1588.[21] It describes Mount Putuo through the eyes of someone who had
greatly influenced its history.

An Account of a Journey to Mount Putuo[22]

Mount Putuo is a remote island off the coast. It is considered the place where the Bodhisattva Guanyin used to preach the Dharma, and since the Tang it has been famous among Chinese and foreigners alike. As time has passed, more and more people have hurried there to pay their respects.

Our family has lived close to the sea for generations, and whenever I heard the elders talk of [Mount Putuo] I felt deep admiration for it. Later, when I took up the responsibilities [of my father], I became extremely busy and worked without rest. I thought I would never have an opportunity to visit that Buddha land.

Hardly did I expect that—as happened some years ago—imperial favor would charge me with the defense of all of Zhejiang.[23] [Every year] during the spring and autumn floods, I take some forces on an inspection tour out on the ocean. Thus, in spring of 1587, I finally was able to pay my respects to the Bodhisattva at the Puji Temple and satisfy my long harbored wish. After I had returned, I wanted to take up the brush and record the event, but then got too busy to follow through.

In spring 1588 there was again a big flood and on March 27th, 1588[24] I assembled my troops and set out on an excursion. On the 28th we left Jiaomen,[25] went past [the island of] Jintang, and in the evening arrived at Port Luotuo. The Assistant Regional Commander Wu led his marines and rendezvoused with us. The next morning [on the 29th] we proceeded to Zhoushan where Wu and I went into town to look around.

Hou's account so far is similar to that of Yin Yingyuan in 1603 (Chapter 1, Exhibit 3). As Censor-in-Chief, Yin was met by the Regional Commander, who "expected Yin with several thousand elite marines." Yin too remarks on the strategic importance of Putuo: "climbing this mountain, one can point out all strategic points from there."[26] At least since the Ming, Mount Putuo has been not only a religious but also a strategic site. In general, the military and the religious identity of Mount Putuo were kept apart, and the temple gazetteers focus on the religious aspects. Nevertheless, five of the seven travelogues of the period in question mention pirates or sea battles.

Zhu Guozhen, for instance, relates a story of a "pirate ship" (*wozhou* 倭舟), which was forced to anchor near the eastern shore of Putuo one day before his arrival on May 31, 1617. The term *wo* is usually associated with pirates from Japan, but judging from the description of the ship, its firearms, and its subsequent course, it could have been European. Zhu reports: "It was all black and its upper parts like a city rampart. No one was seen on deck. It was 15 meters tall and three times as long."[27] After several days it was surrounded and fired on by Chinese ships, but "the bullets were like sand thrown against a wall and bouncing off again." When a small boat was dispatched to close in on them, the larger ship shot at it with "steel bullets," killing five men. That evening the wind turned and the larger ship set sail and left in the direction of Fujian and Guangzhou. Zhu comments laconically: "Our boats trailed it and I saluted them."

Twenty years after Zhu raised his arms in salute to his navy, Zhang Dai relates how, in 1638, the sounds of canon fire alerted him to a naval battle that took place on both sides of Putuo Island. According to Zhang "bandits" attacked fishing boats. In the nightly battle several dozen people were killed, two boats burned, and three were seized. Zhang, always fond of the curious, enjoyed the show: "Who would have thought that by coming here I would be able to observe a sea battle; how extraordinary!"[28] Still today, although not mentioned in the guidebooks and obscured on the maps, a large part of the island is controlled by the People's Liberation Army, including a harbor and the highest peaks, which are closed to visitors. The strategic location of Putuo still plays a role in the stationing of troops in the twenty-first century. Back in the Ming, Hou Jigao continues:

On March 30th we passed the island of "Qinglei Head"; before Qinglei there are thousands of islands, no one can record them all.[29] Continuing further there is Shitongmen, a group of small islands that stand close together. The tides flow in and out between them from all sides, creating sixteen "gates" [through which a boat can pass], which is why the place is also called the Sixteen Gates. Our ship passed via [the one called] the middle gate, which was just wide enough for our war junk (*fuchuan* 福船) to pass through. Left and right ragged riffs stood like teeth. This is a very dangerous spot.

On the following day [the 31st] on leaving Shenjiamen,[30] our boat could not advance, because of adverse wind and rain.

On April the 1st[31] in the early morning the winds were up and our boats sped along. Soon we crossed the Lianhuayang [channel that lies between Zhoushan and Putuo] and arrived at [Mount] Putuo.

Hou's remark on the "thousands of islands" (*qianshan wandao* 千山萬島) that lie beyond Qinglei Head betrays his frustration. These islands were a major headache for him, as they were almost impossible to police against pirates. The complex geography of the archipelago was difficult to model for the navy. The map contained in Hou's work on the coastal defenses in Zhejiang shows that he and his staff did not have the cartographic skills to map the area well.[32]

The passage concerning the Sixteen Gates south of Zhoushan Island reveals that Hou and his soldiers traveled in a *fuchuan* 福船-class war junk.[33] *Fuchuan* were large war ships with two masts. They had a large draft that was well suited for ocean travel but which put them in danger when crossing narrow reefs such as the Sixteen Gates. The *fuchuan* were manned with up to one hundred sailors, and the party of Hou and Wu likely consisted of more than one boat.[34] This is the only hint we get as to the size of the group. The Sixteen Gates do not appear on any of the modern maps I have consulted. They have probably silted up since the sixteenth century, as in general the shore line of the coastal region around Hangzhou Bay has changed considerably.

The route via Dinghai on Zhoushan Island with a last stop at the Shenjiamen harbor has been used consistently throughout the centuries. The German architect Boerschmann went this way in 1907, as did the monk Zhenhua in 1949.[35] Even today, more than 450 years after Commander Hou's journey, travelers to Mount Putuo still pass by the same landmarks. Taking a bus from Ningbo today, however, they cross the ocean via a vast network of bridges that has been erected in the last decade. In a mere three hours they cover the distance that took Commander Hou four days. One still leaves the mainland at Zhenhai, follows the route via the island of Jintang, and stops in Dinghai on Zhoushan Island, where Hou and Wu took a stroll in the city. A taxi takes the traveler to the ferry pier in Shenjiamen. The ferry ride takes some fifteen minutes, and one arrives at the southern tip of Putuo not far from where Commander Hou went to shore.

From the Duangu[36] pier, walking for two to three *li*, we arrived at the Puji Chan Temple, and paid our respects to the Bodhisattva. Then Mr. Wu waited for me at the abbot's quarters, and after we had finished our vegetarian meal [there], we took a leisurely walk. From afar, we saw the staggered mountain ranges, here soaring, there falling steeply. The evening clouds came, their shapes changing rapidly, too quickly for the eye to follow. In front of the [Puji] temple, stones were piled up to make a stūpa. It is called the Prince's Stūpa, because during the Yuantong reign [1333–11 to 1335–12] of the Yuan dynasty Prince Xuanrang gave money to build it.

The Prince's Stūpa (*Taizi ta*太子塔) is today called Duobaofo ta 多寶佛塔 (Prabhūtaratna Buddha Stūpa). It is one of the oldest structures on the island, though not much is left of the original design.[37] Restored many times during the centuries, its most recent renovation took place in 2010–2011.

> South of the stūpa the coast is covered with yellow sand and the place is therefore called "Golden Sand Beach"; it is here where the Bodhisattva appears. Tradition has it that this is the spot where the Purple-bamboo Sandalwood Grove is located.[38]
>
> After about another three *li* we arrived at the Tidal Sound Cave. The stones around the cave soar high, overlooking the great ocean. Up on the top there is an opening from which one can peer down to see the huge breakers crashing into the narrow cave. It sounded as if a large bell was struck suddenly, or the roaring of a wild tiger. Looking out eastward over the ocean, all one could see was sea and sky. It was as though the pointed peaks of the Penglai Islands were rising out of the mist. One felt light, as if riding the wind, carried along by an immortal. There used to be a building and a bridge from which to observe [the breakers coming into the cave], but it is now destroyed.
>
> Further to the left there is the Sudhana Cave, a narrow grotto; peering into its darkness, none of us was able to say how deep it was. According to tradition, the Bodhisattva shows itself in wondrous ways in these two caves. [It is said that] if one prays with deep sincerity, Guanyin can often be seen. To my regret, I am but a warrior, have not left the "burning house," and dare not speciously hope [to encounter Guanyin].

Like most pilgrims, Hou Jigao first visited the Puji Temple, the main devotional center, and then turned southeast to the Tidal Sound Cave (see Chapter 4, Exhibit 2). Only few visitors took a different way. In 1617 Lu Bao, for instance, took a slow, clockwise route around the island and reached the Tidal Sound Cave only on the sixth day of an eight-day journey.

Toward the end of the above passage, the authorial voice switches into a more private register. How are we to understand the statement that Commander Hou regrets being "a warrior" and may not hope to see the Bodhisattva? In other passages Hou speaks proudly of his military exploits. Are we dealing with a rhetorical formula employed by sympathetic Confucians? Or does the line reveal actual devotion to Buddhism? Would Hou in different times have called himself a Buddhist? As member of the military his position did not depend on the examination system and the special form of Confucian conservatism it tried to inculcate in its participants. This might have given him greater liberty in voicing support for Buddhism as long as it did not affect his loyalty and military prowess.

However, there is not much evidence elsewhere that Hou has privileged the Buddhist part of his identity. He is on the record for promoting both Daoist and Buddhist institutions on several occasions[39] but nowhere refers to himself as Buddhist. Neither does it seem that he took up a *jushi* soubriquet, as did the Yuan brothers and his fellow gazetteer editor Tu Long. Hou's main pronouncement on the subject is found in his postscript, which is translated in Chapter 1. As Sakai (2000) and Brook (1993a) have demonstrated, syncretistic ideas and rhetoric were widespread among the literati of the lower Yangzi area, and the sentiment that officialdom does preclude a more contemplative lifestyle is found throughout Chinese history.[40] Still, it is interesting to see General Hou resort to Buddhist rhetoric in his semi-private reflections. After the moment of introspection at the Sudhana Cave, his travelogue continues:

> We turned east[41] again and after three or four *li* came to what is called the Beach of a Thousand Steps. There was a monk called Dazhi who came from the Wutai mountains and took up residence here.[42] He built a hermitage called Ocean Tide. The hermitage had a high building, from where, with opened windows, it looked as if the vast ocean was just a few sitting mats away. The booming sound of the waves resonated in the steep valleys. The name of the hermitage is an allusion to the line in a Buddhist text where it says "the heavenly sound, the sound of the tide, surpasses all worldly sounds."[43] Dazhi has attained insight into the mystery and attained the teachings of the ultimate vehicle. It is fitting that he does not stay together with the average monastic, has built his own abode, and rise above beyond this world of dust. The summit behind the hermitage had a spring, and Dazhi had ordered his disciples to channel the water down through bamboo tubes. The tea prepared with this water was sweet and cooling. Slowly, the sun set, and as the evening came we returned to our boats.

The fact that the party had to "return to the boats" means that they were not staying in or near the temple compound. Hou's party, which arrived with at least one large *fu*-class war-junk, was probably too large; it might have consisted of several hundred men. Individual travelers, such as Zhu Guozhen or Zhang Dai, usually stayed in the main compound at the Puji Temple, which, like many temples, had to provide accommodation for pilgrims. Lu Bao, for instance, who during his eight-day sojourn explored the island more thoroughly than the other travelers, spent the nights in different monasteries. Commander Hou continues:

Once I obtained a painting of the Bodhisattva [Guanyin] [in the style employed] by Wu Daozi 吳道子 (c. 685–758). It was unpretentious and elegant. Recently, I got a painting [of Guanyin in the style of] Yan Liben 閻立本 (c. 600–673).[44] This one was majestic and beautiful. The two were both great calligrapher-painters of the Tang. I had [their two paintings] carved in stone. Yan's work was previously owned by the former prefect of Ningbo, Cai Xiaoqian 蔡肖謙,[45] who inscribed the Heart Sutra on it. The vice-prefect Long Defu 龍德孚 also inscribed a verse.[46] On Wu's work I have myself written a few words of praise.[47] I brought [both carvings] along and at dawn [the next day] we returned to the Puji Temple and erected the steles on the precincts of the "front hall."[48]

After that we went to the Pantuo Rock, which is flat and so broad that more than hundred people can stand on it. Perched on the stone over the ocean one can see the sun rise in the far east.[49]

West of Puji Temple steep cliffs stand together narrowly like sliding doors, the place is called Gate of Heaven. Passing through the Gate of Heaven, one comes to the "Place of Samadhi." Below it boulders were scattered, the grottoes were high and precipitous, so strangely formed that not even a master artisan could imitate them.

Deep within the temple compound there is Zhenxie's Stone. This is where the Chan master Zhenxie [Qing-] liao 真歇清了 (1088–1151) practiced the Way. Right in front of Zhenxie's Stone stands another stone, called the Stone of No-fear. Although it is square and broad, it tilts to one side precipitously and no one is able to scale it. Next to it there is the Lion's Stone. Apart from those there is Good Destination Peak, Vulture Peak, and Guanyin Peak. We viewed all of these, but could not ascend them all. This is about what Putou looks like.

In Chapter 6 we have seen that powerful visitors were often able to inscribe their calligraphy on the landscape of Mount Putuo. Such inscriptions were at times less durable than expected. In 1638 Zhang Dai was still able to visit an inscription that his grandfather had left at a pavilion near the Puji Temple sometime between 1602 and 1611.[50] Only sixty years later, after the almost complete destruction of Mount Putuo in the early Qing, the Qiu-Zhu Gazetteer laconically lists the pavilion as "destroyed."[51] The recurring cycles of destruction and rebuilding that we have outlined in the Introduction are alluded to by Hou as he continues his account:

Ah! More than a thousand years ago the Bodhisattva has miraculously manifested herself on Mei's Peak. The veneration [for this place] has grown from generation to generation. When the eastern barbarians suddenly grew restless, [however,] the region became infested by those sharks, those lizards![52]

In the end the people in charge had to remove all the statues and images, and move them to the Zhaobao Temple [in Zhenhai on the mainland]. All their huts were burned down. This must be the "great crisis" of which the Buddhists speak.

It is only due to the awesome power of his majesty the emperor and the grand secretary, and the comprehensive planning by our imperial administration that the island barbarians were exterminated, and the sea provinces were restored to order.

The Buddhadharma is forever bright; in the end, the teaching cannot be obstructed. During the turn from the Jiajing to the Longqing era [1567–1572] the monk Zhensong 真松 came from the Longshu Temple on Wutai, and greatly promoted Buddhism, reviving its highest aims.

The "eastern barbarians" of which Hou speaks in such an unflattering manner are of course his nemesis, the *wokou* pirates, against whom he battled as late as 1591.

Although in the passage above Hou directs his ire against the pirates, the actual destruction of the sites on Mount Putuo was the work of government troops. In 1557 government forces forcibly evacuated the island, destroyed all dwellings, and dismantled the temples to deny a safe haven to the pirates. In fact, not counting the "Dutch pirates" who raided Putuo in 1665, there is little evidence that "pirates" have ever attacked Buddhist establishments on Mount Putuo.

Details about all these events are scarce. The gazetteers are forthcoming with information about the periods when Mount Putuo was being revived and flourished, but much less about periods of decline. Since the responsibility for the decline lay often with the central government, it was not advisable to be all too specific.

Accordingly, Hou's account does not go into details as to why there was almost no activity on Mount Putuo before 1572. The passage "in the end [the Buddhist] teaching cannot be obstructed" (*jiao bu zhongpi* 教不終否) is a verbatim quote from a stele inscription by Wang Tang 汪鏜 (1512–1588) on the reestablishment of the Puji Temple.[53] The monk Zhensong arrived on Mount Putuo between July 1572 and February 1573.[54] He petitioned the central government to reopen the island for worshippers that Buddhism could prosper again. Only after he gained permission to rebuild the main temple could monastics return to Mount Putuo, and the site started to flourish again. Writing only fifteen years later, in 1588, Commander Hou continues:

In recent years Buddhist activity on the island is several times what it was before. Moreover, last winter her majesty, our saintly mother, the Empress Dowager Cisheng, had Buddhist sutras printed, images gilded, and temple flags embroidered. The [palace eunuchs] Director Zhang,[55] and Vice-Director Meng were ordered to take the imperial edict and bestow it on this [temple].[56]

How wonderful to see the brilliant orders all carved on superb stone, guarding the temple's entrance and the peace of future generations!

Nevertheless, the prudent and profound lessons of the wise remind us to be constantly vigilant.[57] Even though these days under our brilliant ruler and able ministers, peace reigns from South to North and all the regions are free of worries in a time of civil, cultivated governance, since my family has received the kindness of our country, to be entrusted with military duties, how could I not be diligent and alert! The nation maintains soldiers for the sake of the people and from morning to evening I work relentlessly in order not to fail carrying out this intent.

The Grand Coordinators[58] have ordered the realm, pacified the people, and turned this island forever into a prosperous place, in order to protect the country and shelter its people. Thus luckily, we must not feel uneasy about the resurgence of pilgrimage. [Otherwise,] had we relied on the peace [provided by others] had shrunk from our work, feared hardships and dodged our responsibility, we would have been at fault.

On April 2nd 1588 we set out again on the ocean and reached Taohua Island. I wanted to visit the spot where An Qisheng[59] practiced inner alchemy, but none of those who came along knew where it was. So we took a fast brig, and toured the sea beyond the islands before we returned [to Taohua].

In the middle of the night suddenly wind rose and rain started to fall. It did not stop until [the next morning] April 3rd, and our war ship sat on the heaving waves like a little duck. The others ate, but the food quickly came up again.[60] I helped myself to more. Later at night the winds calmed down somewhat. I had to attend to some matters and desired to return to my office. Therefore I parted with Master Wu and on April 4th, before sunrise, gave orders to set sail. My marines warned me: "The winds are not advantageous, please let us wait a while." I said: "Just go ahead," and we left. In the early morning the winds indeed quickened and before midnight we arrived in Zhaobao. From Taohua to here, it is more than 400 *li*!

On the 5th I went to my district office in Zhenhai. Once the people in front of the hall [that were waiting for an interview] had been dealt with, I took up my brush to write this *Account of a Journey to Mount Potalaka*. This written in [the sixteenth[61]] year of Wanli—with the cyclical characters *wuzi*—on the tenth day of the third month of spring.[62]

Commander Hou returned to the island again the following year, and there were probably further visits as he stayed in command of the regional navy for some time. Like Tu Long, his collaborator on the gazetteer, he stayed in touch with the monastic establishment of Mount Putuo, the place that conjoined his military duties with his religious and cultural interests.

Exhibit 3: Xiancheng's "Knowing the Paths of Pilgrimage" (1826)

In the introduction to this chapter we remarked on the absence of travelogues for the time between 1714 and 1895. That pilgrimage, at least to Mount Putuo, declined during the nineteenth century is not surprising. After 1794 numerous uprisings against the weakened Qing dynasty made travel difficult and at times impossible.[63] However, it seems that even before, during the eighteenth century, when the major pilgrimage routes were reopened, pilgrimage to Mount Putuo experienced a relative decline. This is implied by Ruhai Xiancheng's 如海顯承 (d.u.) "Knowing the Paths of Pilgrimage" (*Canxue zhijin* 參學知津 (1826)), a route book detailing fifty-six pilgrimage routes throughout the empire. The highly informative *Canxue zhijin* provides a rare view of how Chinese Buddhists traveled in the late eighteenth and early nineteenth centuries.[64] It lists, for instance, many routes centered on Mount Jiuhua, which became a popular pilgrimage site only in the Ming. Mount Putuo, on the other hand, plays a very minor role. Of the fifty-six pilgrimage routes described in the *Canxue zhijin*, Putuo is only mentioned as one of the stations on the route from Hangzhou to Mount Tiantai:

From [Ningbo's] Taohua ferry station sixteen *li* to Daguankou of Zhenhai district. In the city there is the Zongchi Temple with the Haiyun'an compound.[65] If the pilgrims cannot leave [by boat that day] because of adverse winds or tides they can eat in the Zongchi Temple. Leaving by the Mount Zhaobao estuary, and passing through the Junshui Sea [south of

Zhoushan] one comes to Shenjiamen in Zhenhai district. From there one crosses the Lianhua Sea to the "White Lotus Mountain," i.e. Mount Putuo. From the pier it is three *li* to the 'front temple,' the Puji Temple. There one can ask for a 'gold stamp' [pilgrimage token[66]]. After three *li* one comes to the 'back temple,' the Fayu Temple, where one can ask for a 'jade stamp' and pay respect to the Pearl-jewel Guanyin [image]. After three *li* one comes to the Huiji Temple on Buddha-peak Mountain, where one asks for a 'jade stamp'. From there one proceeds to the Brahma Voice Cave where one pays respect to the true body of Guanyin and then visits Luojia Cave, the Flying Sand Cave, the Mañjuśrī Cave, the Sudhana Cave, the Dawn Cave, the Purple Bamboo Grove, the Peach Blossom Cave and the Pantuo Rock. The *Avataṃsaka Sūtra* says that when Sudhana visited the Bodhisattva he first saw her on this stone.[67]

In the early nineteenth century the standard pilgrimage route had changed considerably from the days of Hou Jigao. While in 1589 visitors went to the Tidal Sound Cave after paying their respect to the Buddha in the Puji Temple, in 1826 they had to visit two more temples first before touring the numinous sites. Once in the north of the island the Brahma Voice Cave was visited before the Tidal Sound Cave. Although the Tidal Sound Cave is traditionally the most important site, the *Canxue zhijin* does not accord it any special status:

> [. . .][One continues to] The Zhenxie Hermitage, the Wuwei Stone, the Lion Cliff, the Vulture Peak, the Tidal Sound Cave, and the Guanyin Leap. This place is to the right of the Purple Bamboo growing at the Purple Bamboo Grove [Temple], which is right of Meihua Stone]. [Then there is] the Two-Frogs-Listening-to-the-Dharma [Stone] and the Paying-Respect-to-the-Sea-God [Stone]. There is no need to explain where these are, once on the island one can ask people and will find them easily.

We have remarked on the increasing influence of the Fayu Temple and the Brahma Voice Cave in Chapter 4. One reason for the shift was a change in the recommended pilgrimage route: as the temples were to be visited first (in the order: Puji, Fayu, and Huiji), visitors were drawn north. From there the logical route back south was by visiting the numinous sites on the eastern shore from north to south, which Xiancheng duly lists, starting with the Brahma Voice Cave.

Xiancheng wrote mainly for his fellow monastics and *Canxue zhijin* is a unique and original work that provides insight into monastic pilgrimage in late imperial China. Monastic pilgrimage was, at least in theory, less concerned with sacred sites than with traveling from monastery to monastery to meet masters and improve one's meditation. The term for this type of monastic travel for study is *canxue* 參學 or *xingjiao* 行腳, rather than *chaoshan* 朝山, although both terms were used. Monks on *canxue* would visit holy mountains for their scenic beauty as well, and at least some lay visitors on *chaoshan* would have heard sermons from the resident monks and asked questions.

We do not know how many monks actually went on pilgrimage during spring and fall, but the practice existed and, in principle, stood open to all members of the Sangha. As part of monastic practice, pilgrimage was regulated by the Vinaya. For a Chinese monk in the nineteenth century, the main rules regulating pilgrimage were contained in the *Fanwang jing* (T.1484). Precept 37 of the minor vows stipulate what items a bodhisattva-traveler may carry:

[Precept 37.] How a Bodhisattva must act regarding the two *dhūtāṅga* periods [of travel in spring and fall].

[At all times] should the Bodhisattva use a willow twig [for cleaning one's teeth], soap, the three robes, a water bottle, a begging bowl, a mat, a staff, an incense burner, a basket for the incense burner, a water strainer, a handkerchief, a razor, a flint stone, pincers, a hammock, *sūtra* and *vinaya*[68] as well as Buddha or Bodhisattva images.[69] Wherever the Bodhisattva goes on his travels during the *dhūtāṅga* periods, be it a hundred or a thousand miles, he should always have these eighteen items with him. During the *dhūtāṅga* periods which last from the fifteenth of the first month to the fifteenth of the third month [in spring,] and from the fifteenth of the eighth month to the fifteenth of the tenth month [in autumn] he should always have these eighteen items with him, like a bird has its two wings.[70]

The *Fanwang jing* was (and is) an influential apocryphon, which presents a set of Bodhisattva vows that are taken by monastics and lay practitioners alike. It is likely that most monks on pilgrimage did indeed carry all or some of these eighteen items. Precept 37 also contains prohibitions against traveling dangerously:

[. . .] During *dhūtāṅga* periods one should not enter any dangerous places, such as bad countries,[71] countries with a bad king, very high or low places, places with dense forest; one has to avoid all dangerous places [where there could be] lions, tigers, wolves, the dangers of water, fire or wind, of bandits and snakes on the road.

After commenting on the Vinaya prescription regulating monastic travel, Xiancheng quotes the *Gandhavyūha sūtra*. The *Gandhavyūha*, besides being a foundational text for Mount Putuo, is one of the main canonical sources for the practice of pilgrimage in Chinese and Tibetan Buddhism. At his 50th station young Sudhana meets Śrīsambhava and Śrīmati, who share their insight in the "illusory nature of all abiding."[72] Xiancheng quotes the part of their conversation that exhort the pilgrim to continue his journey: "May you never tire of visiting good friends, may you never weary of asking them [about the dharma]."[73]

Xiancheng also includes a ten-point essay of his own in which he outlines ten "principles" for Buddhist pilgrimage. The "Ten Principles of Mountain Pilgrimage" (*Chaoshan shiyao* 朝山十要) provide a glimpse of what it meant for a monk to go on pilgrimage in early nineteenth-century China.[74] The text is written from a monastic perspective on religious travel and complements the travelogues written by the literati travelers. The first principle again takes recourse to the *Avataṃsaka*:

[1.] Mountain pilgrimage gives an orientation to the itinerant student. One becomes an itinerant student in order to learn about the ways of the world. As soon as one leaves one's door, one will encounter sorrow and delight, fear and compassion, anger and desire as matters advance more or less smoothly. Even in old times on Sudhana's southward journey, when he visited King Tireless and the Brahmin Utmost-heat, doubts arose in him [about the quality of these "good friends"].[75] How much less so can this be avoided today, in the latter days of the Dharma.

Monks rarely traveled in larger groups or joined lay pilgrimage groups, but neither were they required to travel alone:

[2.] [. . .] If one is traveling with others, to avoid being alone, one should do with one or two to cope with emergencies such as sickness or robberies. Also when one encounters steep crevices or darkness one can assist each other. It should, however, be someone whose mind is firmly established in the Way. This is what is called "When traveling afar, one relies on good friends." "Choosing what is good in people and following that," one becomes "spiritual friends on the same pilgrimage."

Quite the guidebook author, Xiancheng advises the traveler to plan their journey well:

[3.] Before setting out on a mountain pilgrimage one should first learn about the important places of practice. Once one has decided on a route one should stay the course and be committed to it. Some first go to this mountain, then to another mountain. If one does not establish an itinerary and just wanders hither and thither, eastwards in the morning, at nightfall to the west, this is but distracted, idle wandering. [. . .]

Still, Xiancheng allows for a degree of flexibility. If one hears about a teacher while on a journey, one is allowed to change one's route to visit him. The "Ten Principles" include a rare passage that mentions the difference between lay pilgrimage and monastic pilgrimage from the perspective of the Sangha. Interestingly, it is about an utterly material concern: the availability of accommodation. Xiancheng gives detailed instructions of how a monk on pilgrimage was to ask for shelter in the guest quarter of a monastery:

[6.] Going on mountain pilgrimage there is a difference between monks and lay persons. When lay people go on pilgrimage they have ample travel funds, and can readily find shelter. If monastics go on a pilgrimage, their travel funds are meager. [We] can only register in the guest quarter of monasteries. Every time one applies one has to engender a humble and demure attitude. [. . .] If things work out and host and guest get along, one should count oneself lucky. If there is no karmic connection and one is not allowed to take up residence, one must not give rise to anger. Whether it is already after dark, or raining, or the way is still long, one must ask gently for the other's compassion. If in the end one may not stay, one should ask where else one could find shelter. One must persevere and try another place. Under no circumstance is one allowed to become angry and use abusive language, thus harming one's own virtue by trying to sway someone's mind.

As for their provisions, in case one was not able to reside at a monastery or a hostel, monks were allowed to beg:

[7.] Whether one comes to a place which welcomes everybody, or where there is a lot of hustle and bustle and monks are not properly provided for, we [monks] should always adapt to circumstances and not criticize others for not acting in the spirit of the Way. In the villages and hovels that one passes, some will be too poor to make offerings, some might not be believers or merciful, so that one cannot obtain the provisions. But one should never say anything about people not making offerings. If one cannot do otherwise one has to beg at the roadside. It is said: "With one bowl receiving rice from a thousand families, one can wander alone ten-thousand *li*." This is the true style of Buddhist life. It is no cause for shame. The Sanskrit word *bhikṣu* means 'beggar' after all. Inwardly begging for the Dharma to nurture one's nature, outwardly begging for food to nurture one's body. [. . .]

Guest quarters at Buddhist institutions were not the only option for a traveling monk. Buddhist pilgrims were also able to find shelter at local temples and shrines, many of which would have been closer to Daoist ritual practices than to Buddhism. Even if not at Mount Putuo, at many other sacred mountain sites Buddhism shared space with Daoist and folk religious temples and deity shrines. Here, too, traveling monks were allowed to take shelter, if they kept the peace and did not complain about the food:

[8.] You should know that temples and shrines were erected to venerate the Buddhas or deities, they were not put there because of our coming. The food at these places is first of all offered to the Buddhas and immortals and only secondly to the people who stay there. [. . .]

[9.] On a mountain pilgrimage one finds that places where Buddhist and Daoists reside are both on the same famous mountains. The oldest gate is usually called the 'Mountain Gate.' Some buildings are the great temples of famous mountains, some are small hermitages, or Daoist shrines and temples. At all places providing food and shelter [for pilgrims] one should not be picky and award them all full respect and reverence. If there is even a little disregard or arrogance, it will be difficult to have any numinous resonance. In all matter such as recitation, contemplation, maintenance duties, and eating, one should follow the customs of the place. One has to do what everybody else does and may not say: "I am tired from my pilgrimage" and be lazy.

Xiancheng's discussion of monastic pilgrimage, though structured and normative, conveys a lively impression of a monk's life during a journey. His last point admonishes the pilgrim not to break any precepts, especially not to steal: "If there is only a small breach in this regard and one breaks the precept [against not stealing] and soils the reputation [of the Sangha].

Moreover, it makes things difficult for later pilgrims." Pilgrimage travel freed the pilgrim from the tight supervision of their monasteries or homes, but the road offered a degree of freedom as well as temptation.

Conclusion

There are hundreds of poems written on the occasion of a visit to Mount Putuo. Compared to these, travelogues are rare. The prose accounts, however, are less stereotypical and repetitive, and the descriptions provide many details of how literati visitors interacted with the site. Travelogues usually describe pleasant trips, but not all visitors passed through Putuo in happy circumstances. The Wang Liansheng Gazetteer, for example, collects some excerpts from the diary of Chiang Ching-kuo (1910–1988), written during two short stays on Putuo in the fateful year of 1949. Chiang describes his father Chiang Kai-shek "drinking late at night alone on deck with only the moon his company."[76] The passage of Chiang Kai-shek during his retreat, when some monks were pressed into his army and had to follow him to Taiwan, occasioned neither a stele inscription nor a travelogue.[77] Nevertheless, it is documented in the most recent gazetteer, which collects a number of other travelogues from the early twentieth century.

After its "late Qing revival" in the 1870s, the twentieth century started well for Mount Putuo. Foreign travelers like Boerschmann (1911), Johnston (1913), and Crow (1921) report it in good shape. In the 1920s Clara Ho visited the island and left the first travelogue by a women author.[78] Ho's account is upbeat. She praises the scenery by quoting a number of poems and comments on how well the site has been maintained.

The twentieth century, however, eventually turned on the island, as it did on many other religious sites in China. In the Wang Liansheng Gazetteer the difficult times are documented by an absence: no texts were collected for the period between 1963 and 1993. As De Bruyn noted in his discussion of gazetteer writing, "under a political regime, dominated by strong and perhaps tyrannical power, the unsaid is mostly that what cannot be said."[79] Thus, like the other genres collected in the gazetteers, the travelogues trace the changing fortunes of the site and show how developments on the national and regional level affect local communities.

Conclusion

GAZETTEERS DO NOT REALLY conclude. The compilation ends when the compiler, for whatever reason, decides to stop compiling and hand the work off to whomever commissioned it. Having collected what they wanted to collect, at times they recorded afterthoughts in short postscripts (*ba* 跋 or *houji* 後記). I too will be short.

Things Learned

What the lens of the gazetteers brings into focus in the case of Mount Putuo is that its cycles of decline and revival were caused by political interventions rather than by long-term social change. For the last thousand years Chinese Buddhists have always been ready to go on pilgrimage to Mount Putuo. Buddhist monastics, too, never wavered in their commitment to inhabit and maintain the site. Disruptions were mainly caused by political developments, which affected the flow of pilgrims and therefore the support for institutions on Mount Putuo. The ocean embargoes of the early Ming and Qing, the decline of the site in the mid-nineteenth century, and even the destruction during the Cultural Revolution were never aimed specifically at Mount Putuo but resulted from a failure of governance in the maritime borderlands of the Zhoushan archipelago.

The inquiry into how different genres have shaped the textualization of the site has thrown light on a number of developments. Not surprisingly, the gazetteers repeatedly emphasize the importance of local literati and monastic elites (Chapters 1 and 5) for Buddhist institutions. What is new in the case of Mount Putuo is the prominent role of military officials for its revivals during the Ming and Qing. Future research may be able to reveal whether the high level of military involvement was limited to Zhejiang and Fujian or whether it was a nationwide phenomenon. Maps and pictorial depiction (Chapter 2), in the case of Mount Putuo at least, become successively more "scenic" over time, and this move from panoramic to scenic programs was prefigured in the poetic treatment of Mount Putuo. During the late Ming and Qing, in images as well as in poetry, the mountain was textualized as a series of views. Analogous to the division of the Ming-Qing novel into short episodic chapters, this move reduced the growing complexity of information about the site by imposing structure and order. Miracle tales and foundation legends (Chapter 3) were continuously added to gazetteers. It speaks to the strength of the agnostic gazetteer form, with its roots in administrative record-keeping, that even today it manages to include the most recent sightings of the Bodhisattva. More than any other genre, the miracle tales attest to the continued religious vitality of Mount Putuo. Similarly, the role of inscriptions (Chapter 6) has proven to be a constant. In their dual function as record and protective ward, inscriptions were written on the landscape of Mount Putuo throughout its history. What has changed since the Song is that officials have largely lost the freedom to assume a Buddhist identity in their writing.

Whereas some of the genres reflect patterns of continuity below the veneer of events, a closer look at the inventories of places (Chapter 4) reveals the self-reflexive, fractal way in which self-similar copies of places are created and moved about. Against such an analytic, outsider's perspective on the site, the literary record (Chapters 7 and 8) maintains a more intimate view of how elite travelers experienced the site during their visits. Literati impressions of Mount Putuo were couched in Daoist as well as in Buddhist imagery, and increasingly the panoramic view of the poem cycle gives way and the island dissolves into a series of scenic sketches. Although elite travelers were relatively few in number, it is their texts that the gazetteers collect, and thus their experience is privileged over that of the average pilgrim.

Things Obscured

Every focus blurs that what lies beyond itself. Foregrounding how Mount Putuo was textualized in gazetteers has meant consigning other aspects to the background. The museum metaphor narrows our gaze even further by arranging the material into "exhibits." The reason for concentrating on individual cases, rather than attempting a comprehensive historical description, is that the advantage of the vignette, so appreciated by authors in late imperial China, still holds: single events, objects, and persons afford insight by virtue of being particular and typical at the same time. The obvious weakness of such an approach is that it compounds the historian's conundrum: we can rarely be certain of how far our particulars permit us to extrapolate general trends. Although I have tried to collect exhibits that are representative of their time and genre, they do not amount to a comprehensive history of Mount Putuo, which remains to be written. Such a history would have to draw on many other sources beyond the Putuo gazetteers, especially regional archives and clan genealogies.

Another question is how far the Putuo gazetteers are representative of the format of the Chinese Buddhist temple gazetteer as a whole. Having surveyed and edited a number of Buddhist gazetteers, I am convinced that the Putuo series is fairly typical. Due to my own constraints, however, I was not able to do justice to all the topics addressed in it. The most important omission is a discussion of the sections on landholdings, taxation, local produce, and the flora and fauna of the island. These sections come with special challenges that are better addressed in separate studies.

In focusing on Buddhist gazetteers I have also neglected the gazetteers of Daoist sites and Confucian academies. The only systematic overview of Daoist gazetteers (Hahn 1997) shows a number of intriguing parallels and differences between Buddhist and Daoist gazetteers. A comparison of gazetteer traditions would reveal much about what Chinese sacred sites had in common and what features, if any, might be considered "purely" Buddhist, Daoist, or Confucian.

Another promising dimension, which I was not able to explore here, is how the Chinese gazetteer tradition compares to genres of description of sacred sites found in other Buddhist traditions. The Japanese *engi* 緣起 literature and the *tamnan* chronicles of Southeast Asia, especially, are important forms of local Buddhist historiography, and a comparison would further our understanding of how sacred sites were textualized in different Buddhist traditions.

Thus, there are many ways to go from here. In 1977, Michel Strickman deplored that "hardly any of the numerous monographs [i.e., gazetteers] on religious centres are widely accessible."[1] Almost forty years later this is no longer true, and mountain and temple gazetteers are widely available in print and online. I have just scratched the surface. There is much more to do.

CONVENTIONS AND ABBREVIATIONS

The gazetteers are cited to their most widely available edition at the time of writing. The Sheng Gazetteer is referenced to the Taishō edition of the Buddhist canon, and the Zhou and the Wang Hengyan Gazetteer to the widely available reprints in the ZFSH series. For the other Putuo gazetteers I cite fascicle (*juan* 卷) and page numbers according to the reprints in the *Putuo Gazetteer Reprint Series*. Twelve gazetteers of other famous Buddhist sites are now available in a new, improved edition as *The Zhonghua Collection of Buddhist Temple Gazetteers* 中華佛寺志叢書 (Bingenheimer 2013). Though woodblock editions of these can be found in the ZFSH, they (except the Zhou and the Wang Hengyan Gazetteer) will be cited to this new edition, which includes the page numbers of the ZFSH. The early gazetteers of the Ningbo region *Baoqing Siming zhi* 寶慶四明志 (1229), the *Dade Changguozhou tuzhi* 大德昌國州圖志 (1298) and the *Qiandao Siming tujing* 乾道四明圖經 (1169) are cited to the *Song Yuan difangzhi congkan* 宋元地方誌叢刊 edition (Taipei: Dahua 大化書局, 1987).

The names of the two major temples on Mount Putuo have changed over time.[1] To avoid confusion, I will refer to the two major temple sites on Mount Putuo as *Puji Temple* and *Fayu Temple* throughout the text, including in translations, irrespective of their actual names at the time. I will also speak of Ningbo or the Ningbo region when the texts have older names such as Mingzhou or Siming.

Where the sources give a date to the month or the day it is converted to the (proleptic) Gregorian calendar according to the Dharma Drum Time

Authority Database (authority.ddbc.edu.tw/time). Where only a lunar year is given, the main solar year is used, bearing in mind that the actual event might have occurred early in the following solar year. For example, the year Wanli 萬曆 26 appears in the text only as "1598" not as "1598–02–06 to 1599–01–26."

All translations of administrative titles, wherever possible, follow Hucker's *Dictionary of Official Titles in Imperial China* (1985). All translations from primary and secondary sources are my own where not otherwise indicated.

When speaking about Guanyin in connection to Mount Putuo I use the female pronoun, which seems most appropriate in this context. Avalokiteśvara in an Indian or Central Asian setting is referred to with "he," "his," etc. I render *dashi* 大士 (*mahāsattva*) as "Bodhisattva," not as "Great Being," to reduce complexity. In the sources both *dashi* 大士 and *pusa* 菩薩 (*bodhisattva*) are often used interchangeably as epithets for Guanyin.

The educated upper-class of imperial China, denoted by closely related terms such as *shi* 士, *shidaifu* 士大夫, *shenshi* 紳士, or *shishen* 士紳 has in English been called "gentry," "scholar-officials," or "literati." I generally use "literati," defined as people who were able to write according to occasion. "Literati" is more inclusive than either "gentry," which often implies some form of land ownership, or "scholar-official," as only very few of the educated elite actually attained government office.

Era names frequently mentioned in the text include:

Jiajing 嘉靖 (1521–1567)
Longqing 隆慶 (1567–1572)
Wanli 萬曆 (1572–1620)
Kangxi 康熙 (1654–1722)
Yongzheng 雍正 (1722–1735)
Qianlong 乾隆 (1735–1796)
Jiaqing 嘉慶 (1796–1820)
Daoguang 道光 (1820–1850)
Guangxu 光緒 (1875–1908)

Abbreviations (For Detailed Bibliographic Information of the Gazetteers on Mount Putuo, See the Introduction):

CBETA/T.	*Chinese Buddhist Electronic Text Association* edition of the Taishō Canon (Version 2011).[2]
CBETA/X.	*Chinese Buddhist Electronic Text Association* edition of the *Manji zokuzōkyō* Supplement to the Canon (Version 2011).
CBETA/J.	*Chinese Buddhist Electronic Text Association* edition of texts in the *Jiaxing zang* (Version 2011).
MFQ	*Minguo fojiao qikan wenxian jicheng* 民國佛教期刊文獻集成, (Complete Collection of Republican-Era Buddhist Periodical Literature), Huang Xianian 黃夏年 (Ed.). Beijing: 2006.
MFQB	*Minguo fojiao qikan wenxian jicheng bubian* 民國佛教期刊文獻集成. 補編, Huang Xianian 黃夏年 (Ed.). Beijing: 2007.
Putuo Gazetteer Reprint Series	*Putuo shan dianji* 普陀山典籍. Committee for the Management of the Mount Putuo Famous Site District 普陀山風景名勝區管理委員會 (Eds.). 2007. Xylographic reprints in traditional string binding and blue *han*-cases. With introduction and postscript. No ISBN.
T.	*Taishō Shinshū Daizōkyō* 大正新脩大藏經. Tokyo 1924–1934.
X.	*Manji zokuzōkyō/Wanzi xuzangjing* 卍續藏經. Tokyo 1905–1912.
ZFC	*Zhongguo fosizhi congkan* 中国佛寺志丛刊. Yangzhou: Guangling shushe 广陵书社, 2006. Compiled by Zhang Zhi 张智 et al., 130 vols.
ZFSH	*Zhongguo fosi shizhi huikan* 中國佛寺史志彙刊. Taipei: Mingwen shuju 明文書局, 1980–1985. Compiled by Du Jiexiang 杜潔祥, 110 vols.

NOTES

Introduction

1. "Temple gazetteer" is used in this book as a shorthand for local gazetteers dedicated to Buddhist and Daoist sacred sites. It thus translates *sizhi* 寺志, *miaozhi* 廟志, and *guanzhi* 觀志, but also *shanzhi* 山志 (lit. "Mountain Gazetteers"). Gazetteers describe individual or ensembles of sites, sometimes several temples on a "mountain," or a mountainous area. The gazetteers of Mount Putuo are strictly speaking "mountain gazetteers," however, "temple gazetteer" (*sizhi* 寺志) is generally used for such works in Chinese (see, e.g., the titles of the collections ZFSH and ZFC). For the translation of the term and the history of the genre, see the section "What Are Gazetteers."

2. See James Robson's description of how the Chinese sacred mountains were identified with different locations in ancient and early medieval China (Robson 2009: Chs. 1–2).

3. See Ch. 3 (Exhibit 1) for details.

4. See Kanno (2010: 76–84) for a study of the earliest available records on the foundation of Naksan in the *Samguk yusa*. Besides the Naksan on the east coast, there are two other early Guanyin/Potalaka-related sites in Korea. The Pumon Temple 普門寺 on the west coast, founded by Hoejeong 懷正 (635), and the Bori-am 菩提庵 on the south coast, founded by Wonhyo in 683.

5. There are several Fudaraku sites in Japan, the most famous being the Fudarakusan Temple in Kumano. See Kanno (2010: 329–353) for an overview of the *fudaraku tokai* 補陀洛渡海 ritual. In English there is Moerman (2007) and Hino (2012).

6. Roughly at 30° 0′ 34″ N and 122° 23′ 6″ E.

7. Due to the polysemy of the character *shan* 山, *Putuoshan* 普陀山 could be rendered "Putuo Island" as well as "Mount Putuo." I choose the latter, as its name should be understood in context with other "mountain" sites such as Wutai or Emei. The Chinese characters used to transliterate Skr. *potalaka* vary, resulting in a number of different spellings of the name: *Po-* was expressed as 補 or 普. 陀 was generally used to transliterate *-ta-*. Where not omitted altogether, 洛, 落, or 羅 were used for *-la-* and 迦 or 伽 for *-ka*. Throughout the gazetteer tradition the Chinese meaning of "Potalaka" has been glossed as *xiao baihua* 小白華 "little white flower." This error seems to have originated with the early eighth-century commentary to the *Buddhāvataṃsaka* by Li Tongxuan 李通玄

(645–740) and from there found its way into other commentaries and later into the gazetteers (CBETA/T.35.1735.940a1–3, and again (as 小白花) at 981b13–14). Possibly Li, or one of his collaborators, confused the Chinese transcription *budanluojia* 補怛洛迦 for Sanskrit *Potalaka* with the word for "white lotus" (Skt. *Puṇḍarīka*). Though quite distinct in Sanskrit, attested Prakrit forms are more similar (*Pautalaka* vs. *Pauṇḍarīka*). Following Pullyblank's (1991) reconstruction, the characters 補怛洛迦 in Chang'an Late Middle Chinese were pronounced *puə-tat-lak-kia*. However, there was little reason for visitors to Mount Putuo to suspect that the explanation of the name was spurious. Johnston (1913: 271) remarks that "The name of *Hsiao-pai-hua* is certainly an appropriate one, inasmuch as Puto [*sic*] is famous for a certain beautiful and fragrant white flower which grows wild all over the island. This flower is the *gardenia fiorida*." The etymology of the Sanskrit name Potalaka is unclear. Beal (1884: 121) derives from Skr. *pota* ("boat") + *lo(ka)* ("that which holds or keeps"), a generic name for a harbor site. A more interesting thesis has been forwarded by Hikosaka (1998), who identifies the original Potalaka with today's Mount Pothigai in the Annamalai Hills of Tamil Nadu. Hikosaka argues the older Tamil name of the mountain Potiyil is a later Tamil version of a Sanskrit-Tamil hybrid term *bodhi + il* ("place"), which was resanskritized as *bodhi-loka* or *buddha-loka*, which "might have been used as *Potaloka* in Pali and Chinese" (ibid., p. 126). The derivation of Potalaka from *bodhi-loka* is of course tempting but, in the absence of textual evidence, remains speculative.

8. The Xiamen Putuo Temple has its own gazetteer (ZFSH 63). The homonymy has led at times to confusion (see, e.g., Schlegel's (1895) impatient note).

9. See the comprehensive database of Buddhist Temples in Taiwan (buddhistinformatics.ddbc.edu.tw/taiwanbudgis/ (Jan 2015)). There is also a Putuo Temple 普陀寺 in the Haidian district of Beijing and doubtless in many other cities in China today.

10. Once introduced, Guanyin worship spread quickly in Buddhist centers in both North and South China. See Zou (2008) for an interesting geographical analysis of the early miracle tales.

11. One of the earliest studies of the maritime border land in which Mount Putuo is located is Wiethoff (1969).

12. Wu Lai's *Yongdong shanshui guji ji* 甬東山水古蹟記. Included in the Hou-Tu Gazetteer (Fasc. 3, pp. 1a–5a).

13. Shiba (1977: 392).

14. Ōba counts 548 gazetteers that were brought to Japan in the eighteenth century (Ōba 2012: 167). Next to ships from Ningbo and Nanjing, there even were a few ships that gave Mount Putuo as their immediate port of origin (Ōba 2012: 32–33).

15. Moll-Murata (2006) and other essays in Schottenhammer and Ptak (2006), as well as Schottenhammer (2009).

16. Each of the "four great and famous mountains" is considered to be the abode of a celestial Bodhisattva. Wutai is associated with Mañjuśrī, Emei with Samantabhadra, Jiuhua with Kṣitigarbha, and Putuo with Avalokiteśvara. This set of four is fairly recent and was probably not used before the mid-seventeenth century (see Pan 2000: 817–834). The earliest Putuo gazetteer to use the term was the Qiu-Zhu Gazetteer (Fasc. 2, p. 4b, s.a. ZFSH 9, p. 220). Pre-Qing sources usually speak only of "three great and famous mountains" (Wutai, Emei, and Putuo), e.g., in the *Dade Changguozhou tuzhi* of 1298 (Fasc. 7, p. 2a), an inscription of 1587 (ZFSH 9, p. 35), or the *Buxu gaosengzhuan*

補續高僧傳 dated 1647 (CBETA/X.77.1524.514b16). As Robson (2009: 54) and Hargett (2006: 159) have pointed out, there was a tradition that associated the "four famous mountains" with the four elements of Indian Buddhism (*catvāri mahābhūtāni, sida* 四大). This is also mentioned in the Putuo gazetteers (Qiu-Zhu Gazetteer, Fasc. 2, p. 4b). Considering the existence of an earlier set of *san damingshan*, however, there is no doubt that the *da* 大 is to be read 名 and not in a compound with *si* 四. The association with the four elements is clearly a later, playful reading, rather than an older tradition and did not affect the perception of the site by its visitors. At least for Mount Putuo I have found no evidence of visitors mentioning the "Famous Mount of Water" or anything similar.

17. See the dissertation by Bruntz (2014) on the religious tourism industry on Mount Putuo today, which gives an overview of the current state of the site.

18. So far this particular topographic trend in Buddhist Studies has not caught on in Chinese academia. There are regional studies of Buddhist history (e.g., Jianming He 1999, Yan 2000, Xu and Wang 2002, Daojian 2012) and some excellent studies on religious geography (e.g., the works of Zhang Weiran 張伟然), but there are comparatively few academic monographs on sacred sites (a rare example is Li 2011 on the early Buddhist history of Mount Lu). One reason for this is the enduring strength of the gazetteer format, which is still used to present the history of a site.

19. For an overview of the available corpus of Chinese Buddhist Temple gazetteers see Bingenheimer (Chin: 2010, Eng: 2012). A list of Daoist temple and mountain gazetteers has been made available online by Vincent Goossaert (http://www.gsrl.cnrs.fr/taoist-and-temple/). Bibliographic information on Daoist mountain gazetteers can also be found in the dissertation by Hahn (1997).

20. Yü (2001: 374). Strickmann (1977: 16) had earlier emphasized the importance of gazetteer literature for Buddhist and Daoist studies and expressed his hopes for a "systematic inventory and reprint program" of gazetteers.

21. "La séparation méthodologique des différentes monographies du Wudang shan comme autant de témoins privilégiés de combats et de mutations historiques spécifiques a permis de mieux cerner ces discontinuités" De Bruyn (2010:15). Like those about Buddhist sites, gazetteers on Daoist sites are still written and spin their narrative, according to their historical context (Olles 2012).

22. Sometimes written with the variant *zhi* 誌. The modern Mandarin term is *difang zhi* 地方志.

23. Other meanings, of course, are the "gazette" and someone who writes for one. The sinological usage is not listed.

24. E.g., Reiter (1980) or De Bruyn (2010).

25. De Weerdt (2003: 124), Moll-Murata (2001).

26. See Hargett (1996), Bol (2001), and Hahn (1997) on the antecedents of the gazetteer genre before the Ming and references to more extensive literature on gazetteers in Chinese. The mature form of the gazetteer, which aims to provide a comprehensive cultural description of a location, was widely adopted only after the Yuan. For the "localist turn" in Chinese historiography, which was one of the main causes for the development of gazetteers, see Bol (2003). Moll-Murata (2001) gives an excellent overview of Western, Japanese, and Chinese scholarship on gazetteers. In Chinese scholarship "gazetteer studies" (*fangzhi xue* 方志學) are an important branch of historiographic practice (Huang 1993), with its own dictionaries (e.g., Huang 1986), association (the

Chinese Local Records Association 中国地方志学协会), and journal (*Zhongguo difang zhi* 中国地方志).

27. On the production costs of gazetteers in the Ming, see Dennis (2010).

28. The most sustained study of this diachronic process is Moll-Murata (2001), who describes the relationships between eight extant gazetteers of the Hangzhou region (see esp. Tables 26 and 27).

29. Moll-Murata (2001: 219).

30. Brook (2005: 176).

31. The Chinese names for these categories vary greatly; the titles given here are examples taken from the Xu Gazetteer. They are fairly typical but by no means universal.

32. See the introductions for Vols. 1 and 2 of Bingenheimer (2013).

33. For certain approaches, it might be useful, for instance, to distinguish between early proto-gazetteers and mature gazetteers. Below I exclude some nineteenth- and twentieth-century shorter guidebooks, although they are titled *zhi* 志 or *xiaozhi* 小志 "short gazetteer."

34. I use the Taishō edition (T.51.2101), which appends a number of poems that were not collected by Sheng Ximing. Another, largely identical version is included in the *Siku quanshu*. Sheng's text is also partially included as fascicle 2 in the Hou-Tu Gazetteer, but with omissions and additions. Some of the additions are of considerable interest such as the note by Liu Renben (d. 1368) about his journey to Mount Putuo in 1355 (Hou-Tu Gazetteer Fasc. 2, p. 5b–7b).

35. According to Sheng the mantra was made popular in China by the second Karmapa Karma Pakshi (1204/6–1283), an influential propagator of Tibetan Buddhism in Yuan China (T.51.2101.1136a).

36. The Hou-Tu Gazetteer has become available in the *Putuo Gazetteer Reprint Series* (2007) from an unknown original. However, the first fascicle, containing important prefaces and maps is missing. A complete copy can be found in the Naikaku Bunko 内閣文庫 (Access No.史193–17, 漢14903) Library, Tokyo, and this is used for references to the first fascicle. The first edition is probably better dated to 1590, not 1589 as is often assumed, because the latest date found in the main text is 1590–11–26. It is the date given to Tu Long's biography of the monk Dazhi (Fasc. 3, p. 42b) and, because of the page numbering, it is unlikely that the text was added in the reprint. The Naikaku Bunko copy is of a 1598 reprint, as stated in the additional prefaces (dated 1598) by Xu Dashen 徐大紳 and Wang Ming'ao 王明鰲. Though Tu is generally credited as the main compiler, Hou initiated and actively contributed to the edition (in addition to his postscript, travelogue and poems, see, e.g., his comments in Fasc. 2, pp. 15b–17a). The reprint adds some prefaces and perhaps the set of maps (see the discussion on the maps of the Hou-Tu Gazetteer in Fasc. 2).

37. I use the Zhou Gazetteer as found in the *Zhongguo fosi shizhi huikan* series (ZFSH 8) which, according to the editorial remarks, is a reprint of an original found in the National Library, Taipei. From the ZFSH reprint there is a digital TEI edition, which is part of the *Digital Archive of Buddhist Temple Gazetteers* at Dharma Drum (http://buddhistinformatics.ddbc.edu.tw/fosizhi/).The Zhou Gazetteer is also included in the Putuo Gazetteer Reprint Series (2007) from an unknown original. It is also included in the *Siku quanshu*, and the *Siku quanshu* catalog was the first to record the discrepancy between the statement of Zhou in his preface, where he

says the gazetteer has 5 fascicles and seventeen topics (五卷十七門), and the present form of the text which has 6 fascicles (plus prefatory material) and fifteen topics. (普陀山志六卷(兩淮馬裕家藏本) 明周應賓撰 應賓有《九經考》,已著錄。普陀山在浙江之定海,是編因舊志重輯,凡六卷十五門。而應賓自序稱五卷十七門,勘驗卷帙並無闕佚, 未審何以矛盾也。(*Imperial Siku quanshu Catalog* 欽定四庫全書總目. Fasc. 76, p. 11)). Regarding the number of fascicles, what happened was probably that the poetry fascicle (Fasc. 5 in the table of contents) was divided into two fascicles (Fascs. 5 and 6), perhaps at the printer or for the reprint. This assumption is supported by the fact that fascicles 5 and 6 were both proofread by the same editors, while each of the other fascicles were proofed by a different constellation of editors. Concerning the different count of topics one can only speculate. Among the compilers' names Zhou Yingbin is only listed for fascicles 1–3, and it is therefore possible that he did not have a clear idea of the complete work when he wrote his preface, perhaps while the edition was still taking shape. It is easy to see how he could have counted seventeen instead of fifteen topics, considering the less than clear-cut hierarchy in the table of contents, between, e.g., the addendum of immortals (仙附) to the biographies of Buddhist monks or the division of the "imperial texts" fascicle into edicts and prefaces to the canon. A donation record on page 120 indicates that our copy was taken from the blocks after 1641; however, the way the page is laid out, the note could have been simply added to the woodblock. It is possible that this is the only alteration made after 1607. For a more comprehensive account of the production of this gazetteer as well as a modern punctuated and indexed edition, see Bingenheimer (2013: No. 3, xii–xv).

38. The edition used here is the 2007 reprint titled *Qing Kangxi nanhai putuoshan zhi* 清康熙南海普陀山志 in the Putuo Gazetteer Reprint Series, which was made from a woodblock print preserved in the Shanghai Library (as evident from the library's seal on the first page of Vol. 1). It is attributed to Qiu Lian on the cover but is actually the later edition reworked by Zhu and Chen. The Shanghai library copy from which the 2007 reprint is taken itself belongs to a later print run that can be dated by a set of new prefaces (the last dated to 1735) that were added for the occasion. Prefaces were often added later, easily done because pagination generally restarts with each preface. Besides the prefaces, however, the Shanghai Library copy contains some other texts, added after 1705, such as Lao Zhibian's 勞之辨 short travelogue *Duhai zhuli ji* 渡海祝釐記 (1714) (Fasc. 12, p. 47bff.) and others (cf. Hong 1984: 514). Until a copy of the original Qiu gazetteer of 1698 is found, we cannot distinguish the Qiu and the Zhu/Chen editions further. Brook (2002: No. M69) lists copies of the Qiu gazetteer at some libraries, but it is unclear whether these are the original of 1698. For our purpose "Qiu-Zhu Gazetteer" refers to the edited 1735 reprint of the material that was collected first by Qiu (until 1698) and later edited and extended by Zhu and Chen, who published their amalgamated version in 1705.

39. Among the differences seem to be additions that were made to record the donations bestowed on the temples made by the Kangxi emperor in 1703–1705 some of which are described in Ch. 5, Exhibit 3. Another addition is the section on the produce of the island.

40. The Xu Gazetteer too was reprinted in 2007 in the Putuo Gazetteer Reprint Series. The printing of the Xu Gazetteer copy used for the Putuo Gazetteer Reprint Series

is much better than that of the Qiu-Zhu Gazetteer copy. Qiu-Zhu and Xu use the same set of illustrations, but the Qiu-Zhu Gazetteer copy lacks the first two plates.

41. Like the two previous gazetteers the Qin Gazetteer is included in the Putuo Gazetteer Reprint Series of 2007. The reprint was made from an incomplete copy, however, and fascicles 5 and 6, as well as part of fascicle 4 are missing. A complete copy can be found in the collection *Zhongguo lidai guanyin wenxian jicheng* at Vol. 9: 317–761 (Fascicles 1–15), and Vol. 10: 1–425 (Fascicles 16–20), which is the edition referenced here. Brook (2002: No. M 71) lists reprints of the Qin Gazetteer as late as 1915 and 1917. The Wang Hengyan Gazetteer (p. 13) mentions another reprint in 1919 with a preface by Yinguang. The fact that the Qiu Gazetteer was reprinted several times in the early twentieth century indicates increasing interest in Mount Putuo, a demand that eventually led to the compilation of the Wang Hengyan Gazetteer.

42. Qin Gazetteer, 凡例: 3.

43. Wang Hengyan Gazetteer, p. 23.

44. I cite the Wang Hengyan Gazetteer as published in the *Zhongguo fosi shizhi huikan* series (ZFSH 9) For a more comprehensive account of the production of this gazetteer as well as a modern punctuated and indexed edition, see Bingenheimer (2013: Vol. 4-1, xii–xv). From the ZFSH reprint there is a digital TEI edition, which is part of the *Digital Archive of Buddhist Temple Gazetteers* at Dharma Drum (buddhistinformatics. ddbc.edu.tw/fosizhi/).

45. See Chen (2003).

46. According to the editorial remarks by Du Jiexiang, ZFSH 9 is a copy of the original 1924 edition. Because of this and the date of Wang Hengyan's postscript (p. 637), the gazetteer is often dated to 1924. This was indeed the year of the completion of its manuscript, but the gazetteer was probably not published until 1931 (with Guoguang 國光 publishers in Shanghai) after slight changes by Yinguang and his disciple Xu Zhijing. Brook (2002: 188) lists a 1928 edition published in Shanghai and preserved in the Tōyō bunko. To complicate matters further, the Wang Hengyan Gazetteer copy reprinted in the ZFSH is yet another edition, namely one printed 1934 in Suzhou, which contains among other minor changes some added material inserted between fascicles (pp. 80, 338, 494, 522, 556, 638).

47. British Library Access No: 15269, d. 6–12. The item contains six copies of the same single-volume work. The catalog assumes it was published in Hangzhou and dates it tentatively to the eighteenth century. It contains a set of panoramic views of Putuo and short glosses on places on the island. Brook (2002: 188) describes it as a "crudely printed short work [that] provides information on routes and tides, a list of the main sights and buildings, and a 5–page panoramic drawing of the island." It was probably sold as a relatively cheap, portable guidebook to pilgrims on their way to the island. I am grateful to Sara Chiesura for providing me with images of this item.

48. Included in the Putuo Gazetteer Reprint Series (2007). The reprint was made from a copy that was printed from "the blocks kept in the Ruifeng Hall 蕊鳳堂," the private library of the author Zhu Defeng. 1830 is the latest date mentioned in the preface. Judging from style and the fact they are not mentioned in the table of contents, the images were probably added later.

49. Included in the Putuo Gazetteer Reprint Series (2007).

50. For more on Zhu Defeng's and Shi Chenkong's works, see Ch. 7 (Exhibit 4).

51. Cresswell (2004: 7).

52. See Jones (2000: 121–131) for the history, successes, and dangers of the textual metaphor.

53. The first two of these characteristics are loosely based on concepts developed in Luhmann's system theory (Luhmann 1984 [1987], 1998). "Cumulativity" roughly correlates with the idea of "differentiation" and the "increase of complexity" in autopoetic systems (1984 [1987]: 197, 261f.; 1998: 134–144, 595–617), while "self-reflexivity" borrows from "self-reference" and "second-order observations" (especially in the sense of *Reflexion* (Luhmann 1984 [1987]: 601–602)). The idea of "lossiness" is (as "rate-distortion theory") studied as part of general information theory. Allan Grapard has discussed the textualization process under the rubrics of "the textualized mountain" and "the enmountained text" (Grapard 1989: 171–184).

54. Compare, e.g., the history of the different gazetteer series outlined in the prefaces to the twelve gazetteers of Bingenheimer (2013).

55. Counted as "texts" in this chart are units, sometimes several pages long, sometimes only two lines of verse, and usually with a title header, that are subject to "block-level" editorial intervention (preservation, addition, omission, reordering, etc.). The numbers are the output of a bibliographic database on the Putuo gazetteers created in 2010.

56. Moll-Murata (2001: 220), shows a similar pattern for the Hangzhou Prefecture gazetteers in the Ming and Qing. That series however, goes back further and shows a contraction of gazetteer size for the early Ming. This corresponds to the hiatus in religious activity on Mount Putuo at that time.

57. Moretti (2004: 102).

58. Regarding the second-order observation of first-order observations in system theory, see Luhmann (1993: 183–184 or 1998: 374, 879–880), for the function of reflexivity in social systems see Luhmann (1970). For the relationship of system theory with space and territory, see Helmig and Kessler (2007).

59. In computing, an understanding of "lossiness" is relevant in the development and deployment of compression algorithms. In general information theory the phenomenon is dealt with under the heading "rate-distortion theory" (Cover and Thomas 2006: 301–346). The field tries to understand how and how much information is lost in communication and data transformation processes. I use it here as a metaphor to highlight the information loss that occurs between gazetteer generations. This phenomenon is never addressed by the gazetteer tradition itself, where each gazetteer presents itself as cumulatively including all previous versions.

60. Ricoeur (2004: 17).

61. For a literary meditation on the former, see Borges (1944), for a philosophical one on the latter Ricoeur (2004: 412–456).

62. Park (1994: 197f.).

63. Bingenheimer (2012: 68).

64. CBETA/T.51.2101.1137c20ff.

65. Fasc. 7, p. 2a–b. All references to the early gazetteers are to their editions as included in the *Song Yuan difangzhi congkan.*

66. While on some sacred mountains, such as Nanyue, Buddhists and Daoists were co-present and interacted in "both amicable and inimical" ways (Robson 2009: 322),

in the case of Putuo there is little evidence of Daoist presence either before or after the place became used by Buddhists. There are a few place names on the island that allude to Daoist figures (Mei's Peak, Ge Hong's Well), but apart from these toponyms there is little evidence of Daoist activity on the island from the beginning of the textual tradition in the Song either in the gazetteers or official sources. This does not preclude the fact that Mount Putuo was often described in terms of the literary *imaginaire* of Daoist sacred islands such as Mount Penglai 蓬萊山(or 島) or Mount Fangzhang 方丈山.

67. Zhou Gazetteer: 389; Wang Liansheng Gazetteer: 804, 852, 1075.

68. Fasc. 20, pp. 9b–10b. The manuscript for the *Baoqing Siming zhi* was completed in 1227 and cut in 1229. An imprint of 1272 is in the National Library of China (Cao, Zhang, et al. 1990: 28).

69. *Dade Changguozhou tuzhi* (Fasc. 7, pp. 1a–3b).

70. *Dade Changguozhou tuzhi* (Fasc. 7, p. 2a).

71 A contemporary of Zhang Bangji, the emissary Xu Jing visited Mount Putuo on his way to Korea. His travelogue is translated in Ch. 8 (Exhibit 1). Another witness for the early period is a description of Putuo quoted in the *Fozu tongji* (T.49.2035.388b–c) (translated in Yü (2001: 371–372)). The quote is from the (now lost) *Caoan lu* 草菴錄 by Nanhu Daoyin (1090–1167). The *Caoan lu* must have been written between 1146 and 1167. Still another witness from the twelfth century is a description of Mount Putuo by Zhao Yanwei 趙彥衛 (*jinshi* 1163) contained in his *biji* collection Yunlu manchao 雲麓漫鈔 (1193) (quoted in the Wang Liansheng Gazetteer, p. 654).

72. Wang Liansheng Gazetteer, p. 654 (partially in the Wang Hengyan Gazetteer, p. 557).

73. Wang Jinping (2011: 172–174).

74. T.51.2101.1136a.

75. For a comprehensive overview of Yuan dynasty Buddhism, see Ren Yimin (2005).

76. The history of institutional Buddhism during the Ming is often told in terms of decline and revival. For the revival of Buddhism in the late Ming with a focus on the activities of the eminent monk Zhuhong, see Yü (1981). Brook (1993a) analyzes the changing relationship of the local gentry with Buddhism in the late Ming. Araki (1975 and 2006 [1995]) contextualizes the Buddhist revival with developments in Neo-Confucian thought. Personally, based on quantitative evidence from temple construction, ordination numbers, production of texts, and other indicators, I have no doubt that a revival took place; correlated with the increasing population figures, and a drop of these same indicators for the mid-Qing, however, this revival appears to be rather a short blip in a long-term decline of institutional Buddhism after the Yuan. The fact alone that we see stagnating numbers of Buddhist actors and textual production, in spite of a much larger population, indicates a decrease in the relative size of the Sangha in Late Imperial China.

77. Jiang (2005: see especially Articles 83, 120, and 180). In English the best overviews of Ming Buddhism are Yü (1998) and Brook (1997). A comprehensive, through rather traditional, history of Ming Buddhism is Ren (2009).

78. For a list, see Kawamura (1977: 111).

79. One early overview is Ryūchi (1939). See also He (2002 and 2007).

80. Brook (1997: 168).

81. Shen (2011: 557).

82. See Elman (1997: 76) on the "triumph of Dao Learning as state ideology" in the early Ming.

83. The "Japanese pirate" (*wokou* 倭寇) problem was first caused by the power vacuum during the protracted fall of the Yuan, with whom the Japanese had a history of conflict. It was exacerbated by early Ming restrictions placed on international and private commerce, which resulted in a long-term economic depression of the Ningbo region. Only after the restrictions on overseas trade were lifted in 1567 did the region again grow rapidly (Shiba 1977: 399ff.). In the late fourteenth century many of the official exchanges among China, Korea, and Japan express concerns about piracy (Verschuer 2006 [1988]: 110ff.).

84. Huang 1981: 163ff. By the sixteenth century the "Japanese pirates" were mainly Chinese, though this ethnic distinction probably hardly mattered to the seafaring folk of the south Chinese sea, whose identity was defined by regional and clan affiliations.

85. Wang Liansheng Gazetteer, pp. 1078–1079. On Yu Dayou, see Liu Tingyu (2012).

86. For the avenues available for a fashionable lifestyle in the late Ming, see Brook (1998: 153–237) and Clunas (1991).

87. See Bol (2001, 2003) for the changing perception of the late Ming period in historiography, the rise of local historiography, and the specific characteristics of the Confucians' "Localist Turn" in the late Ming.

88. See Smith and von Glahn (2003) for how the late Ming connects to trends that were present in the Song. For the causes of the economic contraction in the early and mid-Ming, see the exchange between Schneewind (2007) and von Glahn (2007). Evidence from religious history confirms von Glahn's diagnosis. It seems indeed that Hongwu's (and Yongle's) policies and regulations were primarily responsible for the contraction of institutional Buddhism either directly, by restricting ordination and temple construction, or indirectly, by weakening and impoverishing local elites, who otherwise could have supported local or regional institutions. The revival of religious institutions in the late Ming thus confirms the thesis of a continuation of Song-Yuan modes of development after a hiatus between c. 1400 and 1550.

89. See Chen Yunü (1995: 35–102) for a detailed analysis of the impact of Jiajing's policies, based on a wide range of sources.

90. The complex relationship between Wanli and his mother was not without friction, and support for Buddhism was one of the dimensions in which the vicissitudes of their relationship played out. See Zhang Dewei (2010) for details on the favors and dangers that court patronage brought for Buddhist monks during the reign of Wanli. Apart from being encouraged by his mother, the Wanli emperor could rely on ample precedent of imperial patronage of Buddhism in former dynasties (see Kieschnick 2003: 192–194).

91. On the role of the eunuchs in Ming dynasty Buddhism, see Chen Yunü (2001), He Xiaorong (2000), and Ma and Du (2004).

92. For a firsthand account of these negotiations, see Struve (1993: 114–121). The gazetteers remember the episode in a more legendary fashion (Wang Hengyan Gazetteer, p.188).

93. Wang Hengyan Gazetteer, p. 189. The Dutch are first mentioned in the Xu Gazetteer (Fasc. 5, p. 7b). There, in a short miracle tale, the invaders drown after having sold the stolen images in Japan. Butler's (1879: 114–115), and Johnston's (1913: 344ff.)

more detailed accounts of the raid and how the Dutch came to steal a large temple bell are based on the Qin Gazetteer (Fasc. 13, p. 4a–5a). The Dutch had first gained a foothold in Taiwan in 1624 and held the island as a colony for some decades until they were driven out by the Ming loyalist Koxinga in 1662. In a last attempt to gain a base in the South Chinese Sea, they reoccupied the harbor of Jilong in north Taiwan between 1664 and 1668 (Wills 2000). During this period Dutch privateers attacked ships and settlements along the coast of South China, sometimes allied with the Qing against the forces of Koxinga's son Zheng Jing (1642–1681).

94. Wang Liansheng Gazetteer, p. 1084.

95. De Bruyn 2010: 15.

96. In 2010 a forth, large Buddhist temple complex, the *Baotuo jiangsi* 寶陀講寺, was completed on the northern shore of the island.

97. Most of the information about him stems from the texts collected in the Qin Gazetteer (Fasc. 16, p. 86a). I calculate his birth year is calculated based on the title of a poem congratulating him on his sixtieth birthday (ibid., p. 88b).

98. Wang Hengyan Gazetteer, p. 23. Note also that only the Puji Temple appears in the map part of the Qin Gazetteer. The northeastern part of the island with the Fayu Temple was left out on purpose.

99. Qin Gazetteer, fascicle 3.

100. Regarding miracle stories, the Qin Gazetteer is almost completely derivative of its predecessor, the Xu Gazetteer, implying that no new visions of Guanyin were recorded between 1740 and 1832. The better edited Wang Hengyan Gazetteer (1924) includes merely seven miracle stories culled from various sources for the period between 1740 and 1898, but is unable to date them. Only for its more recent past, within the memory of its compilers, does the Wang Hengyan Gazetteer present new miracle stories prefixed by reign and year.

101. First from July 5, 1840 to March 1841, and again from October 1, 1841 to July 25, 1846. For an overview of the British movements, see Tythacott (2011: 51–64).

102. Apart from Fortune, who is cited below, see Rondot (1847) and Huc (1862 [1854]: Vol. II, pp. 232–233).

103. Fortune (1847: 183).

104. Fortune (1847: 182).

105. Fortune (1847: 181).

106. For a comprehensive account of how this ensemble came to England, see Tythacott (2011).

107. For a helpful overview article on the study of Qing Buddhism, see Qiu (2003), who estimates that there were not more than ten specialists working on this period world-wide in 2003. For the Yongzheng emperor's involvement with Chan, see Wu (2008: 163–183). His son Qianlong was much interested in Tibetan Buddhism but had little sympathy for Chan (Bingenheimer 2014: 208).

108. In the eighteenth century the basis of taxation was shifted to landholding rather than population. Thus the number of (tax-exempt) monastics became of little concern. Also in the relatively peaceful eighteenth century the demand for corvee (of which monks were exempted) was not as strong as in other periods (Wu 2008: 166 and Zelin 2002: 213).

109. For the use of the term "civil war," see Meyer-Fong (2013: 11).

110. Welch (1968), and in greater detail the excellent dissertations by Eric Hammerstrom (2010) and Gregory Scott (2013).

111. Welch (1968: 1–23, 222–253, and especially 254–271). To describe a tradition in terms of oscillating cycles of rise and decline is a common trope among historians. Traditional Chinese historiography conceives of national history in terms of the rise and fall of dynasties, but it is debatable in how far the model can be applied to religious life. By using the term "revival" with regard to Mount Putuo, I assert increased religious activity at the site after a period of relative decline. Popular sentiments toward Buddhism might not have changed much, but its local, institutional development in terms of ordination numbers, temple construction, and the production of texts can to a degree be measured and described as increase or decline. With regard to Mount Putuo, for instance, the fact that Mount Putuo was reestablished and flourished in the Wanli period, must, if anything, count as revival. For the Qing, Jiang Wu (2008) has shown how the late Ming revival of Chan Buddhism carried over into the first decades of the Qing and then failed to preserve its momentum. The revival petered out in the early eighteenth century and the production of Buddhist texts dropped accordingly. Among other problems, the Chan discourse in the seventeenth century was marked by an overreliance on textual manipulation and an idealized view of its own past. Both Buddhist and non-Buddhist circles lost interest in this form of discourse when the intellectual mood swung toward historical research and philology (Wu 2008: 245–268).

112. Crow (1921: 128) described Mount Putuo thus: "Among foreigners living in Shanghai it is known as the nearest bathing beach, to Chinese Buddhists it is the most sacred place in East China." One of the earliest "baigneurs" was Jules Arène (1875), who left a jolly account of his excursion in 1872.

113. Butler (1879: 120).

114. Johnston (1913: 316–317). Boerschmann speaks of 1500 (1911: 12).

115. E.g., along the lines of Chün-fang Yü's documentary movie "K'uan-yin Pilgrimage" (1988) or her collection of women pilgrims' songs (Yü 2001: 505–509).

116. Welch (1972).

117. Wang Liansheng Gazetteer, p. 1095.

118. Kouamé and Goossaert (2006) offer an incisive analysis of the role of the state in the recurrent vandalism of religious sites in China and Japan. (The term *vandalisme* was indeed created in the late eighteenth century to denote the destruction of religious buildings and objects by the state.) The authors propose a typology of five modes of state vandalism, some of which can be applied to the case of Mount Putuo. The late Ming evacuation and destruction of Mount Putuo might be considered a reorganization in the use of local space (*détruire pour réorganiser un espace local*, ibid., 182ff.) The Cultural Revolution, on the other hand, with its nation-wide vandalism against all religious establishments, can be understood as an attempt to redefine or reinvent the role of religion in society (*détruire pour réinventer la religion*, ibid. 204ff.). However, the destruction in the early Qing and the dilapidation in the mid-nineteenth century was a side effect to violence elsewhere. They were the result of a lack of government rather than an intentional act of state vandalism.

Chapter 1

1. See Exhibit 4 in this chapter.

2. For more on Xingtong see Ch. 5, Exhibit 3.

3. Elman (2013: 161–163).

4. Kieschnick (2003: 186).

5. The genres used by Chinese Buddhist historiographers are without exception drawn from already existing precedents. Although Buddhism strongly influenced Chinese language and literature, it did not develop a distinct way of writing history. On the use of genre in Buddhist historiography, see Schmidt-Glinzer (1982) and Bingenheimer (2009).

6. Elman (1997).

7. Elman (1997: 61). Officialdom itself was widely seen as desirable and success in the examinations was an immensely coveted aim. Even if Ho Ping-ting's statement that "Ming-Ch'ing society's one ultimate status-goal was attainable only through academic-bureaucratic success" (Ho 1964: 89) must be seen in perspective—it was, for instance, not necessarily true for religious believers—the imperial bureaucracy had certainly managed to imbue its membership with considerable prestige. Prestige aside, the landholding gentry, which produced most literati, had practical reasons to stay within the Confucian fold. The best way to perpetuate the status of the family and exercise power on a local, regional, or even national level was to secure government office for some members of the clan.

8. Araki (1975) and Chu (2010 (2011)).

9. Yuan Zongdao 袁宗道 (1560–1600), Yuan Hongdao 袁宏道 (1568–1610), and Yuan Zhongdao 袁中道 (1570–1624). On the brothers, especially Yuan Hongdao, see Hung (1997).

10. See, e.g., Kubota (1931 [1986]: 608–660), Araki (1975 and 2006), and Brook (1993a,b) for Buddhist–Confucian relations in the Ming.

11. Brook (1993a: 90).

12. For Wang Yangming's contemporary and later critics, who considered his philosophy as "tainted by Buddhism," see T'ang (1973) and McMorran (1973).

13. Even a favor like that asked of Yang Yongjian would have been remunerated in one way or another, mostly without naming a price. A similar concern with literati interests is evident in the literati interaction with Daoist sites (Olles 2003).

14. For a selection of translations of prefaces from secular gazetteers, see Moll-Murata (2001).

15. Chapter 4 of the Zhou Gazetteer (1607), for instance, contains the prefaces of the Hou-Tu Gazetteer (1590) (ZFSH 8: 312–389).

16. Bingenheimer (2013, Vols. 8, 9, or 11).

17. Bingenheimer (2013, Vol. 2: 11).

18. Bingenheimer (2013, Vol. 1: 2).

19. Bingenheimer (2013, Vol. 7–1: 3).

20. Searching the digital gazetteer corpus (buddhistinformatics.ddbc.edu.tw/fosizhi (Aug 2015)) the term 吾儒 appears in 73 out of 206 gazetteers.

21. Qiu Gazetteer (Fasc. 12, p. 34a). Written between 1695 and 1705. The phrase "generously provide for and assist others" 博施濟衆 is from the *Analects* (Ch. *Yongye*). For Kangxi's pronouncements see, e.g., Ch. 6, Exhibit 3.

22. Endorsements gave the monastery a quasi-legal backing to approach prospective donors and presumably were helpful in raising money from among the gentry. See Brook (1993a: 196–213) for other examples of such fundraising appeals.

23. ZFSH 86: 240–242. For Ye's biography see Goodrich (sub voc. 1976); on his role in late Ming politics see He (1994).

24. Huangbo, under its abbot Zhongtian Zhengyuan 中天正圓 (1537–1610), received one of only six sets that were given to various monasteries on this occasion. For a comprehensive study of Buddhism in the Wanli era, especially the roles of the empress dowager and the emperor, see Zhang (2010).

25. ZFSH 86: 241–242.

26. ZFSH 86: 264–265.

27. Cited in Peterson (1998: 753).

28. The indictment of Li Zhi (first translated by Franke [1938: 23–24]) by the censor Zhang Wenda 張問達 (d. 1625) is fiercely critical of literati families practicing Buddhism.

29. ZFSH 32: 298–302.

30. Probably the monk Dagui 大圭 (fourteenth century).

31. ZFSH 62: 4–8.

32. *Qingliang shan zhi* 清涼山志 (ZFSH 81) (1933), *Emei shan zhi* 峨眉山志 (ZFSH 49) (1934), *Jiuhua shan zhi* 九華山志 (ZFSH 77) (1938). Yinguang was also involved in the planning of the *Putuoluojia xin zhi* 普陀洛迦新志 (ZFSH 9 = Wang Hengyan Gazetteer) (1924). For the history and background of these editions, see Chen Jianhuang (2003).

33. Yinguang steered his gazetteer editions away not only from Confucian but also from Daoist influences. His edition of the Mount Emei Gazetteer explicitly extirpates material on the Daoist sites and legends contained in earlier versions (see his preface to the Emei Gazetteer, ZFSH 49: 7–8).

34. ZFSH 77: 32.

35. ZFSH 77: 31.

36. See the exchange of letters between Yinguang, Tao Yong, and Wang Hengyan in the Wang Hengyan Gazetteer (pp. 628–636).

37. Five before the main text: *Butuoluojiashan zhi xu* 補陀洛伽山志序 by Liu Shangzhi 劉尚志 (*jinshi* 1571) (dated 1589 spring second month); *Butuoluojia zhi xu* 補陀洛伽志序 by Long Defu 龍德孚 (1531–1602) (dated 1589–06–27); *Chongke Butuoluojiashan zhi xiaoxu* 重刻補陀落伽山志小序 by Xu Dashen 徐大紳 (1585–1653) (dated 1598); *Chongzi Butuoluojiashan zhi xu* 重梓補陀洛伽山志序 by Wang Ming'ao 王明鰲 (d.u.) (dated Sept.–Oct. 1598); *Butuoluojiashan zhi xu* 補陀洛伽山志序 by Tu Long 屠隆 (1543–1605) (dated 1589–06–28). Three are appended after the main text: *Butuoluojiashan zhi houxu* 補陀洛伽山志後序 by Hou Jigao 侯繼高 (1533–1602) (dated June 28, 1589); *Butuoluojiashan zhi xu* 補陀洛伽山志序 by Wang Yingtai 汪應泰 (*jinshi* 1586) (dated winter 1589); *Ba Butuo zhi hou* 跋補陀志後 by Wang Yitai 王一邰 (d.u.) (dated spring 1589).

38. Hou-Tu Gazetteer, *Tuxu* 屠序, p. 1.

39. The other two being Mount Wutai and Mount Emei.

40. *Chongxiu putuo shan zhi* 重修普陀山志 1607. 6 *juan*. Reprinted 1980 in ZFSH Vol. 9. Reprint 2007: Putuo Gazetteer Reprint Series. New edition Bingenheimer (2013, Vol. 1), with notes and indices.

41. *Chongxiu putuozhi shu* 重修普陀志敘 by Zhou Yingbin 周應賓 himself (dated May 11, 1607); *Butuoshanzhi xu* 補陀山志序 by Fan Wangjia 樊王家 (d.u.) (dated April–May 1607 "second month of summer"); and *Chongqin Butuo zhi xu* 重鋟補陀志序 by Shao Fuzhong 邵輔忠 (*jinshi* 1595) (not dated).

42. Not included are the two prefaces written by Xu Dashen and Wang Ming'ao for the reprint of 1598, as well as the postscript by Wang Yitai, the former two probably because Zhou did not use the reprint from 1598 to which they had been added. Wang Yitai's postscript is the very last text of the Hou-Tu Gazetteer and might have been missing from the copy used for the Zhou Gazetteer.

43. The phrase *gufo zailai* 古佛再來 is an epithet of Guanyin.

44. For this mistake see the section on bibliographical details of the Zhou Gazetteer in the introduction.

45. Zhou Gazetteer (pp. 3–6).

46. To Rujiong 如迥, the abbot of Puji Temple (see Ch. 7, Exhibit 3); to Xinghai 性海, who would became abbot in 1614; and to Xingbao 性寶. Zhou Gazetteer (pp. 547, 550, 572). None of these poems were included in the Wang Hengyan Gazetteer.

47. Zhou Gazetteer (p. 135).

48. See, e.g., the stories at X78n1542p101b13–101c6.

49. There was ample resistance even when Putuo was first reopened during the 1570s. Comprehensive accounts of the whole story, told here only from the perspective of what remains of it in the gazetteers, are Ishino (2005) and Xu (2007: 474–491).

50. Wang Liansheng Gazetteer (pp. 170–172) includes four memorials or prohibitions: from 1574, 1596, 1599, and 1602. Unfortunately, the source of these texts is not given. One of the authors was Fan Lai 范淶 (c. 1560–1610), identified in the 1599 document (Wang Liansheng Gazetteer (p. 172)) as Circuit Surveillance Commissioner for the navy (cf. *Mingshi* pp. 2416, 5904, 7292).

51. Wang Liansheng Gazetteer (p. 172).

52. Ibid.

53. Zhou Gazetteer (p. 183).

54. Wang Liansheng Gazetteer (p. 169).

55. Wang Liansheng Gazetteer (pp. 172–173).

56. Dudbridge (1992: 48).

57. Jiang (2005: 214ff.).

58. See, for instance, the stories collected in the *Sengni niehai* 僧尼孽海 (Rummel 1992; Huang and Blasse 1992), but also some of the tales in the popular *Liang Pai* 兩拍 collection by Ling Mengchu (Hu 2003). For an overview of the literary depiction of monastic debauchery, see Rummel (1992: 85–117) and Durand-Dastès (2002). Goossaert's (2002) analysis of anti-clericalism in a late nineteenth-century Shanghai newspaper shows that these sentiments existed at least into the late Qing. The discourse about the imagined debauchery of monastics is an example of how conservative anxiety about female sexuality is connected with worries about social control in general. As Goossaert says: "Cette altérité, cette liberté imaginée de l'autre (car en réalité rien n'est plus régulé que la vie monastique) provoque la peur d'une contagion, directe, par débauche bien sur, mais aussi diffuse, par influence."

59. Levy (1997: 263–277).

60. Dudbrigde (1992: 50).

61. These laws were echoed in administrative handbooks. See, for instance, the chapter "Prohibiting Women from Visiting Temples" in the *Complete Book Concerning Happiness and Benevolence* (Huang and Chu 1984: 608).

62. Goossaert (2002: 118); also Yü (1981: 151).

63. Goossaert (2002: 118).

64. Brook (1998: 630).

65. Wang Liansheng Gazetteer (p. 173). Stridently anti-Buddhist memorials were not uncommon in the Ming (see Noguchi 1965: 189).

66. The document is the main witness for the "Anti-Putuo faction," and it contains a number of interesting aspects not preserved in the gazetteers. Unfortunately, the edition in simplified characters presented in the Wang Liansheng Gazetteer (pp. 173–178) and the lack of references is far from satisfying, as has been remarked by Ishino (2005: 30n18), who has successfully tracked down all references. Nevertheless, it must be remembered that it is traditional for gazetteers to edit texts freely and dispense with source references. What is innovative is that documents critical of the site were included at all in the Wang Liansheng Gazetteer.

67. The temples were first desacralized by moving the Buddhist images to Ningbo's Qixin Temple 棲心寺. Tang He was not persecuting Buddhism as such. Zhou Gazetteer (p. 138).

68. Imperial forces under General Yu Dayou had regained control of Zhoushan only in 1558, after the remnants of Wang Zhi's forces had retreated south to find new bases on the Fujian coast. Even this victory was not won without intrigue and backbiting among the leaders of the imperial forces, and Yu was later accused of letting the pirates slip away (Geiss 1988: 503; Liu 2012).

69. Wang Hengyan Gazetteer (p. 452).

70. Used here like 巡撫 (see Hucker sub voc. *tu-fu* and *hsün-fu*). Yin was acting as special delegate from the central government to settle the issue of rebuilding.

71. Zhou Gazetteer (p. 463).

72. *Sansheng* 三生. A Buddhist term denoting past, present, and future lives.

73. Zhou Gazetteer (pp. 376–378).

74. Zhou Gazetteer (p. 25).

75. Zhou Gazetteer (p. 31).

76. *Yuzhi chongjian putuosi bei* 御製重建普陀寺碑. Zhou Gazetteer (pp. 53–65).

77. For a detailed overview of Ming religious government institutions and their development, see Zhao (2008: 122–144); for a chronological account of court interactions with Chinese Buddhism based mainly on the Mingshi lu 明實錄, see ibid. (pp. 145–164).

78. Page numbers for the Hou-Tu Gazetteer (postscript is inserted after Fasc. 6). Passages that are not italicized can be found in the Zhou Gazetteer (pp. 333ff.).

79. Besides Mount Wutai and Mount Emei. The set of "Four Great Famous Mountains" of Chinese Buddhism had not yet been formed, Mount Jiuhua was added only during the Qing.

80. This refers to the poems that figure so prominently in the Hou-Tu Gazetteer.

81. This summarizes the first three chapters of the Sheng Gazetteer.

82. Here Hou has *zhongshi* 中使, a mistake that Zhou corrects silently to *neishi* 內使.

83. *Haixian* 海憲. Not in Hucker. 憲 (sub voc.) is an unofficial reference to a censor. According to his preface, Liu's position was surveillance vice commissioner in 1589. The Surveillance Commission was closely associated with the Censorate.

84. Tu thus became the main compiler, but Liu and Long contributed prefaces.

85. This is quoting a passage advocating military action in the *Shujing* (Ch. Yinzheng 胤征). Legge (1865: 169) translates: "When sternness overcomes compassion, then things are surely conducted to a successful issue. When compassion overcomes sternness, no merit can be achieved."

86. Verbatim quote from Liu Shangzhi's preface (Hou-Tu Gazetteer, Fasc. 1).

87. *Jiwang* 既望, the sixteenth day of the lunar month (HDC sub voc.).

88. From the *Analects* (Ch. *Xianwen* 憲問).

89. The phrase 死有重於泰山,或輕於鴻毛 appears in Sima Qian's biography in the *Hanshu* 漢書. The idea is that those who readily sacrifice their lives when (Confucian) moral principle demands it die a meaningful death.

90. Idiomatic expression, here written 厠足 (= 廁足), which is explained in CBETA/ J.34.B296.49a13 as 側足.

91. There are two major versions of this difficult passage. I translate the text as found in the Xu Gazetteer (Fasc. 15, p. 43b), which also has been copied by Wang Hengyan (p. 481), because the Xu Gazetteer seems overall better edited. Cf. Qin Gazetteer (Fasc. 12, p. 44a).

92. *Sanshan chanshi yibo taming* 三山禪師衣鉢塔銘. First included in the Qiu Gazetteer (Fasc. 12, p. 43a).

93. De Bruyn (2010: 16–17).

94. The steles and their inscriptions are analyzed in Ishino (2010).

Chapter 2

1. Zhou Gazetteer (pp. 71–72). 古九州之域,蓋鑄諸鼎。今白華固海上靈境, 將必有天造地設者,非圖何以傳大千？ 若曰「苦海無邊， 回頭是岸」；「有形皆壞, 不爛虛空」，則何必不白華?何必白華? 此山此圖，一齊掃却! The line 有形皆壞, 不爛虛空 seems to be taken from Tu Long's *Shaluo guan qingyan* (Wang Chaohong 2012, Vol. 6, p. 541).

2. Bingenheimer (2013) Vols. 12, 1, and 6. For the close relationship between maps and landscape paintings, see Cahill (1992), who remarks that topographical paintings in China "are often more maplike than properly pictorial" and acknowledges the importance of "schemata for the representation of noted places as we can see these in local guide books" (ibid., p. 253).

3. Cosgrove (2008: 15).

4. For the history and role of cartography in East Asia, see the contributions in Harley and Woodward (1994) and especially Yee (1994b) on the close connection between Chinese cartography and the visual and literary arts.

5. Bingenheimer (2013, Vol. 2: 11). That gazetteer originally included the lavish illustrations of the *Eshan tuzhi* 峨山圖志 a late nineteenth-century guidebook for Mount Emei. The *Eshan tuzhi* is the only such work that has been translated into English. It was published 1936 as *Xinban eshan tuzhi* 新版峨山圖志/*A New Edition of the Omei Illustrated Guidebook* (ZFSH 50) in Chengdu. The translator, Dryden L. Phelps, taught at the West China Union University, a missionary university in Chengdu.

6. Another example for an illustrated guide is the *Pingshantang tuzhi* (ZFSH 40), which is not centered on one Buddhist site, but takes the reader along a tour of a waterway near Yangzhou.

7. For pilgrim maps of Mount Putuo, see, e.g., Boerschmann (1911: 15) or the specimens at the American Museum of Natural History (ASIA/0578, 70/11655), which were printed in the late nineteenth or early twentieth century (the steamboat in the lower right of 70/11655 did start to service the island only after 1875). 70/11655 is published in Poser (2010: 94) and Lucic (2015: 59). For a reproduction and discussion of ASIA/0578, see Lucic (2015: 61). Such printed and hand-colored maps were probably produced in great quantities and sold relatively cheaply to pilgrims on their way to Mount Putuo. Pilgrim guidebooks such as the *Nanhai shengjing putuoshan zhi* 南海勝境普陀山誌 in the British Museum (Access No: 15269) would have been somewhat more expensive. Similar pilgrim maps and guidebooks were available at other sites. For a nineteenth-century pilgrim map of Mount Wutai, see Chou (2007).

8. See, for example, the different maps in the later edition of the *Shang tian-zhushan zhi* 上天竺山志 (ZFC 88) the *Hangzhou shang tianzhu jiangsi zhi* (ZFSH 24) 杭州上天竺講寺志; or the different editions of the *Guangxiao si zhi* 光孝寺志 (ZFSH 85 and ZFC 160).

9. See, e.g., the numerous maps contained in the Wang Liansheng Gazetteer.

10. T.51.2087.932a14–23.Translation Beal (1884 [1983], Vol. 2, p. 233), slightly adapted.

11. T.49.2035.314b–c. On these maps, see Park (2010). For an overview of how Buddhist cosmography was mapped in China and Japan, see Wong (2008). For a discussion of an early mural "map" of Mount Wutai, see Heller (2008). For the "dozens" of general maps of the Chinese empire from the twelfth and thirteenth centuries, see De Weerdt (2009).

12. The actual location of the Malaya Mountains is probably near the Cape of Comorin, the southernmost tip of India. Beal discusses the position of the Potalaka and believes the place that Xuanzang describes from hearsay refers to Adam's Peak (Sri Pada) in Sri Lanka (Beal 1883: 338). The Chinese and Japanese cartographers imagined Mount Putuo as a different island west of what is Sri Lanka in their maps. Against this Hikosaka (1998) locates the beginnings of Potalaka on the South Indian mainland. For a summary of other theories about the original location of Xuanzang's Potalaka, see Kanno (2010: 21–22).

13. The oldest of these (dated 1364) is the "Map of the Five Regions of India" *Go tenjiku zu* 五天竺図 produced by the monk Genshunbō Jūkai 源春房重懷 (b. 1297).

14. See Moerman (forthcoming). I am grateful to Max Moerman for sharing images of rare Japanese maps and some unpublished material.

15. Cao, Zheng, et al. 1990, esp. Fig. 130 (*Fujing tu* 府境圖) and Fig. 137 (*Changhuo xian jingtu* 昌國縣境圖).

16. It is not clear under what circumstances the *Budaluo shengjing* came to Nagano; an inscription on the back dating to 1576 states the painting has been in the possession of the temple for "many years" (Ide 1996: 40). The following description of the *Budaluo shengjing* owes much to Ide's study of the work (Ide 1996). I am grateful to Liao Chaoheng (Academia Sinica, Taipei), who made a large-scale reproduction of the painting available to me. For more examples of map-paintings, see Yee (1994b: 147ff.). For a discussion of a topographic painting of the Guanyin site at Kumano, see Moerman (2005: 24–41).

17. Okasaki (1977: 80–82) mentions several such paintings that are owned by Japanese temples. None of these, however, show the Mount Putuo near Ningbo.

18. Ide (1996: 46) points out the influence of contemporaneous maps on the unusual composition and the depiction of landscape and ocean.

19. Ide (1996: 41). There is a typo giving 1269 instead of 1369 for the second year of Hongwu. One label on the *Budaluo shengjing* contains the place name Changguo Prefecture 昌國州. In the second year of Hongwu Changguo was demoted to district status (*xian* 縣).

20. The legend that connects Somachattra to the Willow-branch Guanyin is told in the *Qing Guanshiyin pusa xiaofu duhai tuolounizhou jing* 請觀世音菩薩消伏毒害陀羅尼呪經 (T.20.1043.34b–c). In the Ming and Qing the Dragon Girl and Sudhana eclipsed all other pairs of attendants for Guanyin. Before that Sudhana was sometimes combined with other figures. Somachattra and Sudhana as Guanyin attendants, however, are attested for Song China (Foulk 1993: 170) and early Edo Japan (Mujaku Dōchū and Murata (1909 [1715]: 512). A thirteenth-century statue of Somachattra as attendant of Guanyin that was brought from the Ningbo area and perhaps from Putuo is preserved in the Sennyū Temple in Kyōto (see the essay by Nishitani in Nara Kokuritsu Hakubutsukan 2002: 100, 260–261, 303). Another attendant pair that lost traction in later imperial China is that of Sudhana and Elder Daquan (see Ch. 3, Exhibit 2).

21. *Dade Changguozhou tuzhi* (7: 2a).

22. Ide (1996: 45) identifies the iconographic type as "Lotus Boat Guanyin" (*lianzhou guanyin* 蓮舟觀音).

23. Zhou Gazetteer (p. 155). Qiu-Zhu Gazetteer (Fasc. 3, p. 11b).

24. CBETA/T.9.262.57c5–6.

25. CBETA/T.51.2101.1138.a27. Prince Xuanrang was a grandson of Kublai Khan. His gift is only one example of the imperial patronage of Mount Putuo under the Yuan.

26. See Hou Jigao's travelogue (Ch. 8, Exhibit 2).

27. To the west of the Fenfeng Stūpa, the *Budaluo shengjing* shows a smaller stūpa called Duobao Stūpa, which was not rebuilt in the Ming. Both its position (west of the main gate of Puji) and its form make it unlikely that this was the stūpa associated with the Prince of Xuanrang.

28. In 1369 Changguo, which is referenced on the *Budaluo shengjing* as "prefecture" (*zhou* 州), lost its prefecture status (Ide 1996: 41).

29. Wang Liansheng Gazetteer (p. 134).

30. The first photo of the stūpa was published by Shufeldt (1899: Fig. 4). Boerschmann's picture is clearer (1911: Plate 6), but his estimate for the height of the stūpa (31m) is widely off the mark (Boerschmann 1911: 27) (perhaps a printing mistake for 13m).

31. Wang Hengyan Gazetteer (p. 475).

32. Wang Liansheng Gazetteer (p. 134).

33. T.51.2101.1136c02.

34. As mentioned in the introduction, the first fascicle, which contains the maps, is taken from the Naikaku bunko copy of the Hou-Tu Gazetteer, which was printed around 1600.

35. Pregadio (2008: sub voc.). The Three Officials were an important motif in Daoist art (Huang 2001 and 2012: 292–340). Their popularity in South China in the late Ming is also attested by the fact that they are mentioned prominently in the first European history of China (Mendoza 1586: 35–36).

36. Zhou Gazetteer (p. 117).

37. Huang (2012: 318–325). The idea of "crossing the ocean" *(duhai* 渡海*)* is connected to "crossing to the other shore" *(du. . . bi an* 度/渡. . .彼岸*)*, a common Buddhist metaphor for salvation.

38. Robson (2011).

39. Robson (2009: 322).

40. Robson (2011: 97).

41. Bingenheimer (2015).

42. See Boerschmann (1911: 194) for a picture and description.

43. It is also possible that the names refer to two different adjacent piers.

44. Edicts ordering coastal bans were issued relatively frequently between the fourteenth and seventeenth centuries.

45. The Korean connection is remembered in a minor place name, though: the "Silla Reef" shown east of the island on the Hou-Tu maps. On this see Park (2003).

46. T.51.2101.1136b21.

47. Wang Hengyan Gazetteer (p. 108).

48. In late imperial China, Sudhana and the Dragon Girl were firmly associated with the legend of Miaoshan and associated with Mount Putuo. See de Groot's telling of the story (1886: 193–197).

49. See Idema (2008: 161–189) for the story of Sudhana and the Dragon Girl as it appears in *baojuan* literature. On references to Mount Putuo, see especially pp. 162, 168, and 182–183.

50. Even the maps in the Hou-Tu Gazetteer were not drawn to scale, however. Gazetteer maps before the Qing rarely were "intended for presenting quantitative information" (Yee 1994a: 91).

51. The printing of the copy available to us is not of sufficient quality to allow for reproduction here. They can be found online (buddhistinformatics.ddbc.edu.tw/fosizhi).

52. Except No. 14, the second half of which was left empty or is missing in the Zhou Gazetteer (after p. 101).

53. *Jizushan zhi* 雞足山志 (1692: 53–60), *Huayin shan zhi* 華銀山志 (1865: 46–49). See buddhistinformatics.ddbc.edu.tw/fosizhi.

54. A close relationship between poetry and visual arts can also be observed at other famous sites (Cahill 1992: 281).

55. Qiu Gazetteer (Fasc. 10, p. 13a–b).

56. Guanyin is here given the epithet "Buddha" instead of "Bodhisattva." This common usage can be observed elsewhere in canonical literature as well as the gazetteers. In iconography too Guanyin is at times treated equivalent to a Buddha (Yü 2001: 77). This is mostly based on the encounter of the Bodhisattva with the Buddha Guanshiyin as told in the Chinese *Śūraṅgama Sūtra* (starting at T.19.945.128b15).

57. The name *Duangu daotou* 短姑道頭 means literally "Pier of the Rebuked Younger Sister-in-Law," below shortened to "Pier of the Sister-in-Law." The legend here is told according to the Wang Hengyan Gazetteer (p. 180).

58. The Xu Gazetteer (Fasc. 5, p. 5a) includes the tale as the last story in the section of Yuan dynasty miracle tales.

59. Wang Hengyan Gazetteer (pp. 516, 518).

60. The Qiu-Zhu Gazetteer also contains the first entry for the Brahma Voice Cave and mentions the "endless prostrations" devotees practiced there (Qiu-Zhu Gazetteer, Fasc. 2, p. 13b–14a).

61. Wang Hengyan Gazetteer (p. 96).

62. Qiu-Zhu Gazetteer (Fasc. 10, p. 14b).

63. Zhu (1619 [1991]: Fasc. 26, p.14a).

64. Wang Liansheng Gazetteer (p. 419).

65. T.51.2101.1139c5.

Chapter 3

1. See Exhibit 4 of this chapter.

2. Guanyin miracle tales are well studied, and especially the work of Robert Campany (2012) absolves me from saying more about the history and characteristics of the genre. Concerning the term "miracle," although like many English words first used in a Christian context, I agree with David Fiordalis that it is a viable term for the study of Buddhism (Fiordalis 2008: 1–9). See also Campany (2012: 15n58).

3. Bingenheimer (2013, Vol. 1: 155–173).

4. Bingenheimer (2013, Vol. 7-1: 20–40, 104–110).

5. Bingenheimer (2013, Vol. 6: 281–291 (Buddhist), 292–298 (Daoist)).

6. The last miraculous incident in the Mount Jiuhua Gazetteer (1938), for instance, is dated 1931, while the last miracle tale in the Mount Huangbo Gazetteer (1824) is dated 1654.

7. Bingenheimer (2013, Vols. 8 and 9).

8. In Chinese and Buddhist studies, in lieu of a better term, *ganying* is often translated as *stimulus-response* or *sympathetic resonance*. See the overviews in Sharf (2002: 77–133) and Birnbaum (1986: 134–137); for *ganying* as pertaining to miracle tales, see Yü (2001:153–158) and Campany (2012: 49). For studies and translations of early Guanyin miracle tales, see Campany (1996), Rice (2008) and Yü (2001: 163–173). The early history of the notion in China until the second century has been studied comprehensively in Le Blanc (1979). Closely related and virtually synonymous to *ganying* is the term *gantong* 感通, the notion that phenomena mutually affect (*gan*) each other and reach into, communicate with, or penetrate (*tong*) each other.

9. The closest South Asian relative of *ganying* is the "Act of Truth" (Skt. *satyakriyā*, Pāli *saccakiriya*), but South Asian Buddhism deals with miraculous events in a different key. For miracle tales in Indian Buddhist literature and associated reasoning, see the comprehensive treatment by Fiordalis (2008). For *satyakriyā*, see esp. pp. 101–107.

10. These early supernatural tales appear in various places. Zou Yan 鄒衍 of Qi is found in the *Liezi* (Ch. *Tang Wen* 湯問). Duke Yang of Lu 魯陽 is from the Huainanzi (Ch. *Xianmingxun* 覽冥訓).

11. Bo Juyi ([1979], Vol. 3: 998).

12. I am using "apparition" or "vision" throughout this chapter, preferring them slightly over "manifestation," "appearance," or "epiphany." The original semantics of "epiphany," the appearing (gr. *epiphaneia*) of a divine being, would have been an ideal fit, but the word has come to mean different things in our time.

13. Yijing, *Xici* 繫辭 commentary, Part I, 10.

14. Teiser (1994: 62) comments on how Chinese Buddhism had to "look" both "westward" to India and "to the east" in the use of foundation texts for the concept and practice of the Ten Kings of Hell.

15. Läänemets (2006: 302ff.) believes that the relatively minor role of Avalokiteśvara in this text is due to the fact that the *Gaṇḍavyūha* was composed before his cult became widespread. The *Gaṇḍavyūha* circulated originally independently but in the versions available to us (Sanskrit, Chinese and Tibetan) is part of the *Buddhāvataṃsaka*.

16. Skr: *atha khalu sudhanaḥ śreṣṭhidārako [. . .] anupūrveṇa yena potalakaḥ parvatastenopasaṃkramya potalakaṃ parvatamabhiruhya avalokiteśvaraṃ bodhisattvaṃ parimārgan parigaveṣamāṇo'drākṣīdavalokiteśvaraṃ bodhisattvaṃ paścimadikparvatotsaṅge utsasaraḥprasravaṇopaśobhite nīlataruṇakuṇḍalaka jātamṛduśādvalatale mahāvanavivare vajraratnaśilāyāṃ paryaṅkaṃ baddhvā upaviṣṭaṃ nānāratnaśilātalaniṣaṇṇāparimāṇabodhisattvagaṇaparivṛtaṃ dharmaṃ deśayamānaṃ sarvajagatsaṃgrahaviṣayaṃ mahāmaitrīmahākaruṇāmukhodyotaṃ nāma dharmaparyāyaṃ saṃprakāśayantam* [Gaṇḍavyūha sūtram Ch.30 (Text: Digital Sanskrit Buddhist Canon Version (http://www.dsbcproject.org/node/4514 (Jan 2015))); Translation: Läänemets (2006), slightly adapted]. There are three Chinese versions of this passage: The earliest translated by Buddhabhadra 佛陀拔陀羅 et al. in Ch'ang-an 418–420 CE (CBETA/T.9.278.718a–718c); the second by Śikṣānanda 實叉難陀 et al. also working in Ch'ang-an 695–699 CE (CBETA/T.10.279.366c–367b); a third version is by Prajña 般若et al., again Ch'ang-an, 796–798 CE (CBETA/T.10.293.732c–735c).

17. The depiction of Mount Potalaka as an island is found only at the end of the previous section in the sutra, where Sudhana is given directions to Avalokiteśvara's Bodhimaṇḍala. While the second Chinese translation speaks of an island in the sea (*hai shang you shan* 海上有山) (CBETA/T.10.279.366c6), the (later) Sanskrit text has the more poetic "amidst the 'king of stormy waters'" (*śirījalarājamadhye*). The two characters 海上 are missing in the Taishō edition of the earlier version of the Huayan jing (CBETA/T.9.278.717c28); they are, however, part of the Chinese editions. There are a number of other texts in the Chinese canon that associate Mount Potalaka with the ocean.

18. For an overview, see Kanno (2010: 10–14).

19. Both the Qiu-Zhu and the Qin gazetteers collect the scriptural references to Mount Potalaka/Mount Putuo in a single fascicle titled "scriptural evidence" (*jing zheng* 經證), in which the *Buddhaāvataṃsaka* and the Chinese *Śūraṅgama Sūtra* feature prominently.

20. Egaku's name is spelled with different variant characters in the sources. The first character appears as 慧 or 惠, the second as 鍔, 愕, or 蕚. The earliest sources agree, however, in the use of 惠蕚, thus this should be considered the normative spelling (Tanaka 2011: 6–7).

21. The scare quotes around the "welcome" are by me. I believe it was widely understood by the readers of the gazetteer that the prefect in effect pilfered the numinous image.

22. Zhou Gazetteer (p. 144).

23. *Xuanhe fengshi gaoli tujing* 宣和奉使高麗圖經, Fasc. 34 ("The sea route" 海道).

24. Pu and Xu (1991: 72).

25. Sheng Gazetteer (T.51.2101.1137c).

26. The story of Egaku was long hidden in a difficult tangle of partially contradicting information preserved in a wide array of Japanese and Chinese sources. Only recently

has a dedicated research project under Tanaka Fumio (Tanaka 2011) clarified many of the questions surrounding Egaku's journey's to China.

27. Kimiya (1955: 124–125) lists three journeys, while Tanaka (2011: 52) believes we have firm evidence for five trips, possibly seven.

28. For Zhang Bangji, see the Introduction; for Nanhu Daoyin see Ch. 4 and Yü (2001: 372f).

29. See Verschuer (2006 [1988]) for the premodern trade among Japan, Korea, and China, and Bingenheimer (2001) for biographical information on the early Japanese student-monks that traveled to China. Recent scholarship has concluded that the "Tang" merchant Li Linde/Rhee Rindeok 李隣德, who gave passage to Egaku several times, was probably part of the Korean community in Ningbo (Tanaka 2011: 16).

30. The story of Egaku was recently turned into a movie: *Bukenqu Guanyin* 不肯去観音 (Eng. title *Avalokiteshvara*) (released in 2013) is directed by Zhang Xin 張鑫 and partly filmed on Mount Putuo. Another example for the presence of Mount Putuo in modern Chinese popular culture is Wei Hui's novel *Wo de chan* 我的禪 (*Marrying Buddha* (London: Robinson, 2005)), which is partly set on Putuo.

31. Fasc. 11, p. 10a.

32. T.49.2035.388b16–c05.

33. It is no surprise that the story of Egaku at Mount Putuo features prominently in the *Genkō shakusho* 元亨釈書 (1322). Its author the learned Kokan Shiren 虎関師錬 (1278–1346) was a student of Yishan Yining a former abbot of Mount Putuo, who was sent to Japan in 1299 by the Yuan rulers.

34. Wang Liansheng Gazetteer (p. 1119). Wei was a student of Liu Yuxi and the son-in-law of Yuan Zhen, part of a famous clique of poets, therefore, who were favorably disposed toward Buddhism.

35. Fasc. 11, p. 10b.

36. Some sources have 858 (e.g., the *Fozu tongji* CBETA/T.49.2035.388b), others 859 or 863, and again others say Egaku visited during the Later Liang in 916 (e.g., the Sheng and the Zhou gazetteers). The Later Liang date can be excluded as it does not align with the complicated dating of Egaku's journeys (Peri and Maspero 1909). 916 is rather the founding date of a permanent temple for the image (Tanaka 2011: 47). Of the first three, 863 CE seems most likely (Wang Liansheng Gazetteer, p. 1120), because only for 863 do we know for certain that Egaku passed through Ningbo (Kimiya 1955: 125; Tanaka 2011: 52). Nevertheless, the sources are ambivalent, and 859 remains a possibility. Park (2003: 40–41) and Xu (2007: 460) recommend 858 as the most likely date, but according to Tanaka's (2011: 47–49) detailed discussion of the matter, 858 (Dazhong 大中 12) should be considered a mistake for 859 (Dazhong 大中 13).

37. The last two miracle tales in the Xu Gazetteer, for instance, are said to have taken place in 1731 and 1738. They are both missing in the Qin Gazetteer, which does not include any story after the Kangxi period.

38. Canonical sources often point out that Guanyin appears in many forms. The most popular Guanyin text—the *Pumen* chapter of the Lotus Sutra—describes thirty-three manifestations, which today can be seen as sculptures surrounding the central Guanyin image in the main hall of the Puji Temple. The rationale for different manifestations is understood to be the *upāya*, the "expedient means," of helping others in a form they can relate to, or that is most appropriate in their circumstance of distress. Thus Guanyin appears as *nāga* to

*nāga*s, to laywomen as a nun, to beings that "enjoy discussing" as a scholar. Accordingly, in the tale of "Guanyin and the Rebuked Sister-in-Law" the Bodhisattva appears to the hungry women waiting on the boat as an elderly lady selling food.

39. A vision or salvific effect is often caused by the recitation of her name or Guanyin related *dhāraṇī*s. Regarding images, see Dudbridge (1998) for examples of miracle tales surrounding Guanyin images in the Tang dynasty. Also Campany (2012: 56–58).

40. See also Yü (2001: 385–388) and Johnston (1913: 298–302). For summaries of other miracle tales from the Mount Putuo gazetteers, see Yü (2001: 398–399).

41. Wang Hengyan Gazetteer (p. 179).

42. Tales of retribution appear characteristically at moments of dynastic transition. For the Yuan-Ming transition, the gazetteers preserve a tale about General Tang He, who laid waste to Mount Putuo in 1383. In the legend, however, Tang's expedition has the opposite result, as his boats are stopped by iron lotuses and the emperor changes his orders to make him *repair* the temples instead of burn them to the ground (Wang Hengyan Gazetteer, p. 181). For the Ming-Qing transition the gazetteers adapt the story of Ruan Jun, who attempted to sell the Tripitaka of the Fayu Temple to Japan in order to raise troops for the Southern Ming (Wang Hengyan Gazetteer, p. 188). In the legend his boats were blocked by giant fish and had to return. In fact Ruan did sent a ship to Nagasaki, but the Japanese were not interested in exchanging soldiers for another set of the Tripitaka (see Struve 1993: 114–121).

43. Zhou Gazetteer (p. 154). Wang Hengyan Gazetteer (p. 181).

44. Mujaku Dōchū and Murata (1909 [1715]: 530).

45. Bingenheimer (2013: Vol. 7-1, p. 232). Daquan is mentioned, however, a few times in the poems of the *Continued Aśoka Temple Gazetteer* (Bingenheimer 2013: Vol. 7-2, p. 336).

46. Nakaseko (1993: 232).

47. The entry in Soothill-Hodous, e.g., associates him with King Aśoka instead of the Aśoka Temple. Reliable information can be found in the entry *Daquan Xiuli Pusa* and *Zhaobao Qilang* in Div. 5 of Mujaku Dōchū's 無著道忠 (1631–1744) encyclopedic compendium of monastic culture the *Zenrin shōki sen*禅林象器箋 (see Mujaku Dōchū and Murata 1909: 146ff.). See also the studies by Durt (1984), Sasaki (1988), and Nakaseko (1993).

48. One of these, dated the sixteenth to seventeenth century, is in the Metropolitan Museum of Art (Accession Number: 13.100.123), the other in the Philadelphia Museum of Art (Accession Number: 1929–40–40). The paintings are almost identical and were almost certainly created by the same artist.

49. Wang Hengyan Gazetteer (p. 193).

50. The University of Chicago owns one fascicle of a draft for a commentary by his hand (Acc. No. 9110.28 2372: 5.2), which was published in 1917.

51. See, e.g., Sima Qian's biography of Zhang Liang (*Shiji* Fasc. 55). For canonical and noncanonical Buddhist deities in East Asia that appear as old men, see Kim (2014: 211–248).

52. The tale is referenced to the "Jewel Mirror of the Compassionate Mind" (*Cixin baojian* 慈心寶鑑), a four-fascicle work first published in 1781.

53. Campany (2012: 58).

54. T.53.2122.533b26.

55. Campany (2012: 150).

56. Yü (2001: 94–97).

57. Idema (1999, 2002, and esp. 2008: 33–34, 185–186). The earliest known association of the parrot with Guanyin in art goes back to the thirteenth century (Yü 2001: 443–445).

58. Qiu-Zhu Gazetteer (Fasc. 5, pp. 4a–6b), Wang Hengyan Gazetteer (pp. 202–203). The texts in these two versions differs slightly.

59. Qiu-Zhu Gazetteer (Fasc. 5, p. 4a–4b).

60. Sharf (2001: 119–125).

61. For instance, by Yinguang (Wang Hengyan Gazetteer, p. 14).

62. The *Yijing* text for hexagram 31 (*Xian* 咸) equates 咸 with 感.

63. In the *Buddhāvataṃsaka* (T.9.278.433a26) and elsewhere.

64. In the Lotus Sutra (T09n0262_p0057c12).

65. Pei Xiu 裴休 (791–864) was never actually prime minister, but was at times highly influential at court and a lifelong supporter of Buddhism.

66. T.48.2015.399a5.

67. Qiu-Zhu Gazetteer (Fasc. 5, p. 4b–5a).

68. Qiu-Zhu Gazetteer (Fasc. 5, p. 5a).

69. A skeptical view on visions and apparitions by the geographer Wang Shixing 王士性 (1547–1598) is cited in Ishino (2005: 13).

70. E.g., in the *Liji* (Ch. *Zhong Yong* 中庸, Section 27).

71. Mencius (Ch. *Jin Xin* 盡心, Section 2).

72. Qiu-Zhu Gazetteer (Fasc. 5, p. 5b).

73. This saying seems first attested in the biography of Li Gu 李固 in the *Hou hanshu* 後漢書. There, however, King Yao is seen in both cases (on the wall and in the soup).

74. Qiu-Zhu Gazetteer (Fasc. 5, pp. 5b–6a).

75. Wu (1992).

76. Wu (1992: 82).

77. The praise of the rustic and simple in topoi such as the unsullied mind of an infant (*chizi* 赤子) or the unhewn piece of wood (*pu* 樸) was already celebrated in the *Daode jing*.

78. Yijing, *Xici* 繫辭 commentary, Part I, 5.

79. The most elaborate version of his story is told in the *Dhammapāda* Commentary (*Appāmada* Chapter, No.3 (PTS ed., Vol.1, p. 239)). Cūḷapanthaka is the standard example for those with dull faculties, who nevertheless make progress (e.g., in the Mahāvibhāṣa T.27.1545.210b08).

80. Qiu-Zhu Gazetteer (Fasc. 5, p. 6a–6b).

81. Qiu-Zhu Gazetteer (Fasc. 5, p. 6b).

82. Wang Liansheng Gazetteer (p. 38).

Chapter 4

1. 名山大川固雖天造地設莫不因人而傳而重者也 (CBETA/X.86.1609.652a08). On Tongxu, see Ch. 5, Exhibit 1.

2. Tea was produced on Mount Putuo probably already in the Song. It is first mentioned in the Sheng Gazetteer (T.52.2101.1136b).

3. Zhang (1638 [1935]: 50). The rock formation, west of the Pantuo Rock, can still be visited today.

4. Bingenheimer (2013, Vol. 5: 61–103 (natural landscape), 113–153 (buildings)). Moll-Murata (2001: 219) has observed that gazetteers list features that rise above ground (mountains, hills, etc.) always before waters (rivers, lakes, etc.).

5. Bingenheimer (2013, Vol. 5: 214–234). The Mount Tiantai Gazetteer (1894 [1601]), ecumenic as well as encyclopedic, even contains an extensive section on Daoist temples (*gongguan* 宮觀) (Bingenheimer 2013, Vol. 6: 91–97).

6. Wang Liansheng Gazetteer (1999: 93–129).

7. Hahn (1997: 159).

8. The earliest maps (see Ch. 2) do not suggest that the island continued in the northeast (Hou 1593: No. 31–99 and 31–100). In the Qing set of the twelve views of Mount Putuo the Tidal Sound Cave and the Brahma Voice Cave were shown as on separate shores. In the undated lithography included in the Wang Hengyan Gazetteer (1924–1932), the two parts of the island are also clearly not yet connected. All the visual evidence suggests that the Brahma Voice Cave was on a separate island until quite recently. In text, the separation of the two parts of the island was still remembered in 1913 when Reginald Johnston visited Mount Putuo (Johnston 1913: 315n1). The separation between what is today the northeastern part and the main island is also mentioned in a 1916 text (Wang Liansheng Gazetteer, p. 705).

9. While Boerschmann's well-documented photos of his travels in China have been published several times in German and English (1923 [1982]), the photo collection associated with Shufeldt is less well known. The local museum on Mount Putuo displays some reprints (mis-)labeled "Major Robert Wilson." The originals are kept at the United States National Anthropological Archives (Inventory Nos: 04513300–04537900), where they were credited to Robert Wilson Shufeldt, Jr. (1850–1934). The younger Shufeldt, however, had never been to Asia. The pictures might have come into his possession via his father Rear Admiral Robert Wilson Shufeldt (1822–1895), who traveled in the Zhoushan archipelago during his first commission in China in 1866 and 1867 (Drake 1984: 96, 112). Shufeldt senior would later return to Asia (1880–1882) and play an important role in the so-called opening of Korea. Shufeldt junior published some of the photos in an article (1899). These are, to my knowledge, the first published photos of Mount Putuo.

10. He Zhanglian (1934: 7).

11. Eliade (1957: 11–13).

12. T.49.2035.388c03. Cf. Yü (2001: 373). The *Fozu tongji* cites Nanhu Daoyin's 南湖道因 (1090–1167) now lost *Caoan lu* 草菴錄. See also Ch. 6, Exhibit 1 for another early account.

13. The two appear together also in the Chinese *Śūraṅgama sūtra* where a vase in form of a flying *kalaviṅka* is used in a simile for emptiness (T.19.945.114c07).

14. One famous painting by Muqi (1210–1269) shows Guanyin on the Potalaka. A copy of this painting is preserved in the Daitoku Temple 大德寺, Kyoto (s. Yü 1994). The motif was also used in Korean Buddhist art. Perhaps the earliest depiction of Guanyin in Europe can be found in Athanasius Kircher's *China Illustrata* (1667: 140). Kircher calls her "Pussa" (< ch. *pusa* = bodhisattva), and the eccentric image shows Guanyin sitting on a lotus, complete with Sudhana and the vase in the middle of an ocean. To the right there is land, perhaps a distant echo of Mount Putuo.

15. See Ray (1994: 41–42).

16. Accounts of such encounters are, for instance, collected in the *Shenxian ganyu zhuan* 神仙感遇傳 (DZ 592).

17. Soymié (1956: 88–93).

18. On the grotto-heavens, see Verellen (1995) and Pregadio (2008, sub voc. "Dongtian and Fudi"). On the genesis of the *Dongtian fudi yuedu mingshan ji* and its author Du Guangting 杜光庭 (850–933), see Verellen (1989).

19. Sporn (2010: 556, 570).

20. For an example, see Jones (2005: Vol. 5, after p. X).

21. A comparative study of the pilgrimage sites of Guanyin and Saint Mary would yield many more parallels, but this is far out of scope.

22. See Saitō (2004: 22). Also Ch. 6, Exhibit 1.

23. For a list of other replicas of Mount Putuo and temples that were at various times meant to serve as surrogates for the island site, see Wang Liansheng Gazetteer (pp. 446–449).

24. The Fayu temple was described in great detail by the German architect Ernst Boerschmann (1911). Because of the age of existing structures, the Fayu Temple is ranked as a "Province-level Cultural Heritage Protection Site" (Wang Liansheng Gazetteer 1999: 537), while the older and traditionally more powerful Puji Temple is in a lower tier.

25. The earliest account of this event seems to be Tu Long's *Butuo shan lingying zhuan* 補陀山靈應傳, which is only included in the Hou-Tu Gazetteer (Fasc. 3, pp. 36a–42b).

26. A number of other poems attest to Dazhi's popularity among the literati. The Hou-Tu Gazetteer alone contains ten poems on Dazhi by eight different authors, among them a contribution by the prolific Wang Shizhen 王世貞. The well-connected Dazhi is also the only monk mentioned in Hou Jigao's travelogue (see Ch. 8, Exhibit 2).

27. A strong story is difficult to suppress. Even though Tu Long's account was dropped from the gazetteer tradition, in 1617, thirty-five years after the fact, Zhu Guozhen was still very much aware of the details of this story and retold the tale with relish in his travelogue. Zhu (1619 [1991]: Fasc. 26, p. 10).

28. Zhang Dai (1638 [1935]: 48).

29. Qiu-Zhu Gazetteer (Fasc. 2, p. 13b). Lan Li's vision of Guanyin is told at Fasc. 5: 12b. There are poems both by monks (e.g., Fasc. 15, p. 6a) and laypeople (e.g., Fasc. 14, p. 4a) on the Brahma Voice Cave.

30. Ledderose (2013). On the assimilation of Indian Buddhist cosmology in China, see Deeg (1999).

31. Birnbaum (1989: 136); Hargett (2006: 161).

32. An earlier source for the association of Mount Wutai and Mañjuśrī is the *Mahāparinirvāṇa Sūtra* (Sen 2003: 76–78).

33. Evidence for this kind of "doubling" also appears in Japan where the long Shikoku pilgrimage trek was miniaturized and copied at three other sites between 1686 and 1857 (Tanaka 1981: 247–248).

34. Cartelli (2013: 195).

35. Traveling in the 1920s Clara Ho remarks that "only four huts are on this island, but only thirty years ago it was completely deserted" (He Zhanglian 1934: 11–12).

36. 無傳人則無傳地矣. Zhang Dai (1638 [1935]: 44).

37. Sometimes relics share the fate of the place where there are enshrined. The Dissolution of Monasteries (1536–1541), on orders of Henry VIII, e.g., resulted in the end of the cults of some martyrs irrespective of whether their bodies were preserved (as with St. Cuthbert in Durham) or scattered (as with St. Edward the Martyr). The cults did not survive the end of the institutions that maintained them.

38. Tanaka (1981: 248–249) mentions that fourteen of the eighty-eight stations of the Shikoku pilgrimage have moved since the middle of the sixteenth century and that at "each new site the assemblage of physical landscape-markers, with their symbolic meaning, has been reconstructed to consecrate the site."

39. T.51.2101.1136c2–4.

40. Wang Hengyan Gazetteer (p. 108); Wang Liansheng Gazetteer (pp. 96, 103).

41. Hou Jigao describes the Sudhana Cave in his travelogue (see Ch. 8, Exhibit 2) as "unfathomably deep."

42. Hou-Tu Gazetteer (Fasc. 1, p. 27a)

43. Yü (2001: 83, 440). The textual basis of the association of Sudhana with Guanyin is the *Buddhāvataṃsaka*; the Dragon Girl appears prominently in the twelfth chapter of the Lotus Sutra and esoteric sutras.

44. See De Visser (1913) for a comprehensive overview. Sea and island goddesses were often seen as "dragon daughters" (e.g., De Visser 1913: 197, 236). See, e.g., the Tang dynasty story of the "Legendary Marriage at Tung-t'ing" (Ma and Lau 1991: 346–355).

45. Idema (2008: 42, 182).

46. Hou-Tu Gazetteer (Fasc. 5, p. 29a).

47. Wang Hengyan Gazetteer (p. 108).

48. Wang Liansheng Gazetteer (p. 96).

49. Jones (2000: 228).

50. Only the most recent gazetteer provides detailed ground plans and architectural drawings (Wang Liansheng Gazetteer, pp. 343–413).

51. Boerschmann (1911). During his visit to Mount Putuo in 1908, Boerschmann measured, photographed, and sketched many monuments on the island, especially the Fayu Temple, down to transcribing the inscriptions on temple plaques. For a comprehensive discussion of the temple architecture on Mount Wutai, see Wei-cheng Lin (2014).

Chapter 5

1. "Der Beobachter erster Ordnung sieht die Unterschiede der Menschen und ihrer Schicksale und fragt nach Gerechtigkeit. Auf der Ebene zweiter Ordnung kann man beobachten und beschreiben, daß und wie die Gesellschaft selbst reguliert, welche Positionen sie Personen zuweist und wie sie dies rechtfertigt" (Luhmann 1998: 1075).

2. How these were realized in print varies. The organization of lists ranges from stringing names together in one single paragraph (e.g., in the Hou-Tu Gazetteer, Fasc. 1, p. 23b) to elaborate tables (Wang Hengyan Gazetteer, pp. 428–448). Lineages are often presented as a series of biographies (e.g., in the Mount Huangbo Gazetteer (Bingenheimer 2013: Vol. 10)). An interesting artifact of lineage construction is the Dharma lineage poem that decides the first character in the Dharma names of succeeding generations. Members of the first generation have the first character of the poem in

common, members of the second generation the second character, etc. For a collection of Caodong lineage poems in the canon see CBETA/X.86.1603.484c20. In the gazetteers see, e.g., the lineage poems in the Mount Huangbo Gazetteer (Bingenheimer 2013: Vol. 10, p. 11).

3. Used in Chinese historiography since Sima Qian (d. 86 BCE), the *zhuan* was adopted by Chinese Buddhists in the sixth century, and a number of substantive collections of "biographies of eminent monks" (*gaoseng zhuan* 高僧傳) are among the most important sources for the history of Chinese Buddhism (Kieschnick 1997). The information in biographies was often based on tomb stūpa inscriptions and miracle tales (Shinohara 1988). For caveats regarding the use of *zhuan* literature as historical sources in the study of religion, see Bumbacher (2010). For a detailed, digital edition of *Gaoseng zhuan* literature that visualizes events recorded in biographies both geographically and as social networks, see Bingenheimer, Hung, and Wiles (2011).

4. See Yanagida (1983) for an overview of early *yulu* literature, and Wittern (1998: Ch. 2) for a discussion of the use and development of the term in Chan/Zen scholarship. *Yulu* were often based (at least ideally) on private notes taken by students of their masters' work.

5. About 15 percent of the Wang Hengyan Gazetteer consists of biographical information. The Hou-Tu and the Zhou Gazetteers are atypical in that they only contain a bare minimum of information about monks associated with the island (c. 2 percent of the page volume). Created by a group of local literati, they tend to foreground *belles-lettres* and local or imperial patronage. Against that about 30 percent of pages in the Mount Huangbo Gazetteer (Bingenheimer 2013, Vol. 10) or the Quanzhou Kaiyuan Temple Gazetteers (Bingenheimer 2013, Vol. 11) contain biographical information.

6. Bingenheimer (2013, Vol. 2: 204–210).

7. Bingenheimer (2013, Vol. 6: 98–203 (Buddhists), 205–236 (Daoists and Hermits)).

8. His Dharma name was Qingliao, but it was by his sobriquet Zhenxie that he was remembered in the toponyms on Mount Putuo. On the revival of the Caodong School, see Schlütter (2008: 78–103).

9. On one occasion Dahui criticized Qingliao even in his own monastery in front of his students (Schlütter 2008: 123–129).

10. Qingliao on Pure Land: CBETA/T.47.1973.318c21. Zhuhong on Qingliao CBETA/T.51.2072.151a22. Zhuhong's claim seems, as so often, unburdened by evidence.

11. His *yulu* is titled *Zhenzhou Changlu liao chanshi qiewai lu* 真州長蘆了禪師劫外錄 (X.1426). It includes the commemoration inscription titled *Chongxian Zhenxie Qingliao taming* 崇先真歇了禪師塔銘 (CBETA/X.71.1426.777c3). The stele inscription, authored by Qingliao's Dharma brother Hongzhi Zhengjue 宏智正覺 (1091–1157), used to be at the Tiantong Temple, which alongside the Aśoka Temple and Mount Putuo itself was one of the most important temples of the Ningbo region.

12. CBETA/X.71.1426.778a6.

13. CBETA/T.51.2101.1137c23.

14. Foulk (1993: 163–167).

15. Belonging to a documented lineage of Chan transmission remained a condition of eligibility for abbotship at major monasteries into the twentieth century (Welch 1963: 95). For the *zutang*, see Foulk (1993: 172–176).

16. Hou-Tu Gazetteer (Fasc. 1, p. 23a).

17. *Putuo lie zu lu* 普陀列祖錄, X.1609.

18. CBETA/X.86.1609.652a16.

19. *Chaoyin heshang zhongxing putuosi ji*潮音和尚中興普陀寺記. Qiu-Zhu Gazetteer (Fasc. 12, p. 17b).

20. According to the Zhou Gazetteer (p. 114), the former abbots were venerated in the same hall as the Bodhisattvas Mañjuśrī and Kṣitigarbha and the Temple guardian spirit (*qielan* 伽藍).

21. Wang Liansheng Gazetteer (pp. 324 and 336).

22. The text has Jingliao 靜了, but this is due to the strict taboo character conventions in the Qing. Using the name Qingliao 清了, which might be read as "the Qing are finished," was not recommendable. There are other common variations found in the text, e.g., all 玄 are written 元, because the character 玄 was part of Kangxi's taboo name (*Xuanye* 玄燁).

23. 凡七處說法. The presentation here draws on the idea that the *Buddhāvataṃsaka* was taught in seven different places to different gatherings of gods and humans.

24. Qiu-Zhu Gazetteer (Fasc. 6, pp. 2b–3a).

25. See Wu (2008: Appendixes 2 and 3) for how questions of lineage construction led to serious disputes.

26. Wang Hengyan Gazetteer (pp. 341–342).

27. The Wang Liansheng Gazetteer duly notes the affiliation with the Chan School but, like Wang Hengyan, simply lists the abbots of the temples on Mount Putuo chronologically without concern for lineage. Wang Liansheng Gazetteer (pp. 504ff.).

28. Naquin (2000: 306). The "religious activism" of the Qing emperors also appears in the temple-building activities in Beijing (ibid., 331–332).

29. Wang Hengyan Gazetteer (p. 190). The first mention of this legend is in the Xu Gazetteer (Fasc. 5, p. 8).

30. *Huang gong ci ji* 黃公祠記. Wang Hengyan Gazetteer (p. 466).

31. Wang Hengyan Gazetteer (p. 466).

32. The Fayu Temple had been (re-)associated with the Chan School three years earlier with the arrival of Bie'an Xingtong.

33. For translations of some documents concerning this conquest—Shi Lang's invasion plan, proclamations to the inhabitants, and his advice as to how to incorporate Taiwan into the Qing empire—see Wiethoff (1969). Shi Lang also was an avid supporter of religious sites and was responsible for the restoration of the Southern Putuo Temple 南普陀寺, an important regional site in Xiamen that was named after Mount Putuo (ZFSH 63: 3).

34. "The Record on the Commemorative Shrines for Master Lan, built during his lifetime at the front temple [Puji] and the back temple [Fayu]." 普陀前後兩寺藍公生祠記 Qiu-Zhu Gazetteer (Fasc. 12, p. 21b).

35. This is probably true in general for patronage of Buddhism during the Qing. As subjects of the Manchu empire, Confucians could not safely argue that Buddhism was a foreign, barbarian creed. They thus lost the "cultural" argument against Buddhism. As the Chinese, Mongols, and Tibetans were forced to live peacefully under their Manchu rulers, their internal divisions were much reduced. The Qing policy of appropriating religious expression for imperial use did not leave much room for infighting among traditions. In

this light, the many depictions in Qing literature of Buddhism as degenerate, decadent, and erotically deviant might be understood as the suppressed voices of the xenophobic, nationalist strand of Confucian literati society, which had been banned from political discourse.

36. *Dayuanhou* 大元侯: According to Hucker (1985 sub voc.) an "unofficial reference to a Provincial Military Commander." Most sources have Lan Li as "Regional Commander," however, and the use of *dayuanhou* might be eulogistic here.

37. First included in the Wang Hengyan Gazetteer (pp. 468–469).

38. Wang Hengyan Gazetteer (p. 143).

39. Wang Hengyan Gazetteer (p. 261). Tu Cuizhong belonged to the 12th generation of the Ningbo Tu clan; Tu Long, editor of the Hou-Tu Gazetteer, belonged to its 8th generation.

40. These lists are variously titled *banci* 頒賜, *enci* 恩賜, *enlai* 恩賚, *tanna* 檀那, *tanshi* 檀施, etc.

41. Qiu-Zhu Gazetteer (Fasc. 8); Xu Gazetteer (Fasc. 4).

42. Qiu-Zhu Gazetteer (Fasc. 8, pp. 2b–3a).

43. For the history of the rosary and its use in Qing court culture, see Kieschnick (2003: 116–138).

44. Needless to say, this kind of official status was highly desired, not only by the Sangha but also by the local gentry (Gernet 1995: 4–5). Not only emperors and high-ranking officials wrote gate plaques. Famous artists like Dong Qichang (1555–1636) were at times also invited, perhaps more for aesthetic reasons than for patronage. Person and calligraphy were closely associated, and Dong's calligraphy was at one point slashed by rioters during a land dispute (Kraus 1991: 52).

45. See, e.g., the stūpa inscriptions at CBETA/J.39.B444.343a01 and CBETA/J.39. B438.252c01. Like Xutong, Xingtong also actively contributed to the lineage discourse. According to Wu (2008: 362n69), he wrote the massive *Xudeng zhengtong* in forty-two *juan* in order to legitimize his lineage.

46. See Kraus (1991) for how Communist rulers have continued the tradition.

47. For an eyewitness account of Kangxi writing, see Kraus (1991: 3). On the performative aspects of Kangxi's and Qianlong's visits to Mount Tai, see Dott (2004: 157–193).

48. The Qiu-Zhu Gazetteer (Fasc. 8, p. 3b) mentions the little-known Haian 海安 as representative for the Puji Temple. Forty years later the Xu Gazetteer (Fasc. 4, p. 3b) highlights Xinming as the recipient of three imperial inscriptions.

49. These are only listed in the Qiu-Zhu Gazetteer (Fasc. 8, p. 3b) that was finalized in 1705. For the compilers of the Xu Gazetteer in the 1740s it was not advisable to dwell too much on the various princes listed forty years earlier, as by then many of them had fallen out of favor.

50. The two earliest sources for Xinming's life are Fan Wei's 范煒 *Keyue chanshi xiaozhuan* 珂月禪師小傳 (before 1740) and Yan Yudun's 嚴虞惇 (1650–1713) *Yitang heshang liuzhi shou xu* 繹堂和尚六袠壽序. The former is not contained in the Gazetteers but in two versions of the Xianjue Temple 先覺寺 Gazetteer (ZFC 120 and 192).

51. To give but a few examples: There is a poem by Shao Cheng 邵城 (*jinshi* 1568) in the Hou-Tu Gazetteer (Fasc. 5, p. 30) and one by Shao Fenglai 邵鳳來 in the Zhou

Gazetteer (p. 449). An especially ardent supporter was Shao Buzhong 邵輔忠 (*jinshi* 1595), who contributed a preface and many poems to the Zhou Gazetteer. His grandson Shao Yuanguan 邵元觀 (*juren* 1695) wrote a friendly poem for Xinming, who might have been a close relative of the same generation (Qiu-Zhu Gazetteer, Fasc. 14, p. 44b). About thirty years later another member of the clan, Shao Ji 邵基 (*jinshi* 1721), vice minister in the Ministry of Personnel, contributed a preface and added a poem to the reprint of the Qiu-Zhu Gazetteer (Fasc. 14, p. 46b). The poem is in a much more eulogistic voice befitting Shao Ji's position as a younger family member but also reflecting Xinming's great influence at the time.

52. Xu Gazetteer (Fasc. 15, pp. 53a–54b).

53. The schematic drawing of a stūpa with the characters of the Heart Sutra (*xinjing ta* 心經塔) is a playful and fairly common form of the Heart Sutra, which is often used decoratively on objects.

54. The fact that Xinming was at Jehol in 1709 is reported not in the list of imperial gifts but in a short essay on the Fahua building by Gu's fellow emissary Sun Wencheng. It was first included in the 1735 reprint of the Qiu Gazetteer (Fasc. 12, before p. 35). See also Wang Hengyan Gazetteer (p. 298).

55. Wang Hengyan Gazetteer (p. 223).

56. Huc (1862 [1854]: Vol. II, pp. 232–233).

57. Huc (1862 [1854]: Vol. II, p. 232).

58. See Silas Wu (1970).

59. For an example, see Spence (1966: 122–123).

60. For Cao Yin, see Spence (1966). Sun Wencheng's palace memorials are collected in Chuang (1978).

61. Wang Hengyan Gazetteer (p. 222).

62. The memorials are preserved not in the Putuo gazetteers but in a transcript of the Xianjue Temple Gazetteer (ZFC 120: 1–53). The Xianjue Temple, located some 10 miles northwest of Ningbo, was rebuilt by Tongxu during the *haijin*, and Xinming had continued his master's work by supporting the smaller temple after he became abbot at Putuo. He is even listed as the author-compiler of the 1721 edition of the Xianjue Temple Gazetteer (ZFC 192), though the lack of a preface by him and the inclusion of his biography make the attribution dubious.

63. Spence (2002: 168).

64. Döll (2010: 115–133).

Chapter 6

1. "Da aber für meine Zwecke das Eingehen auf die Inschriften unerläßlich war, glaubte ich es wagen zu müssen, die Übersetzungen zu bringen." Boerschmann (1911: XVI).

2. Boerschmann, who found them locked, photographed them in 1908 (Boerschmann 1911: 17–18).

3. On *moya* and landscape, see Harrist (2008). For a characteristically Chinese Buddhist development of the commemorative stele, see Wong (2004). A long-term project under Lothar Ledderose (Heidelberger Akademie der Wissenschaften) that studies and documents Buddhist *moya* in unprecedented detail has started to publish the first volumes of what promises to become a major series (Ledderose and Wang 2014).

4. As always there are exceptions—the Mount Huangbo Gazetteer of 1824 (Bingenheimer 2013, Vol. 10) is largely unconcerned with imperial rescripts and inscriptions in general.

5. Mount Emei Gazetteer (Bingenheimer 2013, Vol. 2).

6. Aśoka Temple Gazetteer (Bingenheimer 2013, Vol. 7-1).

7. The museum on Mount Putuo displays some historic photographs of the site. One of them shows the *moya Zhendan diyi foguo* 震旦第一佛國 ("Premier Buddha Land in China" overwritten with the inscription *Zhongguo gongchandang wansui* 中国共产党万岁 ("Long live the Communist Party of China"). According to the caption on the photo, the original inscription was restored in 1979–1980.

8. The attribution is doubtful. The first mention of Zhenxie's Spring is in the Qiu-Zhu Gazetteer (Fasc. 15, p. 23a), which, however, does not mention Shi Hao. Only some forty years later in the Xu Gazetteer (Fasc. 1, p. 19b) is his name associated with the seal script *moya*. See the photo section of the Wang Liansheng Gazetteer for a picture.

9. This inscription is first attested in the Zhou Gazetteer (p. 108). Another "Buddha Land between Sea and Sky" inscription greets visitors today at the landing pier. Inscribed on a large boulder some 7 or 8 feet high, it is by Jiang Zemin, the President of China from 1993 to 2002.

10. Halperin (2006: 28).

11. Wang Liansheng (1999, pp. 562–573) lists twenty-eight inscriptions alone for the period between 1984 and 1999.

12. The Wang Liansheng Gazetteer (p. 542) quotes one earlier inscription that is said to have been "re-cut" in the twentieth century because it was worn away and no longer legible. This inscription is, however, not mentioned in previous gazetteers and is therefore of doubtful authenticity.

13. The Shi were one of the most powerful clans of the Ningbo region during the Southern Song and uniquely successful in the official examination system. Over several generations the Shi produced seventy-two *jinshi* holders, and not only Shi Hao but also his son and grandson became prime ministers (Shi Meilu 2006: 8). For a comprehensive study of Shi Hao's involvement with Mount Putuo, see Saitō (2004).

14. Cao Hengde and Yang Guchang in Shi Meilu (2006: 130).

15. See, e.g., his questions to Zhilian 智連 (1089–1164) recorded at X.77.1524.384a20. He is also mentioned in the *Huangbo shan* gazetteer (ZFSH Vol. 86: 54), and a short biography of him is included in the *Tiantai shan fangwai* gazetteer (ZFSH Vol. 89: 450). For a list of texts related to Buddhism among Shi Hao's extant works, see Saitō (2004: 6–7).

16. Saitō (2004: 21).

17. Alongside commercial activities, donations were a second important source of income for monasteries. For an analysis of the dynamics of donations given out of religious fervor, see Gernet (1995: 195–228).

18. Zhou Gazetteer (pp. 197–199).

19. T.51.2101.1137a15–23. Inscriptions were sometimes made directly—brush on stone—by the authors or calligraphers, before they were carved (Harrist 2008: 25–26). The story of Shi Hao's visit has also been included in many other local gazetteers (Saitō 2004: 17).

20. Wang Hengyan Gazetteer (pp. 542–598).

21. *Baosuo* 寶所. An allusion to his idiosyncratic transcription for Putuo: *Bao*tuo shan寶陀山.

22. *Dongqin'an* 東秦岸. Originally denoting the Shandong region, but here probably referring to the Maqin 馬秦 Mountain on Zhujia jian, an island close to Putuo. Maqin, during the Song and Yuan, was associated with hermits.

23. Probably a *dhāraṇī*, perhaps the *Mahā Karuṇā Dhāraṇī/Dabei zhou* 大悲咒 (T.1111–1113).

24. Reading *xi* 夕 with the Hou-Tu Gazetteer (Wang Hengyan Gazetteer: *ri* 日). Shi Hao means that the party approached the Tidal Sound Cave again "at sunset," after the attempt to see Guanyin in the morning failed.

25. Reading *jiao* 教 with the Hou-Tu Gazetteer (Wang Hengyan Gazetteer: *fang* 放).

26. The translation is based on the text as found in the Hou-Tu Gazetteer (Fasc. 4, p. 3b) ("Leaving a Stele Inscription at the Baotuo Chan Temple" (*Liuti baotuo chansi bei*留題寶陀禪寺碑)) and collated with the version in the Wang Hengyan Gazetteer (p. 177). The *Qiandao Siming tujing* (7: 2a–b) of 1169 attributes the eulogy to Huang Guinian 黃龜年 (1083–1145), another renowned Song official. The eulogy is also under Huang's name in the Qiu-Zhu Gazetteer (Fasc. 11, pp. 3–4), but the text there is in bad shape and corrupted in places. The Wang Liansheng Gazetteer also lists the eulogy as by Huang Guinian (p. 798) while also including the text as part of the Shi Hao's inscription (p. 574). Given that the Siming Gazetteer of the Qiandao period is an early source, it cannot be discounted lightly. It is possible that Shi Hao was merely quoting Huang Guinian's eulogy (without attribution) in his inscription and only added the preface about his own visit. Against that stands the fact that the narrative of the preface and the eulogy is consistent, and the text clearly says 迺作偈 "thus [I/we] composed a eulogy." In any case, all gazetteers associate the prose text with Shi Hao, and only Qiu-Zhu and Wang Liansheng list the eulogy separately under Huang Guinian.

27. Gimello (1992).

28. Weidner (2001b: 126) mentions the involvement of eunuchs in the production of temple art. The Zhihua Temple in Beijing was founded through the efforts of the eunuch Wang Zhen in 1443, and his shrine there was still active until the late eighteenth century. See He (1996: 304) for a reproduction of the stele image of Wang at the Zhihua Temple. See also He (2000: 25–26).

29. Naquin (2000: 162). The most comprehensive case study of eunuch patronage in Ming Buddhism is Chen Yunü (2001).

30. He (1996: 286).

31. Dated to autumn 1607, it was perhaps too late to be included in the Zhou Gazetteer; or perhaps Zhang Sui, who arranged the printing, felt it was inappropriate to include his own laudatory inscription.

32. Wang Liansheng Gazetteer (p. 430).

33. The *Han Jingchang* 漢經廠 was a eunuch-run printing press housed near the imperial palace during the Ming. It was the pendant to the *Fan Jingchang* 番經廠, which printed Buddhist scriptures in languages other than Chinese (e.g., Tibetan).

34. *Dao ke min* 鳥可民. In all later versions 鳥可泯 (Xu, Qin, Wang Liansheng Gazetteers). I believe Zhou uses 鳥 as a rare variant for 島 here (HDC *sub voce* 鳥).

35. 謙. Perhaps pronounced *qie* here.

36. Qiu-Zhu Gazetteer (Fasc. 11, pp. 14b–16a).

37. Neither inscription was included in the Qiu-Zhu Gazetteer. They might have arrived too late to make it into the first print (1705), but it is surprising that the inscriptions were not added to the reprint (1735).

38. Xu Gazetteer (Fasc. 卷之首, p. 2b). For a rather free translation of Kangxi's inscription for the Puji Temple, see Butler (1879: 116–117).

39. An allusion to a line by Li Bo ("A golden rope lines the street to enlightenment, the jewel raft ferries us across the river of confusion" 金繩開覺路, 寶筏度迷川). Li Bo's poem in turn draws on imagery from a passage in the Lotus Sutra, which describes the Pure Land of Buddha Padmaprabha (T.9.262.11c18).

40. *Hengsha* 恆沙 is of course the "sands of the river Ganges," but, as with some of the other references in this allusive text, a more literal reading seems preferable.

41. The mythical Daoist islands of Penglai 蓬萊, Fangzhang 方丈 (or Fanghu 方壺/Fangzhu 方諸), and Yingzhou 瀛洲 are often evoked in connection with Putuo (see also Ch. 7).

42. *Qingning* 清寧, "bright peace" as well as "the peace of the Qing." Also an allusion to a verse in the *Daodejing* 道德經 (Ch. 39): *Heaven attained unity and became bright* (清), *Earth attained unity and became tranquil* (寧).

43. This line probably alludes to the gift of roof tiles from the imperial palace in Nanjing that Kangxi made to Mount Putuo in 1699 (see Ch. 5, Exhibit 3). Together with the next line the passage blends imagery of the underwater palace of the Dragon King with that of the rebuilt temple (see HDC sub voc. 貝闕珠宮, and 貝闕).

44. Xu Gazetteer (Fasc. 卷之首, pp. 1a–3a).

45. Yü (2001): 21. See also ibid. 233–247.

46. Wang Liansheng Gazetteer (pp. 330 and 548). The Fang Gazetteer (p. 66) mentions the existence of an earlier Kangxi stele that Xingtong had carved in 1699 from a handwritten poem that he had received from the emperor. This stele too was broken during the Cultural Revolution. Its pieces are still preserved in the Fayu Temple.

47. Xu Gazetteer (Fasc. 卷之首, 3a–5a).

48. There is a photo of this occasion, reproduced in the Fang Gazetteer (p. 319).

49. The text was considered authentic enough to warrant inclusion in his complete works (*Sun Zhongshan Quanji*, Vol. 3, p. 352). The best version of the text seems to be Sun (1937) and Sun (n.d.). Cf. Wang Liansheng Gazetteer (p. 708). Where not otherwise indicated, I follow the text as preserved on the stele.

50. Daojie 道階 (1870–1934) was an influential monk in the early Republican period.

51. Liaoyu 了餘 (1864–1924, abbot 1915–1919), see Wang Liansheng Gazetteer (pp. 492–493). For a preface by him, see Shi Chenkong (1948: 25f).

52. The 輿 ("carriage") is written only in Sun (1937). All other texts, including the stele and Sun (n.d.), omit the 輿. 筍 is here read *xùn,* with the meaning of "bamboo carriage." For a nineteenth-century sketch of such a "mountain chair" used in the Ningbo region, see Fortune (1847: 167).

53. *Beiju zhi jie* 備舉之捷. Except Sun (1937) and the *Sun Zhongshan Quanji*, all texts, including the stele, have the wrong 絡 instead of 備.

54. See the early accounts by Zhang Bangji (see Introduction), the Sheng Gazetteer, and Shi Hao, which concede that people see different things.

55. Soong (1997).

Chapter 7

1. "Il y a donc un sens à dire, sur le plan de une philosophie de la littérature et de la poésie òu nous nous plaçons, qu'on 'écrit une chambre', qu'on 'lit une chambre', qu'on 'lit une maison.'" (Bachelard 1961: 32).

2. He (1934: 7–8).

3. Wang Hengyan Gazetteer (p. 517).

4. Elman (2013: 3).

5. The only comparable European genre is the sonnet, which spread across Europe from Italy starting from the twelfth century. Even the sonnet, however, was never nearly as pervasive within Europe poetry as the *shi* was in China.

6. Although women were not as mobile as men, they developed distinctive styles of travel writing in the Ming and Qing (Wang 2013). Chang (1997: 147) remarks that with more than three thousand collections by women poets, China has the largest corpus of women's poetry of all nations. Poetry collections by women writers became popular only in the late Ming. There has been a wealth of research in English on women's writing in China (Ko 1994, Widmer and Chang 1997, and Idema and Grant 2004, to name only a few). An important digital collection of Ming-Qing women authors has been online since 2005 (digital.library.mcgill.ca/mingqing/english/) (Jan 2014).

7. Cai (2008: 308 and 354).

8. Bingenheimer (2013: Vol. 9, Vol. 10).

9. Bingenheimer (2013: Vol. 11, p. 62).

10. These are the numbers given in the "Edition Principles" (*fanli* 凡例). My count of the authors in the table of content is very different, however: the book actually contains poems by 752 authors. Such a corpus was matched by other famous sites. Brian R. Dott cites figures for poems on Mount Tai, according to which 1,190 poems on Mount Tai were written in the Ming and Qing by 497 poets (Dott 2004: 198).

11. Not all poems are strictly about the site, e.g., the piece by Su Shi (Wang 2008: 15; see also his preface, p. 18). On the other hand, Wang did not include all of the poems in the Hou-Tu Gazetteer (he omitted, for instance, those by Hou Jigao and Long Defu).

12. The first half of Tian's book on travel writing can be read as an introduction to the poetic conventions that underlie the poems in this chapter. Cartelli has translated and decoded a large number of poems on the eminent Buddhist site of Mount Wutai and analyzed its depiction as a pilgrimage site in poetry. In a way the examples in this chapter are an extension of the history of poetic depiction of landscape and travel from the early beginnings in the fourth to the sixth century as described by Tian and the poem cycles on Mount Wutai translated by Cartelli, which were written between the fifth and the eleventh centuries. The poetic record of "visionary journeys" to Mount Putuo begins in the early twelfth century, where the texts described by Cartelli leave off.

13. Elman (2013: 161).

14. Hou-Tu Gazetteer (Fasc. 3, pp. 1aff.; Fasc. 5, pp. 1aff.). The poems discussed below are at Fasc. 5, pp. 6aff. Tu Long actually included four poems by Wu. The last one of the set, in a typical example of lossiness, was omitted in the Zhou and all following Putuo gazetteers, and even in the large collection of Mount Putuo poems by Wang (2008). Only the first three, which are translated here, were anthologized after 1607.

15. Zhang Dai (1638 [1935]: 51).

16. Or: "the countless green isles stretch into the distance."

17. This phrase references a number of other poems. The Yunmeng marshes 雲夢澤 include the Dongting Lake, which for many centuries was the largest lake in China.

18. Both *panmu and fusang* are place names that sometimes appear in the legendary geography of China's "Eastern Sea." Of the two, *fusang* is more widely used and has at times been used as a poetic name for Japan. Both place names seem to have originated in the names of trees, and Wu Lai exploits this ambivalence here for poetic effect.

19. Also Xian Mengao 羡門高. An immortal mentioned in the *Shiji* (Annals of Xiaowu 孝武本纪) together with An Qisheng.

20. Cai (2008: 95).

21. For the tale of Mahākāśyapa's smile, which originated in China in the tenth or the eleventh century, see Welter (2000). For how Potalaka was taken to mean "little white flower," see the Introduction.

22. See, however, the remarks on the *Sanguan* Hall in Ch. 2, Exhibit 2.

23. Lu (1980: Vol. II, 113). For the role of scenic sights in modern Chinese tourism see Nyíri (2006).

24. Hou-Tu Gazetteer (Fasc. 5, p. 20b).

25. Wang probably did not visit Mount Putuo, though he came close when he was on Zhoushan in 1507.

26. None of the information on him in English (Goodrich (1976: sub voc.), Nienhauser (1986: sub voc.)) does mention his active promotion of Buddhism, for example. The most comprehensive study to date is Wu Xinmiao (2008). Wu offers a comprehensive discussion of Tu Long's role in the literary debates of his time but does not even mention his editorship of the Hou-Tu Gazetteer. Tu Long's works have recently appeared in an authoritative new edition (Wang Chaohong 2012).

27. The attribution of the *Kaopan yushi* is disputed, and it is not included in Tu Long's Collected Works (Wang Chaohong 2012). An excellent annotated and illustrated edition of the *Kaopan yushi* is Tu and Zhao (2012). For a translation of a similar compendium by Li Yu, see Dars (2003). For the literati culture surrounding these "precious things" or curiosities in the late Ming and early Qing, see Clunas (1991 [2004]).

28. Brook (1993a: 272).

29. Searching the Digital Archive of Buddhist Temple Gazetteers (Ver. January 2014). See also the collaboration of Daoists and Buddhists in Tu's play *Tanhua ji* (esp. Scene 7). Cf. Brook (1993a: 66–68).

30. *Mingzhou ayuwang shanzhi* (p. 259).

31. For a summary of Tu's critique, see Kubota (1931 [1986]: 649–660).

32. Kubota (1931 [1986]: 642) believes Zhenyi is a *nom de plume* of Tu Long himself, but that is unlikely. First, Zhenyi is not among the known pseudonyms of Tu, and second, he could not have called himself "monk" (*shamen* 沙門, Skt. *śramaṇa*). The author of the preface, who signed himself 沙門真一, was in all likelihood not Tu Long but the Zhenyi mentioned in other places in the Putuo gazetteers (see Dharma Drum Person Authority Database sub voc. 真一).

33. The Qiu-Zhu PT Gazetteer contains a set of twelve poems on the same sites by the monk Huanmin 幻敏 (1639–1707) (Fasc. 15, pp. 6a–b).

34. Except where otherwise indicated the text is from the Hou-Tu Gazetteer (Fasc. 6, pp. 13aff.).

35. Cai (2008: 220). The rhyme is imperfect in poem 11 (津 does not rhyme with 輪); this is perhaps balanced out by the reduplication of the first two characters in poems 11 and 12.

36. Mount Luofu in Guangdong was considered a famous Daoist grotto-heaven (*dongtian* 洞天). Tu Long here echoes a line by Su Shi from his poem *Zaiyong 'Songfeng ting xia meihua sheng kai' yun* 再用"松風亭下梅花盛開"韵: "In the Plumblossom Village at the foot of Mount Luofu // the jade-white snow turns into bone-white ice and spirits" 羅浮山下梅花村, 玉雪爲骨冰爲魂. The "plum" points to Putuo's older name Mount Meicen, and the image of the "white blossoms" to the Chinese nickname of Mount Putuo: "Little White Blossom." Neither is mentioned explicitly, readers were expected to know their Su Shi.

37. Zhang (2011: 24) believes the color red in the text comes from the red blossoms of the 山茶華 tree, which he obviously believes to be the tea plant. The tea plant (*Camellia sinensis*) blossoms white, however, and the 山茶華 is rather the Rose of Winter (*Camellia japonica*), a different shrub. The *xian zhu ren* 獻珠人, "the person gifting the pearl" is of course the Dragon Girl.

38. "Hearer" (originally a translation of *śrāvaka*) is in the context of Chinese Mahāyāna a term for a "Hīnayāna" practitioner, who was considered inferior compared to practitioners of the Bodhisattva way. Pun is intended therefore when the line says that the monks are not "hearers," although they attain enlightenment while listening to the waves.

39. A lake at the foot of Tea Mountain (Zhou Gazetteer, p. 111), later known as Feishayu 飛沙隩.

40. This is a reference to a story in the Zhuangzi (Chapter *Waiwu* 外物) and other early works, which the audience would have immediately recognized and connected with the place name in the title. The tale is about a "spirit turtle" (*shengui* 神龜) who appears to the Ruler of Song in a dream revealing itself as "ambassador from Clear-Water to the River Earl" and in need of help because it was caught by a fisherman. The King of Song takes the turtle from the fisherman, but instead of setting it free has it killed and its carapace used for divination. The carapace was said to be "five cubits in circumference," and the number is echoed in the second line which refers to the *five signs*-method of divination, an allusion that I have not translated.

41. Meant here is the "Eastern Gate of Heaven," one of three heavenly gates on Putuo Island (Wang Hengyan Gazetteer, p. 104).

42. Guanyin is often depicted with a tame dragon. The topos is based on passages in the Lotus Sutra, which say praying to Guanyin protects from the damage that can be wrought by dragons (see, e.g., CBETA/T.9.262.58a3–5, or CBETA/T.20.1052. 67b20–22). In China dragons were connected to wind and rain and brought storms and devastation (Loewe 1994: 142–159; Brook 2010: 6–23) at least since the Han dynasty. Asking Guanyin to subdue the dragons was therefore often equivalent to asking for good weather, preventing storms, or ending a flood, all matters of considerable concern for the people of Zhejiang and Jiangsu. The iconography also illustrates the assimilation of the Chinese "dragons" into the Buddhist cosmos. By conflating the Chinese dragon with the Indian *nāga* serpent spirits, Buddhism applied the same move twice: similar to the

inclusion of the *nāgas* into Buddhist lore that happened earlier in India, the subjugation of the rain-bringing dragons by the Dharma in China asserts its dominance over local cults. The very words "subdued poisonous dragon" (*zhi dulong* 制毒龍), e.g., are also used in a *jātaka* story about the Buddha in a previous life as an evil *nāga*/dragon, who is reformed by the precepts (see, e.g., *Da zhidu lun* CBETA/T.25.1509.162a11). Dragons feature prominently in the poetic imagery around Mount Putuo. In addition, see, e.g., poem No. 10 or Hou Jigao's poem on the Fayu Temple (Hou-Tu Gazetteer, Fasc. 5, pp. 28a–b). In an insightful essay Bernard Faure (1987) has proposed that *nāgas* should be seen as representing local, territorial cults, whereas the Bodhisattva or traveling monk that tames (or at times kills) them stands for the supra-spacial side of Buddhist doctrinal ideology.

43. "Precious raft" *baofa* 寶筏 is a metaphor for the Dharma teachings that ferry sentient beings over to the "other shore." The Hou-Tu Gazetteer (Fasc. 6, p. 14b) has *wà* 襪—the socks or leggings (*pādaveṣṭanikā*) allowed by the Vinaya that are part of the attire of Chinese monastics. 寶襪 seems unusual ("[clad] in precious hose"?), and later editions of this poem have the common 寶筏, which I translate here (e.g., Wang Hengyan Gazetteer, p. 115). This might be a *lectio facilior.*

44. The lotus pond where people are reborn in Amitābha's pure land.

45. The Beryl World (琉璃界 *vaiḍūrya-dhātu) appears in texts connected to the pure land of the Medicine Buddha, also known as King of Beryl Radiance (*Vaiḍūryaprabhārāja*). Like Mount Putuo, the Beryl World is said to be in "the East" (CBETA/T.19.926.42a23). Here, however, Tu Long is also hinting at one of the manifestations of Guanyin. As Beryl Guanyin 琉璃觀音, or King of Fragrance 香王, this manifestation is depicted as floating on a lotus flower, which ties it into the imagery evoked in the first line.

46. "Incense Cauldron" was the name of a small island (*Xianglu shan* 香爐山). It appears on the map in the Zhou Gazetteer (p. 75) and in Hou Jigao's work on the defenses of Zhejiang (Hou 1593 [1995]: 31–99/100).

47. *Boshan* 博山, next to Penglai 蓬萊 and Yingzhou 瀛洲, was one of the three fabled Daoist islands of the immortals. *Boshan* is also short for Boshan stove 博山爐, a special type of censer in the shape of a mountain, understood as depicting the Daoist paradise (for images, see Munakata 1991: 72–81). Whenever incense or sandal wood is burned inside the censer, the smoke rises through holes in the "mountain," making it seem like clouds. This is alluded to in the next sentence. I am grateful to Liu Tingyu for alerting me to the Boshan stove allusion.

48. This poem too is about a smaller island close to Mount Putuo (*Jin boyu shan* 金鉢盂山). The name alludes to the legend of a golden begging bowl (*jin boyu* 金鉢盂) that appeared floating in the sea during the early Hongwu reign (c. 1370) (e.g., Zhou Gazetteer, pp. 153–154).

49. Like Incense Cauldron and Golden Bowl, this poem is about a smaller island close by Mount Putuo. While the former two islands are not currently connected with Mount Putuo, Luojia Shan is still associated with it. There are daily ferries from Mount Putuo to Luojia, and it still plays a role in the pilgrimage-tourism offerings at today's site where advertisement boards announce "No journey to Mount Putuo is complete without a visit to Luojia!"

50. I was not able to find a translation of *lingming* 靈明 that reflects all its nuances. "Numinous light of wisdom" tries to cope with the *double entendre* of 明, but another

meaning of the compound denotes the "charioteer of the sun" (HDC sub voc.), linking it with the previous sentence. Understood as "numinous Ming," the line 萬劫靈明應不滅 becomes a wish for the continuity of the dynasty. Tu Long here weaves together religious, political, and astronomical imagery in a single verse.

51. Zhou Yingbin edited, for instance, the gazetteer of the Hanlin Academy in Nanjing, the *Jiujing cilin zhi* 舊京詞林志 (1597).

52. Zhou Gazetteer (p. 446).

53. For literati patronage of Buddhist institutions in the wider Ningbo region, see Brook (1993a: 266–277). For the larger network of gentry society in Ningbo see, Brook (1990: 27–50).

54. Zhou Gazetteer (p. 576).

55. The World Benefactor of the Left was the most senior of eight high-ranking offices in the Sangha Registrar Office 僧錄司 (Zhao 2008: 122ff.). The office was ranked 6a in the official hierarchy, which amounted to a very powerful position for a Buddhist figure in a Confucian institution. On the inviting or sometimes even "drafting" of monks into government service see Zhou (2005: 230–236).

56. A detailed first-person account of this process is included in the autobiography of the monk Zhenhua (Chen-hua 1992: 194–203).

57. Shi Chenkong (1948 [2007]: 2–3). This is contradicted by a contemporary account that describes the island as a place of comparatively lax monastic rules, where even monks could be seen eating meat and drinking (Chen-hua 1992: 188–190). For 1908/1909 Boerschmann reports a strictly vegetarian diet. He had to dispatch his servant to smuggle in some chicken meat (Boerschmann 1911: 166).

58. Zhu Defeng (1830 [2007]: 1b).

59. Viewing a space through its history is called *langu* 覽古 ("contemplation of antiquity") in Chinese poetic theory (Tian 2011: 77).

60. For a detailed analysis of this case, see Ukai (2000). Xie Lingyun seems to have hit a nerve, and this boast proved his undoing. Ukai reckons his feud with Meng Kai contributed considerably to the decline of his career that ended in his execution in the market of Guangzhou.

61. In Liu's poem *Meng fang furu* 夢方孚若 (成佛却居靈運先).

62. My dating of her birth is based on the poem *Bingzi shuhuai* 丙子述懷. Written in the *bingzi* year 1696, she mentions her age as "49 springs."

63. *Ziyongru chanshi yulu* 子雍如禪師語錄 (*Jiaxing Canon* B465).

64. Their communities and poetry have been documented and described by Beata Grant. For the chapter on Ziyong Chengru, see Grant (2009: 165–184); for translations of more of her poems, see Grant (2003: 134–142).

65. CBETA/T.11.310.126a20-21.

66. CBETA/X.73.1456.806b15.

67. A well-known phrase from Su Shi's *First Ode to the Red Cliff* 前赤壁賦 that has entered modern Chinese parlance.

68. This line and the previous alludes to the nine levels of practitioners in the *Guan wuliangshou jing*, of which the highest was the "Upper-upper level rebirth" (*shangpinshang sheng* 上品上生). The different levels of people reborn in Sukhāvatī, were variously depicted in the art of the Pure Land school, e.g., in the Taima Maṇḍala.

69. For another example, see Tu Long's Poem No. 7 in Exhibit 1.

70. Wang (2008: Preface, p. 19). The ratio between monastic and secular authors varies widely between dynasties, but again the impact of the early Ming suppression of Buddhism is visible. For the Song and the Yuan we have more monastic than secular authors (Song: 10 monastic vs. 8 secular; Yuan: 14 vs. 13). In the Ming the relative number of monastic authors drops precipitously (25 vs. 153), while for the Qing and the Republican Period about one third of authors were monastics (Qing: 110 vs. 372, Republic: 13 vs. 33).

71. There are also a number of independent poetry collections by monks. An example by an author who lived and practiced on Mount Putuo is the collection *Linyue ji* (Haiguan 1611) discussed in Xu (2007: 520–524).

Chapter 8

1. Turner (1973: 213). Cohen (1992) comments on the applicability of Turner's model to Buddhist pilgrimage sites in Thailand.

2. There have been various attempts made at describing and categorizing religious pilgrimage and its relationship to tourism. In a study of the role of religion in modern tourism, Stausberg distinguishes between *religiöser Tourismus*, religiously motivated tourism, and *Religionstourismus*, which he defines as tourism to religious sites (Stausberg 2010: 21). Another attempt at categorization is Erik Cohen's four-fold schema consisting of pilgrim, pilgrim-tourist, tourist-traveler, and traveler (Cohen 1991). For an assessment of how the state controls domestic tourism in China, especially the definition and creation of scenic sites, see Nyíri (2007). For a discussion of the dynamics of the tourism industry on Mount Putuo today, see Courtney Bruntz (2014).

3. In English, the best overview of pilgrimage in China is Naquin and Yü (1992a). See also Magnin (1987) and Lagerway (1987).

4. See Strassberg (1994: 1–57) and Landt (1994: 15–33) for an overview of the development and characteristics of the genre and some translations. The most comprehensive discussion of Chinese travelogues in a European language is Eggert (2004). For an example of a travelogue relating a journey to a Daoist Mountain, see Soymié (1956: 44–50). For a virtual journey to a "standard" Daoist mountain site, see Hahn (1988).

5. *Wutaishan ji* 五台山記 included in Xu and Huang (2008: 212–213), translated in Strassberg (1994: 357ff.). Though included in an anthology of travelogues, it is doubtful the text is actually a travelogue, i.e., a first person account of a journey. Nothing implies that Gu Yanwu actually went there; his main concern is the depiction of Wutai in various historical records.

6. "What a pity that I do not have the leisure to stay and rest here for ten days. I could invite Taibo and Yuxi and converse with them among the clouds." In Xu and Huang (2008: 219).

7. Wu (1992: 82–85). See also Brook's remark on how the taste for visiting Buddhist temples seems to have faded in the early Qing (Brook 2005: 179–180).

8. On Japanese medieval travel diaries (*kikō* 紀行), see the extensive study by Plutschow (1982).

9. The German Karl Gützlaff visited as early as 1833 (Gützlaff 1834: 438–446), his account was followed by those of Medhurst (1838: 482–488), Rondot (1847), Fortune (1847: 180–187), Huc (1862 [1854]: Vol. 2: 229–240), Arène (1875), and others. The first

European image of Mount Putuo, supposedly showing the "Grand Temple at Poo-too, Chusan," was published by Wright and Allom (1843: Vol. 4: 28). It bears only passing resemblance with the Puji Temple.

10. For the term route book and its connection to gazetteers, see Brook (2002: 3). A modern edition with some annotation and a useful introduction is Pu and Xu (1991).

11. Embassies during the Song were organized in three ranks. The party would have been about thirty-five people strong not counting sailors.

12. The first gazetteer to include this account is Wang Liansheng (p. 681). However, the text in this edition is (as so often) not reliable. The translation here and below is based on the text in the *Siku quanshu* edition (*Shibu* 史部 (地理類, 外紀之屬), Fasc. 34, pp. 8b–9b), although even this version is problematic. For the complex textual history of the *Xuanhe fengshi gaoli tujing* see Qi (1996).

13. For footprints in Buddhism, see, e.g., Quagliotti (1998) and Arsland (2006).

14. As discussed in Chapter 3 (Exhibit 1), the reference to the Southern Liang (502–557) is a mistake. For all we know, Mount Putuo was established not in the sixth century but in the late Tang.

15. See the exhibits and essays in Nara Kokuritsu Hakubutsukan (2002). For the Ming, which saw much less traffic, see Chen Xiaofa (2009).

16. Nishitani (2002). The statues are enshrined in the Sennyū Temple in Kyōto.

17. I use the title "Commander" for Hou since that was his rank when he wrote his travelogue. As for his actual responsibilities and later career, it would be equally correct to call him General or perhaps Admiral. Information about Commander Hou was hard to come by until recently. He does not appear in any print biographical dictionary or index. In addition to all biographical reference works for the period listed in Wilkinson (2000: 893–894), I have consulted the *Mingdai difangzhi zhuanji suoyin* 明代地方志傳記索引 (30,000+ entries from 299 gazetteers) to no avail. Li (2006) has found some references to Hou in the *Mingshilu* mainly pertaining to his promotions. However, as so often now, an online search quickly produced Hou's life dates and a biographical sketch. The biography on the internet originated on a blog and was subsequently copied to other sites (crucially to Baidu, the largest Chinese online encyclopedia) and edited. When we contacted the author of the original blog post, he turned out to be Hou Yaoming (1938–2011) a private historian and descendant of Hou Jigao, who used the published collection of remaining Ming dynasty archives (*Zhongguo mingchao dang'an zonghui* 中國明朝檔案總匯) as well as unpublished material from clan histories and local libraries in Zhoushan for his research in family history. The biography in the original post titled *Hou Jigao Zhuan* 侯继高传 is therefore based on thorough, original research and contains an overview and a number of important details concerning Hou's career, especially regarding his relationship to religion (this part was deleted in the Baidu entry). In 2012 a posthumous private edition of a clan history of the Hou family (Hou Yaoming 2012) appeared, which included the material published online and adds still more information on Hou Jigao and the Hou clan.

18. Hou Yaoming (2012: 81).

19. See Kyoto Daigaku Kokubungakkai (1961) and Li (2006).

20. Hou Yaoming (2012: 89).

21. The first took place in 1587; Hou made a third journey in 1589 (Hou Yaoming 2012: 90).

22. Translated from the authorial version in the Hou-Tu Gazetteer (Fasc. 3, pp. 5–11). The text is also included in the *Gujin tushu jicheng* 古今圖書集成 collection and (carelessly, with omissions) in the Wang Hengyan Gazetteer (pp. 130–133).

23. Hou Jigao was appointed Regional Commander (*zongbing guan* 總兵官) of Zhejiang in 1585 (Hou Yaoming 2012: 88).

24. 季春甲申朔. "Third month of spring on the day *jiashen*, the first day of the month." This is probably a mistake by Hou; the first day of the lunar month fell on March 26, 1588, the *jiashen* day was one day later on March 27.

25. Today's Zhenhai 鎮海.

26. Zhou Gazetteer (p. 378). Another navy commander who was involved with Mount Putuo during this period was He Rubin 何汝賓 (active in the region 1622–1627). Monastics and colleagues erected a memorial stele for him (Qiu-Zhu Gazetteer, Fasc. 11, p. 48).

27. Zhu (1619 [1991], Fasc. 26, p. 13a).

28. Zhang Dai (1638 [1935]: 50).

29. The mapping of the Zhoushan Archipelago was only completed in the twentieth century. Today it comprises 1,390 islands (Moll-Murata 2006: 109, 120).

30. All place names ending on 門 here are small harbors.

31. *jichou* 己丑. Some versions of the text have *yichou* 已丑, which is wrong.

32. Hou (c. 1594 [1995]: 100).

33. The Wang Gazetteer (p. 131) has 偪船 in a *lectio facilior*.

34. For an image and a detailed description of the "Large Fuchuan class" (*da Fuchuan shi* 大福船式), see Zheng (1624 [1990]: 1203–1204 (Fasc. 13, pp. 3c–4a)).

35. Though they came via the same route, the two journeys ended very differently. While Boerschmann spent three pleasant weeks on the island doing research on the temple architecture of Mount Putuo, Master Zhenhua was drafted into the Republican army at gunpoint. (Boerschmann 1911: 5, 199–203; Chen-hua 1992: 181–203).

36. The pier was used into the twentieth century. Today, however, visitors arrive at a new pier to its west.

37. See Ch. 2, Exhibit 1.

38. The "Purple Bamboo Grove" (*Zizhu lin* 紫竹林) is the place where Sudhana meets Guanyin in the *Buddhāvataṃsaka*. The addition of the fragrant "Sandalwood" to the name is a mistake.

39. Hou Yaoming (2012).

40. For the development of this trope see Berkowitz (2000). Hou's words "to my regret I am only a warrior" 余愧武人 are closely echoed in a poem by Zhu Yi'e朱一鶚 titled "Traveling to Mount Putuo" (first included in the Zhou Gazetteer, p. 463): "To my regret I have the position of an official—looking back into emptiness, how pitiful—our horses and chariots in the dust." 自慚身是宰官身, 回首空憐車馬塵.

41. The Thousand Step Beach is north of the Tidal Sound and the Sudhana Cave. The party walked along the eastern shore of the island.

42. For Dazhi's relationship with the group around Hou Jigao and the founding of the Fayu Temple, see Ch. 4, Exhibit 2.

43. From Kumārajīva's translation of the Lotus Sutra (T.9.262.58a26).

44. Yan Liben and Wu Daozi were the two foremost figure painters of the early Tang (Lawson 1973: 4–7). Already during the Song, the eminent painter Mi Fu complained that

many paintings were wrongly attributed to Yan (Ning 2008:103). The difference between original paintings and copies was not always articulated by collectors and patrons, and considering there are hardly any originals left of Yan's art there can be little doubt that the passage here refers to paintings in the Yan Liben style, not to an original. Yan's style is characterized by the use of fine, even-width lines, which is indeed how the Guanyin on the stele in the Yangzhi Hermitage is drawn.

45. Cai Guiyi 蔡貴易 (1538–1597, *jinshi* 1568). His chosen name is elsewhere only attested as 肖兼.

46. Here referred to by his *hao* Long Quyang 龍渠陽. His title is given as 二守, which is not listed in Hucker (1985), but we know that Long served as vice prefect (*juncheng* 郡丞) of Ningbo. Long's verse is preserved in the Hou-Tu Gazetteer (Fasc. 4, pp. 17a–b).

47. Hou's verse is preserved in the Hou-Tu Gazetteer (Fasc. 4, p. 7a).

48. For the fate and whereabouts of the steles see the note in the Wang Hengyan Gazetteer (p. 572). Apparently both steles were destroyed, but a copy taken in 1608 of the carving based on the painting allegedly by Yan Liben is preserved today in the Yangzhi Hermitage 楊枝庵.

49. *Fusang* 扶桑. Sometimes meaning Japan, but here just the eastern limit of the horizon. The term is often used in the Putuo gazetteers. Though it is not possible to see Japan, which is some 465 miles to the east, Japan must have "felt" close on Mount Putuo, which was situated directly on the shipping lane to Ningbo, the main port of entry for Japanese traders and scholar monks since the Tang dynasty. See Nara Kokuritsu Hakubutsukan (2009) for the Sino-Japanese exchanges around Ningbo.

50. Zhang Dai (1638 [1935], p. 47).

51. The stele text is preserved in the Wang Hengyan Gazetteer (pp. 238–239).

52. *Jingni* 鯨鯢. Actually, whales and salamanders. *Jingni* is used here to describe a hated foe (cf. HDC s.v. *nijing* 鯢鯨).

53. Zhou Gazetteer (p. 363).

54. Ibid. (p. 139).

55. Both were probably benefactors of Buddhism independently of the emperor's order. Zhang is mentioned by Hanshan Deqing as having donated money to rebuild a temple. *Hanshan laoren mengyou ji* 憨山老人夢遊集, Fasc. 22 (CBETA/X.73.1456.622b3).

56. For details of this gift, see the Wang Hengyan Gazetteer (p. 209).

57. This paraphrases two *diangu* 典故 similes in the text.

58. *Futai* 撫臺 probably equals *xunfu* 巡撫. Perhaps this is meant in the singular and refers to one particular Grand Coordinator, a position in charge of overseeing regional administration. Since the mid-Ming it was seconded to the military regional command. In the present context Hou is referring to the military successes against the pirates.

59. A legendary Daoist master in Qin-Han times.

60. *Hù* 嗀 'vomit' (HDC, s.v.). The rare character, which has a number of other meanings, can also be read *qiào* "to attack what is below from above" which might be the way a humorous navy commander describes vomiting from the deck of a boat.

61. The year number has been added only in the Xu Gazetteer and included in the following editions. The Qiu-Zhu Gazetteer has mistakenly Wanli 4, but that was a 丙子 not a 戊子 year.

62. The tenth day of the third lunar month would equal April 4, not 5. This is probably a mistake by Hou.

63. The largest uprisings were the White Lotus rebellion (1794–1804), the Opium Wars (1839–1842 and 1856–1860), the Nien rebellion (1851–1868), the Taiping rebellion (1850–1864), and the Hui rebellions (1862–1877 and 1895–1896). Especially the Opium Wars and the Taiping had an impact on the Ningbo region.

64. The authorial preface is dated 1826, two other prefaces are dated 1827, and the edition used here was printed in 1876. Johnston (1913: 149ff.) mentions other "pilgrims guides" and summarizes one he used in his explorations of Chinese Buddhist sites.

65. According to the Wang Hengyan Gazetteer (p. 418), the Haiyun'an was built to shelter traveling monks.

66. To my knowledge, these tokens, stamped in booklets or on pennants (*xiangqi* 香旗), have not been researched so far. Collecting stamps or tokens on a pilgrimage is attested for other pilgrimage cultures as well. Cf. the *Credencial del Peregrino*, a stamp book for pilgrims that documents their journey to Santiago de Compostella. In pre-modern Japan a pilgrim's "passport" (*ōraitegata* 往來手形) served as identification and permit (Kouamé 2001: 70ff.) and today it is quite common for visitors to temples to have a *shuin* 朱印 "vermillion seal" stamped and calligraphed into a booklet (*shuinchō* 朱印帳) by a priest at the temple.

67. Ruhai Xiancheng (1826: Fasc. 2, pp. 26bff.).

68. *Jinglü* 經律. Glossed by Xiancheng as meaning the *Fanwang jing* and the *Sifenlü* Vinaya.

69. Explained as images of Amitabha, Guanyin, and Mahāsthāmaprāpta. Xiancheng: "Usually on a small scroll that can be folded up. For use in places where there are no Buddha images. One can also hang it when one recites the precepts or during the morning and evening rites."

70. T.24.1484.1008a13–b7. Quoted by Ruhai Xiancheng (1826: Introductory chapter, 16aff.) with commentary.

71. Xiancheng: "Where there is hunger for example."

72. T.10.279.419c14ff.

73 T.10.279.421a04.

74. Ruhai Xiancheng (1826: Introductory chapter, 6b–10a). A similar list is mentioned in Magnin (1987: 299–300).

75. Station 17 (King Anala) and 9 (Jayoṣmāyatana).

76. Wang Liansheng Gazetteer (p. 711).

77. For an eyewitness account of a monk drafted at gunpoint, see Chen-Hua (1992: 198–202).

78. He Zhanglian (1934: 4–12).

79. De Bruyn (2010: 17).

Conclusion

1 Strickman (1977: 14).

Conventions and Abbreviations

1. Official names of the Puji Temple were: *Bukenqu guanyin yuan* 不肯去觀音院 (910–1079), *Baotuo guanyin si* 寶陀觀音寺 (1080–1605), *Huguo yongshou baotuo chansi* 護國永壽寶陀禪寺 (1605–1699), *Puji chansi* 普濟禪寺 (1699–today). In addition

to that there were colloquial usages; Xu Jing, e.g., in 1123 calls the temple *Baotuo yuan* 寶陀院. The Fayu Temple was officially referred to as: *Haichao an* 海潮庵 (1580–1592), *Haichao si* 海潮寺 (1592–1606), *Huguo yongshou zhenhai chansi* 護國永壽鎮海禪寺 (1606–1699), Fayu chansi 法雨禪寺 (1699–now).

2. Order of references is volume.text.page.row.line. E.g., CBETA/T.11.310.126a20-21 means the passage is in volume 11, text 310, on page 126, row a, lines 20 to 21. Dto. for CBETA/X., CBETA/J., T., and X.

BIBLIOGRAPHY

Ambros, Barbara. 2008. *Emplacing a Pilgrimage—The Ōyama Cult and Regional Religion in Early Modern Japan.* Cambridge, MA: Harvard University Asia Center.

Andrews, Susan. 2013. "Representing Mount Wutai's 五臺山 Past: A Study of Chinese and Japanese Miracle Tales about the Five Terrace Mountain." PhD thesis, Columbia University.

Araki, Kengo. 1975. "Buddhism and Confucianism." In: Wm. T. De Bary (ed.), *The Unfolding of Neo-Confucianism*, pp. 39–66. New York: Columbia University Press.

Araki, Kengo 荒牧典俊 (ed.). 2000. *Hokuchō Zui Tō Chūgoku bukkyō shisō shi* 北朝隋唐中国仏教思想史. Kyoto: Hōzōkan 法蔵館.

Araki, Kengo 荒木見悟. 2006 [1995]. *Mingmo Qingchu de sixiang yu fojiao* 明末清初的思想與佛教. Taipei: Liang Jing 聯經. Translated by Liao Chao-heng 廖肇亨. Original: *Chūgoku shingaku no kodō to bukkyō* 中国心学の鼓動と仏教 (Tokyo: Chūgoku shoten 中国書店 1995).

Arène, Jules. 1875. "Excursion de Deux Baigneurs Européens a l'Ile Sacrée de Poutou." *L'Explorateur* Vol. 20.1: 467–471.

Arsland, Markus. 2006. *The Sacred Footprint—A Cultural History of Adam's Peak.* Bangkok: Orchid Press.

Bachelard, Gaston. 1961. *La poétique de l'espace.* Paris: Presses Universitaires.

Beal, Samuel. 1883. "Two Sites Named by Hiouen-Thsang in the 10th Book of the Si-yu-ki." *Journal of the Royal Asiatic Society of Great Britain and Ireland, New Series*, Vol. 15.4 (Oct.): 333–345.

Beal, Samuel. 1884 [1983]. *Si-yu-ki. Buddhist Records of the Western World—Translated from the Chinese of Hiuen Tsang (AD 629).* London: Trübner, 1884 [Delhi: Munshiram, 1983].

Benn, James, Jinhua Chen, and James Robson. 2012. *Images, Relics, and Legends: The Formation and Transformation of Buddhist Sacred Sites.* New York: Mosaic Press.

Berkowitz, Alan. 2000. *Patterns of Disengagement: The Practice and Portrayal of Reclusion in Early Medieval China.* Palo Alto, CA: Stanford University Press.

Bingenheimer, Marcus. 2001. *A Biographical Dictionary of the Japanese Student-Monks of the Seventh and Early Eighth Centuries. Their Travels to China and their Role in the Transmission of Buddhism.* Munich: Iudicium (Buddhismus-Studien/Buddhist Studies 4).

Bingenheimer, Marcus. 2009. "Writing History of Buddhist Thought in the 20th Century—Yinshun (1906–2005) in the Context of Chinese Buddhist Historiography." *Journal of Global Buddhism* Vol. 10: 255–290.

Bingenheimer, Marcus (as 馬德偉). 2010. "Zhongguo fosizhi chutan ji shumu yanjiu 中國佛 志初探及書目研究." *Hanyu foxue pinglun* 汉语佛学评论 Vol. 2: 377–408.

Bingenheimer, Marcus. 2012. "Bibliographical Notes on Buddhist Temple Gazetteers, Their Prefaces and Their Relationship to the Buddhist Canon." *Chung-hwa Buddhist Journal* Vol. 25: 49–84.

Bingenheimer, Marcus (ed.). 2013. *Zhonghua fosizhi congshu*中華佛寺志叢書 (The Zhonghua Collection of Buddhist Temple Gazetteers). No. 1–12. Taipei: Xinwenfeng 新文豐. Vol. 1: 清涼山志 *Mount Qingliang Gazetteer*, Vol. 2: 峨眉山志 *Mount Emei Gazetteer*, Vol. 3: 重修普陀山志 *Revised Gazetteer of Mount Putuo*, Vol. 4: 普陀洛迦新志 *New Gazetteer of Mount Putuo*, Vol. 5: 九華山志 *Mount Jiuhua Gazetteer*, Vol. 6: 天台山方外志 *Mount Tiantai Gazetteer*, Vol. 7-1: 明州阿育王山志 *Aśoka Temple Gazetteer*, Vol. 7-2: 明州阿育王山續志 *Continued Aśoka Temple Gazetteer*, Vol. 8: 寒山寺志 *Hanshan Temple Gazetteer*, Vol. 9: 玉岑山慧因高麗華嚴教寺志 *Huiyin Temple Gazetteer*, Vol. 10: 黃檗山志 *Mount Huangbo Gazetteer*, Vol. 11: 泉州開元寺志 *Kaiyuan Temple Gazetteer*, Vol. 12: 雞足山志 *Mount Jizu Gazetteer*.

Bingenheimer, Marcus. 2014. "A History of the Manchu Buddhist Canon and First Steps Toward Its Digitization." *Central Asiatic Journal* Vol. 56 (2012/2013): 203–219.

Bingenheimer, Marcus. 2015. "The Digital Archive of Buddhist Temple Gazetteers and Named Entity Recognition (NER) in Classical Chinese." *Lingua Sinica* Vol. 1.8: 1–19.

Bingenheimer, Marcus, Jen-Jou Hung, and Simon Wiles. 2011. "Social Network Visualization from TEI Data." *Literary and Linguistic Computing* Vol. 26.3: 271–278.

Birnbaum, Raoul. 1986. "The Manifestation of a Monastery: Shen-Ying's Experiences on Mount Wu-t'ai in T'ang Context." *Journal of the American Oriental Society* Vol. 106.1: 119–137.

Birnbaum, Raoul. 1989. "Secret Halls of the Mountain Lords: The Caves of Wu-t'ai shan." *Cahiers d'Extrême-Asie* Vol. 5: 115–140.

Bo, Juyi 白居易. [1979]. *Bo Juyi ji* 白居易集. 4 vols. Beijing: Zhonghua Shuju.

Boerschmann, Ernst. 1911. *P'u T'o Shan—Die Heilige Insel der Kuan-Yin der Göttin der Barmherzigkeit.* Berlin: Georg Reimer (Die Baukunst und Religiöse Kultur der Chinesen, Band 1).

Boerschmann, Ernst. 1923. *Baukunst und Landschaft in China. Eine Reise durch zwölf Provinzen. Mit 288 großformatigen Aufnahmen.* Berlin: Ernst Wasmuth (Republished 1982 as *Old China in Historic Photographs: 288 Views.* New York: Dover Publications).

Bol, Peter K. 2001. "The Rise of Local History: History, Geography, and Culture in Southern Song and Yuan Wuzhou." *Harvard Journal of Asiatic Studies* Vol. 61.1: 37–76.

Bol, Peter K. 2003. "The 'Localist Turn' and 'Local Identity' in Later Imperial China." *Late Imperial China* Vol. 24.2: 1–50.

Borges, Jorge Luis. 1944. "Funes el memorioso." In: J. L. Borges, *Ficciones*, pp. 51–56. Buenos Aires: Sur.

Brook, Timothy. 1990. "Family Continuity and Cultural Hegemony in Ningbo: The Chinese Gentry, 1368–1911." In: Joseph Esherick, Mary Rankin (eds.), *Chinese Local Elites and Patterns of Dominance*, pp. 27–50. Berkeley: University of California Press.

Brook, Timothy. 1993a. *Praying for Power—Buddhism and the Formation of Gentry Society in Late-Ming China*. Cambridge, MA, and London: Council on East Asian Studies Harvard University.

Brook, Timothy. 1993b. "Rethinking Syncretism: The Unity of the Three Teachings and their Joint Worship in Late- Imperial China." *Journal of Chinese Religions* Vol. 21: 13–44.

Brook, Timothy. 1997. "At the Margin of Public Authority: The Ming State and Buddhism." In: Theodore Huters, R. Bin Wong, and Pauline Yu (eds.), *Culture and State in Chinese History: Conventions, Accommodations and Critiques*, pp. 161–181. Stanford, CA: Stanford University Press.

Brook, Timothy. 1998. "Communications and Commerce." In: Twichett and Mote (eds.), *The Cambridge History of China*, Vol. 8: 582–707.

Brook, Timothy. 2002. *Geographical Sources of Ming-Qing History*. Ann Arbor, MI: University of Michigan, Center for Chinese Studies. (Michigan monographs in Chinese Studies; 58) [First edition 1988].

Brook, Timothy. 2005. "Buddhism in the Chinese Constitution: Recording Monasteries in North Zhili." In: T. Brook, *The Chinese State in Ming Society*, pp. 158–181. London: Routledge.

Brook, Timothy. 2010. *The Troubled Empire—China in the Yuan and Ming Dynasties*. Cambridge, MA: Harvard University Press.

Brook, Timothy. 2013. *Mr. Selden's Map of China—Decoding the Secrets of a Vanished Cartographer*. New York: Bloomsbury Press.

Bruntz, Courtney. 2014. "Commodifying Mount Putuo: State Nationalism, Religious Tourism, and Buddhist Revival." PhD thesis, Graduate Theological Union.

Bumbacher, Stephan P. 2010. "Zum religionsgeschichtlichen Quellenwert des literarischen Genres *zhuan* ("Lebensbeschreibung") in Daoismus und chinesischem Buddhismus." In: Schalk and Deeg, *Geschichte und Geschichten*, pp. 57–95.

Butler, John. 1879. "Pootoo Ancient and Modern—A Lecture Delivered before the Ningbo Book Club, January, 29, 1879." *Chinese Recorder and Missionary Journal* Vol. 10: 108–124.

Cai, Zong-qi. 2008. *How to Read Chinese Poetry*. New York: Columbia University Press.

Cahill, James. 1992. "Huang Shan Paintings as Pilgrimage Pictures." In: Susan Naquin and Yü Chün-fang (eds.), *Pilgrims and Sacred Sites in China*, pp. 246–292. Berkeley: University of California Press [Reprint Taipei: SMC Publishing, 1994].

Campany, Robert F. 1996. "The Earliest Tales of the Bodhisattva Guanshiyin." In: Donald Lopez (ed.), *Religions of China in Practice*, pp. 82–96. Princeton, NJ: Princeton University Press.

Campany, Robert F. 2012. *Signs from the Unseen Realm—Buddhist Miracle Tales from Early Medieval China*. Honolulu: Hawaii University Press.

Cantor, Theodore. 1842. *General Features of Chusan—With Remarks on the Flora and Fauna of that Island.* London: Taylor.

Cao, Ganghua 曹刚华. 2011. *Mingdai fojiao fangzhi yanjiu* 明代佛教方志研究. Beijing: Zhongguo renming daxue 中国人名大学出版社.

Cao Wanru 曹婉如, Zheng Xihuang 郑锡煌, et al. 1990. *Zhongguo gudai ditu ji: Zhanguo—Yuan* 中国古代地图集 战国—元 *(An Atlas of Ancient Maps in China—From the Warring States Period to the Yuan Dynasty (476 B.C. – A.D. 1368)).* Beijing: Cultural Relics Publishing House.

Cartelli, Mary Ann. 2013. *The Five-Colored Clouds of Mount Wutai: Poems from Dunhuang.* Leiden: Brill.

Chang, Kang-i Sun. 1997. "Ming and Qing Anthologies of Women's Poetry and Their Selection Strategies." In: Ellen Widmer, Kang-i Chang (eds.), *Writing Women in Late Imperial China,* pp. 147–170. San Francisco: Stanford University Press.

Chavannes, Édouard. *Le T'ai Chan—Essai de monographie d'un culte chinois.* Paris: Éditions Ernest Leroux, 1910.

Chen-Hua. 1992. *In Search of the Dharma—Memoirs of a Modern Chinese Buddhist Pilgrim.* New York: State University of New York Press.

Chen, Jianhuang 陳劍鍠. 2003. "Sida mingshan shi de xuanxie guocheng ji qi zongjiao yiyi 大名山志的撰寫過程及其宗教意義." *Pumen xuebao* 普門學報 Vol. 15 (2003–5): 109–145.

Chen, Xiaofa 陈小法. 2009. "Riben qian Ming shi yu Putuo shan 日本遣明使与普陀山." In: Guo and Zhang, pp. 18–33.

Chen, Yunü 陳玉女. 1995. "Mindai bukkyō shakai no chiiki teki kenkyū: kajō manreki nenkan o chūshin toshite 明付仏教社會の地域的研究—嘉靖•萬暦年間(1522–1620)を中心として" PhD thesis, Kyūshū University.

Chen, Yunü 陳玉女. 1996. "Mingdai zhongye yiqian huanguang, sengguaan yu tingchen de lianjie guanxi—tongguo 'fensi' yu 'diyuan' wenti de tantao 明代中葉以前宦官、僧官與廷臣的連結關係-透過對 「墳孝」與「地緣」問題的探討" *Chengong daxue lishi xuebao* 成功大學歷史學報 Vol. 22: 283–304.

Chen, Yunü 陳玉女. 2001. *Mingdai ershi si yamen huanguan yu Beijing fojiao* 明付二十四衙門宦官與北京佛教 (Eunuchs of the Twenty-Four Yamen in the Ming Dynasty and Buddhism). Taipei: Ruwen 如聞.

Cheng, Irene. 1976. *Clara Ho Tung: A Hong Kong Lady, Her Family and Her Times.* Hong Kong: The Chinese University of Hong Kong.

Chou, Wen-shing. 2007. "Ineffable Paths: Mapping Wutaishan in Qing Dynasty China." *Art Bulletin* Vol. 89.1: 108–129.

Chu, William. 2010 (2011). "The Timing of the Yogācāra resurgence in the Ming Dynasty (1368–1643)." *Journal of the International Association of Buddhist Studies* Vol. 33.1–2: 5–27.

Chuang, Chi-Fa 莊吉發. 1978. *Sun Wencheng zouzhe* 孫文成奏摺. Taipei: Wenshizhe 文史哲.

Cohen, Erik. 1991. "Pilgrimage and Tourism: Convergence and Divergence." In: E. A. Morinis (ed.), *Journeys to Sacred Places,* pp. 47–61. Westport, CT: Greenwood Press.

Cohen, Erik. 1992. "Pilgrimage Centers: Concentric and Excentric." *Annals of Tourism Research* Vol. 19: 33–50.

Cosgrove, Denis E. 2008. *Geography and Vision—Seeing, Imagining and Representing the World.* London: I.B. Tauris.

Cover, Thomas M., and Joy A. Thomas. 2006. *Elements of Information Theory.* 2nd ed. Hoboken, NJ: Wiley, pp. 301–348.

Cresswell, Tim. 2004. *Place—A Short Introduction.* London: Blackwell.

Crow, Carl. 1921. *The Travelers' Handbook for China (Including Hongkong).* 3rd ed. New York: Dodd, Mead and Co.

Cuevas, Bryan J., and Jacqueline I. Stone. 2007. *The Buddhist Dead: Practices, Discourses, Representations.* Honolulu: Hawaii University Press.

Daojian 道堅. 2012. *Chongqing Zhongzhou fojiao yanjiu* 重慶忠州佛教研究. Beijing: Zhongjiao wenhua 宗教文化出版社.

Dars, Jacques. 2003. *Les Carnets Secrets de Li Yu.* Arles, France: Editions Philippe Picquier.

De Bary, William (ed.). 1975. *The Unfolding of Neo-Confucianism.* New York and London: Columbia University Press.

De Bruyn, Pierre-Henry. 2010. *Le Wudang Shan—Histoire des récits fondateurs.* Paris: Les Indes Savantes.

De Visser, Marinus Willem. 1913. *The Dragon in China and Japan.* Amsterdam: Johannes Müller.

De Weerdt, Hilde. 2009. "Maps and Memory: Readings of Cartography in Twelfth-and Thirteenth-Century Song China." *Imago Mundi: The International Journal for the History of Cartography* Vol. 61.2 (1913): 145–167.

De Giorgi, Manuela, Annette Hoffmann, and Nicola Suthor (eds.). 2013. *Synergies in Visual Culture—Bildkulturen im Dialog. Festschrift für Gerhard Wolf.* Munich: Wilhelm Fink.

Deeg, Max. 1999. "Umgestaltung buddhistischer Kosmologie auf dem Weg von Indien nach China." In: Dieter Zeller (ed.), *Religion im Wandel der Kosmologien*, pp. 241–254. Frankfurt: Peter Lang.

Dennis, Joseph. 2010. "Financial Aspects of Publishing Local Histories in the Ming Dynasties." *Princeton East Asian Library Journal* Vol. 14.1/2: 158–244.

De Weerdt, Hilde. 2003. "Regional Descriptions: Administrative and Scholarly Traditions." In: Patrick Hanan (ed.), *Treasures of the Yanching*, pp. 122–153. Cambridge, MA: Harvard-Yenching Library.

Döll, Steffen. 2010. *Im Osten des Meeres: Chinesische Emigrantenmönche und die frühen Institutionen des japanischen Zen-Buddhismus (East of the Ocean: Chinese Emigrant Monks and the Early Institutions of Japanese Zen Buddhism).* Stuttgart: Franz Steiner.

Döll, Steffen. 2012. "Manifestations of the Mountain: Preliminary Remarks on the Utopian Study of Potalaka in Pre-modern East Asia." *Review of Asian and Pacific Studies* Vol. 37: 83–102.

Dott, Brian R. 2004. *Identity Reflections—Pilgrimages to Mount Tai in Late Imperial China.* Cambridge, MA, and London: Harvard University Press.

Drake, Frederick C. 1984. *The Empire of the Seas—A Biography of Rear Admiral Robert Wilson Shufeldt, USN.* Honolulu: University of Hawaii Press.

Dudbridge, Glen. 1991. "A Pilgrimage in Seventeenth-Century Fiction: T'ai-shan and the 'Hsing-shih yin-yüan chuan'." *T'oung Pao* Vol. 77.4/5: 226–252.

Dudbridge, Glen. 1992. "Women Pilgrims to T'ai Shan: Some Pages from a Seventeenth-Century Novel." In: Naquin and Yü, 1992, pp. 39–64.

Dudbridge, Glen. 1998. "Buddhist Images in Action: Five Stories from the Tang." *Cahiers d'Extrême Asie* Vol. 10 (1998): 377–391.

Durand-Dastès, Vincent. 2002. "Désirés, raillés, corrigés: Les bonzes dévoyés dans le roman en langue vulgaire du XVIe au XVIIIe siècle." In: Vincent Goossaert (ed.), *L'Anticléricalisme en Chine*, pp. 95–112. Saint-Denis, France: Presses Universitaires de Vincennes.

Durt, Hubert (H•デュルト). 1984. *"Nihon zenshu no gohōjin: Daiken shuri bosatsu ni tsuite* 日本禅宗の護法神：大権修利菩薩について*." Indogaku bukkyō gaku kenkyū* 印度学仏教学研究 Vol. 64: 128–129.

Eberhard, Wolfram. 1964. "Temple Building Activities in Medieval and Modern China." *Monumenta Serica* 23: 264–318.

Eggert, Marion. 2004. "Der Reisebericht (*youji*)." In: Marion Eggert, Wolfgang Kubin, Rolf Trauzettel, and Thomas Zimmer (eds.), *Die klassische chinesische Prosa Essay, Reisebericht, Skizze, Brief—Vom Mittelalter bis zur Neuzeit* (Geschichte der chinesischen Literatur Vol. 4), pp. 117–202. Munich: K. G. Saur Verlag.

Eichman, Jennifer. 2005. "Spiritual Seekers in a Fluid Landscape: A Chinese Buddhist Network in the Wanli Period (1573–1620)." Unpublished PhD thesis, Princeton University.

Eliade, Mircea. 1957. *The Sacred and the Profane—The Nature of Religion*. Orlando, FL: Harcourt.

Elman, Benjamin A. 1997. "The Formation of 'Dao Learning' as Imperial Ideology During the Early Ming Dynasty." In: Theodore Huters, R. Bin Wong, and Pauline Yu (eds.), *Culture and State in Chinese History: Conventions, Accommodations and Critiques*, pp. 58–82. Stanford, CA: Stanford University Press.

Elman, Benjamin A. 2013. *Civil Examinations and Meritocracy in Late Imperial China*. Cambridge, MA: Harvard University Press.

Faure, Bernard. 1987. "Space and Place in Chinese Religious Traditions." *History of Religions* Vol. 26.4 (May): 337–356.

Fiordalis, David V. 2008. "Miracles and Superhuman Powers in South Asian Buddhist Literature." Unpublished PhD thesis, University of Michigan.

Forêt, Philippe, and Andreas Kaplony (eds.). 2008. *The Journey of Maps and Images on the Silk Road*. Leiden: Brill.

Foulk, T. Griffith. 1993. "Myth, Ritual, and Monastic Practice in Sung Ch'an Buddhism." In: Patricia B. Ebrey and Peter N. Gregory (eds.), *Religion and Society in T'ang and Song China*, pp. 147–208. Honolulu: Hawaii University Press.

Franke, Otto. 1938. *Li Tschi* 李贄 *- Ein Beitrag zur Geschichte der Chinesischen Geisteskämpfe im 16. Jahrhundert*. Berlin: De Gruyter (Abhandlungen der Preussischen Akademie der Wissenschaften Jahrg. 1937. Phil.-hist. Klasse Nr. 10).

Fukushima, Kosai 福島光哉. 1979. "Chigi no kannōron to sono shisōteki haikei 智顗の感応論とその思想的背景" Ōtani Gakuhō 大谷学報 Vol. 49.4: 36–49.

Fortune, Robert. 1847. *Three Years' Wanderings in the Northern Provinces of China, including a Visit to the Tea, Silk and Cotton Countries*. London: John Murray.

Geiss, James. 1988. "The Chia-ching reign, 1522–1566." In: Mote and Twitchett (eds.): *The Cambridge History of China* Vol. 7: 440–510.

Gernet, Jacques: *Buddhism in Chinese Society—An Economic History from the Fifth to the Tenth Century.* New York: Columbia University Press, 1995.

Gimello, Robert M. 1992. "Chang Shang-ying on Wu-t'ai Shan." In: Naquin and Yü (eds.), *Pilgrims and Sacred Sites in China*, pp. 89–149.

Goodrich, L. Carrington. 1976. *A Dictionary of Ming Biography.* New York and London: Columbia University Press.

Goossaert, Vincent. 2000. "Counting the Monks—The 1736–1739 Census of the Chinese Clergy." *Late Imperial China* Vol. 21.2 (December): 40–85.

Goossaert, Vincent. 2002. "Anatomie d'un discourse anticlérical: le *Shenbao*, 1872–1878." In: Vincent Goossaert (ed.), *L'Anticléricalisme en Chine*, pp. 113–131. Saint-Denis, France: Presses Universitaires de Vincennes.

Grapard, Allen G. 1989. "The Textualized Mountain—Enmountained Text: The *Lotus Sutra* in Kunisaki." In: Tanabe and Tanabe (1989), pp. 159–190.

Grapard, Allen G. 1992. *The Protocol of the Gods.* Berkeley: University of California Press.

Groot, Jan Jakob Maria de. 1886. *Les Fêtes Annuellement célébrées à Émoui (Amoy).* Paris: Leroux 1886 (Annales du Musée Guimet No. 11) (Transl. C. G. Chavannes) [Reprint San Francisco: Chinese Material Center Reprint Series No. 77, 1977.]

Grootaers, Willem A. 1945. "Les temples villageois de la region au sud-est de Tat'ong (Chansinord), leurs inscriptions et leur histoire." *Folklore Studies* Vol. 4: 161–212.

Grootaers, Willem A. 1948a. "Temples and History of Wan-ch'üan (Chahar), the Geographical Method Applied to Folklore." *Monumenta Serica* XIII: 209–316.

Grootaers, Willem A. 1948b. "Catholic University Expedition to Hsüanhua (South Chahar)—Preliminary Report." *Folklore Studies* 7: 135–138.

Grootaers, Willem A. 1951. "Rural Temples Around Hsüan-hua (South Chahar), Their Iconography and Their History." *Folklore Studies* 10:1: 1–3, 6–17, 26–48, 54–61, 68–73.

Guo, Wanping 郭万平; Zhang, Jie 张捷. 2009. *Zhoushan Putuo yu dongya haiyu wenhua jiaoliu* 舟山普陀与东亚海域文化交流. Hangzhou: Zhejiang University Press 浙江大学.

Gutzlaff, Charles [Gützlaff, Karl F. A.]. 1834. *Journal of three voyages along the coast of China, in 1831, 1832, & 1833, with notices of Siam, Corea, and the Loo-Choo islands.* London: Frederick Westley and A. H. Davis. Preface by William Ellis.

Hahn, Thomas. 1997. *Formalisierter Wilder Raum—Chinesische Berge und ihre Beschreibungen (shanzhi* 山志). Unpublished PhD thesis, Heidelberg University.

Hahn, Thomas. 1988. "The Standard Taoist Mountain and Related Features of Religious Geography." *Cahiers d'Extrême-Asie* Vol. 4: 145–156.

Haiguan 海觀. 1611. *Linyue ji* 林樾集. Included in *Chanmen yishu (xu bian)* 禪門遺書 續編. Taipei: Hansheng 漢聲, 1987. Vol. 3: 1–42.

Halperin, Mark. 2006. *Out of the Cloister—Literati Perspectives on Buddhism in Sung China 960 – 1270.* Cambridge, MA: Harvard University Asia Center.

Hammond, Kenneth J. 2001. "Beijing's Zhihua Monastery: History and Restoration in China's Capital." In: Weidner (ed.), *Cultural Intersections*, pp. 189–208.

Hargett, James M. 1996. "Song Dynasty Local Gazetteers and Their Place in the History of *Difangzhi* Writing." *Harvard Journal of Asiatic Studies* Vol. 56.2: 405–442.

Hargett, James M. 2006. *Stairway to Heaven—A Journey to the Summit of Mount Emei.* Albany: State University of New York Press.

Harley, J. B., and David Woodward. 1994. *The History of Cartography, Vol. 2, Book 2: Cartography in the Traditional East and Southeast Asian Societies.* Chicago: University of Chicago Press.

Harrist, Robert E. 2008. *The Landscape of Words—Stone Inscriptions from Early and Medieval China.* Seattle: University of Washington Press.

Hasebe, Yūkei 長谷部幽蹊. 1987. *Min Shin bukkyō kenkyū shiryō—bunken no bu* 明清仏教研 究資料. 文献之部. Nagoya: Komada Insatsu 駒田印刷.

He, Jianming 何建明. 1999. *Aomen Fojiao: Aomen yu neidi fojiao wenhua guanxi shi* 澳门佛教: 澳门与内地佛教文化关系史. Beijing: Zongjiao wenhua 宗教文化出版社.

He Xiaorong 何孝荣. 1994. "Ye Xianggao yu mingmo zhengju 叶向高与明末政局." *Fujian luntan (renwen shehui kexue ban)* 福建论坛(人文社会科学版) Vol. 3: 62–66.

He Xiaorong 何孝荣. 2000. "Mingdai huanguan yu fojiao 明代宦官与佛教." *Nankai xuebao* 南开学报Vol. 1: 18–27.

He, Xiaorong 何孝榮. 2012. "Yuanmo Mingchu mingseng Laifu shiji kao 元末明初名僧來復事跡考." *Lishi jiaoxue* 歷史教學 Vol. 12 (December): 14–21.

He, Jianming 何建明. 1999. *Aomen Fojiao: Aomen yu neidi fojiao wenhua guanxi shi* 澳门佛教: 澳门与内地佛教文化关系史. Beijing: Zongjiao wenhua 宗教文化出版社.

He, Zhanglian 何張蓮 (Clara Ho). 1934. *He Zhanglian mingshan youji* 何張蓮名山遊記. Hongkong: Lianhua 聯華.

Heine, Steven, and Dale S. Wright (eds.). 2000. *The Kōan—Texts and Contexts in Zen Buddhism.* New York: Oxford University Press.

Heller, Natasha. 2008. "Visualizing Pilgrimage and Mapping Experience: Mount Wutai on the Silk Road." In: Forêt and Kaplony (eds.), *The Journey of Maps and Images on the Silk Road*, pp. 29–50.

Helmig, Jan, and Kessler, Oliver. 2007. "Space, Boundaries, and the Problem of Order: A View from Systems Theory." *International Political Sociology* Vol. 1.3: 240–256.

Hikosaka, Shu. 1998. "The Potiyil Mountain in Tamil Nadu and the Origin of the Avalokiteśvara Cult." In: *Buddhism in Tamil Nadu: Collected Papers*, pp. 119–141. Chennai, India: Institute of Asian Studies.

Hino, Takuya. 2012. "Ocean of Suffering, Boat of Compassion: A Study of the *Fudaraku Tokai* and *Urashima* in Anecdotal (*setsuwa*) Literature." *Journal of the American Academy of Religion* Vol. 80.4 (December): 1049–1076.

Ho, Ping-Ti. 1964. *The Ladder or Success in Imperial China.* New York: Science Editions [first edition, New York: Columbia University Press, 1962].

Hong, Huanchun 洪換椿. 1984. *Zhejiang fangzhi kao* 浙江方志考. Hangzhou: Zhejiang renmin 浙江人民.

Hou, Jigao 侯繼高. 1593 (according to Hou Yaoming 2012: 91) [1995]. *Quan Zhe bing-zhi* 全浙 兵制. Manuscript from the Tianjin Library included in *Sikuquan shu cunmu congshu* 四庫全書存目叢書; "Master," Part 子部, Fasc. 31: 95–236.

Hou, Yaoming 侯耀明. 2012. *Jinshan xiang Houshi jiazupu* 金山鄉侯氏家族譜. Privately published.

Hu, Lenny (Transl.). 2003. *In the Inner Quarters.* Vancouver: Arsenal Pulp.

Huang, Jun 黃鈞, and Chen Manming 陳滿銘 (eds.). 2010. *Xinyi Soushen ji* 新譯搜神記. Taipei: Sanmin 三民書局.

Huang, Liu-Hung. 1984. *Complete Book Concerning Happiness and Benevolence.* Translated by Djang Chu. Tucson, AZ: University of Arizona Press.

Huang, Ray. 1981. *1587—A Year of No Significance. The Ming Dynasty in Decline.* New Haven, CT, and London: Yale University Press.

Huang, San, and Jean Blasse. 1992. *Moines et nonnes dans l'océan des péchés.* Arles, France: Picquier.

Huang, Shih-shan Susan. 2001. "Summoning the Gods: Paintings of Three Officials of Heaven, Earth, and Water and Their Association with Daoist Ritual Performance in the Southern Song Period (1127–1279)." *Artibus Asiae* Vol. 61.1: 5–52.

Huang, Shih-shan Susan. 2012. *Picturing the True Form—Daoist Visual Culture in Traditional Culture.* Cambridge, MA, and London: Harvard University Asia Center.

Huang, Wei 黄苇. 1986. *Zhongguo difangzhi cidian* 中国地方志词典. Hefei: Huangshan shushe.

Huang, Wei 黄苇. 1993. *Fangzhixue* 方志学. Shanghai: Fudan chubanshe.

Huc, Évariste Régis. 1862 [1854]. *L'Empire Chinois.* 2 vols. Paris: Gaume & Duprey.

Hucker, Charles O. 1985. A Dictionary of Official Titles in Imperial China. San Francisco: Stanford University Press.

Hung, Ming-shui. 1997. *The Romantic Vision of Yuan Hung-tao, Late Ming Poet and Critic.* Taipei: Bookman.

Ide, Seinosuke 井手誠之輔. 1996. "Nagano Jōshōji shozō Fudarakusan seikyōzu 長野 定勝寺 所藏 補陀洛山聖境図." *Bijutsu kenkyū* 美術研究 Vol. 365: 39–49.

Idema, Wilt L. 1999. "Guanyin's Parrot: A Chinese Buddhist Animal Tale and Its International Context." In: Alfredo Cadonna (ed.), *India, Tibet, China: Genesis and Aspects of Traditional Narrative*, pp. 103–150. Florence: Leo S. Olschki.

Idema, Wilt L. 2002. "The Filial Parrot in Qing Dynasty Dress: A Short Discussion of the Yingge baojuan [Precious Scroll of the Parrot]." *Journal of Chinese Religions* 30: 77–96.

Idema, Wilt L. 2008. *Personal Salvation and Filial Piety: Two Precious Scroll Narratives of Guanyin and her Acolytes.* Honolulu: University of Hawaii Press.

Idema, Wilt L., and Beata Grant. 2004. *The Red Brush—Writing Women of Imperial China.* Cambridge, MA: Harvard University Asia Center.

Ishino, Kazuharu 石野一晴. 2005. "Mindai Banreki nenkan ni okeru Fuda san no fukkō— Chūgoku junrei shi kenkyū josetsu 明代萬暦年間における普陀山の復興— 中國巡礼史研究序説." *Tōyōshi kenkyū* 東洋史研究 Vol. 64.1: 1–36.

Ishino, Kazuharu 石野一晴. 2010. "Fudaraku san no junreiji—Sekkōshō Fuda san ni okeru nanajū seiki zenban no kudokuhi o megutte 補陀落山の巡礼路— 浙江省普陀山における17世紀前半の功徳碑をめぐって(Making the Path in the Chinese Potalaka: Introduction to 17th Century's Two Inscriptions of Donations for the Putuoshan)." *Higashi Ajia bunka kōshō kenkyū* 東アジア文化交渉研究 (文化交 渉学教育研究拠点) Vol. 3: 143–160.

Jiang, Yonglin. 2005. *The Great Ming Code.* Seattle: University of Washington Press.

Jin, Enhui 金恩輝; Hu, Shuzhao 胡述兆. 1996. *Zhongguo difangzhi zongmu tiyao* 中國地方志總目提要. Taipei and New York: Sino-American Publishers 漢美圖書. 3 vols.

Johnston, Reginald Fleming. 1913. *Buddhist China.* London: Murray.

Jones, Lindsay. 2000. *The Hermeneutics of Sacred Architecture—Experience, Interpretation, Comparison. Vol. 1: Monumental Occasions*. Cambridge, MA: Harvard University Center of the Study of World Religions.

Jones, Lindsay (ed.). 2005. *Encyclopedia of Religion*. Detroit: Thomson Gale.

Kanno, Tomikasu 神野富一. 2010. *Fudaraku shinyō no kenkyū* 補陀洛信仰の研究. Tokyo: Sankibo.

Keika Atsuyoshi 桂華淳祥. 1995. "Chihōshi ni kisai sareru iori no kiroku yori mita MinShin bukkyō—Sekkō chihō o chūshin ni 地方誌に記載される庵の記録 よりみた明清仏教—浙江地方を中心に (Ming and Qing Buddhism in Chapels Recorded in Local Gazetteers, with Special Reference to Zhejiang Area)." *Ōtani gakuhō* 大谷學報 Vol. 75.1: 13–25.

Kieschnick, John. 1997. *The Eminent Monk—Buddhist Ideals in Medieval Chinese Hagiography*. Honolulu: University of Hawaii Press.

Kieschnick, John. 2003. *The Impact of Buddhism on Chinese Material Culture*. Princeton, NJ: Princeton University Press.

Kim, Sujung. 2014. "Transcending Locality, Creating Identity: Shinra Myōji, a Korean Deity in Japan." Unpublished PhD thesis, Columbia University.

Kimiya, Yasuhiko. 1955. 木宮泰彦: *Nichika bunka kōryūshi* 日華文化交流史. Tokyo: Toyamabō 富山房.

Kircher, Athanasius. 1667. *China monumentis qua sacris qua profanis, nec non variis naturae et artis spectaculis, aliarumque rerum memorabilium argumentis illustrata*. Amsterdam: Weasberge & Weyerstraet.

Kleeman, Terry F. 1994. "Mountain Deities in China: The Domestication of the Mountain God and the Subjugation of the Margins." *Journal of the American Oriental Society* Vol. 114.2: 226–238.

Ko, Dorothy. 1994. *Teachers of the Inner Chambers—Women and Culture in Seventeenth-Century China*. Stanford, CA: Stanford University Press.

Kraus, Richard Curt. 1991. *Brushes with Power—Modern Politics and the Chinese Art of Calligraphy*. Berkeley: University of California Press.

Kubota, Ryūon 久保田量遠. 1931 [1986]. *Chūgoku Ju Dō Butsu sankyō shiron* 中国儒道佛三教史論. Tokyo: Kokusho.

Kouamé, Nathalie. 2001. *Pèlerinage et société dans le Japon des Tokugawa. Le pèlerinage de Shikoku entre 1598 et 1868*. Paris: École Française d'Extrême-Orient.

Kouamé, Nathalie, and Goossaert, Vincent. 2006. "Un vandalisme d'État en Extrême-Orient? Les destructions de lieux de culte dans l'histoire de la Chine et du Japon." *Numen* Vol. 53.2: 177–220.

Kyoto Daigaku Kokubungakkai 京都大學國文學會. 1961. *Riben fengtu ji* 日本風土記. Kyoto: Kyoto University. (The only known copy of the *Riben fengtu ji* is appended as fascs. 4 and 5 to the *Quan Zhe bingzhi* 全浙兵制 copy of the Naikaku bunko. This edition is a xylographic reproduction of these two fascicles with a helpful introduction and index.)

Läänemets, Märt. 2006. "Bodhisattva Avalokiteśvara in the Gandavyūhasūtra." *Chung-Hwa Buddhist Studies* Vol. 10: 295–338.

Lagerway, John. 1987. "Le pèlerinage taoïque en Chine." In: Jean Chélini and Henry Branthomme (eds.), *Histoire des pèlerinages non chrétiens—Entre magique et sacré: le chemin des dieux*, pp. 311–327. Paris: Hachette.

Landt, Frank A. 1994. *Die Fünf Heiligen Berge Chinas—Ihre Bedeutung und Bewertung in der Ch'ing Dynastie*. Berlin: Verlag Dr. Köster.

Lawton, Thomas. 1973. *Chinese Figure Painting*. Baltimore: Freer Gallery of Art.

Le Blanc, Charles. 1978. "The Idea of Resonance (Kan-ying) in the Huai-nan tzu." Unpublished PhD thesis, University of Pennsylvania.

Ledderose, Lothar. 2013. "Eine *translatio loci* von Indien nach China." In: De Giorgi et al., *Synergies in Visual Cultures*, pp. 155–166.

Ledderose, Lothar; Wang, Yongbo. 2014. *Buddhist Stone Sutras in China (Shandong Province 1)*. Wiesbaden, Germany: Harrassowitz.

Lévy, André. 1997. *Amour et Rancune—Les Spectacles Curieux du Plaisir*. Arles, France: Editions Philippe Picquier.

Li, Qinhe 李勤合. 2011. *Zaoqi lushan fojiao yanjiu* 早期廬山佛教研究. Nanchang: Jiangxi renmin 江西人民出版社.

Li, Xiaolin 李小林. 2006. "Hou Jigao ji qi Riben tufeng ji 侯继高及其《日本风土记》." *Journal of Lanzhou University* 兰州大学学报 Vol. 34.1: 47–51.

Lin, Wei-cheng. 2014. *Building a Sacred Mountain—The Buddhist Architecture of China's Mount Wutai*. Seattle: University of Washington.

Liu, Tingyu 刘婷玉. 2012. "Nei wu yinghuan, wei you neng li gong ming yu wai zhe—you Yu Dayou kang wo qijian de dejiu, qifu tanqi 内无应援, 未有能力功名于外者由俞大猷抗倭期间的得咎, 起复谈起." In: Zhao, Yifeng 赵轶峰; Wan, Ming 万明 (eds). *Shijie da bianqian shijiao xiade mingdai zhongguo* 世界大变迁视角下的明代中国 (Collected Articles of the International Conference of Ming China under the Perspective of Global Transformation). Jilin renmin 吉林人民出版社, pp. 370–382.

Loewe, Michael. 1994. *Divination, Mythology and Monarchy in Han China*. Cambridge: Cambridge University Press.

Lu, Xun 鲁迅. 1980. *Lu Xun—Selected Works*. 2nd ed. Translated by Yang Xianyi and Gladys Yang. 4 vols. Beijing: Foreign Language Press [first edition 1957].

Lucic, Karen. 2015. *Embodying Compassion in Buddhist Art: Image, Pilgrimage, Practice*. Poughkeepsie, NY: Frances Lehman Loeb Art Center.

Luhmann, Niklas. 1970. "Reflexive Mechanismen." In: Soziologische Aufklärung 1. Opladen: Westdeutscher Verlag.

Luhmann, Niklas. 1984 [1987]. *Soziale Systeme—Grundriss einer allgemeinen Theorie*. Frankfurt/M.: Suhrkamp.

Luhmann, Niklas. 1998. *Die Gesellschaft der Gesellschaft*. 2 vols. Frankfurt/M.: Suhrkamp.

Magnin, Paul. 1987. "Le pèlerinage dans la tradition bouddhique chinoise." In: Jean Chélini and Henry Branthomme (eds.), *Histoire des pèlerinages non chrétiens—Entre magique et sacré: le chemin des dieux*, pp. 278–310. Paris: Hachette.

Mair, Victor (ed). 2008. "The Cult of the Bodhisattva Guanyin in Early China and Korea." *Sino-Platonic Papers* Vol. 182 (September).

McDaniel, Justin. 2002. "Transformative History: The Nihon Ryōiki and the Jinakalamalipakaranam." *Journal of the International Association of Buddhist Studies* Vol. 25.1: 151–207.

McMorran, Ian. 1973. "Late Ming Criticism of Wang Yang-ming: The Case of Wang Fu-chih." *Philosophy East and West* Vol. 23.1/2: 91–102.

McNair, Amy. 2007. *Donors of Longmen: Faith, Politics, and Patronage in Medieval Chinese Buddhist Sculpture*. Honolulu: University of Hawai'i Press.

Medhurst, Walter H. 1938. *China: Its State and Prospects with Especial Reference to the Spread of the Gospel*. London: John Snow. Illustrations by G. Baxter.

Meyer-Fong, Toby. 2013. *What Remains—Coming to Terms with Civil War in 19th Century China*. Stanford, CA: Stanford University Press.

Mingzhou ayuwang shanzhi 明州阿育王山志. Compiled by Guo Zizhang 郭子章 (1543–1618). Available in the Digital Archive of Buddhist Temple Gazetteers (http://buddhistinformatics.ddbc.edu.tw/fosizhi).

Moerman, D. Max. 2005. *Localizing Paradiese—Kumano Pilgrimage and the Religious Landscape of Premodern Japan*. Cambridge, MA, and London: Harvard University Asia Center.

Moerman, D. Max. 2007. "Passage to Fudaraku: Suicide and Salvation in Premodern Japanese Buddhism." In: Cuevas and Stone, *The Buddhist Dead: Practices, Discourses, Representations*, pp. 266–296.

Moerman, D. Max. Forthcoming. *Geographies of the Imagination: Buddhism and the Japanese World Map*. Cambridge, MA: Harvard University Asia Center.

Moll-Murata, Christine. 2001. *Die chinesische Regionalbeschreibung: Entwicklung und Funktion einer Quellengattung, dargestellt am Beispiel der Präfekturbeschreibungen von Hangzhou*. Wiesbaden, Germany: Harrassowitz.

Moll-Murata, Christine. 2006. "Sundry Notes on the Zhoushan Archipelago: Topographical Notation and Comparison to the Braudelian Islands." In: Angela Schottenhammer and Roderich Ptak (eds.), *The Perception of Maritime Space in Traditional Chinese Sources*, pp. 109–124. Wiesbaden, Germany: Harrassowitz.

Moretti, Franco. 2004. "Graphs, Maps, Trees—Abstract Models for Literary History—Part 2." *New Left Review* Vol. 26 (March): 79–103.

Mote, Frederick W., and Denis Twichett (eds.). 1988. *The Cambridge History of China—The Ming Dynasty, 1368 - 1644, Part 1*. Vol. 7. Cambridge: Cambridge University Press.

Mujaku Dōchū 無著道忠 (auth.), Murata Mudō 村田無道 (ed.). 1909 [1715]. *Zenrin shōki sen* 禅林象器箋. Kyoto: Baiyō shoten 貝葉書院.

Munakata, Kiyohiko. 1991. *Sacred Mountains in Chinese Art*. Urbana and Chicago: University of Illinois Press.

Nakaseko, Shōdō 中世古 祥道. 1993. "Shobō shichirō Daiken shuri bosatsu ni tsuite 招宝七郎大権修理菩薩について" *Journal of Soto Zen Studies* 宗学研究 Vol. 35: 232–237.

Naquin, Susan. 2000. *Peking—Temples and City Life*. Berkeley: University of California Press.

Naquin, Susan, and Yü Chün-fang (eds.). 1992. *Pilgrims and Sacred Sites in China*. Berkeley, CA: University of California Press [Reprint Taipei: SMC Publishing, 1994].

Naquin, Susan, and Yü Chün-fang. 1992a. "Pilgrimage in China." In: Naquin and Yü (eds.), *Pilgrims and Sacred Sites in China*, pp. 1–38.

Nara Kokuritsu Hakubutsukan 奈良国立博物館 (ed.). 2009. *Tokubetsuten—Seichi Ninpo: Nihon bukkyō 1300 nen no genryū* 特別展 聖地寧波: 日本仏教1300年の源流. Nara: Kokuritsu Hakubutsukan.

Ning, Qiang. 2008. "Imperial Portraiture as Symbol of Political Legitimacy: A New Study of the 'Portraits of Successive Emperors'." *Ars Orientalis* Vol. 35: 96–128.

Nienhauser, William H. (ed.). 1986. *The Indiana Companion to Traditional Chinese Literature*. Bloomington: Indiana University Press.

Nienhauser, William H. (ed.). 1998. *The Indiana Companion to Traditional Chinese Literature—Vol. 2*. Bloomington: Indiana University Press.

Nishitani, Isao. 2002. "Sennyū-ji sō to fudasan shinkō—Kannon bosatsu zazō no shōrai ito 泉涌寺僧と普陀山信仰—観音菩薩坐像の請来意図." In: Nara Kokuritsu Hakubutsukan (ed.), *Tokubetsuten—Seichi Ninpo: Nihon bukkyō 1300 nen no genryū*, pp. 260–263.

Noguchi, Tetsurō 野口鉄郎. 1965. "Mindai Chūki no bukkyōkai: hidari zensei Keigyō o megutte no nōto 明付中期の佛教界-左善世繼曉をめぐてのノ-卜." *Tōyōshi ronshū* 東洋史學論集 Vol. 7: 189–232.

Nyíri, Pál. 2007. *Scenic Spots—Chinese Tourism, the State, and Cultural Authority*. Seattle: Washington University Press.

Ōba, Osamu. 2012. *Books and Boats—Sino-Japanese Relations in the Seventeenth and Eighteenth Centuries*. Portland, ME: Merwin Asia.

Olles, Volker. 2003. "Der unsterbliche Lehrmeister: Chinesische Literati und religiöses Verdienst in einer Inschrift von 1858 auf einem heiligen Berg der Daoisten im Kreis Pujiang (Provinz Sichuan)." *Zeitschrift der Deutschen Morgenländischen Gesellschaft* Vol. 153: 395–416.

Olles, Volker. 2012. "The Gazetteer of Mt. Tianshe—How the Liumen Community Reshaped a Daoist Sacred Mountain." In: Philip Clart (ed.), *Chinese and European Perspectives on the Study of Chinese Popular Religions*, pp. 229–289. Taipei: Boyang Publishing.

Okasaki, Jōji. 1977. *Pure Land Buddhist Painting*. Tokyo, New York: Kodansha.

Ono, Katsutoshi 小野勝年, and Oyafumi Hibino, 日比野丈夫. 1942. *Godaisan* 五臺山. Tokyo: Zauhō Kankōkai 座右寶.

Orzech, Charles, Henrik Sørensen, and Richard Payne (eds.). 2011. *Esoteric Buddhism and the Tantras in East Asia*. Leiden: Brill.

Overmyer, Daniel L. 1976. *Folk Buddhist Religion － Dissenting Sects in Late Traditional China*. Cambridge, MA: Harvard University Press.

Pan, Guiming 潘桂明. 2000. *Zhongguo jushi fojiao shi* 中國居士佛教史. Beijing: Chinese Academy of Social Science 中國社會科學.

Park, Chris C. 1994. *Sacred World—An Introduction to Geography and Religion*. London: Routledge.

Park, Hyeongyu 朴現圭. 2003. "Zhongguo fojiao shengdi Putuoshan yu Xinluojiao 中国佛教圣地普陀山与新罗礁." *Journal of Zhejiang University (Humanities and Social Sciences)* 浙江大学学报（人文社会科学版）. Vol. 33–1 (January).

Park, Hyunhee. 2010. "A Buddhist Woodblock-printed Map in 13th Century China." *Crossroads* Vol. 1/2: 57–78.

Peri, Noël, and Henri Maspero. 1909. "Le Monastére de la Kouan-Yin qui ne veut pas s'en aller." *Bulletin de l'École française d'Extrême-Orient* Vol. 9.4: 797–807.

Peterson, Willard. 1998. "Confucian Learning in Late Ming Thought." In: Twichett and Mote (eds.), *The Cambridge History of China*, Vol. 8: 708–788.

Plutschow, Herbert Eugen. 1982. "Japanese Travel Diaries of the Middle Ages." *Oriens Extremus* Vol. 29 (1982): 1–136.

Poser, Adriana (ed.). 2010. *Pilgrimage and Buddhist Art*. New Haven, CT, and London: Yale University Press.

Pregadio, Fabrizio. 2008. *The Encyclopedia of Daoism*. London: Routledge.

Pu, Qinghui 朴庆辉 (ed.); Xu Jing 徐兢 (author). 1991. *Xuanhe fengshi gaoli tujing* 宣和奉使高丽图经. Changchun 长春: Jilin wen shi chu ban she 吉林文史出版社.

Pulleyblank, Edwin G. 1991. *Lexicon of Reconstructed Pronunciation in Early Middle Chinese, Late Middle Chinese and Early Mandarin*. Vancouver: University of British Columbia Press.

Quagliotti, Anna Maria. 1998. *Buddhapadas*. Kamakura, Japan: Institute of Silk Road Studies.

Qi, Qingfu 祁庆富. 1996. "'Xuanhe fengshi gaoli tujing' banben yuanliu kao '宣和奉使高丽图经' 版本源流考"*Tushuxue yanjiu* 图书学研究 Vol. 3: 229–234.

Qiu, Gaoxing 邱高興. 2003. "Qingdai fojiao yanjiu xiankuang清代佛教研究現況." *Pumen Xuebao* 普門學報. Vol. 16: 311–322.

Ray, Himanshu Prabha. 1994. "Kanheri: The Archaeology of an Early Buddhist Pilgrimage Center in Western India." *World Archaeology* Vol. 26.1: 35–46.

Reiter, Florian. 1980. "Bergmonographien als geographische und historische Quellen, Dargestellt an Ch'en Shun-yüs 'Bericht über den Berg Lu' (Lu-shan chi) aus dem 11. Jahrhundert." *Zeitschrift der Deutschen Morgenländischen Gesellschaft* Vol. 130: 397–407.

Ren, Yimin 任宜敏. 2005. *Zhongguo fojiaoshi—Yuandai* 中国佛教史 元代 [History of Chinese Buddhism—The Yuan Dynasty]. Beijing: Renmin 人民出版社.

Ren, Yimin 任宜敏. 2009. *Zhongguo fojiaoshi—Mingdai* 中国佛教史 明代 [History of Chinese Buddhism—The Ming Dynasty]. Beijing: Renmin 人民出版社.

Rice, Jeffrey. 2008. "Records of Witness of Responses of Guan(g)shiyin in Three Collections: Image, Icon, and Text." *Sino-Platonic Papers* Vol. 182 (September): 4–24.

Richthofen, Ferdinand von. 1907. *Tagebücher ans China*. 2 vols. Berlin: Reimer.

Ricoeur, Paul. 2004. *Memory, History, Forgetting*. Chicago, IL: University of Chicago Press.

Ríos Peñafiel, María Elvira. 2015. "El reflejo de la luna en la montaña: el budismo en Nanwutai-shan." Tesis Doctoral, El Colegio de México, A.C. Centro de Estudios de Asia y África.

Robson, James. 2009. *Power of Place: The Religious Landscape of the Southern Sacred Peak (Nanyue* 南嶽*) in Medieval China*. Cambridge, MA: Harvard University Asia Center (Harvard East Asian Monographs).

Robson, James. 2012. "Changing Places: The Conversion of Religious Sites in China." In: Benn, Chen, and Robson (eds.), *Images, Relics, and Legends*, pp. 90–111.

Rondot, Natalis. 1847. "Excursion à l'île de Pou-tou (province de tché-kiang) 7 et 8 Octobre, 1845." *Séances et travaux de l'Académie de Reims* Tome 5 (Mai 1846–Aout 1846).

Ruhai Xiancheng 如海顯承. 1826. *Canxue zhijin* 參學知津. Authorial preface dated 1826–08–21. Copy preserved in the Fusinian Library, Academia Sinica, Taipei, printed in 1876.

Rummel, Stefan M. 1992. *Der Mönche und Nonnen Sündenmeer—Der buddhistische Klerus in der chinesischen Roman- und Erzählliteratur des 16. und 17. Jahrhunderts*. Bochum, Germany: Chinathemen.

Saitō Seijun 佐藤成順. 2004. "Nansō no saishō Shi Kō no Fudarakusan Kannon shinkō ni tsuite 南宋の宰相史浩の補陀洛山観音信仰について." *Odai shigaku* 鴨臺史學 Vol. 4.

Sakai, Tadao 酒井忠夫. 2000. *Zōho Chūgoku zensho no kenkyū* 増補中国善書の研究. Tokyo: Kokusho 国書.

Sasaki, Shōkaku 佐佐木章格. 1988. "Nihon sōtōshu to Daiken shuri bosatsu 日本曹洞宗と大権修理菩薩." *Bulletin of the Institute for Sōtō Zen Studies* 曹洞宗宗学研究所紀要 Vol. 1: 32–45.

Schalk, Peter, et al. (eds.). 2010. *Geschichte und Geschichten—Historiographie und Hagiographie in der Asiatischen Religionsgeschichte.* Uppsala, Sweden: Uppsala University Library (Acta Universitatis Upsaliensis—Historia Religionum Vol. 30).

Schlegel, Gustav. 1895. "The Temple of Pootoo." *T'oung Pao* Vol. 5: 447–448.

Schlütter, Morton. 2008. *How Zen Became Zen—The Dispute over Enlightenment and the Formation of Chan Buddhism in Song-Dynasty China.* Honolulu: University of Hawai'i Press.

Schmidt-Glintzer, Helwig. 1982. *Die Identität der Buddhistischen Schulen und die Kompilation Buddhistischer Universalgeschichten in China.* Wiesbaden, Germany: Franz Steiner.

Schneewind, Sarah. 2007. "Ming Taizu ex Machina." *Ming Studies* Vol. 55: 104–112.

Sen, Tansen. 2003. *Buddhism, Diplomacy and Trade—The Realignment of Sino-Indian Relations 600 – 1400.* Honolulu: University of Hawaii Press.

Sharf, Robert H. 2001. *Coming to Terms with Chinese Buddhism: A Reading of the Treasure Store Treatise.* Honolulu: University of Hawaii Press.

Shi Chenkong 釋塵空. 1948 [2007]. *Putuo shan xiao zhi* 普陀山小志. Shanghai: Dafalun shuju 大法輪書局/The Maha Dharmacakra Bookstore. [Reprint in: *Putuo Gazetteer Reprint Series*, 2007]

Shi, Meilu 史美露 (ed.). 2006. *Nansong siming shishi* 南宋四明史氏。 Chengdu: Sichuan meishu 四川美术出版社.

Shiba, Yoshinobu. 1977. "Ningpo and Its Hinterland." In: William Skinner (ed.), *The City in Late Imperial China*, pp. 391–440. Stanford, CA: Stanford University Press.

Shen, Weirong. 2011. "Tantric Buddhism in Ming China." In: Orzech, Sørensen, and Payne (eds.), *Esoteric Buddhism and the Tantras in East Asia*, pp. 550–560.

Shinohara, Koichi. 1988. "Two Sources of Chinese Buddhist Biographies." In: Phyllis Granoff and Koichi Shinohara (eds.), *Monks and Magicians—Religious Biographies in Asia*, pp. 119–194. Oakville, Ontario: Mosaic Press [Delhi: Motilal, 1994].

Schottenhammer, Angela (ed.). 2009. *The East Asian "Mediterranean": Maritime Crossroads of Culture, Commerce and Human Migration.* Wiesbaden, Germany: Harrassowitz.

Schottenhammer, Angela, and Roderich Ptak (eds.). 2006. *The Perception of Maritime Space in Traditional Chinese Sources.* Wiesbaden, Germany: Harrassowitz.

Shufeldt, Robert Wilson, Jr. 1899. "The Pagoda and other Architecture of China." *Overland Monthly and Out West Magazine* Vol. 33–196 (April): 4–13.

Skinner, William (ed.). 1977. *The City in Late Imperial China.* Stanford, CA: Stanford University Press.

Song Yuan difangzhi congkan 宋元地方志叢刊. Taipei: Zhonghua shuju 中華書局, 1990.

Soong, Irma Tam. 1997. "Sun Yat-sen's Christian Schooling in Hawai'i." *The Hawaiian Journal of History* Vol. 31: 151–178.

Soper, Alexander C. 1991. "Yen Li-Pen, Yen Li-Te, Yen P'i, Yen Ch'ing: Three Generations in Three Dynasties." *Artibus Asiae* Vol. 51.3/4: 199–206.

Soymié, Michel. 1956. "Le Lo-feou chan: étude de géographie religieuse." *Bulletin de l'Ecole Française d'Extrême-Orient* 48: 1–139.

Spence, Jonathan D. 1966. *Ts'ao Yin and the K'ang-hsi Emperor, Bondservant and Master.* New Haven, CT: Yale University Press.

Spence, Jonathan D. 1988. *Emperor of China—Self-Portrait of K'ang-hsi.* New York: Vintage Books [first edition: New York: A. Knopf, 1974].

Spence, Jonathan D. 2002. "The K'ang-hsi Reign." In: Willard J. Peterson (ed.), *The Cambridge History of China,* Vol. 9: 120–182.

Sporn, Katja. 2010. "Espace naturel et paysages religieux: les grottes dans le monde grec." *Revue de l'histoire des religions* Vol. 227.4: 553–571.

Strassberg, Richard E. 1994. *Inscribed Landscapes—Travel Writing from Imperial China.* Berkeley: California University Press.

Stausberg, Michael. 2010. *Religion im Modernen Tourismus.* Berlin: Insel Verlag.

Strassberg, Richard E. 1994. *Inscribed Landscapes—Travel Writing from Imperial China.* Berkeley: California University Press.

Strickmann, Michel. 1977. "Bibliographic notes on Chinese Religious Studies, II." *Society for the Study of Chinese Religions Bulletin* Vol. 4: 10–19.

Struve, Lynn A. (ed.). 1993. *Voices from the Ming-Qing Cataclysm—China in Tigers' Jaw.* New Haven, CT, and London: Yale University Press.

Sun, Yat-sen. 1937. "You Putuo zhi qi 遊普陀誌奇." *Foxue banyuekan* 佛學半月刊 Vol. 154 (July): 14–15 [Reprinted in MFQ Vol. 54: 184–185].

Sun, Yat-sen. n.d. "Zongli yimo 'You Putuo zhi qi' 總理遺墨「遊普陀誌奇」." *Rongxian foxue yuekan* 榮縣佛學月刊 Vol. 25: 10–11 [Reprinted in MFQB Vol. 50: 524–523].

Sun Zhongshan quanji 孫中山全集. Beijing: Zhonghua 中华书局1981–1986. 11 vols.

Tanabe, George J., and Willa J. Tanabe. 1989. *The Lotus Sutra in Japanese Culture.* Honolulu: University of Hawaii Press.

Tanaka, Fumio 田中史生. 2011. "Nittō sō Egaku no guhō katsudō ni kan suru kisoteki kenkyū 入唐僧惠萼の求法活動に関する基礎的研究." Unpublished research report (available in the Kanto Gakuin University Library). 2011.3. 2007年度-2010年度科学研究費補助金基盤研究成果報告書.

Tanaka, Hiroshi. 1981. "The Evolution of a Pilgrimage as a Spacial-Symbolic System." *The Canadian Geographer* Vol. 25.2: 240–251.

T'ang, Chün-i. 1973. "The Criticisms of Wang Yang-ming's Teachings as Raised by His Contemporaries." *Philosophy East and West* Vol. 23.1/2: 163–186.

Tay, C. N. 1976. "Kuan-yin: The Cult of Half Asia." *History of Religions* Vol. 16.2: 147–177.

Teiser, Stephen. 1994. *The Scripture of the Ten Kings—And the Making of Purgatory in Medieval Chinese Buddhism.* Honolulu: The Kuroda Institute.

Ter Haar, Barend. 1992. *The White Lotus Teachings in Chinese Religious History.* Leiden: Brill.

Tian, Xiaofei. 2011. *Visionary Journeys—Travel Writings from Early Medieval and Nineteenth Century China.* Cambridge, MA: Harvard University Asia Center.

Tu, Long 屠隆 (author); Zhao, Jing 赵菁 (ed.). 2012. *Kaopan yushi* 考槃餘事. Beijing: Jincheng 金城出版社.

Turner, Victor. 1973. "The Center out There: Pilgrim's Goal." *History of Religions* Vol. 12.3 (February): 191–230.

Tuttle, Grey, and Johan Elverskog (eds.). 2011. *Journal of the International Association of Tibetan Studies* Vol. 6. Special Issue on *Wutai Shan and Qing Culture*.

Twichett, Denis, and Frederick W. Mote (eds.). 1998. *The Cambridge History of China—The Ming Dynasty, 1368 - 1644, Part 2*. Vol. 8. Cambridge: Cambridge University Press.

Tythacott, Louise. 2011. *The Lives of Chinese Objects—Buddhism, Imperialism and Display*. New York: Berghahn Books.

Ukai, Mitsuaki 鵜飼光昌. 2000. "Sha Reiun to Yuimakyō 謝霊運と維摩経." In: Araki (ed.), *Hokuchō Zui Tō Chūgoku bukkyō shisō shi* 北朝隋唐中国仏教思想史, pp. 89–122.

Verellen, Franciscus. 1989. *Du Guangting (850 - 933): Taoiste de cour a la fin de la Chine medievale*. Paris: De Boccard (Memoires de l'Institut des hautes etudes chinoises Vol. 30).

Verellen, Franciscus. 1995. "The Beyond Within: Grotto-Heavens (*dongtian* 洞天) in Taoist Ritual and Cosmology." *Cahiers d'Extrême-Asie* Vol. 8: 265–290.

Verellen, Franciscus (ed.). 1998. *Culte des sites et culte des saints en Chine*. Special issue of *Cahiers d'Extrême-Asie* Vol. 10.

Verschuer, Charlotte von. 2006 [1988]. *Across the Perilous Sea: Japanese Trade with China and Korea from the Seventh to the Sixteenth Centuries*. Translated by Kristen Lee Hunter. Ithaca, NY: Cornell University Press (Cornell East Asia Series No. 113) [First published as *Le commerce extérieur du Japon des origines au XVIe siècle*. Paris: Maisonneuve & Larose, 1988. (Bibliothèque de l'Institut des hautes études japonaises)].

von Glahn, Richard. 2007. "Ming Taizu ex Nihilo?" *Ming Studies* Vol. 55 (Spring): 113–141.

Walsh, Michael J. 2010. *Sacred Economies—Buddhist Monasticism & Territoriality in Medieval China*. New York: Columbia University Press.

Wang, Jinping. 2011. *Between Family and State—Networks of Literati, Clergy and Villagers in Shanxi, North China 1200 - 1400*. Unpublished PhD thesis, Yale University.

Wang, Liansheng 王連勝. 2008. *Putuo shan shici quanji* 普陀山詩詞全集. Shanghai: Shanghai Cishu 上海辭書出版社.

Wang, Yanning. 2013. *Reverie and Reality: Poetry on Travel by Late Imperial Chinese Women*. Plymouth, UK: Lexington.

Wang, Chaohong 汪超宏 (ed.). 2012. *Tu Long ji* 屠隆集. 12 vols. Hangzhou: Zhejiang guji 浙江古籍出版社.

Weidner, Marsha (ed.). 2001a. *Cultural Intersections in Later Chinese Buddhism*. Honolulu: Hawaii University Press.

Weidner, Marsha. 2001b. "Imperial Engagements with Buddhist Art and Architecture: Ming Variations on an Old Theme." In: Weidner, *Cultural Intersections*, pp. 117–144.

Welch, Holmes. 1963. "Dharma Scrolls and the Succession of Abbots in Chinese monasteries." *T'oung pao* Vol. 50: 93–149.

Welch, Holmes. 1968. *The Buddhist Revival in China*. Cambridge, MA: Harvard University Press.

Welch, Holmes. 1972. *Buddhism under Mao*. Cambridge, MA: Harvard University Press.

Welter, Albert. 2000. "Mahākāśyapa's Smile: Silent Transmission and the Kung-an (Kōan) Transmission." In: Heine and Wright (eds.), *The Koan*, pp. 75–109.

Widmer, Ellen, and Kang-i Chang (eds.). 1997. *Writing Women in Late Imperial China*. Stanford, CA: Stanford University Press.

Wiethoff, Bodo. 1969. *Chinas Dritte Grenze—Der traditionelle chinesische Staat und der küstennahe Seeraum*. Wiesbaden, Germany: Harrassowitz.

Wilkinson, Endymion. 2000. *Chinese History: A Manual, Revised and Enlarged*. Cambridge, MA: Harvard University Asia Center.

Wills, John E. 2000. "The Dutch Reoccupation of Chi-lung, 1664–1668." In: Blundell, David. *Austronesian Taiwan*. Berkeley: University of California.

Wittern, Christian. 1998. *Das Yulu des Chan-Buddhismus—Die Entwicklung vom 8.bis zum 11. Jahrhundert*. New York: Peter Lang.

Wong, Dorothy C. 2004. *Chinese Steles—Pre-Buddhist and Buddhist Use of a Symbolic Form*. Honolulu: University of Hawaii Press [Chinese translation (with the original text of inscriptions) 王靜芬. 2011. 中國石碑 一种象征形式在佛教转入之前与之后的运用. 北京：商務印書館].

Wong, Dorothy C. 2007. "Guanyin Images in Medieval China, Fifth to Eighth Centuries." In: William Magee (ed.), *Bodhisattva Avalokiteśvara (Guanyin) and Modern Society*, pp. 254–302. Taipei: Dharma Drum Publishing.

Wong, Dorothy C. 2008. "The Mapping of Sacred Space: Images of Buddhist Cosmographies in Medieval China." In: Forêt and Kaplony (eds.), *The Journey of Maps and Images on the Silk Road*, pp. 51–79.

Wong, Dorothy 王靜芬. 2014. "Qi ba shiji Guanyin zaoxiang de fanyan 七、八世紀觀音造像的繁衍." In: Shi Shouqian 石守謙, and Yan Juanying 顏娟英 (eds.), *Yishushi zhong de Han-Jin yu Tang-Song zhi bian* 藝術史中的漢晉與唐宋之變, pp. 193–224. Taipei: Shitou 石頭.

Wright, George N., and Thomas Allom. 1843. *China, in a Series of Views, Displaying the Scenery, Architecture, and Social Habits of That Ancient Empire*. 4 vols. London: Fisher, Son & Co.

Wu, Jiang. 2008. *Enlightenment in Dispute—The Reinvention of Chan Buddhism in Seventeenth-Century China*. New York: Oxford University Press.

Wu, Pei-yi. 1990. *The Confucians Progress—Autobiographical Writings in Traditional China*. Princeton, NJ: Princeton University Press.

Wu, Pei-yi. 1992. "An Ambivalent Pilgrim to T'ai Shan in the Seventeenth Century." In: Susan Naquin and Yü Chün-fang (eds.), *Pilgrims and Sacred Sites in China*, pp. 65–88.

Wu, Silas. 1970. *Communication and Imperial Control—Evolution of the Palace Memorial System*. Cambridge, MA: Harvard University Press.

Wu, Xinmiao 吳新苗. 2008. *Tu Long yanjiu* 屠隆研究. Beijing: Wenhua yishu 文化艺术出版 社.

Xu, Sunming 徐孙铭, and Chuanzong Wang 王传宗. 2002. *Hunan fojiao shi* 湖南佛教史. Changsha: Hunan renmin 湖南人民出版社.

Xu, Yizhi 徐一智. 2007. "Mingdai Guanyin xinyang zhi yanjiu 明代觀音信仰之研究." Unpublished PhD thesis, National Zhongzheng University, Taiwan.

Xu, Yizhi 徐一智. 2010. "Mingdai zhengju bianhua yu fojiao shengdi Putuoshan de fazhan 明代政局變化與佛教聖地普陀山的發展." *Xuanzang Foxue Yanjiu* 玄奘佛學研究 Vol. 10.4: 25–88.

Xue, Yu 學愚. 2014. *Zhongguo fojiao de shehuizhuyi gaizao* 中國佛教的社會主義改造. Hong Kong: Chinese University Press 香港中文大學出版社.

Yan, Gengwang 嚴耕望, and Qiwen Li 李啟文 (eds.). 2005. *Wei Jin Nanbei chao fojiao dili gao* 魏晉南北朝地理稿. Taipei: Academia Sinica 中央研究院歷史語言研究所.

Yan, Yaozhong 严耀中. 2000. *Jiangnan fojiao shi* 江南佛教史. Shanghai: Shanghai renmin 上海人民出版社.

Yanagida, Seizan. 1983. "The Development of the 'Recorded Sayings' Texts of the Chinese Ch'an School." Translated by John McRae. In: Whalen Lai and Lewis Lancaster (eds.), *Early Ch'an in China and Tibet,* pp. 185–205. Berkeley, CA: Berkeley Buddhist Studies Series.

Yang, Ming 杨明, Yunwei Pan 潘运伟, and Qian Zhao 赵谦. 2011. *Fojiao yu siyuan jingji lüyou guihua chuyi* 佛教与寺院经济旅游规划刍议. Beijing: Zongjiao wenhua 宗教文化.

Yee, D. K. Cordell. 1994a. "Chinese Maps in Political Culture." In: J. B. Harley and D. Woodward (eds.), *Cartography in the Traditional East and Southeast Asian Societies*, pp. 71–95. Chicago, IL: University of Chicago Press.

Yee, D. K. Cordell. 1994b. "Chinese Cartography among the Arts: Objectivity, Subjectivity, Representation." In: J. B. Harley and D. Woodward (eds.), *Cartography in the Traditional East and Southeast Asian Societies*, pp. 128–169. Chicago: University of Chicago Press.

Yü, Chün-fang. 1981. *The Renewal of Buddhism in China: Chu-hung and the Late Ming Synthesis.* New York: Columbia University Press.

Yü, Chün-fang. 1988. "Kuan-yin Pilgrimage," video documentary (58 min), filmed in 1987 [Available as DVD (2004) Columbia University Press].

Yü Chün-fang. 1992. "P'u-t'o Shan: Pilgrimage and the Creation of the Chinese Potalaka." In: Susan Naquin and Yü Chün-fang (eds.), *Pilgrims and Sacred Sites in China*, pp. 190–245.

Yü Chün-fang. 1994. "Guanyin: The Chinese Transformation of Avalokiteshvara." In: Weidner and Berger, *The Latter Days of the Law—Images of Chinese Buddhism,* pp. 151–182.

Yü, Chün-fang. 1998. "Ming Buddhism." In: Twichett and Mote (eds.), *The Cambridge History of China,* Vol. 8.2: 893–952.

Yü, Chün-fang. 2001. *Kuan-Yin: The Chinese Transformation of Avalokiteśvara.* New York: Columbia University Press.

Yu, He 余兢, and Song Huang 黄松 (eds.). 2008. *Youji juan* 游记卷. Beijing: Qinghua daxue 清华大学. (Series: Zhongguo gudian sanwen jingxuan zhuyi 中国古典散文精选注译)

Zelin, Marianne. 2002. "The Yong-cheng Reign." In: Willard Peterson (ed.), *Cambridge History of China: The Ch'ing Empire to 1800*, Vol. 9.1: 183–229.

Zhang, Dai 張岱. 1638 [1935]. "Haizhi 海志" In: *Yuanhuan wenji* 瑯嬛文集. Shanghai: Shanghai Zazhi Gongsi 上海雜誌公司, 1935.

Zhang, Dewei. 2010. *A Fragile Revival—Buddhism under the Political Shadow, 1522 – 1620.* PhD thesis, University of British Columbia, Vancouver.

Zhang, Jian. 张坚. 2001. "Tu Long yu Putuo shier jing 屠隆与普陀十二景." *Journal of Zhejiang Ocean University (Human Science)* 浙江海洋学院学报 (人文科学版). Vol. 18.1: 23–26.

Zhao, Tiefeng 赵铁峰. 2008. *Mingdai guojia zongjiao guanli zhidu yu zhengce yanjiu* 明代国家宗教管理制度与政策研究. Beijing: Chinese Academy of Social Sciences 中国社会科学出版社.

Zheng, Ruozeng 鄭若曾. 1624 [1990]. *Chouhai tubian* 籌海圖編. In: Wang Chunsheng 王纯盛 (ed.), *Zhonghuo bingshu jicheng* 中国兵书集成, Vol. 16. Beijing: Jiefangjun 解放軍出版社.

Zhongguo   lidai   guanyin   wenxian   jicheng   中國歷代觀音文獻集成. Beijing: Zhonghua quanguo tushuguan wenxian suowei fuzhi zhongxin 中華全國圖書館文獻縮微復制中心, 1998. 10 vols.

Zhou, Qi 周齊. 2005. *Mingdai fojiao yu zhengzhi wenhua* 明代佛教与政治文化. Beijing: Renmin 人民出版社.

Zhu, Guozhen 朱國禎. 1619 [1991]. *Yongchuang xiaopin* 湧幢小品 [Reprint Taipei: Guangwen shuju 廣文書局].

Zhu, Defeng 祝德風. 1830 [2007]. *Putuo quansheng* 普陀全勝 [Reprint in: *Putuo Gazetteer Reprint Series*, 2007].

Zuo, Lala. 2008. "A Geographical Study of the Records of the Verifications of the Responses of Guanshiyin in Three Volumes." *Sino-Platonic Papers* Vol. 182 (September): 25–55.

Putuo Gazetteers

Sheng Gazetteer. 1361. Cited to the Taishō edition.

Hou-Tu Gazetteer. 1590 [1598]. Fasc. 2–6 cited to the copy reprinted in the *Putuo Gazetteer Reprint Series*. Fasc. 1 to the Naikaku Bunko 內閣文庫 copy.

Zhou Gazetteer. 1607 [1641]. Cited to the page number of the copy reprinted in the *Zhongguo fosi shizhi huikan* series (ZFSH 8). A punctuated edition of this with detailed indices and references to the original pagination is Bingenheimer (2013, Vol. 3).

Qiu-Zhu Gazetteer. 1698–1705 [1735]. Cited to the copy reprinted in the *Putuo Gazetteer Reprint Series*.

Xu Gazetteer. Dated 1740. Cited to the copy reprinted in the *Putuo Gazetteer Reprint Series*.

Qin Gazetteer. 1832. In the *Putuo Gazetteer Reprint Series* fascicles 5 and 6, as well as part of fascicle 4, are missing. Here cited to a complete copy reprinted in the *Zhongguo lidai guanyin wenxian jicheng* at Vol. 9: 317–761 (Fasc. 1–15), and Vol. 10: 1–425 (Fasc. 16–20).

Wang Hengyan Gazetteer. 1924–1934. Cited to the copy reprinted in the *Zhongguo fosi shizhi huikan* series (ZFSH 9). A punctuated edition of this with detailed indices and references to the original pagination is Bingenheimer (2013, Vol. 4).

Fang Gazetteer. 1995. Shanghai: Shanghai shudian 上海書店.

Wang Liansheng Gazetteer. 1999. Shanghai: Shanghai shudian 上海書店.

INDEX

Adam's Peak (Sri Pada), 211n.12
Addenda, 10
Amalgamation Order of 1391, 20
Ancestral temple (*ci* 祠), 135
Anti-clericalism, 208n.58
Apparitions
    ganying as conceptual basis for, 79
    in grottoes, 98–99
    at Tidal Sound Cave, 84–87, 98
    visitors' interaction with, 87
    Zhu Jin essay on, 89–93. *See also*
        Visions
Architecture, lack of discourse
    on role of, 107
"Armchair traveling," (*woyou* 臥遊) 54
Aśoka Temple 阿育王寺
    assigned to Chan School, 111
    Daquan as guardian deity of, 85–86
Aśoka Temple Gazetteer, 32
    on Daquan, 85–86
    miracle tales in, 77
    poetry in, 146
Autographs, 31
Avalokiteśvara, Bodhisattva
    associated with oceanic travel and
        littoral pilgrimage centers, 98
    pronoun used for, 192
    Sheng Gazetteer eulogies to, 16
    throne of, 80. *See also* Guanyin,
        Bodhisattva

Avataṃsaka Sūtra, 14
    association of Potalaka and Putuo in, 17
    Gandavyūha passage about
        Sudhana in, 80
    on Pantuo Rock, 163
    Sudhana Cave in, 65
    and textualization of Mount Wutai, 103

Bachelard, Gaston, 145
Baoqing Siming zhi 寶慶四明志, 17, 57,
    82–83, 191
Baotuo Pagoda, 74, 75
Baotuo Yuan 寶陀院, 82, 239n.1
Beijing, study of temples in, 4
Bie'an Xingtong 別庵性統, 24
    biography of, 119–125
    continuation of teacher's lineage by, 51
    on Lan Li, 117–118
    and stele inscriptions, 138, 228n.46
Biographies
    basis of information in, 222n.3
    of Bie'an Xingtong, 119–125
    categorizing people associated
        with site, 109
    of famous visitors, 7
    of Huang Dalai, 115–117, 119
    of Lan Li, 115, 117–119
    of laypeople, 7, 108, 109
    of military officials, 114–119
    of monks, 7, 108–109, 119–125

Biographies (*Cont.*)
    of patrons, 7, 109
    in Song and Yuan dynasties, 36
    of Yitang Xinming, 119–125
    of Zhenxie Qingliao, 110–113
    zhuan-type, outside of lineage,
        108–126, 222n.3
Birnbaum, Raoul, 103
Boerschmann, Ernst, 4, 27, 64, 175,
        236n.35
    on condition of Mount Putuo, 187
    descriptions and images by, 221n.51
    on inscriptions, 127
Bo Juyi 白居易, 78–79, 130
Bori-am 菩提庵, 195n.4
Boshan 博山, 232n.47
Brahma Voice Cave 梵音洞
    and copy mode of
        textualization, 99–104
    gate plaque for, 119, 120
    increasing influence of, 182
    location of, 219n.8
    on maps, 66
    on pilgrimage route, 182
    in "Twelve Views of Putuo," 69, 70
British occupation of Zhoushan, 25
Brook, Timothy, 4
    on Amalgamation Order of 1391, 20
    on Confucian literati, 31
    on support for Buddhism, 52
    on Tu Long's support of
        Buddhism, 152
Bu ken qu guanyin 不肯去觀音 "Guanyin
    Who Did Not Want to Leave", 81–
    83, 159, 171
Budaluojia guanyin xianshen shengjing
    補怛洛迦觀音現神聖境 (*Budaluo
    shengjing*), 57–60, 71, 211n.16,
    frontispiece
    sites on, 100, 106
    "Twelve Views" compared to, 76
Buddhism
    academic study of sacred sites, 4–5
    agreement between Daoism and, 62, 64
    appropriation of island by, 17
    attitudes toward death in, 50–52
    beginning activity of, 17

conflation of Daoism and, 33
Confucian attitudes toward, 30–35
earliest connection of Mount Putuo
    with, 83
"Four Great and Famous
    Mountains" of, 4
ganying in, 78, 79
interest of eunuchs in, 135
late-Ming revival of, 31
in local and regional administration, 19
during Ming, 19–23, 202n.77
Mount Putuo as major pilgrimage
    site, 4, 16
Neo-Confucian attitude toward, 30–31
patronage of, 223n.35
pilgrimages in, 166
during Qing, 26
during Republican era, 37
revivals of, 202n.76, 203n.88
rhetoric toward Confucianism in, 35–38
sacred sites in, 104
support for institutions of, 19
Tibetan, 20
transmission from China to Japan, 3
Tu Long's support of, 152
voicing sympathy/tolerance toward, 130
Zhou Yingbin on survival of, 137–138.
    See also Chan Buddhism; Chinese
    Buddhism; Pure Land Buddhism;
    Tibetan Buddhism
Buddhism texts
    Hongwu's control over, 20
    translation into Mongolian, 19
Buddhist canon
    gifting of, 123
    Ruan Jun's attempted sale of, 23
Buddhist historiography, 5, 190, 206n.5
Buddhist sacred sites
    literati reasons for visiting, 167
    miracles at, 77
    at or near Daoist shrines, 62, 64
Buddhist temple gazetteers, 1, 190
    as adaption of Confucian genre, 30
    Confucian literati as writers of, 29–35
    fascicles of, 7
    maps in, 54. *See also* Mount Putuo
        gazetteers

Buddhist temples, 196n.9
  descriptions in official gazetteers, 6
  pirate-traders' raiding of, 23
  during Taiping Rebellion, 26
  temple or mountain gazetteers
    about, 6–7
Buddhist traditions, 5
Butler, John, 27
Butuoluojiashan ji 補陀洛迦山記
  (Tu Long), 168

Cai Guiyi 蔡貴易, 237n.45
Calligraphy
  association of person and, 224n.44
  inscriptions made in, 117, 178
  as instrument of rulership, 120
  on Pantuo Rock, 71
  prefaces and postscripts in, 8, 31
  in woodblock editions, 31
Cantor, Theodore, 26
Canxue 參學, 183
Canxue zhijin 參學知津 "Knowing the
  Paths of Pilgrimage" (Xiancheng),
  181–187
Caoan lu 草菴錄 (Daoyin), 202n.71,
  212n.12
Caodong lineage, 110, 221n.2
Cao Yin 曹寅, 124
Cartelli, Mary Ann, 103, 147, 229n.12
Catholicism
  Lourdes miracles in, 99
  sacred sites in, 104
Central Asia, knowledge about
  geography of, 56
Chan Buddhism
  and abbotship of monasteries, 222n.15
  first transmission of, 150
  and "innate knowledge," 30
  "moon in the pond" trope in, 74
  Pure Land Buddhism and, 91, 113
  transmission to Japan, 78
  Zhenxie Qingliao biography, 110–114
  and *zhuan*-type biographies, 108
Chaoshan shi yao 朝山十要 "Ten
  Principles of Mountain Pilgrimage"
  (Xiancheng), 184–186
Chaoyin Tongxu 潮音通旭, 111

  appointment by Lan Li, 117
  and inscription for Huang Dalai,
    116–117
  on Qingliao, 112
  "Record of the Lineage of Putuo
    Patriarchs," 12, 111–113
  on remembering mountains and
    rivers, 95
  Xinming as novice under, 121–122
Chavannes, Édouard, 4
Chen Chenhai 陳辰海, 161
Cheng Hao 程顥, 30, 31
Cheng Yi 程頤, 30, 31
Chen Shikai 陳世凱, 115, 118
Chen Xuan 陳璿 / 陳璇, 9
Chiang Ching-kuo 蔣經國, 187
Chiang Kai-shek 蔣介石, 187
Children, on pilgrimages, 71
China
  academic study of Buddhist sites
    in, 4–5
  calligraphy in, 120
  dragon king's daughter trope in, 105
  dragons in, 231–232n.42
  education and examination system
    in, 147
  education system during Ming, 21
  embassy traffic between Korea and, 171
  Guanyin worshiped in, 2
  lineage in, 109
  miracle tales in, 83
  Mount Potalaka in, 2–3
  Ningbo as trading hub for, 3
  pilgrimages in, 166
  poetry in, 145–146
  Potalaka sites in, 2, 3
  "Putuo" or "Southern Putuo"
    temples in, 3
  Song-Yuan transition in, 19
  state's role in vandalism of religious
    sites in, 205n.118
  women's poetry in, 229n.6
Chinese Buddhism
  characteristics of sacred mountains
    in, 103
  "Four Great and Famous
    Mountains" in, 4

Gazetteer of Yongkang County, 93
Gazetteers (*zhi* 志 / 誌), 197–198n.26
  as container genre, 14
  definitions of, 5–6
  earlier formats replaced by, 36
  lack of discourse on architecture in, 107
  limit of genre, 13, 14
  for Mount Putuo (*See* Mount Putuo
    gazetteers)
  of Mount Wudang, 5
  origin of, 6
  topography sections of, 96
  usage of term, 5
of Confucian academies, 190. *See also*
    individual gazetteers; *specific types*,
    e.g.: Temple gazetteers
Ge Hong Well 葛洪井, 64
Generation loss, 14–15
Geography of Mount Putuo, 100. *See also*
    Landscape
Ginseng, as gift, 122
Grapard, Allan, 201n.53
Grootaers, Willem, 4
Grottoes, 99
Grotto-heaven 洞天, 98–99
Groundplans, 7
Grouping famous views, 150–151
Guan Daxun 管大勳, 151
Guangxi Peak 光熙峯
  "On Guangxi Peak after snowfall,"
    161–162
  in "Twelve Views of Putuo," 74, 75
Guan wuliangshou jing 觀無量壽經,
    233n.68
Guanyin 觀音, 2
  apparition of, 17 (*See also*
    Apparitions)
  arrival at Mount Putuo, 68, 69
  attendants of, 212n.20
  in *Budaluo shenjing*, 57
  as "Buddha," 213n.56
  Dalai Lamas as manifestations of, 2
  depicted with dragon, 231n.42
  forms of, 216–217n.38
  "Guanyin Who Did Not Want to
    Leave", see *Bu ken qu guanyin*

images of, 219n.14
  on Mount Potalaka, 2–3
  Mount Putuo as abode of, 3
  pronoun used for, 192
  and the Rebuked Sister-in-Law, 68–70,
    84, 160
  triad of Sudhana, Dragon Girl, and,
    105–106. *See also* Avalokiteśvara,
    Bodhisattva
Guanyin Leap (*Guanyin tiao*
    觀音跳), 170
Gu Guang 顧光, 162
Guidebooks for pilgrims, 55
Gu Wenxing 顧問行, 122–123
Guxin Minghu 古心明忞, 121
Gu Yanwu 顧炎武, 167

Haitian foguo 海天佛國 "Buddha Land
    between Sea and Sky", 128–129
Haizhi 海志 (Zhang Dai), 168
Haladai, 84–85
Halperin, Mark, 129
Hangzhou Prefecture gazetteers, 201n.56
Han Jingchang 漢經廠, 227n.33
Hanshan 寒山 (poet), 77
Hanshan Deqing 憨山德清, 31, 163–164
Hanshan Temple 寒山寺
  miracle tales in gazetteers of, 78
  steles of, 128
Han Wudi 漢武帝, 157
Han Yu 韓愈, 167
Hargett, James, 4, 103
Healing motif, in miracle tales, 89
Heaven, 91–92
Heavenly gates, 231n.41
Hermits (*yin*), 47, 109, 170
He Rubin 何汝賓, 236n.26
Hidden information, in prefaces and
    postscripts, 46–50
Hierophanies, 98
Historiography
  Buddhist, 5, 190, 206n.5
  Chinese, 1, 205n.111, 222n.4
  local, 21
  of sacred sites, 5
History chapters (in gazetteers), 7

"we Confucians"/"our Confucianism" in, 32–35
Potalaka, 195–196n.7
    as Guanyin's Pure Land, 57
    location of, 211n.12
    meaning of, 150
Potala palace (Lhasa), 2–3
Prabhūtaratna Buddha Stūpa, *see*
    Duobaofo Stūpa
Precious scroll (*baojuan* 寶卷), 106
Precious Scroll of Good-in-Talent and
    Dragon Girl, 106
Prefaces (*xu* 序), 7, 31, 52–53
    and attitudes of Confucians toward
        Buddhism, 31
    Buddhist rhetoric toward Confucianism
        in, 35–38
    and Confucian writers of
        gazetteers, 29–35
    distortion in, 32
    in Fang Gazetteer, 11
    incongruities between an edition and, 32
    placement of, 31
    as self-referential genre, 32
    textualization of, 31–32
    understanding hidden information
        in, 38–46
    of Wang Hengyan Gazetteer, 27
Prince's Stūpa, *See* Stūpa of the Prince
Prip-Møller, Johannes, 4
Proto-gazetteers, 16, 29
Puji Temple 普濟寺, 24, 191
    abbots' biographical information, 12
    abbots from 1820 to 1875 at, 26
    assigned to Chan School, 110, 111
    bias of Qin Gazetteer toward, 24–25
    in *Budaluo shenjing*, 57
    burning of (1598), 22, 40
    burning of (1675), 23
    embassy members' rituals at, 171
    equal recognition of Fayu Temple
        and, 120
    gate plaque for, 119, 120
    and geographic dynamics of island, 100
    Hou-Tu maps of, 60, 62
    imperial inscriptions for, 127, 138–139

names of, 239n.1
    patriarch hall of, 111–112
    on pilgrimage route, 182
    plans in Qiu-Zhu Gazetteer, 66
    plunder and decay of, 115
    and Qiu-Zhu Gazetteer, 9
    ranking of, 220n.24
    reconstruction after 1598 fire, 40–41,
        43–46, 157
    rivalry between Fayu Temple and, 10,
        25, 100
    roof tiles for, 120
    shrine for Lan Li at, 117
    and stay mode of textualization, 98, 99
    stele repair at, 141
    in "Twelve Views of Putuo," 74, 75
    in Xu Jing's foundation legend, 81–82
    Yongzheng inscription for, 141
    Zhang Bangji on, 19
Pumon Temple 普門寺, 195n.4
Punctuation, 10
Pure Land
    Kalavinka birds in, 98
    Potalaka as, 57
Pure Land Buddhism
    Chan Buddhism and, 91, 113
    Qingliao's engagement with, 110
    rebirth into lotus blossoms in, 164
    Wang Hengyan's attempt to balance
        Chan and, 113
    and *zhuan*-type biographies, 108
Purple Bamboo Grove, 236n.38
Purple Bamboo Hermitage, 106
Putuo Gazetteer Reprint Series, 191
Putuo lie zu lu 普陀列祖錄 "Record of the
    Lineage of Putuo Patriarchs"(Tongxu),
    12, 111–113

Qiandao Siming tujing 乾道四明圖經,
    17, 191, 227n.26
Qianlong 乾隆 emperor
    lifting of Buddhist ordination
        restrictions by, 26
    reign of, 24
    Wang Hengyan references to, 25
    Xu Gazetteer under, 10